Dr. Bob Fischer opens wide a window on the faith, life, and worship practices of the early Nazarene believers. Drawing on a diversity of sources ranging from Post-Exilic rabbinical teaching to the Dead Sea Scrolls and the Church Fathers, he succeeds in unearthing the Jewish roots of Christianity in a manner that will not only cause us to rethink many of our assumptions, but provoke us to a deeper discussion as well.

I would highly recommend his book both for its readability and as a research tool for those who truly wish to learn more about the first century church.

—Rabbi Michael Gertsman
Poriyya Illit, Israel
Renfrew, Canada

History has always survived under the mighty hand of the victors. Unfortunately for us, that leaves us with a panegyric rather than an objective view. It is historically and biblically clear, however, that the Christian church sprang forth from an Upper Room on Mount Zion as an entirely Jewish enterprise and brought with it much of the rich understandings and traditions of the original twelve apostles and their inner circle of 120 who first embraced Christ whom they called by his Hebrew name, Yeshua. At the martyrdom of Stephen in A.D. 35, the gospel went out, being spread equally among the Gentiles and the Jews, often creating a denomination of racial background. Cities where the gospel became prominent divided into churches and synagogues for Christ. Dr. Raymond Robert Fischer, a Jewish believer who was brought to faith in the Gentile Christian church, provides an important and exciting restoration of the understandings and traditions of "The Way" that contributes much to our better undertanding of early church history. Dr. Robert Fischer in his work has captured the flavor of the Christian synagogue and recognized the differing sects within the Jewish Christian community. *The Ways of The Way* is a refreshing history on how a Jewish community of believers would see its purpose and contribution to modern Christianity. *The Ways of The Way* is of particular importance to those many home congregations that are now emerging and seeking to establish themselves on a more clearly understood foundation of the rich Jewish heritage of their faith.

—Jay E. Thompson
Professor of church history
Faith Evangelical Seminary

Bob Fischer is a true apostolic voice in the still-developing area of the Jewish roots of Christianity. With keenness and sensitivity, he addresses issues in *The Ways of The Way* that need to be brought into greater biblical alignment, while offering clear and constructive direction on how this can be accomplished.

"The Way" were the very first Jewish followers of Yeshua. Their foundational understandings, lifestyle, unique practices, and observance of the feasts and festivals effectively shaped their world through the liberty of adherence of the Word of Life. Now, in our greatly troubled world, "The Way's" rich legacy cries out for restoration.

As the church has begun to embrace the return to our Jewish roots, we know there is so much more we need to learn! *The Ways of The Way* is an important next step toward clearing the overgrowth on the ancient paths we have so longed to know.

—Donna McClain Chappell
Prayer Harvest Ministries
Tampa, Florida

I am very excited about Robert Fischer's new book, *The Ways of The Way*! Robert has a very fine mind and is a gifted writer, and possesses an equally outstanding Christian spirit. He calls attention to archaeological remnants of an ancient Jewish Christian synagogue that may have had—I dare to say, *did* have—some level of Jewish-Christian involvement from as far back as [the] late first or early second century of the Christian Era. Even more importantly, he deals well with what it means to honor and model ancient Jewish-Christian heritage in a modern world. How fitting it is that a Jewish Christian living in Tiberias on the shores of the Sea of Galilee is calling attention both to ancient Christian archaeological relics in the Holy Land, while also dealing well with The Way within our day.

—Dr. Lee W. Woodard
Historian and New Testament Specialist

THE WAYS of The WAY

Restoring the Jewish Roots of the Modern Church

An Examination of the History, Theology, and Worship Practice of the First Jewish Believers

THE WAYS of The WAY

Restoring the Jewish Roots of the Modern Church

An Examination of the History, Theology, and Worship Practice of the First Jewish Believers

RAYMOND ROBERT FISCHER

CREATION HOUSE
A STRANG COMPANY

The Ways of The Way by Raymond Robert Fischer
Published by Creation House
A Strang Company
600 Rinehart Road
Lake Mary, Florida 32746
www.strangbookgroup.com

Note to the reader: The biblical term "The Way" as used in this volume is not to be confused with "The Way International," founded by Victor Paul Wierwille and with whom Dr. Raymond Robert Fischer holds no affiliation.

Unless otherwise noted all photographs are by the author.

Design Director: Bill Johnson
Cover design by Justin Evans

Library of Congress Control Number: 2009924726
International Standard Book Number: 978-1-59979-763-2

First Edition

09 10 11 12 13 — 987654321
Printed in the United States of America

With profound thanksgiving I dedicate this work of my heart to the sacred memory of the very first Jewish believers in *Yeshua ha Mashiach* (Jesus the Christ), those who were the twelve apostles and their inner circle who were called The Way; who walked with Him, heard Him speak, and then memorialized what they had seen and heard so that all ensuing generations might have the means by grace through faith to find eternal life in Him.

Acknowledgments

I WOULD LIKE TO EXPRESS my deep appreciation to the many dear ones who stood by my side as this work came forth:

- To Professor Jay Thompson and Dr. Lee Woodard for their guidance and scholarly contributions and for their independent dating of the Tiberias synagogue of The Way to the mid-second century.
- To Robert Crysler, who skillfully and faithfully copyedited the manuscript.
- To Reuven Schmalz, who ensured the historical accuracy of what is written and who helped greatly in keeping my emotions from spilling over into polemics.
- To Rabbi Michael Gertsman and Bill Eldridge, my dear friends and brothers, who read the manuscript and made timely and excellent suggestions.
- And, finally, to Donna Jean Goade Fischer, my darling wife of more than forty-nine years, my most faithful and helpful contributor, who, after Yeshua, is the wellspring of my every joy.

Contents

Part III: The Theology and Doctrine of The Way

Part IV: The Sacred Writings of The Way

Part V: The Praise and Worship of The Way

Part VI: The Ways of The Way as a Guide for Today's Church

Introduction

Among my myriad awesome blessings as a Jewish citizen of Israel and longtime resident of the Galilee, I have often sat on each of a few small boulders at the apex of a natural amphitheater on Mount Ermos ("Mount of Beatitudes") and prayerfully pondered the words spoken there by Yeshua, Jesus Christ, the Creator of the universe. With His holy hand He carved out this perfectly acoustical place as the locale for what, arguably, was His most important publicly delivered message.

A mostly Jewish audience of many thousands heard Him speak that day.

> Do not think that I came to destroy the Law [Torah, instructions] or the Prophets. I did not come to destroy but to fulfill. For assuredly, I say to you, till heaven and earth pass away, one jot or one tittle will by no means pass from the law till all is fulfilled. Whoever therefore breaks one of the least of these commandments, and teaches men so, shall be called least in the kingdom of heaven; but whoever does and teaches them, he shall be called great in the kingdom of heaven. For I say to you, that unless your righteousness exceeds the righteousness of the scribes and Pharisees, you will by no means enter the kingdom of heaven.
>
> —Matthew 5:17–20

Some three and one-half years after He spoke these words, many who had heard Him speak that day followed His twelve disciples and the one hundred and twenty of their inner circle to the Upper Room on Mount Zion. There they formed a mighty, all-Nazarene Jewish movement called "The Way" (Acts 24:14). In the pages that follow, the terms *The Way*, the *Nazarenes*, and the *Nazarenes of the Way* are used interchangeably.

It was there in the heart of Jerusalem that they, guided by the Holy Spirit, carefully reviewed and wrote down many of the things they had seen and heard while they had walked closely by the side of their now risen Lord.

Much of what they heard Yeshua speak was not entirely new to them. They already cherished and embraced the underlying substance of His mighty teachings in the pages of their Holy Scriptures, which they had treasured and studied all of their lives, for they—like He—were deeply committed, *Torah*-observant Jews.

Moreover, all of these first members of this "mother congregation" had first been Essenes, deeply religious members of the ascetic sect who brought with them much of the theology, doctrine, worship practice, and tradition they had memorialized in their sacred scrolls and then hidden away in caves near their home center at Qumran on the western shore of the Dead Sea.

And so it was that this Essenic treasure of wisdom, knowledge, and truth quickly became the very foundation and substance of the belief system of the Nazarenes of The Way. The Essenes had long anticipated the coming of the Messiah, the very Son of God and God Himself who, through the blood of His own willing self-sacrifice, would atone for the sins of the world. When He appeared among them, these who were to become the founding members of The Way recognized and embraced Him. Thus, after He had ascended into heaven before their very eyes, they dedicated themselves to sharing the great wonders they had seen, heard, and received from Him, first with their fellow Jews and then with the nations.

Toward this end, guided by the Holy Spirit, they wrote down many volumes of their recollections. Four such volumes were later canonized as Gospels by the Christian Church to which their witness had given birth.

This inner circle also wrote many letters (twenty-one of which were also later canonized), some addressed to those believing Jews who had already dispersed from Mount Zion, others to Gentile congregations who were newly established in the just-emerging church and were in need of instruction.

Although the apostle Paul was never fully accepted by the Essene-rooted inner circle and for the most part remained aloof from them, he, who had only recently before been Sha'ul of Tarsus, a militant Pharisee bitterly opposing them, was the greatest letter writer of them all. The theology, doctrine, and other guidance Paul included in the fourteen of these twenty-one canonized letters he wrote gave rise to the later, now-legendary quip that he was the very "creator of Christianity."

No matter their differences, the God who had chosen and called them to this inner circle remained with them. He guided them through all manner of persecution and other adversity. He shielded them from the constant barrage of fiery darts hurled at them by Satan and his legion of demons, who were steadfastly determined to prevent the Nazarenes of The Way from accomplishing their divine purpose. And, by His almighty hand they succeeded in two very great ways.

First, after they had blended together the very essence of the Torah as it was fulfilled in the purpose, life, and teachings of Yeshua, they brought this salvational message to their fellow Jews. Many listened and were saved.

Then, as they had been divinely called, they obediently took this same gospel of salvation to the nations, where it was to become the orthodox foundation from which all subsequent expressions of Christianity arose.

Truly, their God was with them through the entire four centuries of their existence until at last, overcome by relentless persecution from their fellow Jews, the successive Roman governments who ruled over them, and the church to which they had given birth, they finally succumbed and vanished from the pages of history. And so it was that the bright and orthodox spiritual torch of the Nazarenes of The Way passed unwittingly to the church fathers—those who had helped to quicken their demise and thus inherited God's sacred call to increase, disciple, and protect what by then, toward the end of the fifth century, had become an almost exclusively Gentile-populated movement.

I genuinely love the Christian church. Without it, not I nor any other Jew or Gentile would have come to know Yeshua and receive eternal life through Him. But so much more than this, the church gave me my spiritual education, my love of the Word, the very meaning and purpose for my life, and my zest to live it. The church showed me how to find and how to express the indescribably wonderful joy of my salvation, brought forth and poured out from the Holy Spirit, who dwells within me.

It is because of this deep appreciation and love I have for the church that it is decidedly not my purpose here to point a finger of derision or blame for the sad state of the body of Christ as it exists in the world of today. My deeply committed central purpose is not to bash, condemn, or destroy but rather to restore!

The Pew Forum on Religion and Public Life seeks to promote a deeper understanding of issues at the intersection of religion and public affairs. The Forum pursues its mission by conducting surveys and delivering timely, impartial information in four key areas of research, including religion.

Most recently, in June 2008, the Pew Forum reported their findings from a "Survey of the United States Religious Landscape." These findings, based on interviews with more than thirty-five thousand American adults, detail the religious makeup, beliefs, and practices of the American public.[1]

I pray that the following summary of the most genuinely shocking results (adapted by the author from the report) will be the basis for a rallying cry from all believers, Jewish and Gentiles alike, for the restoration of the body of Yeshua, the church.

Members in Agreement with the Position Statement: "Many religions (other than Christianity) can lead to eternal life."

Mainline churches: 83%
Evangelical churches: 57%
Catholics: 79%
Jews: 82%

Members in Agreement with the Position Statement: "Scripture (the Bible) is the Word of God, literally true, word for word."

Mainline churches: 22%
Evangelical churches: 59%
Catholics: 23%
Jews (traditional): 10%

Members Reporting Their "Frequency of prayer: daily"

Mainline churches: 53%
Evangelical churches: 78%
Catholics: 58%
Jews (traditional): 26%

Members Reporting They "Attend religious service once or more each week"

Mainline churches: 34%
Evangelical churches: 58%
Catholics: 42%
Jews (traditional): 16%

These responses from the contemporary church beg the question: How would members of The Way have reacted to this same survey from Mount Zion during the mid-first century? They were with Yeshua when they heard him clearly say, "I am the way, the truth, and the life. No one comes to the Father except through Me" (John 14:6).

Can we believe that 83 percent of the members of today's mainline churches and 57 percent of evangelicals do not believe Him? Do they think He was lying? God is incapable of lying (Num. 23:19).

The apostle John tells us, "In the beginning was the Word, and the Word was with God, and the Word was God" (John 1:1). Yeshua is at once the "living Word" and God incarnate. Thus, it follows that the written Word as it was originally given by God, through the power of the Holy Spirit, must also be perfect and without error.

The Didache, an early Nazarene text, instructed the early church to pray the Lord's Prayer three times each day. Paul instructed us all to "pray without ceasing" (1 Thess. 5:17). Again, I find it almost inconceivable that only 53 percent of mainline Christians and 78 percent of evangelicals pray daily.

Members of The Way met each day in their homes and every *Motzei Shabbat* (Saturday evening) as a congregation. How can it be that only 34 percent of modern day mainline church members and 58 percent of evangelicals attend services once each week?

In the face of this devastating report on the condition of the modern day church, consider this also: during the forty years between 1967 and 2007, some 19.2 million members (25 percent) of the top five mainline church denominations left the rolls of their respective churches.[2]

Again, it isn't my purpose or within the scope of this writing to assess blame for this terribly sad, self-destroyed state of the church, the body of Christ. I leave it to the many others who have expressed and continue to express their outrage over a great number and variety of contributing factors.

May I suggest that the way out of the horrendous pit of steeply declining social, cultural, and religious values lies *within* the Church, not in its bashing? I believe that restoring much of the original theology, doctrine, worship practices, and structure that was its first-century foundation will go a long way toward lifting the church, the bride of Christ, back up to her former glory. The journey toward this restoration may not be as long or as arduous as many at first think. The fact is, this restoration has already been under way for a number of years, ever since the mid-1960s, when the great numbers of those who began leaving their mainline church homes began to look for different places of worship.

I believe this quest for new church homes was among the principal causes that gave birth to two movements, both of which emerged in the mid-1960s: the Return to the Jewish Roots of the Church movement, or simply, the Jewish Roots movement; and a parallel movement to create home congregations, also known as home groups and/or home cells, depending upon their organizational structure and setting.

The Jewish Roots movement is populated by a growing number of Christians who have already left their mainline churches and are actively seeking to worship in a setting that would restore the original Jewishness of Christianity. They work toward this restoration, among other ways, by studying the Bible in its Jewish context, observing the Torah to the extent they are able, keeping *Shabbat* rather than Sunday as the Sabbath, and celebrating the biblical festivals.

Sadly, however, the Jewish Roots movement has often been perverted by those Christians who have, in their zeal for Judaism and everything Jewish, crossed over into Rabbinical Judaism by embracing the mistaken understanding that Yeshua is not the divine Son of God and God Himself but rather simply a totally human messiah.[3]

This church-wide Jewish Roots movement has continued to grow with an almost feverish intensity in this opening decade of the new millennium. In turn, it seems evident that this movement has been and remains the prime mover of a parallel phenomenal growth across the entire wide spectrum of Messianic Jewish congregations.

The fact that this growth of contemporary Messianic Judaism has been almost exclusively generated by new Gentile participation gives rise to two concerns regarding the appropriateness of the Messianic Jewish movement as a spiritual sanctuary for those who continue to flock to its rapidly expanding and ever-multiplying congregations. The first of these concerns is that the Messianic Jewish congregations in the United States are in fact a microcosm of the greatly fragmented denominational Christian church that gave them birth. At one extreme of this highly diverse Messianic Jewish body are those congregations whose entirely Jewish membership accept Yeshua as the Messiah while denying His divinity and/or rejecting many New Testament writings, especially those of Paul, as they look beyond the Bible to give precedence and greater authority to the Talmud and other rabbinical writings. At the other end of this spectrum are, in the extreme case, those entirely Gentile led and populated congregations that pay only lip service to the theological and doctrinal Jewish roots of their faith as they flatly reject Jewish tradition and worship practice.

Between these two extremes are the majority of Messianic congregations, each of which embraces its own unique mix of theological, doctrinal, and other related traditions, understandings, and worship practices.

The first problem I see here is this: those who are seriously looking within Messianic Judaism for new, more "orthodox" spiritual homes may indeed find their quest long and difficult.

The second concern that I have is this very Gentile preponderance itself. One need only look to the history of the early planted church at Antioch, which was at first a mixed Jewish and Gentile congregation but very soon became a predominantly Gentile Christian church. Like the rest of the early Gentile Church, which was soon to overtake its Jewish parent in both size and influence, the elimination of any and all things Jewish became an early focus soon after their membership had become predominately Gentile.[4]

I hasten to add that I am not by any means discouraging Gentile participation in Messianic Judaism. I closely adhere to and embrace the "one new man" understanding set forth by the apostle Paul (Eph. 2:15), wherein there is absolutely no spiritual distinction to be made between Jewish and Gentile born-again believers. I am only suggesting that I find it important in congregational settings that such born-again believers be like-minded in expressing their Jewish roots, understandings, and practices.

No matter the depth and breadth of their frustrations, those dear ones who are or who eventually will be searching for new places to worship continue to do so with a passion that has led them, in recent years, to an entirely new and seemingly much more satisfying alternative—the Home Congregation movement, which caught hold in earnest in the United States beginning in the early 1990s. *Time* magazine reports:

> Since the 1990s, the ascendant mode of conservative American faith has been the megachurch. It gathers thousands, or even tens of thousands, for entertaining if sometimes undemanding services amid family-friendly amenities. It is made possible by hundreds of smaller "cell groups" that meet off-nights and provide a humanly scaled framework for scriptural exploration, spiritual mentoring and emotional support. Now, however, some experts look at groups spreading in parts of Colorado, Southern California, Texas and probably elsewhere—and muse, What if the cell groups decided to lose the mother church?
>
> In the 2005 book *Revolution*, George Barna, Evangelicalism's best-known and perhaps most enthusiastic pollster, named simple church as one of several "mini-movements" vacuuming up "millions of believers [who] have stopped going to [standard] church." In two decades, he wrote, "only about one-third of the population" will rely on conventional congregations. Not everyone buys Barna's numbers—previous estimates set house churchers at a minuscule 50,000—but some serious players are intrigued.[5]

The widely acknowledged founder and most influential leader of this worldwide Home Congregation movement is the Reverend Dr. David Yonggi Cho, senior pastor of Yoido Full Gospel Church, reputedly the largest church in the world, located in Seoul, Korea. The congregation numbered over 750,000 in 1997, with more than 50,000 "home cells," as Dr. Cho calls them.

In 1967, when Dr. Cho introduced the cell system, it consisted of 7,750 individuals of 2,267 families organized into 125 cells. By 1973, in just six years, the congregation had increased fivefold to more than 10,000. Only twelve years later, by 1997, the congregation had again exploded with a phenomenal growth of 750 percent to its membership then of 750,000.[6] Reportedly, ten years later, the congregation had continued to grow to its current 850,000.[7] Dr. Cho directly attributes this incredible growth of his church to the structure and operation of his home cell system.[8]

There is no way of knowing the total number of Jewish and Gentile believers in both Israel and the United States who have, for whatever reasons, already begun to establish home congregations or join those that are already established.

This phenomenon should by no means be surprising to any Bible-reading believer. One need only turn to Chapter 2 of the Book of Acts to see that the very first Jewish believers met daily in homes where they centered each meeting on the Lord's Supper, teaching, prayer, and fellowship. Certainly, these daily home congregation meetings were, in a way, supplementary to the gathering of the entire congregation, which took place on the first day of the week, immediately after sundown on *Shabbat* (Saturday evening) for what is known today as a *Motzei* (after) *Shabbat* service. The purpose of these services was to say farewell to the just-ended week and to properly "christen" the new (Acts 20:7–8).

Again, my first purpose in this writing is to encourage the church to return to the model established for it by The Way on Mount Zion.

Toward this end I have provided what I trust is a sufficiently comprehensive, thoroughly documented, multi-faceted examination of the history, writings, theology, doctrine, and worship practices of these first Jewish believers in Yeshua (Jesus) as they coalesced in The Way's expression and fulfillment of traditional Judaism between the years A.D. 30 and 135—during the time they remained on Mount Zion as an orthodox Nazarene Jewish entity.

Let me explain that I have chosen this just over one-century period as my principal focus because it was mainly after A.D. 135, when The Way was widely dispersed, that their orthodoxy fell under the concerted exposure to pagan influences from all sides. Some of these heterodox and, even worse, pagan influences were taken on by various schismatic groups that broke away from the orthodox

Nazarene mainstream and subsequently found expression in their respective belief systems.

Even so, I believe there is much value in examining the historical progression and other aspects of the Nazarenes' post-Mount Zion development as they continued to survive throughout the Diaspora until, under unrelenting persecution, they finally vanished from history toward the end of the fifth century. I have thus done my best to point out any references to such unorthodox sources in this writing as provided for general information rather than as the basis for modern day adaptation.

My second purpose, which in reality is an actualization of the first, is to use these revealed orthodox ways of The Way to offer guidance to those believers who, in seeking new church homes, have determined to create or join small gatherings (home congregations) on The Way's first-century model.

Thus, the goal I have set for this writing is to provide a straight and clear pathway for those who, longing for the biblical and historical authenticity of their understandings and worship practices, are seeking to take the journey back to the first-century upper room on Mount Zion.

What a mighty precedent they would set if only these many millions of believers who have already left their mainline churches were to establish or join such home congregations, organized and operated on the first century model of The Way!

What an enormous potential impact they could have upon the worldwide church, which so far has been seemingly silent and perhaps either unwilling and/or unable to rise to the challenges foisted upon us all by Satan and his legion of demons, who are running roughshod over the body of Yeshua, the holy church we once took for granted as righteous, true, and good. The Lord God of Israel is filled with loving kindness, grace, mercy, and patience. We are promised, according to His Word, that His love will endure forever, but dare we be so certain about the limits of His patience?

Yeshua wept at a moment of His greatest sorrow (John 11:35). Surely, He is weeping once again as He beholds His body, the church, as a great multitude of Christians continue to flee from their mainline congregations while earnestly seeking new, more orthodox spiritual homes where they might at last worship the one true God in spirit and in truth. It is my heartfelt prayer that this book, at least in some small way, might facilitate the accomplishment of their quest.

A Brief Overview of *The Way* From Its Inception on Mount Zion, Circa A.D. 30, to Its Disappearance in Syria During the Closing Decades of the Fifth Century

How very clearly one can see the mighty hand of God upon the Nazarenes, who were first called The Way—the relatively small minority of Jews who were the first born-again believers in Yeshua. Even while they endured relentless persecution from all sides as they frequently moved about the land of their inheritance in an attempt to escape their pursuers, miraculously, they survived for more than four centuries.

But, far more than this, even while they survived under the most difficult imaginable circumstances, The Way and those Nazarenes who came after them who remained orthodox in their understandings created a vast body of theology, doctrine, and worship practice that, when molded together, became the rock-solid, forever enduring foundation upon which all subsequent expressions of Christianity have come forth.

This four-century era of the Nazarenes of The Way was a fascinating, tumultuous, and, arguably the most vitally important period in Judeo-Christian history. In the beginning, during the early spring of the year A.D. 30, before He ascended into heaven, Yeshua appeared to James, His brother in the flesh, and He appointed him as first shepherd of His earthly flock.[9]

I suggest that our Lord may have been pleased as He beheld His entirely Jewish body, the nascent church, during the first three decades of its existence. His newly appointed apostles, James, Peter, and John, and others of the original one hundred and twenty, just as He had commissioned them, were reaping a mighty harvest of souls as they preached His gospel on Mount Zion, from Solomon's court, in the synagogues of the Pharisees (Acts 9:20), and elsewhere throughout the holy city of Jerusalem and environs.

And, thus, the Lamb of God was glorified as many thousands, at first all Jews, responded to embrace Him as their Messiah with all of their hearts, minds, and strength—even three thousand in one day alone (Acts 2:41, 47).

These formative years were challenging, fulfilling, and glorious for those who were called The Way, the Jewish "mother congregation" that was at first held forth from the Upper Room, now called the Cenacle on Mount Zion (Acts 1:12–14). Led by the Holy Spirit, the patriarchs of The Way established for themselves an ecclesiastical structure which, like most aspects of their new movement, was based upon the model of their Essene brothers at Qumran.[10] According to Bellarmino Bagatti, a contemporary Catholic biblical historian who has written extensively on the early church, from the very beginning the Nazarenes diligently recalled and wrote down the words, sayings, and teachings of their beloved Yeshua, which they had heard Him utter with their own ears during the more than three blessed years He had dwelled among them.[11] These writings were assembled to create four later-canonized gospels and many other writings, some canonical and others we now call apocryphal.

Moreover, according to Emmanuel Testa, another contemporary Catholic biblical scholar and authority on the early church, based largely upon their respective Essene models, these first Jewish believers of The Way established an elaborate ritual to initiate new believers into their fellowship that included renunciation of Satan, a profession of faith, a three-immersion water baptism, celebration of the Lord's Supper, and, in conclusion, a festive community meal.[12]

Drawn together into the intimacy of a *mishpakha* (family) by their shared adoration of Yeshua, "They continued steadfastly in the apostles' doctrine and fellowship, in the breaking of bread, and in prayers. Then fear came upon every soul, and many wonders and signs were done through the apostles" (Acts 2:42–43). They celebrated their Lord in this manner when they gathered together for a *Motzei Shabbat* congregational service immediately after nightfall each Sabbath (Saturday) evening. This was, according to their calendar, the beginning of the first day of the new week. Each time they came together, they worshiped the Lord in adoration and praise as they sang together the new, Spirit-filled praise songs of their own composition, known today as the Odes of Solomon, and also the *Hodayoth* (Hymns of Thanksgiving), which had been handed down to them from an earlier generation of Essenes.

> Every day they continued to meet together in the temple courts. They broke bread in their homes and ate together with glad and sincere hearts, praising God and enjoying the favor of all the people. And the Lord added to their number daily those who were being saved.
>
> —Acts 2:46–47, niv

Indeed, during these, their opening decades, The Way, Yeshua's nascent body in Zion, flourished in a Camelot-like setting from which it reflected the very essence of love, joy, peace, and the other fruits of the Holy Spirit. And from this, its anointed and sanctified initiation, the twelve apostles, led by James and Peter, molded the foundation of a theological, doctrinal, organizational, and worship system that would very soon dramatically unfold in its next iteration, leading to the eventual worldwide church. However, not unlike the Camelot of one who was only a mythical king, the halcyon days of the Jewish mother congregation in Jerusalem were not to long endure.

The seeds of what was to become the meteoric growth of the body of Yeshua were seemingly sown with the martyrdom of Stephen, circa A.D. 35. In the wake of this persecution-driven tragedy and in fear of what similar fate might befall them, many members of The Way widely dispersed from Jerusalem in the first of three exoduses from the mother congregation that would together form a second great Diaspora.[13]

Certainly, this early dispersal of The Way from Zion was not happenstance, but rather an integral part of Yeshua's holy plan to develop His earthly body, the Church. Wherever they went, these newly uprooted Jewish believers planted the holy seed of the gospel in newly plowed and fertile soil. That seed would quickly germinate and spring forth as the means for another, much greater harvest—the equally called, anointed, and saved but culturally and traditionally very different Gentile Christian Church.

As I suggested in an earlier writing, *The Door Where It Began*, the first organized expression of Gentile Christianity likely occurred soon after Yeshua's second feeding of the multitude at Tel Hadar, on the eastern shore of the Sea of Galilee circa A.D. 32, some fourteen years before Paul took his first mission outreach journey (Matt. 15:29–39).[14]

There is compelling archaeological and scriptural evidence suggesting that the first Messianic-Gentile synagogue was established at Hippos/Sussita in nearby Bashan, today's Golan Heights, and that this movement, by direction of Yeshua Himself (Mark 5:19–20), quickly spread throughout the entire ten-city region of the Decapolis, then moved eastward to form what today remains as the various eastern churches. It seems quite remarkable that Gentile Christianity most likely actually began some three centuries before Constantine extended his church to Constantinople, the traditionally understood seat of eastern orthodoxy.

Antioch, in northern Syria, as the first main center of Gentile Christianity, was the most notable of these many Jewish-planted Gentile-Christian churches. This church at Antioch was the genesis of a new, predominately Gentile Christian, western church movement. The missionary focus of the apostle Paul and Barnabas, which began with Paul's first mission outreach journey (A.D. 46–48), and their first visit in A.D. 49 to Antioch's still mostly Jewish body underscored this destiny. Following this first visit by Paul and

Barnabas, Antioch, rather than Jerusalem, became the home base for Paul's subsequent mission outreach.[15]

In parallel with the further development of Gentile Christianity at Antioch and elsewhere, there was a steady migration of believing Jews from Zion. This migration began following Stephen's martyrdom circa A.D. 35 and continued through the second Jewish rebellion against Rome (A.D. 132–135), most notably with end locations spread throughout the Galilee and what is now modern day Syria and Jordan.[16] Moreover, the center of what was to remain the predominately Jewish part of the body soon shifted from Jerusalem to "the region of Damascus."[17] This so-called, often cited "region of Damascus" is a very real, historically important though loosely defined area that occupied a considerable part of what is now southwestern Syria.

In his treatment of the *Damascus Document* (CD-A), J. T. Milik, one of the very first and best-known Dead Sea Scrolls scholars, suggests that a large number of the Essenes of Qumran, under the pressure of a great influx of new members to the sect, left Qumran and resettled in this "region of Damascus," where they established a particularly ascetic community with a strong focus on family life, the Sabbath rest, and ritual purity. Milik then goes on to compare the Essenes to the early Jewish believers, pointing to close organizational parallels and other similarities between the two groups.[18]

Thus, if, as Milik suggests, the Essenes already had a well-established base in "thc region of Damascus," most likely even before the first dispersal of The Way from Jerusalem in A.D. 35, this already established Essene community would have been a natural location to which the like-minded refugees from Mount Zion would have been attracted. The martyrdom of James the Just in A.D. 62[19] was another major turning point in the movement of The Way's center from Jerusalem to this "region of Damascus."

With respect to what happened to the leadership of The Way following the death of James in A.D. 62, Eusebius (and most modern day scholarship) is rightfully skeptical about the accuracy of the list of fourteen ethnic Jewish successors as "bishops" of the mother church in Jerusalem. Eusebius references this list from the earlier, no longer surviving writings of Hegesippus. According to Hegesippus, the last of the fifteen Jewish bishops, Judas, was martyred before A.D. 66, which coincides with the beginning of Emperor Hadrian's relentless siege of Jerusalem. If Hegesippus's list, as it is reported by Eusebius, is indeed accurate—which is highly unlikely—this would mean that, following James's untimely death, there was only a four- to five-year total Jewish leadership of the Jerusalem church, making for an average reign of less than five months for each of James's successors.[20] It seems much more likely that circa A.D. 70, due to continuing persecution and other factors, most Nazarenes of The Way had already relocated from Jerusalem, many of them to the Galilee (including Tiberias) and Syria.

This conclusion is reinforced by Eusebius's further challenge of Hegesippus by pointing to his own, separate account that The Way had been supernaturally warned of the impending Jewish revolt and destruction of the temple and thus fled to the safe haven of Pella, a city of the Decapolis, with only a few of the inner circle remaining in Jerusalem.[21]

There is no reliable record concerning the total membership of The Way at the close of the first century. Estimates range widely from as few as three hundred thousand to as many as one million. What can be said with reasonable certainty is that the Nazarenes of The Way, who by that time had relocated mostly to "the region of Damascus" and the Galilee, continued to grow in both size and influence as a major believing Jewish sect.

Moreover, the considerable development of this sect of Jewish believers took place both in parallel with and in considerable opposition to the sect of the Pharisees, which, beginning in A.D. 70 with the destruction of the temple, was quickly emerging as the precursor of modern day Rabbinical Judaism.

The second Jewish revolt against Rome (A.D. 132–135) was a clear benchmark for the beginning of what was soon to become The Way's precipitous decline. Rabbi Akiva, the major voice of the Pharisees and the instigator of the rebellion, called upon the Nazarenes of The Way to join his already formidable military forces under the leadership of one Bar Kochba ("Son of the Star") whom Akiva had personally chosen and anointed as the "true" Messiah of Israel. The Way was certainly no friend of Rome, given that its members were already suffering considerable persecution under their imperial rule and thus may have otherwise ceded to Akiva's call for military alliance against a common enemy. However, Akiva's ill-advised caveat that The Way must first renounce Yeshua as their Messiah in favor of Bar Kochba was an obvious nonstarter. Thus, there continued a now greatly intensified threefold opposition, which ultimately led to The Way's demise.

The pharisaic Rabbis, who had, circa A.D. 90, already begun to curse both Yeshua and His followers in their synagogues three times daily,[22] now made both The Way and its Messiah the written focus of their most vile curses, scorn, and ridicule in the pages of the forthcoming Oral Torah already being redacted and finally completed circa A.D. 220 as the Mishna. These self-same curses and expansive negative commentary directed at the Nazarenes of The

Way, whom the rabbis called *minim* (outsiders within the Jewish community), have to this day carried over into the most recent versions of the Talmud, a tediously detailed, fifteen-thousand-page, thirty-five-volume collection of rabbinical writings.[23]

This rabbinical persecution of these Nazarenes seems child's play alongside the greatly more intense and persistent opposition of all Jews by the Romans. For example, Emperor Hadrian (A.D. 117–138) forbade them and all other Jews from ever again even approaching their beloved Jerusalem.[24] Later, when they assembled to rebuild their holy city, Emperor Constantine (A.D. 306–337) prevented them from doing so, commanded that their ears be cut off, and otherwise subjected them to physical abuse before widely dispersing them.[25]

The Romans' destruction of the temple was equally devastating to both traditional Jews and the Nazarenes of The Way. The rebuilding of the temple in Jerusalem is the central expectation and hope of traditional Judaism. When this occurs, they hold that God's physical presence will be returned to the holy of holies and they will once again be able to sacrifice to Him as they did while the earlier temples stood.

Please remember that the Nazarenes of The Way were fully Torah-observant Jews, as was their Messiah, Yeshua, who regularly taught and performed miracles in its courts. While the temple stood, the Nazarenes of The Way met there each day (Acts 2:46). They were there on the wondrous occasion of Pentecost, which gave them cause to frequently return to this place where there was continuous celebratory singing and dancing.[26]

Like the Nazarenes of The Way, contemporary believing Jews with very good reason long for the reconstruction of the temple. Scripture teaches that Yeshua will rebuild the temple after His second coming.

> Then speak to him, saying, "Thus says the LORD of hosts, saying: 'Behold, the Man whose name *is* the BRANCH! From His place He shall branch out, And He shall build the temple of the LORD; Yes, He shall build the temple of the LORD. He shall bear the glory, And shall sit and rule on His throne; So He shall be a priest on His throne, And the counsel of peace shall be between them both.'"
>
> —ZECHARIAH 6:12–13

The Bible uses the name *the Branch* to identify the King Messiah. Hence, *the Branch* is a term used to signify Yeshua the Messiah, who is a direct descendant of King David. The prophets Isaiah, Jeremiah, and Zechariah all refer to King Messiah as the Branch. It is the Branch of David, King Messiah,

Yeshua who will build the magnificent temple of Ezekiel 40–48, from which He shall rule the nations.[27]

Quite understandably, the Nazarenes of The Way longed for the rebuilding of the temple for a number of reasons, principal among them being that the second coming of Yeshua was prerequisite to this awesome event.

Among other anti-Semitic acts of the Romans that impacted all Jews during these tumultuous times were:

- Hadrian's construction in A.D. 197 of a temple to the pagan god Jupiter on the very ruins of the Jewish temple. In its atrium, Hadrian had placed a giant statue of himself, benefactor and ruler of the world. The sum of all this was the abomination of desolation spoken of in Daniel 11:31 and in the three synoptic Gospels.
- Hadrian's ban on circumcision (which applied to Egyptians and Arabs as well as Jews). As the most hellenized of all Roman emperors, Hadrian regarded circumcision as nothing less than mutilation. Even so, the Jews rightfully regarded this ban as a deliberate attack on their ability to keep the Abrahamic covenant, which stood as one of the principal foundations of their belief system.
- As if this twofold opposition from their fellow Jews and the Romans were not enough, like newly hatched salmon fry, who gain their early life's sustenance absorbing nutrients from the flesh of their dead or near-dead parents, the Gentile Christian church, almost from its very beginning, turned against its Jewish mother, the Nazarenes of The Way, by making every possible effort to marginalize and eventually pound them out of existence.

In the face of this unremitting opposition, they began to fade into the shadow of the Gentile Christian Church. Some scholars cite the end of this terminal process as early as A.D. 70 in the wake of the first rebellion against Rome. Others hold that these Nazarenes of The Way persisted as a viable entity until well after the second rebellion, which ended in A.D. 135. Archaeological evidence, however, disputes the argument that Nazarene Judaism died out quickly after either A.D. 70 or 135. According to Ignazio Mancini and other respected sources, there is evidence of the active presence of the Nazarenes of The Way, especially in the hill county of southwestern Syria and what today is the Kingdom of Jordan, through the fourth century, followed by a continuing decline for another century or perhaps even two.[28]

It is clear that in the beginning and for some time into the future, these persistent Nazarenes of The Way remained the dominant expression of the organized body of Yeshua in the Israel. The archaeological data opens the question of how long it remained so. Some have suggested that it was the dominant organized expression of the faith in the Israel of that day until the time of Constantine (A.D. 306–337) and the arrival of Byzantine Christians. Since many of their sites stand in close proximity to Gentile Christian sites, the archaeological evidence appears to document a struggle for dominance between the native believing Jewish community of the Nazarene's of The Way and the incoming pre-Byzantine and early Byzantine authorities. Thus, Gentile and Nazarene places of worship existed side by side in the same towns dating from the fourth century. Mancini and others hold that it was not until the arrival of the Byzantines that The Way was finally outnumbered, divided, and marginalized, and thus began to slip into heretical sects.[29]

Part I

The Way's Mother Congregation on Mount Zion

Chapter 1
The Founding of the Jewish "Mother Congregation" on Mount Zion

One can hardly blame James for his skepticism regarding the messianic claims of his blood half-brother, Yeshua, which at first must have seemed outrageous.[1] After all, following their mutual growing-up years in Nazareth, they had gone very separate ways. Yeshua had spent much of his first twenty-seven years preparing for what He had very early called "my Father's business" (Luke 2:49), and James had matured into something of a Jewish holy man, an ascetic, whose piety was controlled by ceremonial concerns. He was frequently in the temple, where he prayed constantly for the people. Hegesippus and others depict him as one who was holy from birth, who drank no strong drink, ate no meat, did not shave his head, anoint himself with oil or bathe, and as one who wore only linen. Later, because of his great righteousness he came to be called, with great respect, James "the Just."[2]

Nothing I have found in Scripture, or elsewhere in the vast collective body of the Nazarenes' non-canonical writings, suggests that James was in any way involved with Yeshua's earthly ministry until its very end. Thus, it must have been a giant credibility leap for James to believe his own human senses when, as it was recorded by Jerome from the Gospel of the Hebrews:

> (Soon) after the resurrection of the Savior: And when the Lord had given the linen cloth to the servant of the priest, he went to James and appeared to him. For James had sworn that he would not eat bread from that hour in which he had drunk the cup of the Lord until he should see him risen from among them that sleep. And shortly thereafter the Lord said: Bring a table and bread! And immediately it is added: he took the bread, blessed it and broke it and gave it to James the Just and said to him: My brother, eat your bread, for the Son of man is risen from among them that sleep.[3]

This post-resurrection appearance by Yeshua to His brother James is affirmed by the apostle Paul: "After that He was seen by James, then by all the apostles" (1 Cor. 15:7). Moreover, the apocryphal Gospel of Thomas records Yeshua's appointment of James as the first leader of the Jewish "mother church":

> The disciples said to Jesus, "We know that you are going to leave us. Who will be our leader?" Jesus said to them, "No matter where you are you are to go to James the Just, for whose sake heaven and earth came into being."[4]

It would seem that church politics are not an invention exclusive to modern times. Immediately following Yeshua's awesome ascension into heaven, those who had been closest to Him returned to the Upper Room to prayerfully consider how they should proceed in implementing their Lord's last human-voice instruction to them:[5]

> Go therefore and make disciples of all the nations, baptizing them in the name of the Father and of the Son and of the Holy Spirit, teaching them to observe all things that I have commanded you; and lo, I am with you always, even to the end of the age.
>
> —Matthew 28:19–20

While it seems clear that Yeshua had commissioned His brother James as the initial leader of His body, it is interesting to note how Luke understood the actual relationship between those who had first returned to the Upper Room.

> Then they returned to Jerusalem from the mount called Olivet, which is near Jerusalem, a Sabbath day's journey. And when they had entered, they went up into the upper room where they were staying: *Peter, James,* John, and Andrew; Philip and Thomas; Bartholomew and Matthew; James the son of Alphaeus and Simon the Zealot; and Judas the son of James. These all continued with one accord in prayer and supplication, with the women and Mary the mother of Jesus, and with His brothers.
>
> —Acts 1:12–14, emphasis added

Arguably, it was neither a simple error nor a matter of chance that Luke put Peter's name ahead of James's. Rather, it seems this was most likely done as a natural and instinctive reflection of a well-understood reality: Peter, at the very least, was a strong voice among the twelve apostles. These were those who were to chart the immediate future and ultimate destiny of what was to come forth first as an entirely Jewish body and then coalesce for a time with the emerging Gentile Church of its own creation.

Peter was, after all, appropriated as the *modus vivendi* of the entire Roman Catholic establishment, having been so transformed to this position through what most non-Catholics hold to be the faulty hermeneutical exegesis of a single verse of Scripture. What did Yeshua really mean when He told Peter, "And I also say to you that you are Peter, and on this rock I will build My church, and the gates of Hades shall not prevail against it" (Matt. 16:18–19)? Was it perhaps something on the order of, "I will move you to my throne in Rome, where I will establish you to sit in my place as the first of a continuing line of successors who will be 'the Lord Pope, sweet Christ on earth'?"[6]

It seems to me instead that Yeshua, in this context, was anointing Peter as the first spiritual leader of an evangelical movement charged with taking forth His gospel from the Jewish congregation on Mount Zion to a spiritually blind and pagan world; that is, Peter was being given the awesome overseeing task of activating and then implementing the Great Commission. James, on the other hand, would remain on Mount Zion as the leader of the mother congregation. He would also often be on his knees in the temple making supplication for his people until his execution in A.D. 62 at the hands of the same temple authorities who had brought his older brother to His cross.

Certainly, Peter did not proceed in this alone. Standing with him to meet this enormous missionary challenge were the likes of Paul, Barnabas, and John-Mark.[7] It was the members of this evangelical team who would venture forth from Jerusalem to bring the good news first to a new, entirely Jewish and widely disseminated Diaspora, and then, only later, to Antioch and a wide range of other non-Jewish fertile mission fields that awaited their respective spiritual plantings and eventual great harvests.

To summarize this point of apostolic relationship, it was the rigidly ascetic James who was called by his brother, Yeshua, to establish and bring to life the very first organized body of Yeshua on Mount Zion. While Peter, Paul, Barnabas, John-Mark, and the rest were out planting holy seeds and beginning to reap what would be a great and growing harvest of souls, it was James who envisioned and then set in place the structure and operating mechanisms of the orthodox Nazarene Jewish body of Yeshua who first met on Mount Zion, where they were called The Way.

It was also James, the righteous overseer, who would, assisted by others, set the body's standards and establish its theology, doctrine, and worship practices. Perhaps most enduringly, he would make certain that the awesome signs, wonders, and teachings that had been seen and heard by those who walked with his brother, Yeshua, would be memorialized in what was to become the enormous collection of their sacred writings.[8]

The tragic martyrdom of Stephen in A.D. 35 at the hands of his fellow Jews was a major turning point in the early life of The Way. Stephen was the leader of a group of seven *mebaqqerim* (deacons) who were ordained to conduct the administrative affairs of the congregation and otherwise minister to the body under the direction of the twelve apostles (Acts 6:1–6). While he was being mercilessly stoned to death, Stephen, a deeply faithful, on-fire believer knelt down and cried out with a loud voice, "Lord, do not charge them with this sin" (Acts 7:60). And it was Sha'ul of Tarsus, a seemingly out-of-control rabbinical fanatic, who was among those who cast the first stones as he cheered on his fellow executioners.[9]

May I suggest, on reflection, that perhaps our Lord had a greater, twofold purpose in allowing Stephen, whom He loved, to so greatly suffer and die? First, there seems to be a clear connection between Stephen's martyrdom and the miraculous metamorphosis of Sha'ul, who had been The Way's most fanatical persecutor, into the apostle Paul, who inarguably became the most important evangelist, writer, and theologian of the first century. Moreover, this Sha'ul the Pharisee *cum* Paul the Apostle was to become the principal founder and architect of Christianity and what became the Gentile Christian Church.

How could Sha'ul, the murdering Pharisee, not be greatly moved by the spectacle of so much constancy, so much faith, so much love emanating from Stephen, the saintly man who was being so unjustifiably tortured, abused—cruelly martyred—in part by his own blindly punishing hand? It is hardly too much to agree with Augustine that "the church owes Paul to the prayer of Stephen."[10]

I would suggest that the second potential greater purpose of Stephen's martyrdom was that it provoked a new diaspora, this one comprised of Jewish believers who, only some five years following Yeshua's ascension, fled from Jerusalem out of a well-founded fear that by not doing so they would likely meet the same end as Stephen.

The persecution of *The Way* continued with an increasing intensity immediately following the martyrdom of Stephen. Both Peter and John were arrested as heretics and condemned to flagellation. Eusebius writes:

> Stephen's martyrdom was followed by the first and greatest persecution by the Jews themselves of the Jerusalem Church. All the disciples except

> the Twelve alone were dispersed about Judea and Samaria. Some, as the inspired record says traveled as far as Phoenicia, Cyprus, and Antioch; but they could not yet venture to share the message of the faith with the Gentiles, and proclaimed it to the Jews alone. At the same time, also, Paul was still raging against the Church, entering the homes of the faithful, dragging off men and women, and handing them over for imprisonment.[11]

Eusebius goes on to discuss the outreach of Phillip, one of the seven who were ordained with Stephen as *mebaqqerim*. Phillip dispersed from Jerusalem to the northeast into Samaria, where he encountered the famous Ethiopian eunuch whom, according to Eusebius, he baptized as the first Gentile member of the body.

While one can argue with Eusebius that there were many other Gentiles who embraced Yeshua during His earthly ministry, such as the famous centurion of Capernaum (Matt. 8:5–13) and presumably many of the four thousand Gentiles He miraculously fed at Tel Hadar,[12] the important point here is that there was a mighty new diaspora created throughout the entire land of Israel of that day and well beyond, which formed a God-positioned deployment of ready and well-experienced, on-fire evangelists who were focused, at first, on spreading the gospel among their fellow Jews.

While not at this point mentioned by Eusebius, perhaps the most important aspect of this new diaspora was the many of these Nazarenes of The Way who relocated throughout the Galilee. Perhaps more important still are those who fled even further north and east to the "region of Damascus" and from there, especially, to Kochaba, what in modern times is a little-known, not yet excavated, very large center to which The Way's base of operations began to shift from Jerusalem as early as A.D. 36.[13]

Even so, despite the Eusebius's opinion to the contrary, there is considerable other evidence that a significant contingent of The Way remained on Mount Zion until just before the onset of the first rebellion against Rome (A.D. 66–73) when, having been supernaturally alerted to the impending destruction of the temple and the city, many of them fled to Pella, a city of the Decapolis.[14]

There is also evidence suggesting that many who had fled to Pella returned to Mount Zion after the war, and remained there in some considerable number until the death of Symeon,[15] a Davidic heir and cousin of Yeshua, who replaced James as the leader of the Jerusalem church following James's martyrdom at the hands of the Sadducean temple authorities in A.D. 62.[16]

What can be said with historical assurance is that, on pain of death and by order of the Emperor Hadrian, the last believing Jew from the era of The Way left Jerusalem sometime during or immediately after the second revolt against Rome (A.D. 132–135), when all Jews were permanently banned from entering the city, which was then re-named *Aelia Capitolina* by Hadrian.[17]

According to Eusebius, the first fifteen bishops of Jerusalem were "of the circumcision" (Jews). Even so, the Romans destroyed the last of the Jewish leadership in Jerusalem in A.D. 135 during the second revolt.

However, by no means do I mean to suggest by any of the foregoing sad commentary that any or all of this spelled the end of the Nazarenes of The Way. While it is fair to say that these events foreclosed the tenure of the mother congregation of The Way on Mount Zion, there were still more than four centuries of internal growth and missionary outreach remaining before the last of these stalwart believing Jews finally succumbed to their never-relenting opposition.[18]

It is not possible to say with certainty when, specifically, each of the anointed and perfectly hewn spiritually Jewish stones was set in place on Mount Zion and later in the region of Damascus that together within a few years would create the anointed foundation of Christianity and the church. Sadly however, during the reign of Constantine (A.D. 306–337), paganism that had earlier begun to creep in and be assimilated into the very fabric of the church intensified as "de-Judaization" became the order of the day. For example, Constantine, before his deathbed baptism, had been a lifelong worshiper of Mithra, the sun god. Thus, one of this sun-worshiping emperor's most telling pagan corruptions was his changing the Biblical Sabbath from *Shabbat* (Saturday) to "Sun-day" which also happened to be the birthday of Mithra.

Even so, despite this and all the many other pagan perversions that followed over the centuries, the very Jewish foundational underpinnings of the body of Yeshua, His bride, the church, endure even today as the anointed legacy of its Jewish progenitor, the Nazarenes of The Way, a relatively miniscule gathering of those who first met in the Upper Room on Mount Zion on the very day our Lord ascended into heaven (Acts 1:12).

In summary, looking to the considerable evidence provided by a variety of sources, we can confidently summarize our understandings about the Nazarenes of The Way, an "orthodox" group (they embraced no heretical or apostate understandings) who, under the leadership of James, the brother of Yeshua, emerged from their original gathering of some 120 Jewish believers who first met on Mount Zion immediately following Yeshua's crucifixion and burial.

These Nazarenes of The Way existed as a distinct sectarian group until the late fourth or early fifth century. They evangelized their Jewish brethren in the synagogues and later reached out to both their fellow Jews and Gentiles in a new, widespread Diaspora that began to form circa A.D. 35 with the martyrdom of Stephen against a background of extreme persecution rendered against them by their fellow Jews, the emerging Gentile Church and the Roman government. The Nazarenes of The Way accepted the entire Tenach (Old Testament) and were the exclusive authors of the Brit Hadeshah (New Testament). They acknowledged that God was the Creator of all things and that Yeshua was at once the Messiah, the Son of God, and God Himself. They fully embraced the tri-unity of the Godhead, an understanding they had by divine revelation. They also inherited this same understanding from traditional Judaism (circa 500 B.C.). It had been embraced by their Essene predecessors and was memorialized by them in their Dead Sea Scrolls.

None of their potential detractors could find anything to indicate that they denied Yeshua's virgin birth or His death and resurrection. While they continued to embrace the Torah in its entirety, they did not believe that doing so was essential for salvation. Rather, their motivation in this regard was to be imitators of Yeshua, who, during His walk amongst them, they observed to be a fully Torah observant Jew.

Up until the time of Epiphanius (A.D. 310–403) the Nazarenes were apparently sufficiently orthodox to escape the attention of the heresiologists, those such as Epiphanius and his contemporary, Irenaeus, who meticulously investigated the numerous seemingly Christian sects that had sprung up during their time to make certain nothing heretical or apostate could be found in their understanding and/or practice. It was solely on the basis of the Nazarenes' continued observance of the Torah that Epiphanius and others who followed him mistakenly determined that they were a heretical sect.

Chapter 2
The Organization and Structure of the Nazarenes and Their Mother Congregation of The Way on Mount Zion

The Jewish Roots movement proceeds on the premise that Christianity is not a new religion, but rather a relatively new expression and fulfillment of Judaism. This understanding rings true, as far as it goes, but that isn't far enough to avoid it being an oversimplification. As previously discussed, Christianity, with its literally thousands of denominational variations, some insignificant and others profound, is anything but homogeneous. So also is the Judaism of today, and so was the Judaism both before and during the time that Yeshua took on flesh and walked about the land of Israel.

This oversimplification concerning Judaism during the time of Yeshua begs the question, What were the principal understandings of this religion of the Jews that found fulfillment and new expression in Christianity?

There were three very different principal Jewish sects operating in early first-century Israel: the Sadducees, the Pharisees, and the Essenes. The Sadducees were closely tied to the temple. When it was destroyed in A.D. 70, they quickly vanished from the scene and left no legacy.

By the time of Yeshua's earthly ministry, the Pharisees had already begun to create an elaborate network of synagogues into which they quickly transitioned after the temple was reduced to ruins. It was from this formidable synagogual base that the Pharisees reached out to appropriate the mantle of normative and/or traditional Judaism. However, the Pharisaic rabbis who now preached a new Oral Torah from the *bamot* (synagogual podiums) of the genuinely traditional, written-Torah-centered "sages" of earlier generations were anything but traditional, as evidenced by their radically new version of Judaism, known today as Rabbinical Judaism. In short, the Pharisees had dared to, in some ways; replace the written Torah of God, the Bible, with the law of men (the Oral Torah as it is expressed in the Talmud and other rabbinical commentary).[1]

The Pharisees of His time, including at first Sha'ul of Tarsus, militantly opposed Yeshua and those Nazarene Jewish believers of The Way who followed Him. Sadly, this opposition continues in full force today, especially in Israel, where even those believers in Yeshua who are 100 percent ethnically Jewish are denied Israeli citizenship because of their religious convictions since they are no longer considered to be Jews.[2]

The contemporary reality is that Rabbinical Judaism is the only surviving expression of the Jewish religion that was instituted by God Himself on Mount Sinai when He handed Moses the Decalogue of the written Torah, inscribed on stone tablets by His holy hand. Hence, by default, Rabbinical Judaism is the traditional and/or normative Judaism of today, simply because there are no other numerically significant competing alternative expressions.

During the first-century walk of Yeshua, however, the Essenes offered a strikingly different sectarian alternative. These understandings as they were recorded in the Dead Sea Scrolls mirrored the theological, doctrinal, and traditional understandings of the Judaism that existed during the reign of King Solomon. This was the Judaism that had been understood and practiced by even earlier generations, a traditional Judaism that had begun to take form with the very first ministrations of Abraham, as early as 2000 B.C.

The Essenes were a major Jewish sect of Yeshua's time, and it was the Essenes who clearly embraced the theological, doctrinal, and traditional understandings of the earlier sages as the baseline of their own updated iteration of Judaism. It is this Essenism that was and remains the very foundation and substance of Yeshua's fulfillment of the Torah, that is to say, Christianity as it was originally expressed in orthodox Nazarene Judaism, which He spoke of in His Sermon on the Mount (Matt. 5:17).

Modern day scholars continue to glean rich theological treasures from the still being translated and studied Dead Sea Scrolls, animal skins upon which the Essenes of Qumran recorded their truly traditional/normative Jewish understandings, understandings from which the Pharisees substantially departed and which radically depart from those of modern day Rabbinical Judaism.

For example, the understanding that the Godhead has three distinct members forming a tri-unity was a central teaching of the sages during the first temple period. This same understanding is recorded in the Dead Sea Scrolls.[3] Moreover, while Rabbinical Judaism still awaits the coming of a Messiah whom they hold will appear in a time of trouble to solve the various problems of the world,[4] the Essenes understood that the Messiah would appear as God incarnate who would atone for the sins of men.[5]

Virtually nothing of any significance has come down to New Testament Christian understanding from the specific unique teachings of the Pharisees, while arguably all foundational, orthodox tenets of New Testament Christian theological understanding, doctrine, and worship practice were either first understood and/or are at least to some extent rooted in the understandings of the Essenes.[6]

While the specific theological, doctrinal, and traditional connections between Essenism and Christianity are detailed in later chapters, let us now turn to the remarkable similarity between the organization and structure of the ascetic Essene community at Qumran and the parallel organization and structure of the Nazarene Jewish sect and their congregation that was called The Way.

The Dead Sea Scrolls reveal that the Essenes had a very structured hierarchy, a system that the Nazarenes adopted and put it into practice on Mount Zion. The Qumran community was governed by a council with twelve members that provided top-level supervision over the entire Essene establishment. This Council of Twelve was comprised of "twelve men [elders] and three priests perfected in all that has been revealed from the whole Torah: for practicing truth and righteousness, justice and loving kindness and walking humbly with each other; for keeping faithfulness in the land with firm intention and contrite spirit; for overcoming iniquity by deeds of justice and endurance of fiery trials, and for walking in all things by the standard of truth and the regulation for the occasion."[7]

Below the Essene Council of Twelve were the inspectors or overseers (*mebaqqerim*), whose duties at the Qumran center included presiding at meetings, in particular what was their precursor of Lord's Supper[8] and/or communal feasts. They were also responsible for admitting new members to the community and for administering communal goods.

The *mebaqqerim*'s role in the greater Essene establishment extended well beyond the monastic center at Qumran into the widely dispersed communities of the sect where they functioned as clear antecedents of modern day pastors and congregational leaders. The Damascus Document speaks of a minister called a *mebaqqer* as the leader of each of these outside communities, which were called "camps." The *mebaqqer*'s pastoral duties were:

> This is the rule of the *mebaqqer* of the camp. He shall instruct the many in the deeds of God, and shall teach them his mighty marvels.... He shall have pity on them like a father on his sons, and will heal all the afflicted among them like a shepherd his flock. He will undo all the chains which bind them, so that there will be neither harassed nor oppressed in his congregation. And everyone who joins his congregation he should examine concerning his actions, his intelligence, his strength, his courage and his wealth, and they shall inscribe him in his place according to his inheritance in the lot of light. No one of the members of the camp should have authority to introduce anyone into the congregation without the permission of the *mebaqqer* of the camp.[9]

The connectivity between the organization of the Essene establishment and that of the extended mother Jewish congregation, headed by James, can be found first in James's epistle written to the believing Jewish Diaspora, which dispersed from Jerusalem after the martyrdom of Stephen. The Epistle of James, widely regarded as the oldest book of the New Testament, was written no later than A.D. 50, probably not too long after A.D. 35.[10] In his epistle, James instructed those seeking healing: "Is any one of you sick? He should call the *elders* of the church to pray over him and anoint him with oil in the name of the Lord" (James 5:4, NIV). Since James was a Jew, writing to a Jewish audience, he almost assuredly wrote in Hebrew, which subsequently was translated into Greek and ultimately further was translated into our modern day English language versions. The original Hebrew word in this verse for "elders," as it is also widely used in the Old Testament, is *zaqenem* ("older, senior council members"). In the New Testament, "elders" is the English translation of the Greek word *presbuterous*.

In any event, the Council of Twelve Apostles, with James as its head, was the successor of the Qumran Council of Twelve.

There are numerous other points of connection between the Essene model and the respective ways of The Way. While most of these are theological, doctrinal, and/or relate to worship practice and will be discussed in later chapters, another interesting matter of comparative organization should be mentioned in this context. While I have the highest respect for the giants of Roman Catholic scholarship, such as Italian Franciscan Father Bellarmino Bagatti and French Cardinal Jean Danielou, who devoted much of their professional lives to studying and writing about what they call Jewish Christianity, they and other such church-rooted scholars consistently superimpose Gentile Christian titles and other terminology upon the foundational Jewish model.

The result is at once inaccurate, inappropriate, and misleading.

For example, the very term *Jewish Christianity* itself implies a body of Jews who have embraced the hellenized Christ, when the reality is that the first believers, prior to at least A.D. 35, were all or mostly all Jews who had embraced whom they knew as *Yeshua ha Masiach*, the prophesied Jewish Messiah, Son of God, and God. They had first learned about Him from the writings of their Essene forbearers, and they later had seen Him walking in the flesh among them. They preferred not to be called "Christians," a Gentile appellation, but rather by the Jewish "Nazarenes."

Similarly misleading is the term *bishop*, used by the body of church scholarship to describe James the Just and the fourteen leaders (apostles) who, according to Eusebius, followed him in what they commonly refer to as "the Jerusalem See," with *See* being yet another strictly Roman Catholic expression.

In any event, James and his fourteen Jewish successors would by no means have been known to those mostly Jewish sheep in their keeping as "bishops." Nor would they have been known to them by the later Gentile Church title of "presbyters" or "episcopes." One might, however, speculate that they were called *zaqen,* the Hebrew title of the earlier corresponding Essene office. Or perhaps they were simply called *talmidim,* "disciples," the title ascribed to them by Yeshua in the Gospel of Matthew.

We can also be reasonably certain that none of those early Jewish believers in the service of The Way were known by the hellenized title "deacon," although this title has been widely used by church-rooted scholarship to describe these first-century congregational "worker bees" who performed the many ministerial and administrative functions of their Essene forbearers, the *mebaqqerim*.

On a different, more functional level, The Way was also greatly influenced by the fixing of specific times for the liturgical structure of the day, week, month, and year, which was a direct carryover from their immediate predecessors, the Essenes.[11] For example, The Way established Wednesday and Friday as rigorously observed fast days, as opposed to Monday and Thursday, which are the traditional Jewish Fast Days, calling those who participated in the then-pharisaic schedule "hypocrites." This different fasting schedule seems easily explained by two facts: first, Yeshua Himself called the Pharisees "hypocrites" (Matt. 23:13–15), and second, the Essenes, who were in strong opposition to the Pharisees, gave Wednesdays and Fridays special importance in their liturgical calendar.[12]

Chapter 3
The Way's Understanding and Celebration of Water Baptism

Water baptism, as it was practiced by The Way, is well rooted in the *mikvah* (immersion in running water) of traditional Judaism.[1] Water baptism was a fundamental understanding and practice of The Way that, in turn, became a cherished holy sacrament of the church. This ancient rite was also handed down through the Pharisees to modern day Rabbinical Judaism, where it has always been understood as simply a means of ritual purification.

The Essenes, like their sister sect, the Pharisees, also regularly practiced immersion in water for ritual purification. Josephus writes:

> Then, after working without interruption until the fifth hour, they reassemble in the same place and, girded with linen loin cloths, bathe themselves thus in cold water. After this purification they assemble in a special building to which no one is admitted who is not of the same faith; they themselves only enter the refectory if they are pure, as though into a holy precinct.[2]

Josephus further records that the Essenes had four different levels of initiation.

> They are divided into four lots according to the duration of their discipline, and the juniors are so inferior to their elders that if the latter touch them they wash themselves as though they had been in contact with a stranger.[3]

However, the Dead Sea Scrolls reveal that water immersion was also employed by the Essenes as a part of the process of initiation for those moving between the four "lots" of community membership. Moreover, immersion in water was also used by the Essenes in the process of repentance of those who had, for whatever reason, fallen away from the rigorous religious requirements of the sect and were seeking readmission into the community.[4]

Thus, while the Pharisees' *mikvah* for ritual purification and The Way's baptism by immersion were in many ways similar and arose from the same ancient mainline Jewish roots, the parallels between the initiation of proselytes into the Qumran community and the initiation of new members into the fellowship of The Way are perhaps even more striking. Both were accomplished by supervised self-immersion in running (living) water.[5] Those being immersed by both groups were adorned in white robes,[6] and all who had thus been immersed soon afterward participated in remarkably parallel, festive, spiritually loaded community meals.[7]

Finally, while John was the first New Testament figure to employ immersion in water as a "baptism of repentance for the remission of sins" (Mark 1:4), he was by no means the first historical figure to do so. As we have seen, the Essenes had, long prior to John's emergence on the scene, been using immersion in water for ritual purposes. Interestingly, while they were doing so, John was also baptizing less than six miles away from their center at Qumran, near the place where the Jordan River empties into the Dead Sea.

The Didache was a remarkable book of instruction issued by the Council of Twelve in Jerusalem some time after A.D. 50, probably circa A.D. 74. This urgently needed sixteen-chapter manual of instruction contained succinct guidance for the benefit of the newly emerging, predominantly Gentile churches that were being planted in an ever-expanding geographical area by Peter, Paul, Barnabas, John-Mark, and other evangelists of The Way.

This newly published work contained the following explicit instruction regarding how water baptism was to be administered:

> Concerning baptism, baptize thus:
>
> Baptize in the name of the Father, the Son, and The Holy Spirit in running water. If you do not have running water, baptize in other water; if you cannot in cold, then in warm. But, if you have neither, pour water on the head three times in the name of the Father, Son, and Holy Spirit...[8]
>
> Before the baptism, let the one baptizing and the one being baptized, and any others who are able, fast. Command the one being baptized to fast for one or two days beforehand.[9]

Yet another remarkable carryover from the Essenes was incorporated into The Way's baptismal formula. The *Excerpta ex Theodoto*, an apocryphal writing of Clement of Alexandria, an early Gentile saint of the church, circa A.D. 208, explains that the *taw* was marked as a sign on the forehead of those being baptized as they went down under the water three times, at the separate invocations of the Name of "the Father, the Son, and the Holy Spirit." The *taw*, the last letter of the Hebrew alphabet, at that time took the form of an equilateral cross—"+". The *Excerpta ex Theodoto* further stated, "The faithful bear through Yeshua the Name of God as if it were an inscription. Even dumb animals show by the seal that they bear whose property they are." This seems to be a decisive indication that in Baptism the faithful were marked with the Name of God and this sign could only have been the *taw*, which in Theodotus still kept its old meaning; that is, salvation.[10] Also, the Odes of Solomon make several references to the "seal of God" such as "On their faces I set my seal."[11] This text is understood to mean that the sign of the *taw* was made on the foreheads of those being baptized in The Way's ritual. This in turn makes reference to the sign of the *taw*, "+", or the Greek "x", referenced in Ezekiel 9:4 and confirmed in Revelation 7:2–3, 9:4, and 14:1, which was made on the foreheads of the elect.[12]

Interestingly, The Way used the Greek term *sphragis* as a name for water baptism. Its meaning in traditional Judaism is "circumcision." The Way, who in every way remained steadfast, practicing Jews, retained the practice of circumcision of the flesh on the eighth day, holding that water baptism was the completion of circumcision which they understood to be a sacred act of obedience to God's Word. As a final note on The Way's practice of water baptism, Bagatti writes quite candidly that The Way did not baptize infants or children who had not yet achieved the age of accountability. Infant baptism, of course, is among the core understandings and practices of not only the Roman Catholics but is also embraced by several of the more liberal "high church" Protestant denominations.[13]

Chapter 4
The Way's Understanding and Celebration of the Lord's Supper

The Lord's Supper, also known variously as the Eucharist and Holy Communion, is a central act of worship in virtually all expressions of historical Christianity, which keeps with Yeshua's invitation to do so. This sacrament of the church commemorates His Last Supper as it is recorded in Matthew 26:26–28, Mark 14:22–24, and Luke 22:17–20. It is partaken through the eating of bread (variously, leavened or unleavened) and drinking of either wine or unfermented grape juice, thought either to be or to represent Yeshua's body and blood.

The writings of The Way, including the three synoptic Gospels, make it clear that they understood that the Lord's Supper was instituted by Yeshua Himself in His celebration of the Passover meal on the night before he died and during which He gave thanks. Both the Book of Acts and several Pauline epistles show The Way participating in this sacrament. I believe they did so "*daily* with one accord…breaking bread from house to house" (Acts 2:46, emphasis added).

Roman Catholic theological understandings are often widely different from those of The Way, from which they came forth, and from the Protestant churches that separated from them, principally because of their disagreement with these understandings. These differences are especially apparent with respect to the Lord's Supper.

Nevertheless, setting these differences aside, there remains a remarkable commonality regarding the understanding of the Catholics and The Way with respect to the centrality of the Lord's Supper. This sacrament is the very substance around which the celebration of the Catholic mass is structured. It is quite striking that recent archaeological discoveries of The Way's very early places of worship have revealed the absence of an altar, which in each case has been replaced by a centrally located elevated table, demonstrating that the communal worship services conducted in these places, like those of the Roman Church, were centered on the celebration of the Lord's Supper. The excavated ruins of the third-century "Christian prayer hall" recently unearthed at Megiddo Prison reveal that there was no altar but rather a table located in the very center of the sanctuary.

Photo by Avi Ohayon; Courtesy of Israel Government Press Office

Two inmates of the Megiddo Prison are shown here cleaning the mosaic floor of the "Christian prayer hall." The pedestal, the remains of which are at the very center of the large room, supported a Lord's Supper table, upon which the sacrament was celebrated.[1]

The Didache, as it did with water baptism, provided the emerging church with guidance on how The Way celebrated the Lord's Supper. The actual Lord's Supper prayers as they are preserved in this book of instruction follow.[2]

The First Prayer of the Officiate (Before Blessing the Cup):

> *We thank You, our Father, for the holy vine, David Your son, which You have made known to us through Yeshua, Your Son; to You be the glory for ever.*

The Second Prayer of the Officiate (Before Blessing and Breaking the Bread):

> *We thank You, our Father, for the life and knowledge which You have made known unto us through Yeshua, Your Son; to You be the glory for ever.*

As this broken bread was once scattered on the mountains, and after it had been brought together became one, so may Your Body be gathered together from the ends of the earth unto Your kingdom; for Yours is the glory, and the power, through Yeshua, for ever.

And let none eat or drink of your (Lord's Supper wine) but those who have been baptized in the name of the Lord, for in truth the Lord has said concerning this, Give not that which is holy unto dogs.

The Third Prayer of the Officiate (Before Serving the Elements to Those Gathered Around the Table):

We thank You, holy Father, for Your holy name, which You have caused to dwell in our hearts, and for the knowledge and faith and immortality which You have made known to us through Yeshua, Your Son; to You be the glory for ever.

Thou, Almighty Master, did create all things for the sake of your name, and have given both meat and drink, for men to enjoy, that we might give thanks to You, but to us You have given spiritual meat and drink, and life everlasting, through Your Son.

Above all, we thank You that You are able to save; to You be the glory for ever.

Remember, Lord, Your Body, to redeem it from every evil, and to perfect it in Your love, and gather it together from the four winds, even that which has been sanctified for Your kingdom which You have prepared for it; for Yours is the kingdom and the glory for ever.

Let grace come, and let this world pass away. Hosanna to the Son of David. If any one is holy let him come (to the Lord's Supper); if any one is not, let him repent. Maranatha. (Come Lord Yeshua.) Amen.

There have been a number of differences within the modern day body regarding several aspects of the Lord's Supper, including: how often it should be celebrated; whether wine or grape juice or both should be served; if the wine and/or grape juice should be served from a common chalice or individual small cups; and whether unleavened or leavened bread, or small rice flour wafers should be served.

These denominational understandings not withstanding, let us jump back more than two thousand years to Mount Zion to examine how these matters were addressed by The Way.

Concerning the Frequency of the Celebration

We again turn to Qumran where the Essenes conducted a type of the Lord's Supper at each of their communal meals. Moreover, it was their understanding that the Messiah of Israel was present at each of these at least twice-daily celebrations, when ten or more members of the community were gathered together for a meal. We read in the Scrolls:

> This is the assembly of famous men, those summoned to the gathering of the community council, when God begets the Messiah with them. The chief priest of all the congregation of Israel shall enter and all his brothers and the sons of Aaron, the priests summoned to the assembly, the famous men, and they shall sit before him, each one according to his dignity, according to their positions in their camps and in their marches. And all the chiefs of the clans of the congregation with the wise men and the learned shall sit before them, each one according to his dignity. And when they gather at the table of community or to drink the new wine, and the table of community is prepared and the new wine is mixed for drinking, no-one should stretch out his hand to the first fruit of the bread and of the new wine before the priest, for he is the one who blesses the first fruit of the bread and of the new wine and stretches out his hand towards the bread before them. Afterwards, the Messiah of Israel shall stretch out his hand towards the bread. And afterwards, shall bless all the congregation of the community, each one according to his dignity. And according to this regulation they shall act at each meal when at least ten men are gathered."[3]

It seems quite clear from the New Testament that The Way, as they did in so many other aspects of their understanding, carried over this Essene practice to the extent that they broke bread together daily when, I believe, they met in small home groups of the mother congregation.

> So continuing daily with one accord in the temple, and breaking bread from house to house, they ate their food with gladness and simplicity of heart, praising God and having favor with all the people.
>
> —Acts 2:46–47

Moreover, there is clear scriptural evidence that The Way met as a congregation each Saturday evening, immediately following the end of *Shabbat.*

> Now on the first day of the week, when the disciples came together to break bread, Paul, ready to depart the next day, spoke to them and continued his message until midnight.
>
> —Acts 20:7–8

The first day of the week began for them some forty minutes after sundown on *Shabbat*, when, fully refreshed after having enjoyed the blessings of a work-free *Shabbat* rest, they came together for their weekly congregational service, which often continued well into the night.[4]

The Didache offers still further evidence that the Lord's Supper shared during these congregational gatherings of The Way on *Motzei Shabbat* (Saturday evening) were followed by the equivalent of what are modern day church suppers, after which the well-sated participants were called to give thanks to God for His abundant provision:

> But after it has been completed, so pray ye. We thank thee, holy Father, for thy holy name, which thou hast caused to dwell in our hearts, and for the knowledge and faith and immortality which thou hast made known unto us through Jesus thy Son; to thee be the glory for ever. Thou, Almighty Master, didst create all things for the sake of thy name, and hast given both meat and drink, for men to enjoy, that we might give thanks unto thee, but to us thou hast given spiritual meat and drink, and life everlasting, through thy Son.[5]

Concerning the Use of Wine Versus Unfermented Grape Juice

There is both scriptural and material evidence that The Way most likely consumed fermented wine and used it in their celebrations of the Lord's Supper. Scripturally, the word *wine* appears 193 times in the New King James Version of the Old Testament and 45 times in the New Testament. In each case the respective Hebrew and Greek words are defined as regular fermented wine. There is one use of *grape juice* in the Old Testament (Num. 6:3), which speaks to the Nazirite vow that precludes both the drinking of wine and grape juice. There are no usages of the words *grape juice* in the New Testament.

Yeshua Himself miraculously turned a large quantity of water into wine at a wedding feast, which evidently fermented to a delightful vintage without the passage of time (John 2:6–10). If instead it had been allowed to ferment naturally, it would have created a foul smelling, bubbling mess.

> From a worldly perspective, when grapes are crushed, a natural fermentation process begins almost immediately, and within a matter of hours the first stage of alcoholic wine has been produced. Fermentation is the natural process that converts the sugar in the grape juice into wine. For naturally fermented wine, no additional ingredients are added, as there are natural enzymes contained in the grape skins that effect the change.

> Natural yeast contained in the grape converts the sugar in the grape juice into alcohol and carbon dioxide gas. As the gas escapes, the juice bubbles violently (ferments). For red wine, the skins of the red grapes are left in the fermentation vats longer to absorb the purple color; for white wine, the crushed grapes ferment without their skins. Total fermentation results in a dry wine, while partial fermentation gives a sweet variety.[6]

Thus, it would only have been possible for The Way to have used unfermented grape juice in their celebrations of the Lord's Supper if they had squeezed the grapes on the spot and then consumed the juice almost immediately.

The use of unfermented grape juice in the place of scripturally designated, ordinary fermented wine by those Protestant denominations that choose to do so is only made possible by the modern day availability of artificial preservatives that inhibit the fermentation process.

Concerning the Use of a Common Chalice Versus Individual Cups

There is no Scriptural evidence, stated or implied, to indicate that individual cups were used by The Way for their Lord's Supper wine, and individual cups were first used among Reformed church bodies in the United States during the late twentieth century.[7]

On the other hand, there are abundant Old and New Testament references to the use of a single chalice or cup. First, please consider that the Lord's Supper is the church's response to Yeshua's instruction that we should replicate what He did at the Passover Seder He conducted on Mount Zion the evening before He went to the cross (Luke 22:19–20; 1 Cor. 11:24–25). During that celebration He blessed and distributed four individual cups of wine that were each consumed, in turn, as they were passed from participant to participant.[8] References to the use of the common cup are recorded in the three synoptic Gospels.[9]

Concerning the Use of Unleavened Bread, Leavened Bread, or a Small Wafer

Yeshua used unleavened bread, some homemade precursor of the modern day mass-marketed seasonal Matzo, during the Passover Seder He conducted on Mt. Zion. After all, our Lord was a Torah-observant Jew, as were all of the participants at His table, and the Torah makes it abundantly clear that only unleavened bread is acceptable for consumption during the entire seven-day Passover Feast. All of the temple grain offerings were unleavened except one:

the two leavened loaves of Pentecost.[10] The unleavened bread offered to God was considered more pure and holy.

> Unleavened bread shall be eaten seven days. And no leavened bread shall be seen among you, nor shall leaven be seen among you in all your quarters.
>
> —Exodus 13:6–8

There is, however, no instruction whatsoever, implied or expressed, in either canonical or apocryphal writings that suggests one way or the other what kind of bread should be used for Lord's Supper celebrations at times other than during of the Passover Feast. As a purely practical consideration, it is often difficult to find Matzos for sale, even in Israel, except just prior to and during the seven-day feast. Further, there is no evidence to suggest that the bakeshops of first-century Jerusalem (or of any time since) had gotten around to providing very thin round wafers made of wheat flour, with or without gluten.[11]

Thus, barring any evidence to the contrary, it seems reasonable to conclude that The Way most likely, out of biblical command and practical necessity, used unleavened bread for the Lord's Supper during subsequent Passover Feasts and leavened bread at other times. In any event, there would seem to be no other theological implications regarding this matter, one way or the other.

Chapter 5

The Initiation of New Members of The Way in First-Century Jerusalem

The Way quickly developed a spiritually rich, day-long ceremony and celebration of initiation for the many thousands of new believers who were entering into their fellowship. Sadly, this Spirit-led, unique blending of the holy sacraments of baptism and the Lord's Supper, each of which was separately rooted in the understandings and practices of their Essene forbearers, has long been lost to the later Church.[1] Instead, there is a great deal of contemporary disagreement about the meaning, substance, and administration of these two sacraments individually. Apparently, many have overlooked the divine connection between them as they were first understood, implemented, and then regularly administered in the first century by both male and female *mebaqqerim* (deacons) under the supervision of James and the other eleven *zaqenim* (elders).

There is considerable evidence from several different ancient sources that enables the church of today to trace the history and development of baptism and the Lord's Supper, as well as their unique blending into the rites of initiation as they were practiced by The Way.

Having discussed baptism and the Lord's Supper as they were embraced and practiced by The Way in the preceding chapters, let us now examine these two sacraments in the context of the elaborate, spiritually loaded, day-long initiation process by which new members entered into the first believing fellowship on Mount Zion. What follows is my best effort to reconstruct this initiation process as it was first practiced in a grotto on the grounds of the Upper Room then later, as it was most likely adjusted to fit the varying settings and circumstances of the widely dispersed congregations throughout the new Diaspora.

Preparing New Members for Initiation Into the Fellowship on Mount Zion (Circa A.D. 30–35)

The apocryphal writings of The Way reveal a complete, well-considered preparation of new members before their formal initiation into the fellowship in a ritual that stems directly from the Essene Rule of the Community. Included in this ritual were: a moral instruction arranged on the plan of the "two ways,"[2] a period of fasting, a personal undertaking to observe the precepts that have been taught, and a commitment to break with the old life. As a means to preserve modesty, The Way's entire initiation process was accomplished separately for initiates of each gender under the close supervision of their respective male and female *mebaqqerim*.[3]

Again, following the Essene model,[4] this period of instruction may have been as short as several days or as long as three months.[5] The instruction most likely focused on the great spiritual and symbolic significance of the life-changing process that was about to occur. For instance, from the example of Philip, who explained a chapter of scripture (Isa. 53) to the Ethiopian eunuch and told him about Yeshua before baptizing him in water (Acts 8:32–36), we can reasonably assume that the instructions of the *mebaqqerim* included a reading and exegesis of this and other appropriate and relevant scriptures and traditions.

A central aspect of this pre-initiation instruction was an in-depth explanation of the Essene-rooted understanding of the "two ways," an understanding that forms the basis for most of The Way's theology and doctrine. (See Chapter 27.) The Didache specifically instructs the church to include a teaching on the "two ways" in the *mebaqqerim* pre-initiation instruction.[6] This same instruction, as it is recorded in the Dead Sea Scrolls' Rule of the Community, was also a part of the initiation of traditional Jewish proselytes and a central feature of the initiation ritual of the Zadokite priests.[7]

There were several additions and elaborations to this "two ways" teaching that have come down to us in their early writings. For example, Barnabas, in his Epistle of Barnabas, an apocryphal writing of The Way, introduced a discussion of angelology into this curriculum by adding to the teaching on water baptism: "On the one side (of the cosmic ladder) are stationed the life-giving angels of God, on the other the Angels of Satan."[8] Clement of Alexandria, a respected Gentile teacher (circa A.D. 200), later added the "renunciation of Satan, and all evil" to the pre-initiation instruction. The actual form of this renunciation comes directly from a parallel Essene initiation ritual, as it is recorded in the Rule of the Community.[9] It therefore was most likely also included in The Way's instruction.

Fasting by both those to be initiated and the officiating *mebaqqerim* was also required as part of the pre-initiation preparation. The Didache memorializes this requirement: "But before the baptism let the baptizer fast, and the baptized, and whoever else can; but you shall order the baptized to fast one or two days before."[10]

The Baptism of Fire

The baptism of fire was the first of three separate baptisms administered to the initiates.[11] This elaborate, deeply spiritual, and symbolic rite may have been unique to the "mother congregation" on Mount Zion, where it was implemented soon after the ascension of Yeshua and most likely continued there until the first of the three dispersions following Stephen's martyrdom circa A.D. 35, or perhaps until after the second great dispersion to Pella in A.D. 62.

The network of catacombs with their sacred grottos that underlie Mount Zion provided a unique setting that could not be easily duplicated elsewhere. Moreover, I have found no reference attesting that the baptism of fire continued as a part of the initiation of new members in the new Diaspora. The baptism of fire was not included among the other aspects of The Way's original initiation of new members that were carried over into the initiating process of the emerging Gentile Christian Church.[12]

One can almost feel the spiritually loaded excitement of these very first Jewish believers on Mount Zion who were candidates for initiation. After having been thoroughly instructed, they descended down one of several stone staircases into the catacombs that crisscross under the entire expanse of Mount Zion.[13] Separate groups of men and women, led by respective *mebaqqerim* of their own gender, wound their way through the labyrinth until they arrived at the first grotto of initiation, a large, near-totally darkened cavern that had been hand hewn from the hard, native Jerusalem stone.

After they had quietly disrobed, assisted by a *mebaqqer*, they anointed their entire bodies with oil. When all of them had been thus totally anointed, as a group they renounced Satan and then made a profession of faith.

After this, the *mebaqqerim* handed a small oil lamp to each of them and then lit them, as well as many such oil lamps that had been placed in close-together niches dug in all sides of the chamber.[14] The effect of the sudden burst of fiery illumination must have been breath taking—beyond awesome! The anointed bodies of the initiates danced and sparkled in myriad mystical reflections of the many lamps. They moved about, crying out excitedly in the joy of their new and wonderful unity with He who had created them. Clement of Alexandria wrote that this baptismal fire illuminated and purified the new saints, symbolically burning and destroying the impure things, namely the terrestrial. The soul renounced the "darkness" to betake of the "light;" one divested himself (undressed) in order to be purified; one was liberated from the influence of the demons and re-clothed in the power of Christ.[15] Cyril of Jerusalem writes:

> For as the breathing of the saints, and the invocation of the name of God, like fiercest flame, scorch and drive out evil spirits, so also this exorcized oil receives such virtue by the invocation of God and by prayer, as not only to burn and cleanse away the traces of sins, but also to chase away all the invisible powers of the evil one.[16]

According to Bagatti, the baptism of fire was symbolically intended to repeat the great moment of Yeshua's baptism, when, according to the Gospel of Hebrews, the skies opened and there appeared a great light like a fire.[17]

Several other sources were apparently used by The Way in developing this baptism of fire. Consider the fire and light concepts as they were written in Peter's second epistle:

> But the day of the Lord will come as a thief in the night, in which the heavens will pass away with a great noise, and the elements will melt with fervent heat; both the earth and the works that are in it will be burned up. Therefore, since all these things will be dissolved, what manner of persons ought you to be in holy conduct and godliness, looking for and hastening the coming of the day of God, because of which the heavens will be dissolved, being on fire, and the elements will melt with fervent heat? Nevertheless we, according to His promise, look for new heavens and a new earth in which righteousness dwells.
>
> —2 Peter 3:10–13

The apocryphal 2 Enoch was likely another source.

> And the Lord said to Michael: Go and take Enoch from out of his earthly garments, and anoint him with my sweet ointment, and put him into the garments of My glory. And Michael did thus, as the Lord told him. He anointed me, and dressed me, and the appearance of that ointment is more than the great light, and his ointment is like sweet dew, and its smell mild, shining like the sun's ray, and I looked at myself, and I was like one of his glorious ones.
>
> —2 Enoch 22

Testa offers the delightful insight that the initiates sang baptismal hymns during this baptism of fire.[18] The Odes of Solomon were written by The Way as a whole new generation of psalms in celebration of the coming of their Lord, Yeshua. (See Chapter 29.) Ode 25 is especially germane. One can imagine it being sung by the initiates during this auspicious celebration as they danced about to their own voices while their anointed bodies shone with the fiery reflection of the many brilliant oil lamps.

> I was rescued from my chains, and I fled unto You, O my God. Because You are the right hand of salvation, and my Helper. You have restrained those who rise up against me, and no more were they seen. Because Your face was with me, which saved me by Your grace. But I was despised and rejected in the eyes of many, and I was in their eyes like lead. And I acquired strength from You, and help. A lamp You set for me both on my right and on my left, so that there might not be in me anything that is not light. And I was covered with the covering of Your Spirit, and I removed from me my garments of skin. Because Your right hand exalted me, and caused sickness to pass from me. And I became mighty in Your truth, and holy in Your righteousness. And all my adversaries were afraid of me, and I became the Lord's by the name of the Lord. And I was justified by His kindness, and His rest is for ever and ever. Hallelujah.[19]

As spectacular as it may have been to this point, the baptism of fire was not yet complete. Multiple sources suggest that the concluding act of this first of three baptisms of initiation was the sealing of the initiates with the sign of the *taw* on their foreheads. The Tenach root for this practice is Ezekiel 9:4, which has the Lord commanding: "Go through the midst of the city, through the midst of Jerusalem, and *put a mark on the foreheads* of the men who sigh and cry over all the abominations that are done within it" (emphasis added). Biblical scholars widely agree that this sign marked on foreheads was the *taw* in its ancient form (+).[20] Interestingly, however, the word translated "mark" in the English versions of Ezekiel 9:4 is the word *taw* in the Hebrew Bible.

Once again, a sacred ordinance of The Way is rooted in Qumran. When the Essenes received converts into their community, they baptized them by immersion in water. Then they signed them on their foreheads with a *taw* in recognition that they were now part of the faithful remnant that mourned the sins of Israel and would be spared in the day of God's wrath.[21]

Please remember that John the Baptist was baptizing the many who came to him in the nearby Jordan River. Considering that John and most if not all of those who came to him were observant Jews, they were certainly conversant with the Book of Ezekiel and even familiar with this Essene practice. It thus seems a short leap to suggest that the tracing of a *taw* on the forehead may well have been a part of John's method of baptism and thus came into later church practice from its earlier adoption from the Essenes by The Way.[22]

Bagatti holds that this marking of the *taw* on the foreheads of the initiates was an indelible tattoo[23] and further writes that this custom is still practiced by some oriental Christians.[24] The Apostle Peter seems to be alluding to ceremonies of this kind when he exhorts the initiates not to fear "the fiery trial" because it made them participators in the suffering of Christ (1 Pet. 4:12–14). Moreover, Revelation 14:1 suggests further New Testament confirmation of this early practice when it speaks of the Father and Son's names apparently permanently signed on the foreheads of the 144,000 specially selected Jewish believers.

The Baptism by Triple Immersion in Water

The baptism of fire being concluded, the initiates moved on to the nearby place of water baptism, which was illuminated by a shaft of daylight entering the chamber from an opening above. Here, the initiates, in the presence of many angels, prepared to meet their Lord, Yeshua.

Cyril of Jerusalem (circa A.D. 340) instructed later Gentile initiates for baptism in a manner presumably similar to that used by The Way:

> Up to now, in fact you have remained *extra portam* (outside of the Body of Christ). The time has come for you to be able to say: the King has led me into His treasury—My soul exults in the Lord because He has clothed me in the robe of salvation and with the vesture of joy; like a spouse, He has placed a mitre on my head and like a bride He has adorned me for the world—so that my soul might be found to be without blemish or wrinkle. I do not want to say what comes before you receive grace; but when you receive grace, your conscience, having nothing with which to condemn, you can concur with grace. This is truly a great thing and with much circumspection you must move toward it. Each one of you should go to God, with many armies of myriads of angels present.[25]

The initiates then stood before a very large *mikvah* in the center of the chamber where they beheld, etched in the stone above this place, the tri-part symbol comprised of a menorah, a Star of David, and a fish, known today as "the Messianic Seal of the Jerusalem Church."[26] One by one, guided by the presence of Michael, the angel of light, they descended down the seven steps of the cosmic ladder until they all stood together in the chest-deep water. Their descent into the water was a spiritualized imitation of Yeshua's earlier descent through the seven heavens,[27] first into the womb of Mary, then into His tomb, and then into Sheol (hell). Their descent took place through the seven heavens symbolized by the seven steps into the water.[28]

For these first Jewish believers, the *mikvah* had been mystically transformed into Yeshua's tomb; in their baptism they had been buried with Him. Moreover, their descent also symbolized their descent with Yeshua into hell. In further symbolism, to the initiates the waters of the *mikvah* had become the fecund womb of the body of Yeshua (the church), in which are generated children in the image of the Incarnate Word.[29] Moreover, they believed that the seven steps of their descent into the water represented the seven gifts of the Holy Spirit,[30] which were given to them by Yeshua, who was Himself so empowered at His own baptism when the Holy Spirit alighted on Him.[31]

The initiates, who all stood in the water of their regeneration, were joined by the *mebaqqerim*, who traced the sign of the *taw* on their foreheads with a thumb or forefinger. Then, the *mebaqqerim* symbolically "buried" each of them, in their turn, by supervising their first complete self-immersion, proclaiming as they entered the water, "I baptize you in the name of the Father." When they had come up from the water the process was repeated for the second time, with the *mebaqqerim* proclaiming, "I baptize you in the name of the Son;" and then a third repetition with the accompanying proclamation, "I baptize you in the name of the Holy Spirit."

While the initiates were thus symbolically buried with Yeshua as they were three times immersed, it was in coming up from the water that they "received life and knew the Name of the Son of God."[32] Moreover, "Even the dead received the Son of God—And in the water they descended dead, therefore, but they arise from it alive."[33]

The Baptism of the Holy Spirit

> When the Day of Pentecost had fully come, they were all with one accord in one place. And suddenly there came a sound from heaven, as of a rushing mighty wind, and it filled the whole house where they were sitting. Then there appeared to them divided tongues, as of fire, and one sat upon each of them. And they were all filled with the Holy Spirit and began to speak with other tongues, as the Spirit gave them utterance.
>
> —Acts 2:1–4

It seems apparent that the apostle Luke, who most likely was the author of the Book of Acts, in writing the above verses, was describing his and the collective awesome experience of the Apostles and probably also the 120 others mentioned in Acts 1:15, who were likely those who received this awesome outpouring of the Holy Spirit at Pentecost.

Surely, those who thus were the first to receive this outpouring of the Holy Spirit must have understood that they were walking in the spiritual footsteps of their Lord:

> While Yeshua was emerging from the waters of the Jordan, the Holy Spirit hovered over Him like a dove.[34]
>
> After He had undergone a second birth according to the flesh, having bathed in the Jordan's current, which proceeds with its blue tide, bearing its waves, having escaped from the fire, He (saw) first a favorable God coming, through the Spirit, on the wings of a white dove.[35]
>
> It was on these silvery wings of the dove, surrounded by angels that the newly thrice immersed initiates now proceeded. In the same manner as Yeshua, who had ascended before them, they now began their symbolic climb up the seven step cosmic ladder to seat themselves with Yeshua at the right hand of His Father.[36]

It would be enough, perhaps, to move on from this point; however, there is another deeply significant, almost always overlooked revelation of Scripture that begs mention in this context. Moving further on in Acts 2, we read:

> And there were dwelling in Jerusalem Jews, devout men, from every nation under heaven. And when this sound occurred, the multitude came together, and were confused, because everyone heard them speak in his own language. Then they were all amazed and marveled, saying to one another, "Look, are not all these who speak Galileans? And how is it that we hear, each in our own language in which we were born? Parthians and Medes and Elamites, those dwelling in Mesopotamia, Judea and Cappadocia, Pontus and Asia, Phrygia and Pamphylia, Egypt and the parts of Libya adjoining Cyrene, visitors from Rome, both Jews and proselytes, Cretans and Arabs—we hear them speaking in our own tongues the wonderful works of God." So they were all amazed and perplexed, saying to one another, "Whatever could this mean?"
>
> —Acts 2:5–12

There are several points to be made here. First, we see that Pentecost (the outpouring of the Holy Spirit) occurred in the temple courts where, according to scripture, The Way went each day (Acts 5:41). This place remained sacred to them, as evidenced by the fact that they were there on the wondrous occasion of Pentecost.

Next, the text makes it clear that it was exclusively born-again Jews of The Way who had thus been overcome by the Holy Spirit and as a result were miraculously speaking in many hitherto-unknown foreign tongues. While I am certain that these presumed 132 members of The Way were quite overcome by the awesome things they had personally experienced, it was the multitude who witnessed this miracle that are spoken of in these verses as being "amazed and perplexed" and asking one another, "Whatever could this mean?" The salient point I would make is this: among those who were "amazed and perplexed" there were non-Jews, Arabs, and more than likely other non-Jews among the Jews from the nations who are not specifically identified as such. But, the Arabs referred to here as witnesses to this amazing event, by any definition, were not Jews. Thus, inarguably, there were at least some non-Jews present.

Reading further in Acts 2 we next behold Peter delivering a bold and compelling explanation of the amazing things God had done. In his discourse, Peter cites the prophet Joel, who had foretold the substance of what had just occurred, including God's great promise that He would pour out His Spirit in this manner upon "all flesh" and "that whoever calls on the name of the Lord Shall be saved" (Joel 2:28–32). Having thus passionately shared these great prophetic words with the multitude, Peter went on to deliver what most certainly was an anointed sharing of the gospel.

> "Men and brethren, let me speak freely to you of the patriarch David, that he is both dead and buried, and his tomb is with us to this day. Therefore, being a prophet, and knowing that God had sworn with an oath to him that of the fruit of his body, according to the flesh, He would raise up the Christ to sit on his throne, he, foreseeing this, spoke concerning the resurrection of the Christ, that His soul was not left in Hades, nor did His flesh see corruption. This Jesus God has raised up, of which we are all witnesses. Therefore being exalted to the right hand of God, and having received from the Father the promise of the Holy Spirit, He poured out this which you now see and hear. For David did not ascend into the heavens, but he says himself: 'The LORD said to my Lord, "Sit at My right hand, Till I make Your enemies Your footstool."' Therefore let all the house of Israel know assuredly that God has made this Jesus, whom you crucified, both Lord and Christ." Now when they heard this, they were cut to the heart, and said to Peter and the rest of the apostles, "Men and brethren, what shall we do?" Then Peter said to them, "Repent, and let every one of you be baptized in the name of Jesus Christ for the remission of sins; and you shall receive the gift of the Holy Spirit. For the promise is to you and to your children, and to all who

> are afar off, as many as the Lord our God will call." And with many other words he testified and exhorted them, saying, "Be saved from this perverse generation."
>
> —Acts 2:29–40

And what a great harvest Peter's witness immediately bore: "Then those who gladly received his word were baptized; and that day about *three thousand* souls were added to them" (Acts 2:41, emphasis added).

But what about the unknown number of Arabs and perhaps other non-Jews who had witnessed these very same things and heard these very same anointed words, which had in the blinking of an eye brought three thousand souls into the kingdom? Were these three thousand all Jewish souls? We aren't told specifically what happened to them. We can only speculate concerning the impact upon their souls of what they saw and heard that day. Were they all blinded by the truth and simply turned away?

While it can only be speculative, I can't help but believe that at least one was also born again that day, perhaps even many of those Arabs and other non-Jews who had seen and heard. If indeed such as these were included among the nameless "about three thousand" who were saved that day, they most certainly would not have been welcomed to join the presumed 132 newly born-again Jews who were to return to the Upper Room when all of this excitement had subsided. The battle to bring Gentiles into the kingdom—to be championed by the apostle Paul, who at the time of Pentecost was still very much Sha'ul of Tarsus—would not begin for at least another four years until after Sha'ul's divine appointment with Yeshua on the road to Damascus.

Be that as it may, please consider the profoundly important significance of one or more non-Jews, that is, pagans, Arabs—Gentiles—being saved on this auspicious occasion. This was Pentecost (*Shavuot*), the very first day in the life of the body of Yeshua, the church! It seems at least probable that both Jews and Gentiles became a part of that body simultaneously that day during the very first moments of its existence.

Nevertheless, there remains today an enormous stumbling block, indeed the formidable second wall of separation built by Constantine and others as they were guided by Satan and his legion of demons to remove both Jews and everything Jewish from the church. Yeshua, by His self-sacrifice, had broken down the first such wall (Eph. 2:15). Together at last, if even for a moment, those born-again Jews and Arabs in the temple courts that morning of Pentecost were those who Paul later spoke of as "one new man," created in Yeshua Himself from the two.

These were Semitic cousins, both descended from Abraham who were grafted (equally saved) branches into the same Jewish tree and fed by the same Jewish sap rising from the same Jewish roots. (See Romans 11:17–22.) Some of the Jewish branches had been broken off; these I see as the 99.75 percent of Jews who are not yet born again. Consider also the almost countless Gentile branches who are also not yet grafted in.

And so you may reasonably ask, what is my point in all of this?

On Pentecost, at the very fleeting moment when the Holy Spirit was poured out upon The Way, some three thousand Jews, and I believe one or more Gentiles, became, in fact and in spirit, the unblemished bride of Yeshua, which we are promised it will one day truly and universally become once again. I earnestly pray that the unified Jewish and Gentile congregations of the body that were manifest in the second great Diaspora, such as at Megiddo, presumably at Tiberias and elsewhere, then later, for a time, at Antioch, Alexandria, and beyond might soon become the model for the sadly disunified body (church) of today.

May we all at last lay down our burdens and walk arm in arm along the road that leads to our full and glorious restoration.

> And I heard, as it were, the voice of a great multitude, as the sound of many waters and as the sound of mighty thunderings, saying, "Alleluia! For the Lord God Omnipotent reigns! Let us be glad and rejoice and give Him glory, for the marriage of the Lamb has come, and His wife has made herself ready." And to her it was granted to be arrayed in fine linen, clean and bright, for the fine linen is the righteous acts of the saints.
>
> —Revelation 19:6–8

May we not long tarry, for the time may be very near.

> Truly, these times of ignorance God overlooked, but now commands all men everywhere to repent, because He has appointed a day on which He will judge the world in righteousness by the Man whom He has ordained. He has given assurance of this to all by raising Him from the dead.
>
> —Acts 17:30–31

White Robes and a Floral Crown

As a fitting conclusion to this three-part baptism, when the initiates emerged from the *mikvah,* having thus symbolically ascended the seven step cosmic ladder to be one with Yeshua, seated at the right hand of the Father, each of them, covering their nakedness, was reclothed with a white robe,[37] and a floral crown[38] was placed upon their heads. The Way understood that the archangel Michael was the spiritual agency responsible for this re-clothing.[39]

The Essenes are well known for their one-piece white linen robes, which were issued to them during their initiation into this ascetic sect.[40] White robes are also mentioned in the Apocalypse of John: "Then each of them was given a white robe, and they were told to wait a little longer" (Rev. 6:11, NIV).

Head crowns are also included in John's account: "Around the throne were twenty-four thrones, and on the thrones I saw twenty-four elders sitting, clothed in white robes; and they had crowns of gold on their heads" (Rev. 4:4–5). The Odes of Solomon says, "Come to paradise, make a crown of its tree and put it on your head" (9:7). Interestingly, pre-baptismal anointing with oil and the post-baptismal placing of a floral crown upon the heads of the newly baptized remains a part of the modern day initiation process of the Syrian Orthodox Church.[41]

The *Laminae* and the Messianic Seal Artifacts

Laminae are thin, silver, credit-card sized plates that were used by fully initiated members of The Way as a kind of "pass card" to ensure their *post mortem* passage through the seven heavens into the kingdom of God. Several such *laminae* have been found and dated to the first century.[42]

One such *lamina*[43] is of particular interest because of its very likely connection to the just described three-part initiation ceremony of The Way. It would also seem to be directly associated with the miraculous healing as it is described by James, the first leader of The Way. Moreover, part of the Aramaic inscription on this *lamina* ("For the Oil of the Spirit") is identical to that on one of the eight surviving Messianic Seal artifacts that were recovered from the Mount Zion catacombs circa 1967.[44]

This particular *lamina* was found in the Judean wilderness, south of Jerusalem, by Bedouins in 1962. It was taken to Emanuel Testa for translation of its Aramaic writing and for his further evaluation. Testa was amazed to discover that the top line of the *lamina* translated as, "For the oil of the Spirit."[45]

One of the artifacts bearing an etched in-stone rendition of the Messianic Seal is a brick-sized, hard local marble utensil that also bears the identical inscription in Aramaic, "For the oil of the Spirit," as if it were written by the same hand that inscribed it on the silver *lamina*.

Testa, Bagatti, and other scholars, who at the time of their observations on this subject were not aware of the discovery of the Messianic Seal artifacts, have concluded that these *laminae* were buried with the dead, as previously noted, to secure their free passage into the kingdom of God.[46]

As Reuven Schmalz and I earlier conjectured in our book, *The Messianic Seal of the Jerusalem Church,* it is also reasonable to speculate that such a *lamina* may have been given to each new member of The Way at the completion of their three-part initiation into the fellowship and that these born-again believers carried these "tickets to heaven" with them until their dying day.[47]

The Oblation of Milk, Honey, and Water

The Way of Mount Zion included a deeply meaningful and spiritually loaded first celebratory act for the new members of their community immediately after they had come up out of the water and donned their white robes and floral crowns. At this point in the proceedings, a *zaqen* (elder) entered the scene to bless and serve two cups to each of the newly baptized. The first cup to be served held water, the purpose of which was to perform the same sort of baptismal cleansing of the inner self as had been accomplished on the outer self during the preceding three full-body immersions. Immediately following this first cup of water, a second cup filled with a mixture of milk and honey was served to each of the newly baptized initiates.[48]

It can't be said with certainty when the church dropped water, milk, and honey from their ritual initiation of new believers. It is, however, likely that this very Jewish-rooted understanding was done away with along with many other such Jewish-rooted practices and traditions at some point during the wave of de-Judaization that began long before and continued long after its sharp peak during the Council of Nicea in A.D. 325.[49]

The apocryphal writings of The Way support their understanding of the post-baptismal oblation of milk and honey. For example, consider one of several references in the Epistle of Barnabas and another from the Odes of Solomon:

> What then is the milk and the honey? Because the child is first kept alive by honey, and then by milk, so in like manner we also, being kept alive by our faith in the promise and by the word, shall live and be lords of the earth.
>
> —Barnabas 6:17

> Because Your seal is known; and Your creatures are known to it. And Your hosts possess it, and the elect archangels are clothed with it. You have given to us Your fellowship, not that You were in need of us, but that we are always in need of You. Shower upon us Your gentle rain, and

> open Your bountiful springs which abundantly supply us with milk and honey. For there is no regret with You; that You should regret anything which You have promised; since the result was manifest to You. For that which You gave, You gave freely, so that no longer will You draw back and take them again. For all was manifest to You as God, and was set in order from the beginning before You. And You, O Lord, have made all. Hallelujah.
>
> —Odes of Solomon, IV:7–15

The Lord's Supper Centered Celebratory Feast: Capstone of The Way's Initiation of New Members

In the contemporary Israeli world of unceasing terrorism and the constant threat of war, there is an old Jewish idiom concerning how our people prioritize matters at community gatherings where there is a meal involved. It goes something like this: "We had a war! We won! Let's eat!"

So it was in the opening decades of the first century, when the newly initiated had completed their day-long, rigorous, three-part baptism. While they hadn't endured a war on this, the most important day in their lives, after several intensive hours of spiritually loaded ceremony, all of which had been preceded by at least two days of fasting, these newest born-again members of the kingdom of God were most certainly hungry.

Thus, as their long, joyful day of initiation faded into evening, these newly baptized believers were hosted by their longer-standing brothers and sisters in what had become a traditional, elaborate Lord's Supper feast. The apocryphal writings of The Way as well as other historical records speak to the centrality of the Lord's Supper, which was celebrated at every community meal. The apostle Luke wrote:

> So continuing daily with one accord in the temple, and breaking bread from house to house, they ate their food with gladness and simplicity of heart, praising God and having favor with all the people.
>
> —Acts 2:46–47

Even more poignant was the centrality of this first communion of those who, earlier that day, had been baptized with fire, water, and the Holy Spirit, for by their inaugural taking of the consecrated Lord's Supper elements of the wine and bread they had become full-fledged members of the believing community.

The apostle Paul admonished the Corinthians, presumably at such a communal Lord's Supper feast, because of their overeagerness to get on with the main meal following the Lord's Supper.

> But if anyone is hungry, let him eat at home, lest you come together for judgment. And the rest I will set in order when I come.
>
> —1 Corinthians 11:34

It is also interesting that, according to Hippolytus of Rome, a presbyter of the church at Rome, circa A.D. 200, the Lord's Supper feast continued in church practice until at least the opening decade of the third century. Hippolytus shared Paul's concern about the participants' eating habits. Hippolytus instructs:

> Eat and drink in moderation. Do not drink to drunkenness, so that no one will mock you and so that he who invited you will not be grieved by your disorderly conduct.... When you eat, eat sufficiently and not to excess, so that the host may have some left that he can then send to someone as leftovers of the saints, so that the one to whom it is sent may rejoice. Let the guests eat in silence, without arguing, saying only what the bishop allows. If someone asks a question, it shall be answered. When the bishop answers, all shall remain silent, praising him modestly, until someone else asks a question. And if, in the absence of the bishop, the faithful attend the meal in the presence of an elder (*Zagen*) or a deacon (*Mebaqqer*), they shall eat in the same way, honorably. Everyone shall be careful to receive the blessed bread and from the hand of the elder or deacon. Similarly, the catechumen [those who were newly baptized] will still receive exorcised (the blessed bread and wine elements of their first communion).[50]

Finally, it is interesting to note an apparent early denominational variance that allowed for the rite of milk and honey to be included as a part of the Lord's Supper feast in the event that the water baptism took place in the immediate vicinity of the church rather than at a remote location. In these situations, the milk and honey were served to those who were about to receive their first communion just prior to the serving of the consecrated elements of wine and bread. The Third Council of Carthage, however, did away with this exception in A.D. 397 by forbidding anything but bread, and wine mixed with water to be served in connection with the Lord's Supper.[51]

Part II

The Tiberias Synagogue of The Way

When I was first considering the content and scope of this book, it seemed fitting to include a section on the movements of The Way from the time they left Mount Zion until they had become well settled, mostly in the Galilee and "the region of Damascus." My initial research, however, soon revealed that any meaningful discussion of the many sites involved in this extensive and complex movement would be well beyond the scope of the current writing. Bellarmino Bagatti, for instance, briefly introduced some 576 early sites in his three-volume *Ancient Christian Village* study. Of these, by my own preliminary review, some 222 may first have been "sites" of The Way scattered along the several pathways of their dispersion.

Thus, having quickly concluded that much additional research, extensive hands-on exploration, and at least one if not several separate volumes would be needed to properly investigate, develop, and present this important subject, I prayerfully pondered as to what, if any, extent these many potential sites of The Way should be introduced in the current writing. The Lord gave me a reply via an e-mail from the United States concerning the remains of a fourth to fifth-century Byzantine church that had been discovered about a year earlier in Tiberias and officially identified as such by the Israel Antiquities Authority. This e-mail further explained that the site was about to be preserved and covered over again by the Antiquities Authority, presumably due to the lack of funds needed for its further excavation and development.

Even though the ruins of Byzantine-era churches are fairly common in Israel and are from a time later than The Way's, I felt quickened in my spirit. Thus, camera in hand, I hurried to the site the next morning. Inexplicably, I felt strongly attached to the place at first sight. It was surrounded by a thick overgrowth of wild mustard in full bloom that made it difficult to approach, standing as it did in this sea of golden loveliness. I was instantly amazed, almost overwhelmed, by the striking beauty of the intricate geometric designs and patterns of the polychrome mosaic floors that had so far been exposed. In a flash of revelation it became immediately clear to me that this site was not by any means a fourth or fifth-century Byzantine church but rather the remains of a much earlier synagogue—a Nazarene Jewish synagogue of The Way. After I had excitedly taken the first of several rounds of pictures, I hurried to get Donna and bring her to this place of my by then very great fascination and excitement.

After we returned to the site, I focused first on the mosaics, pointing out to my equally excited wife the frequent use of the ancient Jewish *taw,* the last letter of the Hebrew/Aramaic alphabet, which took the form of a "plus" sign.

It appeared to have been used there as a symbol of the cross.

In the midst of this spontaneous tutorial I pointed toward the remains of an adjacent cistern, which was connected to a large sub-surface chamber accessible by several steps. "Steps!" Donna cried out excitedly. "It must be a *mikvah*!" Then, when for the first time I focused my attention on this wild-flower-covered and debris-littered section of the sanctuary, it was immediately obvious that this was indeed a *mikvah* with an associated water supply. This was a sacred place of ritual purification, which, along with the very telltale mosaic designs, made it absolutely certain that the identification of this site was Nazarene Jewish, not Byzantine.

Inarguably, we were standing in a very early site of the dispersed Nazarenes of The Way, a holy place of believing Jews who had been forced to leave their mother synagogue on Mount Zion and had then become a part of a second great Diaspora. Indeed, this was one of the earliest if not *the earliest* yet discovered place of worship of our Lord Yeshua, Jesus Christ, the King of the universe.

During the next several days, before the site was finally covered over again by the Antiquities Authority, I took more than two hundred high-quality digital pictures to record every detail of the site that had so far been exposed, probably about one-fourth or less of the entire facility. Some of these pictures illustrate the following chapters.

I then shared these pictures with two well-respected friends and colleagues, Professor Jay Thompson and Dr. Lee Woodard, both highly skilled Greek scholars and specialists in ancient inscription interpretation. Jay E. Thompson, PhD, is professor of church history at Faith Evangelical Seminary in Tacoma, Washington. He received his doctorate from the University of California-Berkeley. Professor Thompson is an authority on early Nazarene Judaism and the beginnings of the church. Lee W. Woodard, DMin, received his doctorate from Phillips University Graduate Seminary, where he studied under Professor Kendrick Grobel, one of the most respected New Testament scholars. Dr. Woodard has devoted the past twenty-four years to developing forensic paleography, a new discipline that combines modern day technology with historical and linguistic expertise. He has used this new discipline to unveil the hitherto unknown dating of the four Gospels, as this data has been previously hidden in the nearly two-millennia-old pages of Codex Washington.

My primary purpose in calling upon these two American church scholars was to elicit their separate professional opinions and commentary regarding the exposed inscriptions and mosaics in the Tiberias synagogue as a further means of accurately dating the site. Their separate commentary is integrated into the chapters that follow.

Very early one morning, just before the site was to be covered over again, as the sun was rising over the adjacent Sea of Galilee, I found myself very alone and on my hands and knees on the mosaic floor, bowing down as the first rays of the sunrise provided sufficient light for me to take some close-up photos of the ancient Greek inscription that lay before me. I was suddenly convicted by the power of the Holy Spirit, overwhelmed by the great and precious wonder of where I was and what I was doing. There I was, a born-again Jew, bowing down before the Lord my God in the very same place as had my Nazarene Jewish brothers of The Way some nineteen centuries earlier.

The Tiberias synagogue of The Way has enormous significance! It provides material, tangible evidence that in a wonderfully unique way confirms and certifies that the roots of Christianity are undeniably Jewish. Moreover, this divinely revealed site passionately cries out to my "traditional" Jewish brethren and to the religious and governmental principalities who would disclaim the Jewish body of Yeshua's right to exist while forever banishing its constituents. Let its undeniable message ring out loud and clear to all who have ears to hear! Modern day Messianic Judaism is, most certainly, a legitimate expression of the type of Judaism that was earlier practiced by Nazarene Jewish believers of The Way right here on the shores of the Sea of Galilee during the second century in parallel with the birth and early development of Rabbinical Judaism.

While the Tiberias Synagogue of The Way is the earliest Nazarene Jewish place of worship to so far be discovered, it does not stand alone. There are two others: the house church at Dura Europas in Syria, built around A.D. 230 and discovered in 1932; and the Roman prayer hall, constructed around A.D. 240 and found at Megiddo Prison in 2005.

Considering the huge number of other potential sites pointed to by Bagatti, Eusebius, and others and which have already been preliminarily identified and await exploration and study, I have no doubt that other exciting discoveries like these three will be eventually if not soon forthcoming. I believe it is certain that when these additional long-buried treasures once again find their way into the light of day, they will most certainly confirm the greatly edifying and altogether wonderful existential revelations that cry out from the ancient ruins of Dura Europas, Megiddo, and now, most recently are being proclaimed to the world from the Tiberias synagogue of The Way.

Chapter 6
Discovery and Initial Identification

Early one lovely morning in April 2007, Carrie Hollands, a Christian volunteer from England, was working on an exploratory dig at the "Excavations of the urban center of Roman Tiberias" under the supervision of an Israel Antiquities Authority staff archaeologist. The mission of this small satellite team was to identify and thus protect any potential historically valuable sites along the intended pathway of a new sewer line that was to be installed from the treatment plant at the southern edge of the modern day city of Tiberias to another processing plant on the shore of the nearby Sea of Galilee.

Carrie, who sometimes visits our home congregation, told me of her involvement in the discovery of the Tiberias synagogue of The Way:

> There had been work carried out in one of the areas where two large basalt pillars had fallen, [and] in this location there were also some very beautiful mosaics. I was asked to clean the area, as there was to be some aerial photography of the site. As I was cleaning one of the pillars I noticed that to the side there was a crudely etched cross. I called to my supervisor and drew her attention to this little mark, she became very excited and said, "This hasn't been noticed before, great!" She called on her cell phone to the director of the excavation, Dr. Moshe Hartal, and he came to investigate the pillar. At this time however he was unimpressed with it. Several days later, I was working in another part of the excavation, when my supervisor came across very excitedly and said, "Carrie, it's a church!" I was a bit nonplussed for a moment and then she said, "Under your pillar, there is a cross and an inscription, it's a church!" They had excavated beneath the basalt pillar where I had found the cross inscribed on the side and more of the beautiful mosaic had been revealed, with several crosses in the design.

Later I was privileged to help with the cleaning and revealing of this most important mosaic and it was a wonderful experience to be a part of the team that first found this lovely old Jewish Christian sanctuary.[1]

This is a view of the partially excavated site looking to the west. The site's *mikvah* is unseen immediately to the right. Its cistern water supply, which is immediately to the left, is also unseen.

This is the roughly etched cross that was discovered by Carrie Hollands. Notice that its vertical member is longer than its horizontal, showing that it is not a Nazarene Jewish *taw* but rather later Byzantine.

The following are excerpts from an Israel Antiquities Authority press release on August 8, 2007, entitled "Surprising Finds Were Discovered in the IAA Excavations in Tiberias":

> In excavations that were carried out by the Israel Antiquities Authority in Tiberias impressive and unique finds were uncovered that shed light on the history of the ancient city. The excavations were conducted over the course of the last three months at the request of *Mekorot* (Water Control

> Agency) as part of a project that involves the installation of a sewage pipeline and the transfer of the waste water treatment facility from Tiberias to the southern part of the Sea of Galilee...
>
> In the lower part of the city, a Byzantine church (from the fourth-fifth centuries CE) was exposed that is paved with magnificent polychrome mosaics decorated with geometric patterns and crosses. Three dedicatory inscriptions written in ancient Greek are incorporated in the mosaics. In one of the inscriptions, which were deciphered by Dr. Leah Di Signi of the Hebrew University of Jerusalem, is the line: "Our Lord, protect the soul of your servant..." ["Our Lord" is a reference to Jesus.] One of the mosaics is adorned with a medallion in which there is a large cross flanked by the letters alpha and omega, which are one of the monograms for Jesus ["alpha to omega" meaning "from A to Z" in Greek]. The church's remains were discovered adjacent to ancient public buildings, among them a basilica, bathhouse, streets, and shops that were exposed at the site in the past.[2]

I must confess that I was at first surprised by the IAA's initial identification of this site as a fourth to fifth-century Byzantine church. On reflection, however, it is quite easy to understand and explain how they could have initially missed its correct identity as a much earlier (circa first to second century) Nazarene Jewish site. Archaeologists, much like lawyers, rely very closely on a body of precedents. Lawyers look to earlier cases and decisions as a basis for resolving new issues and matters of law. In much the same way, archaeologists look to earlier discoveries as a basis for identifying and categorizing new discoveries. Thus, never mind that the Tiberias site displayed a wealth of clearly Nazarene Jewish symbols in its mosaics and that there was an immediately adjacent, uniquely Jewish *mikvah*, complete with its own water supply that could only reasonably have been used for traditional Nazarene Jewish ritual cleansing and baptism. The fact is, up to the discovery of this Tiberias site, no other such facility had been previously discovered and identified as such in Israel. Hence, the IAA had no precedent to call upon and must have relied on syllogistic logic:

> a) If it has crosses it must be Christian.
> b) All Christian churches in Israel are Byzantine (from the fourth to seventh centuries).
> c) The Tiberias site has crosses.
> Ergo, the Tiberias site is Byzantine.

Moreover, the IAA's initial investigation of the site was apparently hurried. In their press release on August 8, 2007, announcing the discovery of this site, they report: "Three dedicatory inscriptions written in ancient Greek are incorporated in the mosaics."[3] The fact is that there are only two inscriptions; one of them is "dedicatory," and the other is not.

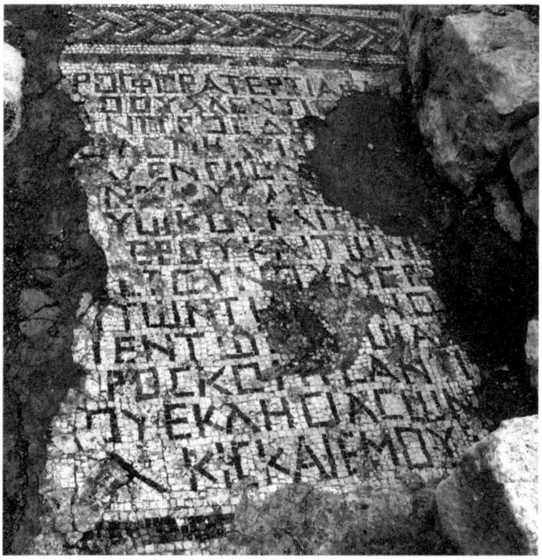

Depicted here is the severely damaged singular dedicatory mosaic inscription, translated to the fullest extent possible by Professor Jay Thompson. He writes:

> The hours that I have stared at this floor have produced not a great translation, because we are only seeing about 1/3 of the inscription. The remainder of it is either destroyed, and also behind the wall that is covering approximately 45% of the floor. This wall is a later addition, not necessarily from the same millennia (8th to 11th century). I think the floor might have been used later for the foundation of a fortress (circa. Crusades Muslim, or Frank). This explains why there was no concern for keeping the floor intact. The Byzantines would have left the floor intact instead of covering over half of it with walls and building structure because they appreciated artwork, and Greek inscriptions were never destroyed. The inscription below is about 33% complete leaving us with not much to go on for interpretation. But this is decipherable:
>
> Line 1: [ ] ΠΡΟΣ ΦΟΡΑ ΤΕΡΤΙΑ Φ[ ]
> TO A THIRD PAYMENT
>
> Line 2: [ ] ΟΟΥ ΑΛΕΝ ΤΙ [ ]
> OF Which WERE FORMED THE WANDERING

Line 3: [ ] N ΠΡΟΣ ΔΕ [ΚΑ]
TO THE TEN

Line 4: [ ] ΩΛΕ ΤΩ ΧΡΙΩ Α [ ]
FOR THE ANNOINTING/JUDGEMENT

Line 5: [ ] ON ΓΗΟΡΗ [ ]
POSSESSION OF THE LAND

Line 6: [ ] N [ ] Y ΚΑΙ N[ ]
AND

Line 7: [TO]Y ΟΙΚΟΥ ΚΑΙ ΤΩΝ [ ]
OF THE HOUSE AND OF THE [THINGS]

Line 8: [ ]ΕΡΟΥ ΚΑΙ ΤΩΝ [ ]
AND OF THE [THINGS]

Line 9: [ ]ΤΣΥΝΟΥ ΜΣΡ [ ]

Line 10: [ ] ΤΩΝ Τ[Ε] ΝΟ[ ]
OF THE

Line 11: [ ] ΕΝ ΤΩ [ΚΑΙΡ]Ω Α[ ]
IN THE MEASURABLE (time?)

Line 12: [ ] ΠΡΟΣ ΚΟΗ [ ]ΣΑΝΤΙ [ ]
TO THE DEED

Line 13: [ ] ΟΥ ΕΚΛΗΣΙΑ ΣΩΝ [ ]
OF THE MEN OF THE CHURCH ALONG WITH

Line 14: [ ]ΛΚΙΣ ΚΑΙ ΕΜΟΥ [ ]
AND OF ME[4]

In commenting further on what we can learn with respect to dating the site from this badly deteriorated inscription, Professor Thompson added:

> Notice the "A," the way it is formed. It is similar to the Rosetta stone alpha, and not like the alpha on the fourth century texts. The "PHI" is also of the same ilk. I would suggest that this is second century and maybe third. But it is not 4th to 7th. In fact it looks like the second century would be more appropriate.[5]

Chapter 7
The Tiberias Messianic Synagogue's Mosaics

The *taw*, the last letter of the Hebrew/Aramaic alphabet in its ancient form was formed as a plus sign, "+", or as an X.

According to the eminent scholar Erwin Goodenough, the Jews knew of and used the sign of the cross as a token for eschatological protection. They carried amulets with crosses, with circles around them, or with dots in the interstices. The X or "+" had significance even for those Jews who lived in the Diaspora, in Rome itself. Discoveries of the tombs of Jewish and Roman bodies reveal these marks on their tombstones. Moreover, the X goes back to an earlier era than the Roman conquest of Judea, where it is found in Ezekiel as the distinctive mark of *taw*. He points out that the Hebrew *taw* was made as a cross, X, or a "+".[1, 2]

It thus seems quite certain that the first Jewish believers of The Way seamlessly transitioned their frequent use of the *taw* from its traditional Jewish understanding to also represent the cross of Yeshua. The several uses of the cross symbol I have seen here in Israel on tombs and in other graffiti that have been attributed to the first Jewish believers, have, without exception, been equilateral in their form (i.e., *taws*).

In Ezekiel 9:4–7 we read how a divine messenger was to go through Jerusalem putting a mark upon the foreheads of the faithful, thus sealing them and protecting them from the divine slaughter of the unrighteous that was to follow. The mark referred to here, in ancient Phoenician script, looks like a "+", which was most certainly later adapted by the early Jewish believers as a symbol of their faith in Yeshua.[3] Moreover, in the English versions of the Bible where the word "mark" appears in Ezekiel 9:4, in the Hebrew Bible it is rendered as *taw*.

There are three relatively large "crosses" in the mosaics of the Tiberias synagogue of The Way, all of which have equilateral members. There are also smaller versions of these equilateral "crosses" placed at the center of three of the many geometrical design patterns that make up the lovely polychromatic presentations. These "crosses" (taws) are shown in the following gallery.

Dr. Woodard points out that there are no other exact duplicates of this form of the *taw* that have so far been found to have been in use circa A.D. 100 but that the one pictured here may well have been the first such usage. The equilateral members of this, what he calls the "fancy cross," are, however, consistent with the other simple versions of the *taw* symbol found throughout the mosaics of this site and with the general body of other such uses circa that era.

Dr. Woodard further explains that the symbol to the right of the *taw* is a combined *aleph* and *taw*, again, a depiction of Yeshua, who called Himself the "first and the last" (Rev. 22:13). He further explains that the "grape vine art" (single ivy leaf/heart shaped symbol) to the left of the *taw* was used first by the early "Holy Land Jewish Christians."[4]

Professor Jay Thompson translates the above inscription as, "Lord Jesus Christ, consider/remember the servants." Based upon his study of this inscription, the other mosaics, and other factors, he dates the site to "about 150 or a little earlier but not earlier than 131, nor later than [A.D.] 230."[6]

Dr. Woodard, the originator of forensic paleography, a relatively new discipline that combines modern day technology with historical and linguistic expertise, has made an exciting discovery with respect to this specific *taw* symbol pictured above. He states, "I am certain that the center tile of the small Tiberias cross includes on the right side a small etched Hebraic letter *Beth* or *Kaph*, followed by additional Hebraic alphabetic forms, but the Hebraic entries are small and difficult to read, and I have not yet been able to decipher it. I will keep trying."[7]

The prominent symbol at the center of the easternmost mosaic panel below is the Solomonic knot, composed of two rings that interlace each other four times, with alternating crossing points that go over, under, over, and under as one traces around each of the rings. King Solomon, according to Italian legend, was on a hill and was charged by God with protecting a village from large boulders that were going to roll down and destroy the village. He was holding three large boulders and took a rope and devised this knot to support the boulders and protect the town.

The design is frequently used in the mosaics of ancient synagogues, which probably gave rise to the symbol's association with King Solomon.

In traditional Judaism it is imbued with mystical meaning as a symbol of eternal motion and the intertwining of space and time. When used by Jewish believers it most often represented the destroyed temple.

Professor Thompson writes:

> The Solomonic knot shows up in many mosaic floors, but unlike the Judaistic synagogue where the Jerusalem temple was depicted by the utensils used in the Temple, the Jewish Christian synagogue used the Solomonic knot to symbolize it. I have some theories on its [two concentric circle] symbolism, as eternal motion, and God's ongoing sustenance of the universe, and every atom, and every connection by which molecules are connected. The resemblance is so remarkable that Dr. Fraser Stoddart of UCLA named such a connection in zinc compounds as 'Solomonic Knots.' Some might poo-poo such symbolism, but I think that the ancients were well aware of atomic and molecular structures, for the Greeks like Aristotle, Plato, and Zenophen held to a clear atomic and molecular theory that our scientists hold to today. They I am sure received such knowledge through ancient sages. The Jews surely would have this understanding that the same power that sustained every atom and molecule preserved the connection of the Jews to the temple even though it was destroyed for it marked the connection of that structure to eternal time.[8]

This interlaced variation of the basic two concentric circle design is shown here set in a square within a square, which is then set within the larger square of the overall mosaic panel. Almost identical versions of this same adaptation are found in the mosaics of the third-century Jewish-Christian Prayer Hall at Megiddo Prison and in the fifth-century Nile Festival House mosaic at Zippori. Notice also that there is a *taw* in each of the five interstices (open spaces) within the design.

Note the simple *taw* at the center of this partially buried geometric square design. Note first that it is shown in the form of a "+" by four white tiles with a blue tile at its center. Now, blink your eyes and look again. You will see that the five blue tiles in the same square display the *taw* in its alternative form as an X.

The Triune Godhead

The Way had a clear understanding of the triune nature of the Godhead. This doctrine was first understood and taught by their traditional Jewish predecessors as early as 515 B.C. Moreover, this Triune conception was passed along to the Essenes, who wrote of it in their Dead Sea Scrolls. Clearly, the foundational Christian doctrine of the Trinity has its roots in these earlier entirely Jewish understandings. As I was reviewing this chapter before publication, I suddenly saw what I had entirely missed during innumerable earlier studies of these mosaics. Here before my eyes was this ancient symbolic depiction of the Triune Godhead that takes the form of a three-dimensional triangle within a larger two-dimensional triangle. Notice that it points directly to the *taw* at its immediate right.

Now please look at the large square immediately above the three-part Godhead symbol. This square encloses a series of unique designs comprised of two concentric circles. There are four rows of two circle images, which in turn are connected in groups of two to form an over-layer of three such groupings in each row. There was obviously something unique about this design that caused The Way to adopt it.

The *Taw* and the Serpent

There is a symbol of the enemy, Satan, depicted in several places as a slithering serpent running between the other various mosaic designs. It seems to be in an obvious counterpoint to the many *taws* that represent Yeshua. Hence,

I believe we have here a depiction of the Essenic "two way" symbolism of light and darkness, good and evil, etc. This particular picture shows a large *taw* within a thick-walled hexagon. To the immediate right there is the serpentine symbol, which terminates in what appears to be the head of the snake. Notice also the smaller *taw* between the serpent and the wall of the hexagon, as if to underscore the symbolism of protection.

Single-Circle Designs

There is also a single-circle design format used within Jewish and Christian art. In its basic form, without beginning or end, it represents the infinite nature of God. To earth-centered, pagan religions, throughout history the circle has represented the feminine spirit or force, the cosmos, or a spiritualized Mother Earth.[9] Moreover, both the two-circle and single-circle "cosmic circle" designs were used by the Essenes.

> Two mysterious Orders of the Essenes, the Sampsonians and Helicaeans, were adept in the calendar mysteries and were named after Samson ["like the sun"] and the Helix, or cosmic circle.[10]

An Essene who wished to meditate would insulate himself from the world by drawing a circle around himself in the sand. Yeshua may have done this before He was ready to judge the men who were stoning to death the woman who was caught in adultery (John 8:2–11).

The Mosaics of the Tiberias site include several striking versions of this single-circle design.

The precise meaning of this partially buried fan design remains a matter for speculation. Please notice the small *taw* at the center of the design and also at the outer extension of each blade of the "fan." Again, the serpentine link border in the midst of so many illustrations of light versus darkness perhaps was intended as an artistic representation of the foundational Essene "two way" understanding, as it was embraced by The Way.

As with the foregoing single circle design, the precise meaning of the adaptation shown here is not immediately apparent. Some have suggested that there is a close resemblance between this design and several of the mysterious crop circles that have appeared in various agricultural fields throughout much of the world in the past several years.[11]

The Fish as a Symbol of Yeshua

The fish, as a symbol of Yeshua and/or His body of believers, has widely been accepted to have first stood alone as a Christian symbol some time before Clement of Alexandria suggested to all his readers in A.D. 150 that they would be well served to include the sign of the fish in their personal seals.[12] Please notice the *taw* at the center of the design.

I have long speculated as to why the three part Messianic Seal (menorah, Star of David, and fish) has not been found beyond Mount Zion, where its original cache of some thirty to forty seal-bearing artifacts were discovered by an old monk, eight of which were subsequently given to Ludwig Schneider.[13] The appearance of the fish as a symbol by itself in the mosaics of this circa A.D. 100–150 Messianic Jewish synagogue of The Way underscores my working hypothesis that the Messianic Seal was created by and for the original orthodox group led by James and that it did not accompany those who widely dispersed from this location of their mother congregation. A number of factors could have contributed to this apparent intentional or unintentional restriction of the Messianic Seal to Mount Zion, such as its complexity of design; the dispersed Way's desire to be integrated, at least to some mutually satisfying degree into the greater body of the church; or to help fend off the growing three-sided persecution that was coming against them from the church, the government, and their fellow Jews.

In Summary

The Westernmost Mosaic Panel

The Easternmost Mosaic Panel

The above two pictures of the western and eastern panels of the mosaic floor, respectively, provide a striking summary of the overall great beauty, superb workmanship, and deep spirituality of those early Jewish believers who planned and effected this genuinely amazing artistic expression of their faith in the risen Jewish Messiah, the Son of God and God Himself incarnate. With very few exceptions, the designs found in the mosaics of this site are entirely unique, as is the site itself, being the first and only Nazarene synagogue of The Way yet to be discovered.

Chapter 8
The *Mikvah* of the Tiberias Synagogue of The Way

The historical roots of the *mikvah* reach all the way back to the Garden of Eden. By eating the fruit, Adam and Eve brought death into the world. Most of the Jewish traditions that relate to impurity are connected to some form of death. Those who come into contact with one of the forms of death must therefore immerse themselves in water, which is described in Genesis as flowing out of the Garden of Eden (the source of life), in order to be cleansed of this contact with death, and by extension, cleansed from sin.[1] Because of its great significance, the many rabbinical authors of the Talmud pontificate at great length and in minute detail on the subject of *mikvah* in an entire large section (tractate) entitled "Mikva'ot."

The Hebrew word *mikvah* in English means "a pool or gathering of water." A *mikvah* may use either stationary rainwater or flowing well water or spring water. Oceans, lakes, ponds, and springs are all natural catch basins of rainwater and thus can be used for this ritual purpose (Lev. 11:36).

Biblically, the word first appears in Genesis 1:10, when God gathers the waters on the third day: "And the gathering [*mikvah*] together of the waters He called Seas." It next appears in Leviticus 11:36 in the context of rules for purification: "Only a spring and a cistern, a gathering [*mikvah*] of waters, shall be ritually pure."

From the dawn of Jewish history, the *mikvah* has been used for ritual purification by post-menstrual women, by men with certain conditions, and by priests before and after participation in their temple rituals. Men traditionally used the *mikvah* for spiritual purification before the Sabbath and *Yom Kippur*. And, brides and converts to Judaism were and continue to use the *mikvah* as a part of these milestone life transformations.

Mikvah purification was, historically, by no means within the exclusive province of traditional and then later Rabbinical Judaism. The Essenes were regular practitioners of daily immersion. Moreover, this Essene practice was adopted by the Nazarenes, who observed daily ritual immersion. The *Clementine Homilies* ("Recognitions of Clement") tell us that Peter always washed, often in the sea, before dawn, which was most likely a practice of all or at least most of the early members of The Way.[2] While members of The Way fully understood and celebrated their salvation by grace through faith in the shed blood of their Messiah, Yeshua, they remained at the same time fully Torah-observant Jews. Hence, *mikvah* purification remained a central feature of their religious understanding and practice.

While there was earlier evidence[3] that pointed to The Way's retention of *mikvah* purification, the *mikvah* and its associated cistern water supply as a central feature of the Tiberias synagogue of The Way provide remarkable, undeniable evidence that this practice continued at least well into the second century.

In the above photo, the *mikvah* is to the left, covered in wild mustard. (Note the nearby sewer pipe that is to be replaced, which prompted this archaeological exploration.) The associated cistern, used to gather and store rainwater for the *mikvah*, is at the right.

Donna Fischer, the author's wife, thrilled with discovery, is shown here seated in the *mikvah*, which we had just cleared of blooming mustard and debris.

Pictured here are the steps leading down into the *mikvah*. One (at the top) of the traditional seven had not yet been exposed. The seven steps symbolize the seven heavens through which Yeshua descended, then ascended, and which He will one day descend again.

Looking west toward the mosaic panels, the flower-covered cistern is to the left and the *mikvah* is to the right.

The drainage port can be seen at the bottom of the cistern, as viewed from the *mikvah*. Water flowed by gravity from the cistern into the *mikvah*. A presumed drain at the bottom remains covered.

And so it is that we must leave this precious site for the time with the great hope and expectation that one day soon private funding will be provided and government approval will be granted for a complete excavation and restoration of this most remarkable Tiberias synagogue of The Way. Until that time, its amazing revelation to the spiritually hungry world must remain concealed from further firsthand view.

The lovely flowers have turned to sticks, everything is dry and thickly covered with dust. The lovely mosaics are buried, well protected by the Antiquities Authority with a thick layer of felt, which in turn is covered with sand, and finally with sand-filled plastic bags. May the Lord God of Israel quickly make a way for this site to once again see the light of day and, having been fully unearthed and restored, become the testimony to Him and to the glorious place it was when the first Jewish believers gathered there together in His name.

Chapter 9
The Way's Presumed Late-First-Century Movement from Mount Zion to Tiberias

The underlying premise of this chapter is the fact—demonstrable by historical reference and the material evidence of the ruins of the Tiberias Messianic Synagogue—that members of The Way found their way to Tiberias, where at some point they established a formal place of worship during the late first or early second century.

While the precise timing, means, and route of The Way's migration from the heart of Judea to the heart of the Galilee can only be speculated, one of several scenarios stands out as perhaps the most plausible. Interestingly, my friend and former colleague, Professor Jay Thompson, independently developed and embraces this very same scenario and felt led to share it with me. Thus, taking his input as a confirmation, I now offer this scenario, however conjectural.

As we examined in earlier chapters, there were two main migrations of The Way from Mount Zion, out of which was formed a new and widely scattered diaspora. In the resulting post-A.D. 70 demographics there were, eventually, two major regional concentrations of The Way; one in the Galilee, the other in "the region of Damascus."

The first of these migrations from the nest of the mother congregation on Mount Zion was provoked by the intense persecution by the Sadducees and Pharisees, which culminated around A.D. 35 with the martyrdom of Stephen. While it cannot be determined with absolute certainty, from what we do know, most of those who first left Jerusalem dispersed to various locations in Judea, Samaria, to the south into the Negev and Egypt, and to the west toward the Mediterranean.[1]

The second phase of The Way's migration from Mount Zion was provoked by yet another tragic death, the devastating martyrdom of their beloved leader, James, in A.D. 62. The loss of James, together with the first revolt against

Rome, which followed just four years later, provided sufficient motivation for all but a handful of believers to flee to safer and potentially more fertile missionary fields.[2]

Most scholars agree the end location of this second phase of the dispersion from Jerusalem was Pella, a city of the Decapolis that was, I believe, then populated by a large community of very early Gentile Christians. As I proposed in my earlier work, *The Door Where It Began*, these on-fire fundamentalist Christians were among the first fruit of the Eastern Church, which had its genesis at Hippos, another city of the Decapolis. In any event, by early A.D. 60 these first-generation Gentile Christians had developed a most impressive city on a mountaintop plateau just north of Scythopolis (modern day Bet She'an) and just east of the Jordan river.

This picture of Pella was taken from the international border looking east into Jordan. The ancient city was set on top of the sizeable hill on the far side of the Jordan River, where it remained a relatively isolated and secure place of sojourn for the Nazarenes of The Way, who fled there from Jerusalem.

As earlier suggested, the many Jewish believers who migrated to Pella were orthodox in their understandings; that is, they held fast to the Torah and to the teachings of James, as these teachings were later to be embraced as foundational theological understandings of the church at large. Perhaps the most important and still the most debated of these is the orthodox understanding that Yeshua was at once the Messiah, the Son of God, and God incarnate.

It was this understanding of Yeshua's divinity that was the primary driver in causing Cerinthius, a cultist whose teachings were to later be deemed heretical by the church father Irenaeus, among others, to form the first major heterodox schism, the participants of which were called Ebionites. This Ebionite schism was followed in turn by the beginnings of several other Gnostic, "heterodox" schisms the common denominator of which was this same denial of Yeshua's divinity.

Thus, it is clear that there was a very significant Ebionite, heterodox movement at Pella from A.D. 70 to 90.[3] Moreover, it can be reasonably surmised that conversions to this heretical heterodox position took a significant toll on this now-dispersed Nazarene community of The Way and posed a continuing threat to them as long as they remained in the relatively restricted boundaries of that mountaintop plateau.

In any event, it seems plausible that toward the end of this period (circa A.D. 80–90) all or at least most of the remaining orthodox believers (Nazarenes) fled from Pella in search of more hospitable surroundings. I further conjecture, as do Professor Thompson and Dr. Woodard, that at least some—perhaps many or even all—of these dear ones ended up in Tiberias.

Herod the Great's son and successor, Herod Antipas, created the city of Tiberias around A.D. 20 on the western shore of the Sea of Galilee as a posh Greco-Roman style city and harbor, and named it after the new Roman Emperor. The decoration of coins found in the earliest strata during the just-concluded three-year excavations of Roman Tiberias reveal that the city's residents at that time were mostly idol-hating Jews who were ruled over by a cautious Antipas, who went out of his way to heed the religious sensibilities of his Jewish subjects. For example, these first coins Herod Antipas struck at Tiberias show the tightrope Antipas walked while he was trying to build a Jewish kingdom in the Roman world. On one side was displayed his own royal image, while on the other were depicted appropriately Jewish symbols, such as reeds, palm branches, and palm trees.

In keeping with his desire to satisfy the sensibilities of his ever-reluctant, almost entirely Jewish population, Herod Antipas built Tiberias without many of the trappings of the classical pagan city, such as statues or pagan temples. Nevertheless, he created a Greco-Roman architectural veneer over the city, which made it a stand-out novelty in the Galilee.[4]

The several challenges that Antipas needed to overcome vis-à-vis his Jewish subjects were anything but simple. Along with an array of worldly considerations, a deep and abiding spiritual cloud hung over this newly constructed, otherwise magnificent city. It seems that Antipas had erected his municipal masterpiece directly over the remains of an ancient Jewish cemetery.[5] It was this enormous, royally perpetrated blunder that made this otherwise highly attractive city an extremely undesirable and religiously forbidden place for Jews to live. This undesirability penetrated to the hearts of even most relatively secular Jews. It was understood to be a redline, and one that persists into modern times.

Jews go to great lengths to honor the dead and to protect their remains. Just recently, Israel traded hundreds of very much alive terrorists with blood on their hands for the remains of two fallen Israeli soldiers who had been kidnapped then died while in captivity.[6] This Jewish passion to bury our people in Israel is rooted in an ancient understanding that by doing so their bodies will eventually turn to dust, mix with the soil, and thus in a very real way become an actual part of the precious land of our inheritance.

Consequently, because of this ancient cemetery, as Josephus tells us, Antipas had to go to great lengths to encourage Jews to relocate to the city. Toward this end, he equipped houses at his own expense and added new gifts of extra land. Tax exemptions were offered, and even the poor and runaway slaves were given citizenship. When even all of these inducements still did not produce Antipas's population expectations, he resorted to outright coercion, physically forcing Jews to abandon their property and relocate to Tiberias.[7] It therefore seems reasonable to conclude that the Jewish population of Antipas's Tiberias was anything but homogeneous and religiously content. It also seems reasonable to conclude it was this same spiritually dark pall hanging over Tiberias that caused Yeshua to consistently bypass the city.[8]

Some scholars hold that the synagogue as a religious institution originated during the Babylonian exile; others contend that it was a later development. The great proliferation of Pharisaic synagogues did not come into being until after the destruction of the temple in A.D. 70. Be that as it may, there were synagogues in the Galilee during the first century, as evidenced, for example, by the archaeological remains of those at Gamala and Capernaum.

While there are no such very early synagogual remains in Tiberias, there was at least one such synagogue in the city during the first century.[9] Josephus presents Tiberias of that time as a magnificent city built in a Roman style with a large palace, baths, *cardo*, and a synagogue he described as "a large edifice, and capable of receiving a great number of people."[10]

It is doubtful, however, that this large synagogue was frequently if ever overcrowded, considering the mostly secular Jewish community from which it had to draw its attendance. Religiously, it seems likely that these Jews of the late-first-century Tiberias were at the most only minimally observant, especially when contrasted with the ultra-religious Pharisees, who were even then creating a whole new Judaism based upon the laws of men as they moved the headquarters of their Sanhedrin ever northward towards Tiberias, where they would ultimately arrive circa 220.[11]

Rabbinic literature makes frequent reference to the many Pharisaic synagogues that sprang up following the destruction of the temple during the next most immediate centuries. For example, the Talmud speaks of an early time when there were eighteen synagogues in Sepphoris as opposed to only thirteen in Tiberias.[12]

It can thus be reasonably concluded that sometime near the end of the first century, when Nazarene believers of The Way arrived in this beautiful, uniquely appointed, tranquil, almost entirely secular Jewish city, it was easy for them to quickly assimilate into the local and for the most part non-religious society without the horror of the multifaceted persecution they had been forced to endure in Jerusalem.

Chapter 10

Tiberias in the Late First Century: The Setting for a New Congregation of The Way

It is highly likely that in the predominately secular Jewish Tiberias of the second and early third centuries, members of the local Nazarene community of The Way lived in close proximity to their non-believing Jewish neighbors, with whom they quickly became bonded by their common, uniquely Jewish underpinnings, especially by the rich Jewish traditions they all shared.[1]

Moreover, it isn't a giant leap to assume that these most recently arrived Tiberias residents continued to meet daily in their homes, just as they had done in Jerusalem and presumably would have continued doing during any interim sojourn in Pella. There is certainly nothing to suggest that these home congregations that met each day and then came together for a communal meeting each *Motzei Shabbat* did not continue these regular meetings well into the Diaspora, until they finally faded from history in the fifth century somewhere in the hills of Coele-Syria or "the region of Damascus."

While it is admittedly also highly conjectural, there is nothing to suggest that this Nazarene community of The Way did not use the very large synagogue spoken of by Josephus as the locale of these weekly *Motzei Shabbat* congregational gatherings.

In any event, there was a period of considerably more than a century from the time these on-fire Jewish believers arrived in Tiberias (late first century) until the arrival of the Sanhedrin (circa A.D. 220), which by any reasonable measure should have been ample time for them to plant a congregation, then grow it into a formidable local body. Please remember that these spiritually charged new arrivals were, presumably, totally dedicated, orthodox Nazarene believers of The Way who most likely were convicted that they had been led by the Lord to relocate to this very fertile mission field, which stood ripe and ready for planting, cultivation, and an eventually great soul harvest.

The scant Jewish history of Tiberias I have been able to find makes no mention of these first Jewish believers in Yeshua, or of their activities in this city, which spanned more than a century. Be that as it may, all of the elements for a spiritual revival of great proportions were seemingly in place.

Beyond these speculations, there is, more importantly, the undeniable material evidence found in the ruins of their obviously once-exquisite synagogue, which clearly confirms that they, an orthodox Nazarene congregation of The Way, were physically present in Tiberias for a considerable time, right in the very heart of the Galilee, worshiping their greatly beloved Yeshua, their Messiah, Son of God, and God incarnate.

I would further suggest the likelihood that this on-fire Tiberias community of Jewish believers vigorously spread the gospel of Yeshua among the large body of their mostly secular Jewish neighbors and that this outreach could well have produced a remarkable harvest of new believers. Using this assumption as a baseline, I would further suggest that such a highly productive missionary outreach to the very large unsaved population of Tiberias generated the clear requirement as well as the considerable resources needed to erect a wonderfully appointed Nazarene Jewish synagogue of their own, the ruins of which we speak.

But there is more exciting archaeological evidence beyond the synagogue itself that gives even greater credence to this scenario. During March 2004, excavations of the urban center of Roman Tiberias were resumed on behalf of the Hebrew University under the supervision of Dr. Y. Hirschfeld and continued in four successive seasons until they ceased in April 2008, soon after Dr. Hirschfeld's death. The northeast corner of the ruins of Roman Tiberias excavated during this period are less then one hundred meters—literally a stone's throw—away from the ruins of the Tiberias synagogue of The Way. Remarkably, this Nazarene Jewish place of worship is set just eighty meters or so further to the northwest, somewhat beyond the northernmost edge of Roman Tiberias, as it was unearthed in the exploration that ended in March 2008.

While much further exploration remains to be accomplished, a longtime volunteer who faithfully worked on this dig during all of its seasons shared with me that, since Dr. Hirschfeld's unfortunate passing, there is currently no further funding budgeted or projected for this project that would thus remain on hold until some unknown time in the future.

Even so, among the extensive ruins of Roman Tiberias that have already been exposed, the most prominent identified is the headquarters and associated facilities of the Sanhedrin, who relocated to this place circa A.D. 220. Among these now-exposed ruins, there is further exciting archaeological evidence strongly suggesting that some one hundred-plus years before the Sanhedrin came to town, some, perhaps a sizable part, of this area may well have been The Way's section of the city. Such a subdivision would have been in keeping with that of many modern day cities, such as Jerusalem, which remain laid out in quarters delineated by ethnicity, such as the Armenian quarter.

The primary evidence that points to this conclusion can be seen in the badly worn mosaic floor of a large salon-size room I came upon, located in the northwestern section of this excavated area. The measurements of what remains of this room are approximately fourteen meters long by four meters wide. While still relatively spacious by Israeli standards, this room was originally even considerably larger. It can clearly be observed that this presumed salon was reduced to its present size by the interruption of thick stone walls that were inserted at a later time on its north, south, and east sides. I would suggest on the basis of their form, substance, and how they fit in with the general layout of this section of the city ruins that these walls were inserted as a part of the reconstruction and conversion of this large area into the new headquarters and supporting facilities of the Sanhedrin circa A.D. 220–230.

As a further testimony to the two widely separated time periods when this room was used, its badly worn mosaic-tiled floor is made up of two distinctively different layers. The original floor was obviously constructed by highly skilled artisans using very small, uniformly cut tiles to create intricate, lovely designs. This suggests that the original occupants of this room, while not likely regal, were nonetheless prosperous.

While some sections of this once-beautiful floor are now exposed, much of the remaining original surface remains overlain with a crudely accomplished, design-free layer made up of irregularly cut, larger, monochrome (dark grey) mosaic tiles. Although it can't be certain, I would suggest that those parts of the original floor that are currently exposed came to be so because of the poor workmanship of their covering layer, large sections of which have apparently broken loose and disappeared over the ensuing centuries, thus exposing sections of the floor beneath. This remarkable room, its floor, and its original mosaic designs are presented in the following gallery.

The Sanhedrin Reception Hall was built in the fourth century as a very large complex of at least two thousand square meters. It had some twenty-five rooms with three main components, a colonnaded courtyard, a passageway, and a reception hall with a semi-circular apse.[2]

The apse of the Sanhedrin reception hall is shown in the center foreground of this general view of the northernmost end of the very large Roman Tiberias. The Sea of Galilee and the Golan Heights form a lovely backdrop for this ancient setting.

Pictured here, looking south, is the north to south oriented *cardo maximus* ("main street"). The large, salon-size room is unseen to the immediate lower left. It is located just to the south of a row of shops that were a part of the later Sanhedrin reconstruction of the site, which began circa A.D. 220–230.

The grey stone steps of the *cardo* are seen in the left-center foreground. The slightly curved wall at right center marks the southern end of the long, salon-size room. These two visible walls at the end of the room, a part of the third-century Sanhedrin complex, were erected directly on top of these badly worn mosaics, which obviously decorated the floor during a much earlier use of this structure.

This view of the large residential room is from the innermost inserted wall, looking north. The wall to the west (left) is original. Presumably, it was during the Sanhedrin reconstruction of the site that the other three walls were inserted directly on top of the original mosaic floor, thus causing extensive damage to the mosaic designs, while greatly reducing room's size.

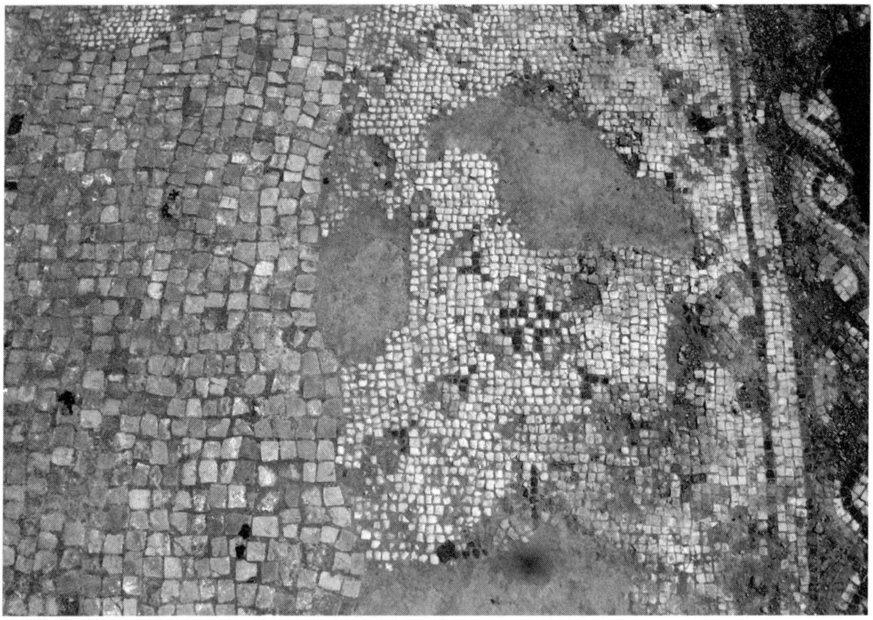

Shown here is the smaller of two distinctly different, high-quality mosaic renditions of the *taw*. They are clearly visible in a section of the original floor that has been exposed as a result of the deterioration of the crudely rendered covering layer. A large remaining section of this covering layer, comprised of unevenly cut, larger tiles can be seen on the left side of this view.

This is a closer view of the smaller of the two *taw* mosaics that adorn the original floor. The arrow symbols seem to be pointing to the centrality of the *taw* from the four principal points of the compass. Dr. Lee Woodard immediately confirmed my own preliminary identification by e-mail:

> Notice again that the cross to which those > symbols are pointing is again of that + style reflected in the other Mosaic [the floor of the nearby Tiberias Synagogue of The Way], which is also the same style used by Jewish Christian Scribe-Artist Barnabas during A.D. 67–74. That style within this new Mosaic is a testament to [its] early age. Do keep in mind that Codex W penmanship and art were by Jewish Christian Barnabas during A.D. 67–74. When we find that same style of cross that Barnabas penned during those dates named above used within those old Tiberias Jewish Facilities adapted or used by Jewish Christians, it seems reasonable to think that those Tiberias facilities were used by Late First and/or Early 2nd Century Jewish Christians.[3]

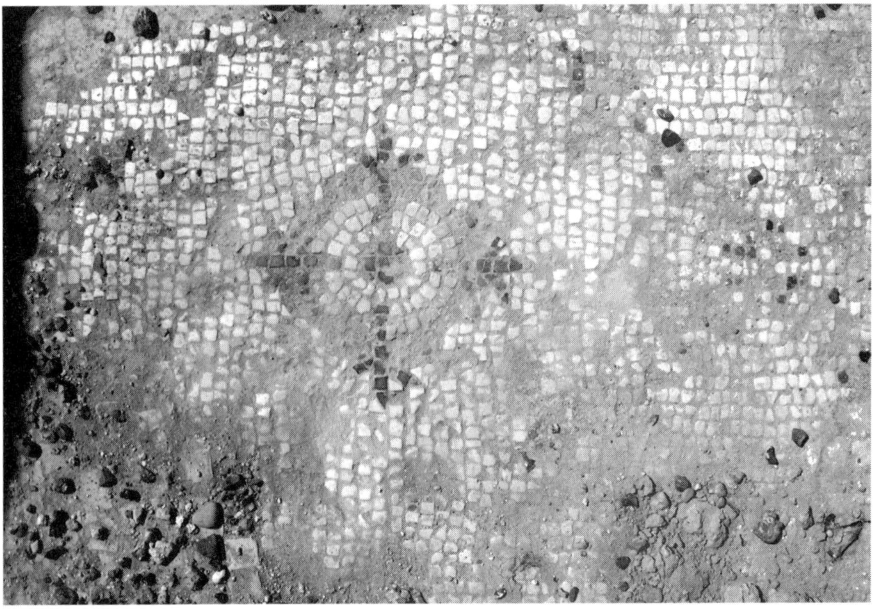

The larger and more striking of the two mosaic renditions of the *taw* with a smaller *taw* at the center is shown here. There are four other visible identical renditions of this design on the remaining floor, all in badly worn condition. Bellarmino Bagatti confirms that the *taw* enclosed in a circle was a frequent graffiti of the early Jewish believers. It was found inscribed on first century tombs at Dominus Flevit, in the mosaics of the old synagogue at Nazareth, and in other locations. Most strikingly, it and the smaller *taw* design cover the entire original floor of a small room of the church at Kursi from the second or third century. They are almost identical to the designs found here in this Roman Tiberias residence. (See Chapter 15.)

This most remarkable mosaic is clearly understood to be a symbol of Yeshua Himself.[4] How awesome! Here it is, a striking symbol of Yeshua inscribed on the floor of a room that was most likely first used by born-again Jews. More than one hundred years later it was crudely covered over, reduced in size by added walls, and then used by the Sanhedrin of the Pharisees, who were the greatest antagonists of the Nazarene Way from their very beginnings on Mount Zion.

While it is of course highly speculative, I would further suggest from the evidence we have seen that this room could have been the salon of a pastor's residence, perhaps even the pastor who oversaw a flourishing Nazarene synagogue of The Way that was literally only a stone's throw away.

This view shows the only place on the entire floor where both versions of the *taw* design are visible together. Also shown here is a small surviving section of the crude tile overlay that was evidently placed there to conceal the tell-tale, prominent Messianic Jewish symbols of the earlier floor beneath.

I would offer a further speculation concerning these two amazing designs with the *taw* as their central feature. First, as a point of departure, these designs as they are situated on this floor are in perfect alignment with the compass. This was certainly not by chance but by obvious deliberate design.

Please take note of the arrow (">") symbols that proceed outward in four directions from the smaller *taw* design, each forty-five degrees off the cardinal directions (north, south, east, west). Then, also note that there is a ">" at each of the four extensions of the larger *taw* design, pointing inward to the small *taw* at its center. I suggest that the smaller *taw* design may depict Mount Zion, Jerusalem, the temple, or Yeshua. The Way was forced by multifold persecution to disperse in all directions from Mount Zion and Jerusalem. The temple was destroyed and their beloved Yeshua ascended into heaven.

I would further suggest that the larger *taw* design may depict a response to what I see depicted in the smaller *taw* design: The Way's greatly longed-for second coming of Yeshua through the seven heavens, depicted here as seven concentric circles, the last two circles being the four members of the small *taw* itself and its center. Next, this design could also represent The Way's longed-for return to Mount Zion and Jerusalem, or perhaps the longed-for reconstruction of the temple.

Chapter 11
The End of an Era: The Way Takes Leave of Tiberias

To everything there is a season,
A time for every purpose under heaven.
—Ecclesiastes 3:1

The Way, it would seem, came to Tiberias sometime between A.D. 80 and A.D. 100 and presumably were quickly assimilated into this peaceful, mostly secular Jewish community, all the while continuing their own home-congregation-focused worship of Yeshua.

They were greatly blessed by sufficient growth and prosperity to build a lovely, perhaps unique synagogue of their own amidst their mostly secular and spiritually open Jewish neighbors. Thus, I believe it is reasonable to surmise that these Tiberias members of The Way brought many, perhaps even thousands, of their neighbors into the kingdom through their century-long witness.

Moreover, just as all of them were blessed to worship together in their lovely synagogue, so are we, the believers of today, greatly blessed by having discovered the still-beautiful remains of their precious place of worship. The Word teaches us, however, that to everything there is a season, a time, and a purpose. Thus, we must consider how it might have been that all of this loveliness began to unravel.

After as many as three generations of blissful, productive peace as fully integrated members of their community, the Tiberias congregation of The Way most likely found it necessary to look for yet another new home. Historical events seem to make it clear that once again either the imminent threat or actual beginnings of persecution by their nemeses, the Pharisees, forced The Way to quit Tiberias and relocate to yet another safe haven.

The rivalry between The Way and the Pharisees may be attributed to multiple factors. In A.D. 62, the vast majority of The Way fled to Pella and elsewhere from Jerusalem and by so doing pointedly refused to join in the first Jewish revolt against the government. Their Pharisee brethren—who were left alone to carry the burden of the ill-fated conflict—were anything but pleased. The Way's bypassing this war was only a part of the growing problem. The Pharisees were obviously also none too pleased to see many of their number, after hearing the good news of Yeshua offered freely by budding evangelists in the temple courts and elsewhere, respond by the thousands to join the ranks of The Way (Acts 2:41). These legions of proselytes who were thus joining the orthodox group on Mount Zion were surely not the end but only the beginning of what must have been explosive growth among the Jews during the remainder of the first century and beyond. From the Pharisees' point of view, every new born-again Jew was one less potential adherent to the Rabbinical Judaism they were bringing forth.

Thus, in A.D. 90, some twenty years after the Sanhedrin had moved to Yavne, they finally got around to officially venting their growing hostility toward those whom they called *minim* ("foreigners, sectarians, or apostates"). These were, quite pointedly, for the most part Jews who had embraced Yeshua and in the process of doing so had, according to the Jewish law promulgated by the Pharisee-dominated Sanhedrin, forgone their Jewish ethnicity and heritage in the process.

Toward this end, "Samuel the Lesser," a member of the Sanhedrin, was commissioned to add an eighteenth "blessing" to the *Amidah*, the central prayer of Jewish liturgy, which came to be called the *Birkat haMinim* ("blessings for the foreigners"). In its original form, this eighteenth blessing, which was read communally three times each day in every Pharisaic synagogue, cried out from the lips of each congregation:

> For the renegades let there be no hope, and may the arrogant kingdom soon be rooted out in our days, and the *Netzarim* [Nazarenes] and the *Minim* [non-Jews] perish as in a moment and be blotted out from the book of life and with the righteous may they not be inscribed. Blessed are you, Lord, who humbles the arrogant.[1]

This "benediction," which was obviously rather a pointed curse on the Nazarenes of The Way, achieved its intended purpose of casting them out of the Pharisaic synagogues since any born-again Jews who attended would be expected to recite a curse upon themselves. Certainly, Yeshua had given them fair warning of the vitriolic opposition that was rising up against them.

> They will put you out of the synagogues; yes, the time is coming that whoever kills you will think that he offers God service. And these things they will do to you because they have not known the Father nor Me.

> But these things I have told you, that when the time comes, you may remember that I told you of them.
>
> —John 16:2–4

Epiphanius, the church father and historian who, as we will see later, was evidently at least somewhat familiar with the events that occurred surrounding the emergence of Christianity in Tiberias, wrote in the fourth century:

> Not only do Jewish people have a hatred of the Nazarenes; they even stand up at dawn, at midday, and toward evening, three times a day when they recite their prayers in the synagogues, and curse and anathemize them. Three times a day they say, "*Elohim* (God) curse the Nazarenes." For they harbor an extra grudge against them, if you please, because despite their Jewishness, they proclaim that Yeshua is Messiah...[2]

The *Birkat haMinim*, softened in the interests of political correctness, as it appears today reads:

> And for slanderers let there be no hope, and let all wickedness perish as in a moment; let all thine enemies be speedily cut off, and the dominion of arrogance do you uproot and crush, cast down and humble speedily in our days. Blessed are you, Lord, who breakest the enemies and humbles the arrogant.[3]

Moreover, the Pharisees had yet another ax to grind with the Nazarenes of The Way. By A.D. 132, Rabbi Akiva, who was now holding forth from Yavne, where the Sanhedrin was then located, took it largely upon himself to instigate a second disastrous revolt against Rome. This time around, however, the revolt took on a clearly religious call to arms. Akiva demanded that all Jews unite around one *Bar Kochba* (Son of the Star), the one whom he had personally proclaimed to be the "King Messiah." To do so, The Way would have had to renounce their salvation in Yeshua—which of course they did not, adding yet another handful of salt to the deep open wound of antagonism the Pharisees had long held toward them.

While we can now say with some assurance why the Nazarenes of The Way left Tiberias, history does not tell us precisely when they pulled up stakes and fled to Coele Syria or "the region of Damascus." What we can say with historical certainty is that the Pharisees, The Way's avowed and long-standing, religiously and politically powerful adversaries had not only decided to move in force to Tiberias but, ironically, had also determined to locate their Sanhedrin and its supporting facilities in the very part of the city that had been the home of the local Nazarene congregation of The Way for over a century. Since there is no historical record telling of any open confrontation between the two groups, which would surely have occurred had they met head-on under these circumstances, it seems reasonable to assume that The Way had departed from Tiberias before the Pharisees, who were called rabbinic sages, entered the city in A.D. 220.

Be that as it may, the fact is, some time prior to A.D. 220, the Nazarenes of The Way fled to the hills of Syria, where they remained in pockets through the fifth century before they vanished into obscurity, having left behind their lovely synagogue and a residential area that may have well been the main attraction that caused the Pharisees to reestablish their Sanhedrin on that very spot.

We can only speculate as to precisely when and how the Tiberias synagogue of The Way fell into ruin.

I could stop right here in recounting this amazing Tiberias chapter in the history of The Way, but there is another, most interesting part of the story that begs telling.

Chapter 12
The Amazing Saga of Count Joseph

Soon after the initial excitement of discovery had begun to settle and I began to examine the ruins of the Tiberias synagogue of The Way more carefully, a very perplexing feature of the site became apparent, defying any immediate explanation. As is evident in the following two pictures, at some point after The Way fled Tiberias, some person or persons began to construct another building directly on top of the ruins of the synagogue, having no regard whatsoever for protecting the lovely mosaics beneath.

The strange thing is this building project evidently came to an abrupt end soon after it began. The only archaeological evidence to be found showing that this inexplicably aborted work was ever undertaken are the remains of three stone block walls that are only one row high (less than one meter) and two grey stone columns that are resting on less than one meter of debris, which separates them from the level of the synagogue beneath.

The view of the easternmost mosaic panel on the previous page shows the beginnings of superimposed stone walls, set directly on top of the mosaics that surround the floor on its east and south sides.

The fallen stone pillar shown here is separated from the floor beneath by a thick covering of debris. This shows that it was a part of the aborted facility that was begun at some time after the synagogue was abandoned and then discontinued soon after this work began.

This fascinating evidence, of course, begs several questions. Who undertook this building project, and when was it begun? Why was the work abruptly aborted? Why did they choose to build directly on top of the ruins of an earlier structure?

The Sanhedrin can reasonably be immediately ruled out as the responsible party. If they had wanted to build on top of the Messianic synagogue so as to conceal what lay beneath, they certainly had the resources needed to complete the project. If they had wanted to simply conceal the tell-tale mosaics, they could have easily done this as well. The Sanhedrin would have had every reason and inclination to destroy or at least hide anything that spoke of Yeshua or The Way within or in close proximity to their new center. Please remember, from what we can deduce, it was they who made what ended up to be a vain attempt to conceal some precious *taw* mosaics on the floor of what likely had been a residence or some other facility of The Way.

So if not the Sanhedrin, then who began only to soon terminate this work, and why? Professor Thompson offers a possible explanation concerning the origin of these walls. He writes:

> This wall is a later addition, not necessarily from the same millennia (eighth to eleventh century). I think the floor might have been used later for the foundation of a fortress (circa. Crusades Muslim, or Frank). This explains why there was no concern for keeping the floor intact. The Byzantines would have left the floor intact instead of covering over half…with walls and building structure because they appreciated artwork, and Greek inscriptions were never destroyed.[1]

While any of these prospective wall builders may have, indeed, been responsible for this desecration of the site and its mosaics, there is still no satisfactory answer here as to why the project was abruptly terminated shortly after it began.

I believe that history offers us another, admittedly still highly speculative but nevertheless plausible alternative explanation. It would seem that Epiphanius of Salmus, an obscure figure from early church history (circa 285–375), may have provided us with the answers to our several questions. Epiphanius, an ordained Catholic priest, is by far best known for his massive, seven-volume work entitled the *Panarion* ("medicine chest"), which seeks to fortify the faithful by describing in great detail eighty specific heresies of the church, among them, the Ebionites, who are criticized because of their heterodox understanding of the Godhead.[2]

While the *Panarion* makes anything but an exciting page-turning read for anyone but the most focused and dedicated scholar, Epiphanius departs from his usual matter-of-fact style in Section 13 of this massive work, where he recounts, in the manner of a storyteller, his encounter with a certain Joseph of Tiberias, whom he met and befriended, circa 355, in nearby Scythopolis (modern day Bet She'an).[3] Epiphanius then goes on to retell some of the stories related to him by Joseph, most of which relate to his conversion from Judaism to Christianity, which took place in his home city, Tiberias, during the latter part of Emperor Constantine's reign (probably circa 335).[4]

It is important to point out that these stories were related to Epiphanius by Joseph when Joseph was over seventy years old, some twenty years after the events they seek to describe took place. They were remembered, sometimes not at all clearly, by Epiphanius as he was writing the *Panarion* some fifteen years after he had first heard these stories.

In the interests of brevity, I will only relate synopses of those stories attributed to Joseph that are relevant to The Way's sojourn in Tiberias. First of all, Joseph was apparently a very resistant candidate for conversion despite the relentless missionary outreaches he recounts, which could only have come from members of some likely continuing home congregations, a presumed progeny of the Tiberias synagogue of The Way, who had left the city at least a century earlier.

Such as these most likely would have been the only believers in the city during this period, when there were as yet no Christian churches. Please remember that Tiberias at that time was the anti-Christian epicenter of the emerging Rabbinical Judaism, which was just then redacting the Gemara, which would, with the already finished Mishna, soon become the Jerusalem (Palestinian) Talmud, the first written version of what had previously been the unwritten Oral Torah.

Joseph speaks of his persistent resistance to all attempts to convert him, which included three separate supernatural visitations by Yeshua Himself. In those visions, Yeshua reportedly declared to this hesitant Jew just who He was and other facts relating to His ministry and purpose. At some point, in the face of this most extraordinary personal outreach, Joseph succumbed and became a faithful and, by his own report, highly productive member of the kingdom.[5]

Prior to his conversion, Joseph had been well connected to the then-reigning Jewish patriarch (head of the Sanhedrin), a close relationship that endured through the patriarch's final days of life. Joseph relates that as the patriarch was nearing his end, he asked that Joseph summon the local bishop. This could only have been the leader of some local home congregation. Joseph goes on to relate how he complied with this request and then peaked through the bedroom door to witness the patriarch's deathbed conversion and baptism.[6]

Later on, before the patriarch died, Joseph relates that he entered the Sanhedrin's library, where he managed to gain entrance to a locked case, wherein he found copies of the Hebrew-language Gospel of Matthew, as well as the Hebrew translations of the Gospel of John and the Book of Acts.[7]

At some point after his conversion, Joseph related to Epiphanius how he had met with the Emperor Constantine, who reportedly was so impressed to find a Jew who was totally sold out to his church that he appointed him to the official royalty level office of "count" and granted him sufficient funding and authority to fulfill his wish to build churches in the Israeli cities of Tiberias,

Sepphoris, Nazareth, and Capernaum.[8] Evidently, Joseph immediately returned to his home in Tiberias, which was still very much the epicenter of Rabbinical Judaism and the headquarters of the Sanhedrin, and undertook to fulfill his commission to build a Christian church in that city.

It is at this point that Epiphanius's recollections get a bit fuzzy. He reports in *Panarion 30* that Joseph proceeded to build a church on the site using the remains of an unfinished pagan temple that had been started to honor the Emperor Hadrian but for some unshared reason had never been completed.[9] Interestingly, we now have compelling evidence that Epiphanius had his facts confused on this very germane point as it relates to The Way and Tiberias. The Israel Antiquities Authority, in summarizing the results of their 2004 Tiberias dig season, wrote, "Stratum VI: The remains of this level dated to the Roman period (second–third centuries C.E.)... Remains of the Hadrianeum... a temple dedicated to Hadrian whose construction was never completed were discovered...."[10] It is only a short leap to make the conclusion that it was not the Hadrianeum that Joseph succeeded in turning into a church. He never even started such a work at this site, which remains unfinished even today. Instead, it seems reasonable to conclude that he began his church-building project right in the front yard, so to speak, of the Sanhedrin, directly on top of the ruins of the Tiberias synagogue of The Way, which had already been abandoned for more than a century.

While of course this entire scenario must remain a supposition, it seems to me at least a good possibility that Joseph's intended rabbinical neighbors would have been none too pleased when they discovered the just-beginning construction of a very early or even pre-Byzantine church right under their very noses. They most likely ran him out of the place forthwith, leaving behind the still just begun walls and fallen columns pictured above.

At some point, probably soon thereafter, Joseph, who no doubt remained under great pressure from the local Jewish officialdom, made his way to Scythopolis. There he established himself and some twenty years later met with Epiphanius, to whom he relayed his remarkable stories.

While his church-building efforts were thus frustrated in Tiberias, I strongly suspect that they were not in at least two other places: his new home city, Scythopolis, as well as in Capernaum. Please remember that Joseph had been commissioned and funded to build churches in four cities, including these two. We have already considered his church-building activity in Tiberias, and I can find no evidence of any such activity in his time in nearby Sepphoris. However, it would seem that in the end he may well have left his mark here in the Galilee.

The "First Christian Church" of Bet She'an

With funds in hand and a frustrated desire to build in his heart, Count Joseph fled Tiberias for the then-much-more-friendly city of Scythopolis (Bet She'an), some forty kilometers to the south on the main route down the Jordan Valley toward Jerusalem. While this major northern city had been the center of many changing cultures and historical events over its long recorded history, it was, just after Joseph's time, to become a major Christian center during the Byzantine Era (fourth to seventh centuries), as attested to by the large number of typically Byzantine Christian churches that sprang up in and near the city during these later centuries.[11]

One of these church ruins that remains, however, is not at all like the others, and its highly unique design and features have been a matter of my own great interest since I first discovered it nestled behind an ancient Roman bath house off the main city tourist trail, apparently generally ignored by most who travel there.

During my first visit to this site, I asked the head state park curator, "Is there anything 'Christian' on the site?" He unhesitatingly told me, "No, but there is the ruin of a large church out of the boundaries of the park." Then, after I found the ruins of this intriguing place well within the park proper, I became all the more curious and researched as far as I could, looking in vain for some documentation concerning this most unusual church.

Finally, as I wrote in my novel, *The Door Where It Began*, I speculated that this "church" was built as a part of the initial outreach and growth of Christianity in the Decapolis, which began in Hippos/Sussita, some fourteen years before Paul took his first missionary journey. (See Mark 5:20.)[12] You will recall that Joseph had relocated to Scythopolis (Bet She'an) and was well re-established there when he was visited by Epiphanius around 355, in the very early Byzantine Era. It thus seems reasonable to suggest that this royally appointed and funded church builder finally had his way as the institutor and financier responsible for building this mysterious church even some years prior to Epiphanius's visit.

This westward-facing view of the ruins of the church that may have been built by Count Joseph shows its singular apse facing east.

The earliest Gentile Christians adopted the Jewish practice of praying toward Eden in the east (Gen. 2:8), the direction from which Ezekiel saw come "the glory of the God of Israel" (Ezek. 43:2, 4). It is the direction in which Yeshua ascended from the Mount of Olives and wherefrom He will return (Acts 1:11), and the direction from whence the angel of the Lord will come in the End Times (Rev. 7:2).[13] The earliest mention of this eastward-facing church orientation is found in the second book of the Apostolic Constitutions (circa 200–250), which prescribes that a church should be oblong "with its head to the East."

Interestingly, however, a system of orientation exactly the opposite of this was adopted in the later basilicas built during the reign of Constantine. The Lateran, St. Peter's, St. Paul's, and San Lorenzo in Rome, as well as the basilicas of Tyre and Antioch and the Church of the Resurrection at Jerusalem, had their apses facing the West.[14] This begs the question, If Joseph was the builder of this church, was he persuaded to build it facing east because of his Nazarene Jewish heritage, which took precedence over his loyalty to his mentor, Constantine?

This adult baptismal, found in the ruins of an ancient church at Bet She'an, is not mentioned in the tourist literature related to the site, nor is there any mention of it that could be discovered after further investigation. It is located directly across from the single apse (pictured above) and is obviously a part of the same facility. The cross above the fount is clearly Gentile Christian; it is not a *taw*. The font itself, however, seems to be intended for a supervised, full-immersion adult baptism, which would be in keeping with the practice of The Way's method of water baptism. Count Joseph would have had no other model upon which to base his conception of an in-church baptismal. It is unlikely that Joseph would have seen the early churches built by Constantine in Jerusalem and Nazareth, which were, I believe, most likely built at a somewhat later time.

The Octagonal Church at Capernaum

Count Joseph may well also have had a hand in planting and building the still-world-famous octagonal church built upon the ruins of Peter's house at Capernaum. Please remember, Capernaum was one of the specific cities where Joseph had been commissioned and funded by Constantine for such ecclesiastical building projects. While the most often quoted dating of the site is early to mid fifth century, based upon some pottery shards found at its strata, such dating can be considered anything but precise. On the other hand, historically we can be certain that by A.D. 90 Peter's house was no longer used as a family residence but rather had already been converted into a house church, perhaps the very first house church, long before Dura Europas. Historically, we can also point precisely to A.D. 350, when Egeria, a pilgrim to the Holy Land, visited this *domus ecclesia*. Interestingly, *Biblical Archaeology* cites the year 400 as the time when the octagonal church was constructed over the remains of the house church.[15]

I can certainly agree with Oskar Skarsuane, who, in introducing his section "Epiphanius on Joseph of Tiberias," offers his view that this material on Count Joseph "has received less attention than it deserves."[16] Please consider the already several-times-demonstrated inaccuracies and even sometimes arbitrary nature of traditional archaeological dating. Then, measure this against what we know historically of Joseph's church-building passion and well-funded commission from the emperor to build a church in that very place. Thus, it seems even probable to me that it was Count Joseph who undertook this great work that even today, some seventeen centuries later, remains a highlight for almost every Christian pilgrim who is blessed to visit the land of Israel.

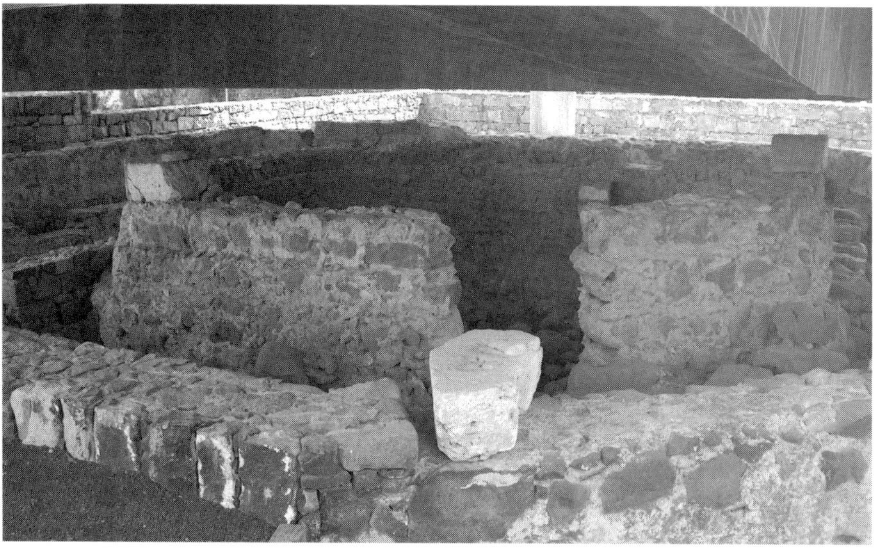

The remains of the Capernaum octagonal church, presumably built by Count Joseph, are seen here, as they have been by countless millions of Christian tourists who have already visited this site from virtually every major reach of the worldwide church.

Chapter 13

The Byzantine Church on Mount Berenice: Another Tiberias Nazarene Site of The Way?

As earlier noted, Herod Antipas had all manner of difficulties in overseeing his anything-but-content constituency in the magnificent city of Tiberias, which he created circa A.D. 20–24. Even so, Antipas was a man of awesome means, and he used some of his great wealth to create a number of getaway summer palaces throughout the Galilee, each one more magnificent than the next. History records that by far the most magnificent of them all was the imposing, bar-no-expense, elegantly appointed monument he erected to himself on the eastern summit of the two-hundred-meter high Mount Berenice, immediately above and in perfect alignment with the somewhat later site of the Tiberias synagogue of The Way. This Tiberias Summer Palace was enclosed within imposing, thick stone walls that surrounded the entire large city, extending all the way up and back down Mount Berenice to give the king's fortress-like palace a fairy tale-like air.

It was thus in 1991 that Yizhar Hirschfeld of Hebrew University, on behalf of the Israel Antiquities Authority, began what was to be his seventeen-season archaeological exploration of Roman Tiberias by seeking first to excavate the magnificent palace overlooking the city. It seems, however, that Professor Hirschfeld and his team were in for somewhat of a surprise when in their early probing they discovered the remains of what they subsequently determined to be a Byzantine Church, which they subsequently dated to the reign of Roman emperor Justinian (527–565).[1] Even in 1991, almost nothing remained of the apparently once magnificent original sixth-century Byzantine church, which was almost entirely leveled in the massive earthquake of A.D. 749. Accordingly, what Hirschfeld found and what can be seen today are the ruins of an even more glorious Byzantine church that was erected on the same site around the eighth or ninth century.

Evidently Yossi Peretz, the mayor of Tiberias at the time of Hirschfeld's discovery, was quite taken with both the palace and the church, to say nothing of greater Roman Tiberias, which lay below the summit. Accordingly, he developed a plan to turn the entire seventy-five-acre area into a landmark archaeological park. He and others apparently invested considerable effort to restore the ruins of the church and then set it up for what they envisioned would be the first phase of the extended, much longer-term development, which would immediately begin to attract Christian pilgrims to the site.

Let me explain that this site is generally understood to be more than just the ruins of an ordinary Byzantine church. Rather, historically it is regarded as one of two possible locations where John the Baptist preached and was imprisoned.[2] According to Josephus, John was actually executed at Machaerus, a fortified hilltop palace located in Jordan fifteen miles southeast of the mouth of the Jordan River on the eastern side of the Dead Sea.[3] However, Josephus has often been discredited by Christian scholars as unreliable. Be that as it may, a case can be made, based largely on longstanding tradition, that the palace at Mount Berenice was the actual location where Antipas presented John's head on a platter to Salome, the daughter of Herodious, who was first his brother's wife (Matt. 14:1–12). I would suggest that the major effort in the early 1990s to turn the Mount Berenice site into a Christian tourist attraction was largely motivated by this traditional understanding.

It was thus that wooden walkways, protected by cast iron side panels, were installed as the pathway of a self-guided tour that took in the entire site; the mosaics were restored to the extent possible; informational signs were strategically located; and a large parking area was created for the benefit of the anticipated caravans of their tour buses, which were expected to deliver large numbers of Christian pilgrims to the site. However, despite all this preparation and anticipation, from the outset the restored site was almost entirely ignored by Christian tour planners and guides. Evidently, the narrow, twisty, unpaved road up the mountain was a turnoff. Even more, the site was significantly off the long-established tourist path and thus was most likely considered insufficiently important to be included as an added attraction.

As a result of this disinterest, the city apparently quickly lost interest in the project and the site was left unattended, thus open to a succession of vandals who over the ensuing years disassembled the once-elaborate walkways, made off with the wood, and otherwise desecrated most everything that once distinguished the place as genuinely worth preserving. Moreover, the lovely mosaics were systematically destroyed and removed by persons and to places unknown.

Pictured here are the ruins of the church on Mount Berenice as they appear today. A segment of the imposing city wall that completely surrounded the seventy-five acre, first-century Roman Tiberias is shown at middle left, and the Sea of Galilee makes a lovely backdrop. What remains of the network of the grated walkways can be seen amidst the ruins.

This is a picture of the modern day city of Tiberias as it is seen from the ruins of the church on Mount Berenice.

Pictured above are the remains of the central apse. There are two smaller apses, one on either side, that were evidently added to the church during its eighth-century reconstruction. Please notice the square foundation with the hole at its center in the left, front, center of this view. Because of its location, well into the sanctuary area, this could only have been the mount for a pedestal that held an altar table, presumably for the service of the Lord's Supper.

Pictured on the previous page is the one surviving mosaic of the church on Mount Berenice as it appeared in March 2004. There is inarguably a *taw* at its center. While this singular *taw* must stand alone in material evidence, I believe that it strongly suggests that it survives as the last recognizable remnant of a very early site of the Nazarenes of the Way, which was the original place of worship built on this site.

If indeed this supposition is correct, then one must wonder why these Jewish believers in Yeshua might have chosen such a remote location. It certainly was anything but convenient to the city that stood at the bottom of the mountain, and as far as we know there was no residential settlement on the summit then, nor is there now.

Moreover, Antipas had gone to his eternal rest in A.D. 39, and his awesome palace had been destroyed during the great Jewish war of A.D. 60–70 because of what was deemed to be the iconoclastic, heretical depictions of its reportedly magnificent mosaics.[4] Thus, if indeed an early Nazarene of The Way site was built in this place it would have stood entirely by itself in an almost inaccessible location, not at all well suited for use as a regular place of worship.

Albeit admittedly highly speculative, my suggestion is that the Nazarenes did indeed build what was probably a small memorial structure on the summit of Mount Berenice and that they did so very early, at some point after their arrival in Tiberias following the Great War between A.D. 60 and 70 and most likely before they built the Tiberias synagogue of The Way. Moreover, I further suggest that they may well have been led to build this memorial structure to mark the place where John the Baptist met the end of his earthly walk. How else could the presence of a first-century Nazarene of the Way site standing by itself on this remote mountaintop be explained?

Chapter 14
Two Other Early Sites of The Way

Any discussion of The Way's movements from Mount Zion into the Diaspora would be incomplete without at least some further mention of two other of their sites, both dated to the third century: the house church discovered at Dura Europas, Syria, in 1932 and dated to A.D. 230; and the Christian prayer hall discovered at the Megiddo Prison, Israel, in 2005 and dated to A.D. 240. Both of these remarkable finds were rightfully touted by the media of their respective times as the earliest discovered places of Christian worship. Remarkably, the Tiberias synagogue of The Way has now been reliably dated as being more than one century earlier than either of these two.

The House Church at Dura Europas

Of the three sites that have so far been clearly identified as having originated with The Way, Dura Europas is the only one that has been described as a house church. The Israel Antiquity Authority describes Megiddo as an ecumenical prayer hall that was shared by Roman soldiers and Jewish believers. It seems highly probable that the Tiberias site was a fully functioning synagogue.

Dura Europas was a Hellenistic and Roman walled city built on an escarpment ninety meters above the banks of the Euphrates River. In the Syria of today, the site ruins are located near the village of Salhiyé, not too far removed from the international border with Iraq. The house church, which dates back to at least A.D. 232, was dismantled and reconstructed at Yale University in the early 1930s. Thus, not much remains to be photographed at the original site other than the basic foundations of the site structures.

In keeping with The Way's earlier model of daily meetings in homes, this house church occupied a typical Roman upper-class house, the central feature of which was a columned courtyard with an open room (*atrium*). There was a pool in the center of the courtyard that was used as a baptismal. In further keeping with the Mount Zion model, there was a raised area for a table near the center of the reception area of the house church, which was apparently used for the regular celebration of the Lord's Supper.[1]

The Christian Prayer Hall at Megiddo Prison

During the early third century, the site of the current Megiddo Prison was at once a village, a Roman military camp, and a city in what was known as the Legio Region. Religiously, three faiths were represented: traditional Judaism and Nazarene Judaism in the nearby community, and Gentile Christianity, which was embraced by some of the Roman soldiers stationed at the centrally located military camp.[2]

In 2005, excavations were conducted on behalf of the Israel Antiquities Authority in a five-hundred-square-meter area of Megiddo Prison, on the highest ground of the ancient settlement. A number of buildings were unearthed, including the quarters of Roman military officers, which have been dated to the third century. During the course of the excavations in this area, the five-by-ten-meter Christian prayer hall was discovered.[3]

An evaluation of the considerable number of coins found in this specific area of the excavations reveal with some certainty the accuracy of the dating of the Christian prayer hall to A.D. 238–244.

From all evidence it seems clear that this facility was used jointly by Roman soldiers who were Christians and by Jewish believers who lived in the adjacent community or may have been employed in various capacities by the local Roman military.

There are at least three material aspects of this facility that suggest its clear connection with The Way: the multiple presence of six nearby *mikvahs* located throughout the area, some of which have been dated to the specific time frame of the Christian prayer hall,[4] at least two clearly Nazarene Jewish symbols in the mosaics,[5] and the Lord's Supper table located in the very center of the room.[6]

This is not to suggest that the site was predominantly Nazarene Jewish. At least two factors speak to Gentile Christian participation. First, the dual fish symbols beautifully rendered in the center of the largest mosaic floor panel are clearly representative of the fish symbol that by now had become the de facto logo of Gentile Christianity. Moreover, one of the mosaic inscriptions gives thanks to one "Gaianus," who was a Roman Centurion, for having financed the lovely mosaics from his own private resources. One really fascinating aspect of this benevolent high-ranking officer is that he may well have been a Jewish believer. There is a tell-tale "shoot" symbol at the beginning of this inscription that was a well-known and often-used identifier of The Way and other Jewish believers in Yeshua. (See Isaiah 11:1.)

Photo by: Moshe Milner. Courtesy of Israel Government Press Office

Several fascinating features are found in this picture. First, side by side are the Gentile Christian fish symbols at the center and four small, distinctly Nazarene Jewish *taw* symbols in a square just to the right of the fish. There is another single *taw* in each of the designs immediately below the upper left-hand corner of the panel. These *taw* symbols appear multiple times in the mosaics of the Tiberias Messianic Synagogue. There are two other mosaic symbols shared by the two sites. First is the Solomonic knot immediately to the left of the square containing the four *taws.* The other is the border "rope" symbol to the immediate right of the *taws'* square, which is very comparable to a similar chain border design at the Tiberias site.

Although they were separated by more than a century, there are two rather striking similarities in the mosaics of this Christian prayer hall and the Tiberias Messianic Synagogue. First, there are the two nearly identical Solomonic knots, and next, the very similar double-roped borders, which appear to be a continuing rendition of the Solomonic knot interlaced oval design.

Tiberias and Megiddo Mosaics Compared

Chapter 15

The Transition From Nazarene to Pre-Byzantine and Early Byzantine Christianity (Circa Late First to Early Fourth Centuries A.D.), as Evidenced by the Original Floor Mosaics at Tabgha and Kursi

I WOULD LIKE TO CONCLUDE Part 2 with a *coda* of sorts by sharing some very new insights that have resolved for me what has been a previously troubling enigma. I have long wondered just when and how the Nazarenes of The Way who formed the second great Diaspora managed to transition over at least two centuries into what became first the pre-Byzantine movement in the late first to early fourth centuries A.D., then later the entirely separate Gentile Christian Byzantine Church (post-A.D. 340). I have recently been blessed to find the answers to these questions written by the hands of the skilled artisans who laid the lovely mosaics of the original sanctuaries at two sites here in the Galilee: the Church of the Multiplication of

Loaves and Fishes at Tabgha and the Church of the Multiplication of Loaves and Fishes at Kursi.

As earlier discussed, Professor Thompson points out that the mosaics of the Tiberias synagogue of The Way for example, as pictured on the previous page, are distinctly not Byzantine in their style. He writes:

> This Tiberias synagogue is to be distinguished from the Byzantine Greek churches in the simplicity of its floor design. The Byzantine mosaics were more lifelike and complex, giving way to portraiture, and the physical form (and naturalistic content including animals, birds, fruit, etc.).[1]

Picking up on Professor Thompson's commentary on Byzantine mosaics, let me point to another apparent misidentification of very early Nazarene Jewish mosaics as being from the later Byzantine Era.

What you see here is a portion of the beautiful mosaic floors of the church at Tabgha that have been dated since the 1980s as early Byzantine (mid-300s). It has been understood up to now that the earliest building at Tabgha was a small chapel (18 by 9.6 meters) from the fourth century. However, only a part of its foundation was uncovered. It has further been understood that during the fifth century, a church decorated with exquisite mosaic floors was built on the site. According to currently accepted history, the church was destroyed in the seventh century and remained buried until the 1980s when "after excavation, the church was restored to its Byzantine form, *incorporating portions of the original mosaics*"[2] (emphasis added).

Please take a closer look at the picture on the previous page. I direct your attention to:

1. the two *taws* immediately above the large bird's fan tail
2. the Solomonic knot-related rope border in the foreground
3. the obvious division of the underlying floor, delineated by an irregular line that runs from border to border, passing just behind the bird's tail
4. the rope border to the right of the dividing line, which appears to be newer and less worn, indicating that the design was an earlier section that was repaired or replaced by a skilled artisan
5. the border on the far side, which has as its central feature the very same serpentine motif as it appears on the floor of the Tiberias synagogue of the Way

I would like to suggest, first, that the *taws* were a part of an earlier, original floor. They are of an almost identical design as the small *taws* on the floor of the residence in the Sanhedrin area. This would suggest a dating of the first structure at Tabgha to the late first or early second century, not the fourth. Moreover, this design would show that those who first worshiped in this place were Nazarene Jews. Second, the bird and plant are distinctly Byzantine and were, I believe, inserted into the original, much earlier mosaics during its fifth century refurbishing and repair. Finally, the two rope designs are distinctly Nazarene Jewish and underscore the original identity of the site.

I feel called to share with you the amazing "God-incident" events surrounding this discovery. First, the picture you see above I took during 2004 as one of only two from the literally hundreds of various naturalistic figures included in the Tabgha mosaics. When I went to my files in search of one of my own pictures of an early Byzantine figure to use in this current context, I came across this image.

I next did a search of the many thousands of pictures in the Israeli National Photo Collection to see if there were any older pictures of the mosaics at Tabgha. I was utterly amazed to find that there was indeed only one such picture of these mosaics presented there from of all of the uncountable many hundreds of other possibilities. It just so happens that this picture, shown below, was taken of the very same figure of the bird after it had been unearthed in 1981 following its most recent burial in the seventh century.

Photo by Herman Chanania.
Courtesy of Israel Government Press Office

Let the mosaics speak for themselves. The picture above was taken April 13, 1981, after these fragments were excavated, having been buried since the seventh century but prior to their restoration on the floor of the church currently standing on the site. Please note, there is a single tile border surrounding the entire bird image, suggesting that this figure was inserted circa the fifth century on the face of the original pre-Byzantine mosaics. Please also notice the section that takes in the bird's head and the area immediately to the right that is made up of more crude, larger tiles than the body of the overall mosaic. I would suggest that this larger tile section was a "repair" made in the fifth century of the original earlier, pre-Byzantine original. Also, the empty space about halfway between the end of the bird's tail and the upper border is significant. May I suggest the obvious—that this blank space was filled in with a *taw* of their own making by skilled artisans who, in the 1980s, restored the floor to its current state? Along with other cosmetic repairs and additions, there is a *taw* that appeared in the original, pre-Byzantine rendition.

There are two points to be taken from the foregoing. First, the original floor was pre-Byzantine, probably dated contemporarily with the Tiberias synagogue of The Way, as evidenced by the appearance of one original *taw* in this section of the mosaic as it appears on the 1981 photograph. Second, the bird figure itself is clearly Byzantine, not Nazarene Jewish, and it seems obvious that it was integrated circa the fifth century with the original pre-Byzantine mosaic.

Now, please take another look at the picture of the bird and plant above. I direct your attention to the obvious "patching," with larger somewhat different color tiles surrounding the plant figure. They are especially obvious around its base. Clearly, it too was inserted in the fifth century over the much earlier Nazarene Jewish/pre-Byzantine original mosaics.

To further illustrate my point as to the pre-Byzantine dating of this site, pictured above is the famous "loaves and fishes" mosaic placed directly in front of the altar to mark the place of the miracle of the first multiplication (Matt. 14:13–21). Please note that the three "crosses" are distinctly *taws. Taws*, as affirmed by a number of scholars, are not Byzantine but rather uniquely Nazarene Jewish. Quite obviously, Nazarenes of The Way who had fled from Jerusalem were the first to identify and worship Yeshua at this site. This mosaic dates the original site to around the second century, nearly contemporaneous with the Tiberias synagogue of *The Way*.

Pictured above are the ruins of the church at Kursi, dated by the IAA as "probably the beginning of the sixth century."[3] The location of Kursi, its architectural features, and the testimony of early travelers identify it as the site where, according to tradition, Jesus healed the demon-possessed man. (See Mark 5:1–20.)

The whole floor of the church was paved with colored mosaics. Preserved mainly in the aisles, square frames are decorated with clearly early-Byzantine floral and faunal motifs, such as grapes, figs, pomegranates, fish, birds, and waterfowl. The faunal representations were almost obliterated, probably by members of the iconoclastic movement, which became active in the early Arab period (seventh century).[4] Also, please notice the presence of *taws* (a clearly Nazarene Jewish symbol) interspersed among the clearly Byzantine figures.

On the south side of the main altar is a room that was, in later Byzantine times, used by clergy. Pictured above is an identical room on the south that was converted to a baptistery room at a later stage (probably the sixth century). It is covered by mosaics on one side, and an oval shaped baptismal (one by one and one-half meters) was inserted on top of the original pre-Byzantine mosaic floor. A nine-line Greek inscription specifically dates the creation of this baptistery to A.D. 582–587.[5]

The surviving mosaics to the left of the later-inserted baptismal basin, while sparse, are nevertheless apparently original. They display a Solomonic knot (distinctly Jewish/Nazarene Jewish), an X version of the *taw*, and smaller "+" versions. These and the entirely geometric designs strongly suggest a pre-Byzantine dating of the site to the early to mid second century.

The entire mosaic floor of the small room to the north of the apse, the twin of the converted baptistery, is entirely comprised of a small and large *taw* design that is nearly identical with that of the "residence" room floor discussed in Chapter 10. Both of these designs that speak to the seven heavens and the temple could not be anything other than Nazarene Jewish. Given their nearly identical rendition, one can only conclude that they are contemporaneous and perhaps were even rendered by the same artisans.

This small panel is placed at the apse end of the southern aisle. It shows a clear, most interesting intermixing of Nazarene Jewish symbology (*taws* and a Solomonic knot), Byzantine crosses, and a pre-Byzantine or Byzantine-Era simple floral design. The *taws* and the Solomonic knot are exclusively Nazarene Jewish, while the floral design and the non-equilateral crosses are clearly pre-Byzantine or Byzantine.

This is one of many such clear and most interesting intermixes of Jewish *taws* with pre-Byzantine and Byzantine symbols throughout both long, colonnaded aisles leading from the entrance to the apse. The *taws* are exclusively Nazarene Jewish, and the bird and partly shown bunch of grapes are exclusively pre-Byzantine and Byzantine. However, these symbols appear together.

The Church at Kursi
Taw Mosaic

Roman Tiberias Residence
Taw Mosaic

Pictured side by side above are the remarkably similar *taw* mosaic designs from the "residence" in the Sanhedrin area of Roman Tiberias and the mosaic floor of the church at Kursi. One can only reasonably conclude that these two sites are contemporaneous (from the first to second centuries) and that they are both of distinctly Nazarene origin.

A *Mikvah* Behind the Church

I have long been a personal friend of a senior Israeli state park manager here in the north who has chosen Kursi as his usual headquarters since the place fascinates him as it does me. I therefore make it a point to stop by and chat with him about our mutual interests in the antiquities.

In early 2002, I stopped by to visit my friend. It had been several months since my last visit, and when we met, he could hardly contain his excitement as he led me to a place immediately behind the existing church ruins that was covered over with a large sheet of corrugated metal. "Wait until you see this!" he exclaimed as he removed the covering and exposed several steps leading down to what he called a small room.

My friend led the way down the several stairs into the open area, where we stood as he explained that this discovery had been unearthed in late 2001 by the Jerusalem Center for Biblical Studies under the direction of Dr. Vassilios Tzaferis of the Israel Antiquities Authority and Dr. Charles Page of the Jerusalem Center for Biblical Studies. He then explained that the team had come to no conclusion about the origin or the purpose of the room, and he suggested that it might be the first revelation of some underground Jewish Christian settlement at the site, which he and I had long speculated about together.

Later, Dr. Page published the "Kursi-Gergesa Excavation 2002 Report," which is posted on the Internet. Dr. Page wrote that the team's original intention was to explore the staircase and where it might lead. However, very early in the exploration, walls began appearing, and the area seemed in danger of collapse. Thus, it was determined any further exploration would likely have to be made from the surface. Even so, as they cautiously continued their exploration, Dr. Page writes:

> Soon we began to discover drain pipes, pools, and water drainage channels. Eventually we found two rooms containing hypocausts (heating systems) and we concluded that we had found a part of a bath complex...
>
> Why a bath complex in a Byzantine monastery? This was a curiosity for me and did not seem consistent with other Byzantine monasteries or churches found in Israel or neighboring countries. In fact, I can think of no other Byzantine monastery in Israel with a bath complex.[6]

A second season of exploration was undertaken in September 2002 by a team under the same authority and direction, the results of which were also reported by Dr. Page, who writes in part, "In 2002 we identified two additional rooms and we removed the fill from all of them. We were disappointed that we could not find doors that might have connected these rooms with other areas. These rooms seemed to have functioned as a one time monumental usage. In the end, we closed the area and refilled the square."[7]

The team went on to open other squares where they found "...walls with a well plastered pipe and, eventually, a small pool which is part of a cold bath (*frigidarium*)." He continued, "In the room we found a beautiful marble floor, a pool with a bench inside for sitting and soaking feet and legs, and a bench around the northern and eastern wall. There was no evidence of a *tepidarium* (warm bath)." Dr. Page concluded the report saying, "...we were surprised to find the bath. Our principal question was why was this here? Finding such a bath in a monastic setting was unheard of. Yet, here it was. Thus far, we have concluded that this bath must somehow be connected to early Christian pilgrimage."[8]

A no doubt brilliant Israeli archaeologist and scholar failed to perceive the *mikvah* at the Tiberias synagogue of The Way when it was right there under her nose. I had initially done the same because of my focus on the mosaics. As earlier conjectured, her mindset, understandably, was apparently that all early Christian places of worship were Byzantine because she had collected little if any data concerning the early Jewish believers experience. Moreover, it is understandable that she was not likely expecting or looking for anything Nazarene Jewish when she encountered what to her seemed to be a Christian church.

In much the same way, I believe that the two eminently well-qualified archaeologists, one Israeli, the other American, who led the Kursi team for two seasons overlooked both the numerous *taws* in the mosaics and what seems to me to be the correct identity of what they found to be a perplexing "bath." To me it seems certain that this "bath" was a first- or second-century *mikvah* that was probably used regularly by a large number of Nazarenes of The Way who most likely lived near or at the site and others who came there to behold the site of the miracle of the swine, which took place in the nearby cave.

In Conclusion

There is a lovely, ecumenical explanation for the unique blending of Nazarene and pre-Byzantine symbols in the mosaics of this greatly important site as well as its *mikvah* located right behind the apse. In my earlier work, *The Door Where It Began*, I suggested, based upon considerable anecdotal evidence that the very first Gentile Christian church was established at nearby Hippos/Sussita, immediately following Yeshua's second feeding of the multitude at nearby Tel Hadar, some fourteen years before Paul took his first missionary journey. Since that writing, further archaeological exploration at Hippos/Sussita would seem to have confirmed my earlier supposition.

After reading *The Door Where It Began*, the chairman of the department of archaeology at a major European university wrote the following to me:

> I should tell you that your novel touched me deeply. I feel that you have been describing your personal experiences... this has been so moving and convicting. I wish I could be in your place (in a position of a person able to prove his/her Jewish roots so as to claim the right to live in the Eretz, yet not abandoning his/her belief in Jesus/Yeshua).
>
> In terms of history/archaeology, your novel opened my eyes to an obvious fact (did anyone discover it before?) that actually, the Gentile Church began at the Decapolis, spreading from the place where the formerly possessed man (your Athanasios) lived (Kursi?) south to Hippos and Gadara, and beyond.

Again, I must confess that while I have visited Kursi almost countless times over the past sixteen years, I was only recently led to actually see this amazing mix of Nazarene and Byzantine symbology in its mosaics and to understand its awesome significance. To me this is just the latest unfolding of the amazing progressive revelation that has continued to bless beyond description my life here in the Holy Land.

I am now certain that there were Nazarenes of The Way living at Kursi who went there, most likely from nearby Bethsaida, Tiberias, and other locations in the Galilee, or perhaps even directly as a part of the dispersion from Jerusalem. It was, I believe, their great calling to disciple these formerly pagan brethren, who brought with them all manner of trappings, which to at least some extent found their way into the symbolism of the first mosaics that were laid at this site.

I can't help but to believe that Kursi was a unique location where Nazarene Jews discipled and worshiped side by side as "one new man" with newly saved Gentile believers in Yeshua. The intensively *taw*-decorated floors, mixed with pre-Byzantine naturalistic symbols, cry out to this understanding. So does what I most certainly believe is the elaborate *mikvah* located right behind the apse.

Let me conclude this chapter rhetorically. Is it reasonable to assume that there was an immediate transition from what began as an entirely Jewish body of Yeshua to what became an almost entirely Gentile body of Christ during some miraculous "overnight" metamorphosis?

I believe there was a gradual transition from what was an originally entirely Nazarene Jewish congregation on Mount Zion to the church that was first called Christian some thirty years later at Antioch. Beyond that, I believe it was much later that the mosaics of the newly established church floors were to be decorated entirely with Byzantine biblical and humanistic scenes in place of entirely Nazarene geometric patterns interlaced generously with *taws*. I can find no other way to explain the amazing, even prophetic, mixture of the symbology at Kursi, which speaks so clearly concerning the Master's divine design of His "one new man" body, wherein one day we all will joyfully dwell with Him.

Finally, I believe that there most certainly must be a great number of other Nazarene of The Way synagogues and other lesser Nazarene sites scattered along the several pathways of their multi-wave dispersion from Jerusalem that cry out for proper identification or reidentification. The several such sites I have pointed to in this current writing only underscore the strong need for an intensive nationwide investigation to uncover and identify what must certainly be literally hundreds of such early Nazarene sites that remain hidden in the rich soil of Israel. Such a massive unveiling, I believe, would finally and unequivocally demonstrate the error of the detractors of modern day Jewish believers, who would deny them both the reality of their legitimate historical Nazarene Jewish roots as well as their God-given right to take up their inheritance and dwell freely here in the Land as fully recognized Jewish citizens.

Part III

The Theology and Doctrine of The Way

THE FOLLOWING DEFINITIONS OF principal terms are provided, as they apply to the forthcoming discussion.

- **Theology**: The study of the nature of God and religious truth; rational inquiry into religious questions
- **Systematic Theology**: Systematic theology answers the question, What does the whole Bible teach us about any given topic? This definition indicates that systematic theology involves collecting and understanding all the relevant passages in the Bible on various topics and then summarizing their teachings clearly.
- **Doctrine**: A code of beliefs or "a body of teachings" or "instructions," taught principles or positions, as the body of teachings in a branch of knowledge or belief system
- **Orthodox**: *Orthodox* is broadly defined in several different ways, including: 1) pertaining to, or conforming to the approved form of any doctrine, philosophy, ideology, etc.; 2) pertaining to, or conforming to beliefs, attitudes, or modes of conduct that are generally approved; [and] 3) sound or correct in opinion or doctrine, especially theological or religious doctrine.

  For the purposes of the following discussion, *orthodox* is defined as the assessment made by the emerging Gentile Christian Church assigned to and regarding any theological understanding, doctrine, or worship practice that was not in heretical or apostate opposition to their own body of theological and doctrinal understandings.
- **Heterodox**: For the purposes of the following discussion, *heterodox* is defined as any theological understanding, doctrine, or worship practice that is in heretical or apostate opposition to the theological and doctrinal understandings of the emerging Gentile Christian Church.

In keeping with the above definitions, it can be said with well-documented assurance that the theological and doctrinal understandings of the Nazarenes of The Way as they were developed, understood, taught, and promulgated in their congregation on Mount Zion were entirely orthodox. It may also be said that they remained so for those of them who continued to be called Nazarenes after they dispersed from Jerusalem in three waves in A.D. 35, 62, and 135, until they vanished from existence in the mountains of Syria early in the fifth century.

Irenaeus, an early church father whose writings strongly influenced the development of Christian theology, wrote:

> The Nazarenes were catholic [orthodox] in every way, believing in the Divinity and the Messiahship of the Lord and strenuously defending the incarnation and virginity of Mary. However, they were attached to Jewish customs, the Davidic family, and the throne of David which they kept on Holy Zion, to the priestly rights of James, who was associated with the Levites, and to several archaic theological schemas.[1]

It also can be said with equal assurance that the first heterodox theological and doctrinal understandings of those Jewish believers who dispersed from Jerusalem did not appear until after A.D. 62, when the great majority of The Way was said to have been divinely forewarned of impending disaster and thus fled as a group to Pella in the Decapolis.[2]

Irenaeus speaks further to this first heterodox schism of the Ebionites[3] when they separated from The Way, most likely during their sojourn in Pella.

> The only true heretics were the [heterodox] Ebionites. In regard to the Trinity, they were rather adoptionist, convinced that there was only one God with his Word, who was not the Son of God but a created being superior to the angels, masculine in gender, and with the Spirit who was an angelic being, feminine in gender. Both descended on the man Jesus on the day of his baptism, divinizing and adopting him while in fact he was the natural child of Mary and Joseph, the Prophet promised by Moses, to whom God will give the power over the "world to come."[4]

Several important observations can be made regarding The Way's truly remarkable theology and doctrine. First, this God-appointed group of the body's first theologians, beginning with the original twelve apostles, led by James, meticulously shared, discussed, wrote down, and organized what they had heard and observed in an enormous body of writings. Those documents eventually became the church's great treasure of canonized and apocryphal gospels, epistles, apocalypses, and other works. It was these writings, in turn, that provided the bedrock foundation upon which the Nazarenes of The Way, in short order, would formulate a remarkably detailed, complete, and anointed orthodox systematic theology.

Moreover, this orthodox Nazarene systematic theology was not created in a vacuum on Mount Zion as a compendium of the mother congregation's self-generated, independent thought. Quite to the contrary, Nazarene theological understandings and the doctrine to which these understandings gave rise were often influenced by the depth and richness of the earlier understandings they had inherited from traditional Jewish sources.

Certainly, some Nazarene theological and doctrinal understandings were situationally dictated and thus entirely original. Even so, I suggest that the resulting highly distinctive Nazarene faith and belief systems, those that were the very underpinnings of later Christian thought, were perhaps most influenced by the very elaborate seminal writings and understandings of the highly prolific Essenes, who were their progenitors at Qumran. These frequent theological and doctrinal points of contact between The Way and the Essenes are well evident in the Dead Sea Scrolls, where they were memorialized by the Essenes, in some cases even multiple centuries before the advent of Yeshua.

In any event, it is reasonable if not compelling to conclude that the very foundation of subsequent Christian theology and doctrine arose from a divinely orchestrated blending of these multiple, entirely Jewish sources. There is, in fact, a growing body of scholarship suggesting that the very basis and even substance of Christianity existed within traditional Judaism long before the Essenes inhabited Qumran. James H. Charlesworth, a highly respected contemporary biblical scholar and historian, points out that eminent Jewish, Roman Catholic, and Protestant scholars who teach in many of the elite universities of the world have become convinced that the Dead Sea Scrolls are essential for understanding the emergence of a sect of Jews who later would be labeled Christians.[5]

Chapter 16
Christology: The Way's Understanding of the Nature of Yeshua

While the Dead Sea Scrolls do not mention Yeshua by name, the Holy One they meticulously describe as their soon-anticipated Messiah is heralded as the divine Son of God, verily God Himself. The following ancient scroll fragment from Cave Four[1] is a clear and succinct statement of the Essenes' Christology:

> ...he shall be great on earth...[all] will worship and will serve [Him]...great he shall be called and by his name he shall be designated. *He shall be named Son of God and they shall call him Son of the Most High.* Like a shooting star of a vision, so shall be their kingdom. They shall reign for some years on the earth and trample everything. One nation shall trample on another nation and one province on another province...until the people of God shall arise and all will desist from the sword. The reign of the people of God will be everlasting; its paths will be in truth and all will have peace; there will be no more wars and all the cities will submit to the people of God. *For the Great God is with them* and He will now subject all enemies to the people of God.[2]

Moreover, there are multiple other scroll references that speak to the nature of the soon-expected Messiah, the sum of which would seem to be a prophetic portrait of Yeshua, who would soon be walking among them. Consider these two striking examples from Cave Four:

> And he will atone for all the children of his generation, and he will be sent to all the children of his people. His word is like the word of the heavens, and his teaching according to the will of God. His eternal sun will shine and his fire will burn in all the ends of the earth; above the darkness his sun will shine. Then, darkness will vanish from the earth,

> and gloom from the globe. They will utter many words against him, and utter every kind of disparagement against him.[3]

> ...for the heavens and the earth will listen to his Messiah, and all that is in them will not turn away from the holy precepts. Be encouraged, you who are seeking the Lord in his service! Will you not, perhaps, encounter the Lord in it, all those who hope in their heart? For the Lord will observe the devout. And call the just by name, and upon the poor he will place his spirit, and the faithful he will renew with his strength. For he will honor the devout upon the throne of eternal royalty, freeing prisoners, giving sight to the blind, straightening out the twisted. Ever shall I cling to those who hope. In his mercy he will judge, and from no-one shall the fruit of good deeds be delayed, and the Lord will perform many marvelous acts such as have not existed, just as he said, for he will heal the badly wounded and will make the dead live, he will proclaim the good news to the meek, give lavishly to the needy, lead the exiled and enrich the hungry.[4]

Please also consider Isaiah 53, as it appears in the great Isaiah scroll.

> Who has believed our report and the arm of YHWH to whom has it been revealed. And he shall come up like a suckling before him and as a root from dry ground there is no form to him and no beauty to him and in his being seen and there is no appearance that we should desire him. He is despised and rejected of men, a man of sorrows and knowing grief and as though hiding faces from him he was despised and we did not esteem him. Surely our griefs he is bearing and our sorrows he carried them and we esteemed him beaten and struck by God and afflicted. And he is wounded for our transgressions, and crushed for our iniquities, the correction of our peace was upon him and by his wounds he has healed us. All of us like sheep have wandered each man to his own way we have turned and YHWH has caused to light on him the iniquity of all of us. He was oppressed and he was afflicted and he did not open his mouth, as a lamb to the slaughter he is brought and as a ewe before her shearers is made dumb he did not open his mouth. From prison and from judgment he was taken and his generation who shall discuss it because he was cut off from the land of the living. Because from the transgressions of his people a wound was to him, and they gave wicked ones to be his grave and rich ones in his death although he worked no violence neither deceit in his mouth. And YHWH was pleased to crush him and He has caused him grief. If you will appoint his soul a sin offering he will see his seed and he will lengthen his days and the pleasure of YHWH in

> his hand will advance. Of the toil of his soul he shall see light and he shall be satisfied and by his knowledge shall he make righteous even my righteous servant for many and their iniquities he will bear. Therefore I will apportion to him among the great ones and with the mighty ones he shall divide the spoil because he laid bare to death his soul and with the transgressors he was numbered, and he, the sins of many, he bore, and for their transgressions he entreated.[5]

Gabriel's Vision: "A Dead Sea Scroll on Stone"

Very recently, during the course of this writing, yet another compelling example of the Jewish foreknowledge of fundamental Christian theological understanding has risen to center stage among biblical scholars.

Yeshua's resurrection three days after His burial is a foundational understanding of Christianity, one that has historically separated it from Judaism and that has long been a great stumbling block in the path of Jewish acceptance of Yeshua as the Messiah. Now it would seem this stumbling block may well be broken down with the surfacing of a mysterious, three-foot grey stone tablet dubbed "Gabriel's Vision," dated to the first century B.C., during the very time when the Dead Sea Scrolls were being written.[6]

The startling central message of the severely worn eighty-seven lines written in black ink on the surface of "Gabriel's Vision" is the prophetic understanding that a messiah will rise from the dead after three days.

Dr. Israel Knohl, professor of Bible Studies at Hebrew University in Jerusalem, focuses on line eighty of the tablet, which he translates, "In three days you shall live. I, Gabriel, command you."[7] To whom is Gabriel speaking? Professor Knohl points out that the next line of the tablet says, "Sar hasarin," meaning "prince of princes." Thus, he contends that the writings are about the death of a leader of the Jews who will be resurrected in three days. Professor Knohl explains:

> I [have] identified a previously unrecognized Jewish notion that the blood of the messiah is necessary in order to bring about national redemption. The idea of a tortured messiah who was resurrected three days after his death was adopted by Judaism before the birth of Jesus.[8]
>
> His mission is that he has to be put to death by the Romans to suffer so his blood will be the sign of the resurrection to come.... This is a conscious view of Jesus himself.[9]

Even so, Professor Knohl would likely not agree that "Gabriel's Vision" offers any proof of the Christian understanding regarding the divinity or the atoning and salvational purpose of the messiah. To the contrary, while referring to Jesus as "the son of Joseph," he states:

> This should shake our basic view of Christianity. Resurrection after three days becomes a motif developed before Jesus, which runs contrary to nearly all scholarship. What happened in the New Testament was adopted by Jesus and his followers based upon an earlier messiah story.[10]

I believe that the "Gabriel Vision" is just what its title implies, biblical prophecy miraculously brought forth into the light.

In any event, the ultimate resolution of what promises to be a long debate on this crucial matter of theology will ultimately be settled by what is already written in the Word of God.

> But although He had done so many signs before them, they did not believe in Him, that the word of Isaiah the prophet might be fulfilled, which he spoke: "Lord, who has believed our report? And to whom has the arm of the Lord been revealed?" Therefore they could not believe, because Isaiah said again: "He has blinded their eyes and hardened their hearts, Lest they should see with their eyes, Lest they should understand with their hearts and turn, So that I should heal them." These things Isaiah said when he saw His glory and spoke of Him.
>
> —John 12:37–41

"Gabriel's Vision" was purchased from a Jordanian antiquities dealer eight years ago by David Jeselsohn, an Israeli-Swiss collector who kept it in his Zurich home. When he recently showed the tablet to Ada Yardeni, who specializes in ancient Hebrew writing, she was overwhelmed. "You have a Dead Sea Scroll on stone," she told him. After performing a chemical analysis of "Gabriel's Vision," Professor Yuval Goren, professor of archaeology at Tel Aviv University, who specializes in the verification of ancient artifacts, said that he knew of no reason to doubt the stone's authenticity.[11]

The Ancient Jewish Understanding of the Triune Godhead

The traditional Judaism of the first temple period also provided some genuinely amazing input to The Way's theologians regarding the nature of the Godhead and the person of Yeshua.

There is, I believe, an almost universal understanding throughout the church regarding the origin of the centrally important and foundational doctrine of the Trinity. It is preached from most pulpits and taught in most seminaries that the understanding of the Tri-unity of God more or less evolved over time, beginning with the progressively more compelling insights of the early church fathers.

The historical fact is, however, that ancient Jewish tradition embraced the remarkable Essene understanding—handed down by YHWH to Abraham—that the nature of the Godhead is distinctly and clearly triune. It will thus certainly come as a shock to many Christians to learn that the doctrine of the Trinity was a Jewish concept that was being widely taught by the Jewish sages as early as 515 B.C., rather than a deduced understanding of the church fathers that was eventually codified by the Council of Nicea in A.D. 325.[12]

The Hebrew word *Kabbalah* translates in English as "received." The Talmud, the central document of Pharisaic-*cum*-modern-day Rabbinical Judaism, uses *Kabbalah* to describe the thirty-four books of the Hebrew Bible that follow the Torah. In post-Talmudic literature, *Kabbalah* was used to describe the Oral Law. (It is of great importance to note, however, that in modern day Rabbinical Jewish usage the word *Kabbalah* has come to describe only Jewish mysticism, a branch of modern day Judaism that is completely separate from Orthodox and other Jewish expression. This is different from the Kabbalah to which I will refer in this chapter.) Ancient Kabbalah was founded in three important ancient books: the Sefer Yetzirah, the Bahir, and the Zohar. However, Jewish mysticism existed long before these books, a fact that is historically well documented in the Dead Sea Scrolls as well as in the writings of the first century Jewish historian, Philo.[13]

The earliest source to which these three ancient books are attributed is the Patriarch Abraham, circa 2000 B.C. As early as the tenth century A.D., commentators of that time widely agreed to Abraham's authorship. A number of very old manuscripts of the Sefer Yetzirah, for example, begin with the subtitle "The Letters of Abraham Our Father." The attribution of this work to Abraham is further supported by the final stanza of the Sefer Yetzirah, which mentions him by name as having "looked and probed" into the words and meaning of the text.[14]

According to Aryeh Kaplan, the noted modern day Jewish historian and scholar, the mystical tradition was more advanced in ancient Israel than in India. Therefore, Kaplan reasons, since Abraham was the greatest mystic and astrologer of his age, it is highly probable that he was conversant with all of the ancient mysteries of Egypt and Mesopotamia; after all, he was born in Mesopotamia, and he also lived in Egypt.[15]

The Targums, ancient Aramaic translations and interpretations of the Hebrew Bible, were read every day in the synagogues during the second temple period and well into the early Middle Ages. According to Christian leader and teacher Grant Jeffrey, these sacred writings taught that there was a profound mystery regarding the triune nature of God, one which was further revealed both in the Targums themselves and in the Zohar.[16]

Following are several examples of these teachings showing how clearly the understanding of the triune nature of the Godhead was being taught by the traditional Jewish sages as early as 515 B.C.

> How can they [the three] be One? Are they verily One, because we call them One? How Three can be One, can only be known through the revelation of the Holy Spirit.[17]

> Come and see the mystery of the word, *Jehova*: there are three steps, each existing by itself; nevertheless they are One, and so united that one cannot be separated from the other.[18]

> The Ancient Holy One is revealed with three Heads, which are united in One, and that Head is thrice exalted. The Ancient Holy One is described as being Three; it is because the other Lights emanating from Him are included in the Three.[19]

Summary

The great significance of all of this to the formulation of The Way's first-century systematic theology, a central message of the Dead Sea Scrolls and Kabbalah, is that there was an ancient Jewish understanding of the divine nature and substance of the triune Godhead.

Hence, the seed that ultimately evolved into the Christian doctrine of the Trinity was, by tradition, first handed down to Abraham by God, then passed along through successive generations of traditional Jewish sages until it ultimately was handed over to the Essenes. It was presumably through this input that the Essenes came to understand the triune nature of the Godhead and the person of each of its three members, all of which they recorded in their Dead Sea Scrolls.[20]

Chapter 17
THE WAY'S UNDERSTANDING OF THE NAME

You shall not take the name of the LORD *your God in vain, for the* LORD *will not hold him guiltless who takes His name in vain.*

—EXODUS 20:7

FOLLOWING THE DESTRUCTION OF the temple in A.D. 70, the Pharisees relocated first to Yavne. It was there that they began the arduous task of redacting the Oral Torah into what was, in written form, called the Mishna. It was completed in Tiberias circa 220, and after being combined with the Gemara commentaries, it finally emerged as the first written version of the Talmud, circa 500.

It was during this time that the Pharisees were giving birth to what has evolved into modern day Rabbinical Judaism. Early on, they began exercising extreme caution so as to avoid violating the third great commandment of God by inadvertently taking the name of God in vain. (See Exodus 20:7.)

In this same Torah context, God quite explicitly told His people His name and how it was to be used.

> And God said to Moses, "I AM WHO I AM." And He said, "Thus you shall say to the children of Israel, 'I AM has sent me to you.'" Moreover God said to Moses, "Thus you shall say to the children of Israel: 'The LORD God of your fathers, the God of Abraham, the God of Isaac, and the God of Jacob, has sent me to you. This is My name forever, and this is My memorial to all generations.'"
>
> —EXODUS 3:14–15

There are more than one hundred other references in the Tenach and New Testament scriptures that speak of God's name and how His people are commanded to actively make it a part of their every day walk with Him. For example:

> I will praise the Lord according to His righteousness, And will sing praise to the name of the Lord Most High.
>
> —Psalm 7:17

> I will declare Your name to My brethren; In the midst of the assembly I will praise You.
>
> —Psalm 22:22

> Blessed be Your glorious name, Which is exalted above all blessing and praise!
>
> —Nehemiah 9:5

> Whoever receives one little child like this in My name receives Me.
>
> —Matthew 18:5

> And in that day you will ask Me nothing. Most assuredly, I say to you, whatever you ask the Father in My name He will give you. Until now you have asked nothing in My name. Ask, and you will receive, that your joy may be full.
>
> —John 16:23–24

The Talmud departs greatly from these biblical imperatives as it teaches, regarding the Tetragrammaton (YHWH, the name of God): "Not the way I am written am I pronounced. I am written with yod heh, and I am uttered with alef dalet."[1] Thus, according to the Talmud, God's name, expressed with the Tetragrammaton, is not to be pronounced phonetically but rather to be read as if it were written *Adonai*, which means "the Lord." This is the word that, in fact, actually appears in all major English versions of the Bible and in the Siddur, the Hebrew Jewish prayer book. Moreover, the Talmud places a time limit on this restriction, teaching that the name of God must be disguised in this world.[2]

In an earnest effort to implement this restriction, the most often used expression of the sacred name—YHWH—within modern day Rabbinical Judaism, as it evolved from the religion of the Pharisees, is written "G-d" and "L-rd," with a dash taking the place of *o*, the appropriate vowel. Another universally practiced rabbinical tradition, rooted in these same Talmudic teachings, is the substitution of the Hebrew word *haShem,* meaning "the Name" in English, for the word *God*, even though *God* is a generalized designation pointing to YHWH and cannot be reasonably construed to be His actual, personal name. Thus, for example, the commonly used English expressions to render thanks unto God, "Praise God!" and "Thank God!" are, by tradition, most often rendered within all forms of Judaism as *Baruch haShem*, or "Blessed be the Name."

The Name in the various expressions of traditional Judaism refers to YHWH. For The Way, however, *the Name* referred to Yeshua. In both cases the theology of the Name becomes a person distinct from the Father.[3] There are many such usages of *the Name* in the Old Testament that are quoted in the New Testament.

> "That they may possess the remnant of Edom, and all the Gentiles who are called by My name," Says the LORD who does this thing.
>
> —AMOS 9:12 (QUOTED IN ACTS 15:17)

> "Now therefore, what have I here," says the LORD, "That My people are taken away for nothing? Those who rule over them Make them wail," says the LORD, "And My name is blasphemed continually every day."
>
> —ISAIAH 52:5 (QUOTED IN ROMANS 2:24)

The Way often quotes Old Testament verses where *the Name* in their original context could only mean YHWH but when quoted take on their understanding that the Godhead is triune in nature and that YHWH expressed as the Father has the same meaning and essence as Yeshua, His Son, the difference being a matter of functionality. For example in Joel 2:32, the reference is clearly made to the Father but also refers prophetically to Yeshua: "Whosoever shall call upon the name of the LORD shall be delivered" (KJV). When this verse is quoted in Acts 2:21 and Romans 10:13, the term specifically refers to Yeshua. Moreover, this functional shifting from Father to Son is explained in Acts 4:12: "Nor is there salvation in any other, for there is no other name [than Yeshua] under heaven given among men by which we must be saved."

Another example of this functional shifting within the same essence of the three members of the triune Godhead is found in the Gospel of John. John 17:11 says, "Holy Father, protect them by the power of your name—the name you gave me—so that they may be one as we are one" (NIV).

The apocryphal writings of The Way also speak to the Name, as it is understood to mean Yeshua. *The Name* as a specific reference to Yeshua appears in 1 Clement, the Shepherd of Hermas, the Epistle of James, and the Gospel of Truth.[4] For example, Hermas writes:

> The Name of the Son of God is great and infinite, and sustaineth the whole world. If then all creation is sustained by the Son of God, what thinkest thou of those who bear the Name of the Son of God?...Sees thou what manner of men He sustaineth? Even those who bear His Name with their whole heart. He Himself then has become their foundation and He sustaineth them gladly, because they are not ashamed to bear His Name.[5]

As previously discussed, traditional Jews were making the sign of the *taw* on their foreheads to denote the Name, a symbol of salvation,[6] as early as 590 B.C. This practice is recorded in Ezekiel 9:4[7] and further developed in Revelation 7:2, 14:1, and 22:4. This understanding, quite unsurprisingly, became central to The Way's systematic theology. According to Danielou, The Way understood the sign of the cross to be a symbol of Yeshua physically standing with outstretched arms as He did during His passion. Therefore, they regarded the Name and the *taw* to be synonymous expressions since they both signified Yeshua.[8]

The Way's understanding that *the Name* was synonymous with Yeshua is well illustrated in their liturgy of the Lord's Supper as it is recorded in the Didache: "We give Thee thanks O Holy Father, for thy Holy Name which thou hast made to tabernacle in our hearts."[9] Here we have a clear suggestion of The Way's understanding that it is the name of God in a *homoousios* ("of the same essence") expression of the entire Godhead, which comes to dwell within us at the time of our salvation.

Chapter 18
The Way's Understanding of Redemption

A key understanding of The Way's theology is that Yeshua descended through the seven heavens, hiding Himself from the angels who watched over the transit between these levels. Several writings of The Way agree that Yeshua descended through the heavens, and as He was about to pass through each, He changed His appearance in such a way that He could pass through unrecognized. The Father ordered Him to do this so that He "mayest judge and destroy the princes and angels and gods of that world."[1] Obviously, if He had not disguised His identity in this manner, the angels who looked over these places would have intervened and protected Him from going to the cross and thus disrupted the plan of the Redemption.[2] This understanding carried over into the New Testament. (See 1 Corinthians 2:8 and Ephesians 3:10–12.)

We read in the Ascension of Isaiah (circa A.D. 150–200), "This hath been hidden from all the heavens and all the princes...And, I saw: In Nazareth he sucked the breast as a babe and kept in all things the common law of life in order that He might not be recognized."[3]

In the *Epistle of the Apostles* (circa A.D. 140–150) the Word is said to descend clothed in the wisdom of the Father. This wisdom, as in the writings of Theophilus of Antioch (circa 170–180), is understood to be the Holy Spirit, the third person of the Trinity.[4]

Yeshua's Descent into Hell

Yeshua's post-Resurrection descent into hell is a part of The Way's theology. The purpose of this descent, they held, was to enable Yeshua, after His death, to preach salvation through Him to the righteous who were there imprisoned. This doctrine appears to be unknown in canonized New Testament scriptures, where His descent is understood to be His passing from heaven to Earth, in which He entered into the womb of Mary in order to make Himself "in the likeness of men" (Phil. 2:7).

The doctrine of the descent into hell was also excluded from the Nicene Creed, formulated at the Council of Nicea in A.D. 325, where the Nazarenes' participation was purposefully excluded. This doctrine was also excluded from the Apostles' Creed, first written in the early 1500s. However, because of a strong carryover of Jewish originated tradition, it was included in later versions of this creed and remains in the current version. Even so, while it was finally included in the creed, the church did not consider the doctrine of Yeshua's descent into hell to be salvational. (This doctrine was, however, considered to be salvational by the Nazarenes of The Way.)

Rather, the common understanding among Christian denominations is that Yeshua, on this occasion, took the souls of those who had died trusting in the promises made under the old covenant—Abraham, Moses, David, Elijah, Isaiah, and many others—and brought them out of the realm of the dead directly into heavenly glory. But the creed is not concerned with this point. The reference to the descent into hell is included in this context to make it clear that the death of Yeshua was not just a swoon or a coma but death in every sense of the word.[5]

Several writings of The Way speak to their salvational understanding of Yeshua's descent into hell. For example, Irenaeus, quoting the "Elder," affirms The Way's view: "...His advent there also and the remission of sins received by those who believe in Him." Also, from the Gospel of Peter (circa A.D. 70) we read, "...hast thou preached to them that sleep?"[6]

The Odes of Solomon, Ode 42, which they most likely sung to a now long-lost melody, provides a lovely summary of this doctrine.

> Sheol saw me and was overcome; Death suffered me to return and many with me. I was gall and bitterness to him, and I went down with him to the utmost of his depths. I held an assembly of living men among the dead, and I spake to them with holy lips; and those who had died ran towards me, they cried and said: Son of God, have pity on us and deal with us according to thy loving kindness; bring us out from the bonds of darkness, and open to us the door, that we may come forth to thee. For we see that our death has not come nigh thee. As for me, I heard their voice, and I traced my name upon their heads; therefore they are free men and they are mine.

The Way's Understanding of the Cross

The centrality of the cross in my own personal understanding took on its very deep meaning on the first evening I attended graduate study classes at Faith Seminary in Tacoma, Washington. It was pouring down rain when I arrived and parked my car. I was wracked with uncertainty about my ability to undertake this new calling at the age of fifty-seven. After I prayed, I exited the car and began to run toward the nearby door of the seminary. Suddenly, I stopped short. I am certain I was divinely directed to look toward the huge wooden cross planted in the front lawn, some distance away from where I was standing in the downpour in my three-piece tailor-made suit getting soaked to the skin. Even so, mesmerized, I made my way to the cross and embraced it, my own tears of joy and renewed confidence blending with the rain pouring down my cheeks.

In my uncountable succeeding visits to this institution both as a student and a teacher, I have never failed to stop for a moment to once again be renewed in this lovely, intimate way with my wonderful Yeshua, who gave Himself to me and to the world on a tree such as this.

The Way surely must have understood that the cross, in both its shape and substance, was a sign of the risen Yeshua working in the body with the Spirit to achieve the divine purposes. There is a deep irony in this understanding, in that many if not most modern day Jews have a negative view of the cross as a Christian symbol with little or no positive meaning for any Jew. To my knowledge, some of my Jewish brothers and sisters who claim to be born-again in the very blood that was shed on such a cross share these seemingly inbred negative feelings.

To many Jews, unsaved and saved alike, the cross of Yeshua represents the horrendous things done against our people almost from the very beginning of the church. For example, there were the infamous Crusades, which began in 1095. On the road to Jerusalem, the crusaders encountered the Jewish communities of the Rhineland. They called out, "Why rush to Jerusalem to conquer the infidel when here he lives among us?" With the same fury and passion with which they left their homes, they massacred the entire large Jewish communities of Mainz and Speyer. The violent affirmation of Christian truth that they had set out to achieve at the expense of the Muslims in Jerusalem was first directed at the Jews. The symbol of the destroyed temple was recreated as the synagogues of western Europe were burned down with countless hundreds of Jewish men, women, and children locked inside them by men carrying shields decorated with crosses who all the while loudly sang out Christian hymns in order to drown out the agonized screams of those entire congregations of Jews they were burning alive.[7]

Then there were the pogroms, which began in Russia in 1881, when Jews were forbidden by law from living in or acquiring property except in predetermined locales. Once again in a so-called Christian country, more than two million Jews were forced to leave everything they owned behind while they fled for their lives from the land of their birth under the banner of the cross and in the name of Jesus.[8]

Then of course, there was the Holocaust of annihilation perpetrated by the Nazis, who were cheered on by the Arab fathers of those who to this day are denying that over six million Jews were slaughtered by men wearing belts with the logo "God Is With Us," serving a frenzied madman who was inspired by a supposedly Christian theology gone wild. The following excerpt may seem like a piece of Nazi paraphanalia, but it was written by Martin Luther, considered the father of Protestantism.

> They [rulers] must act like a good physician who, when gangrene has set in proceeds without mercy to cut, saw, and burn flesh, veins, bone, and marrow. Such a procedure must also be followed in this instance. Burn down their synagogues, forbid all that I enumerated earlier, force them to work, and deal harshly with them, as Moses did...If this does not help we must drive them out like mad dogs.[9]

But in the beginning, before any of these horrendous things had occurred, many writings of these first Jewish believers attested to their great love and deep theological understanding of the cross of Yeshua:

Irenaeus, a second-century church father, writes in a moving ecumenical call:

> For we lost Him by means of a tree, by means of a tree again He has been manifest to all, showing the height, the length, the breadth, the depth of Himself; and, as one of predecessors has said reuniting the two peoples in one only God by the stretching forth of his hands. For there were two hands because there were two peoples scattered to the ends of the earth; and there was but one head as there was but one God.[10]

This writing well illustrates The Way's insight that the cross was a sign of the life-giving power of Yeshua. There are two allusions here. First, the cross speaks of "the breadth and length and height and depth of the love of Jesus" (Eph. 3:18). Second, it demonstrates that Yeshua "has broken down the middle wall of partition having abolished in His flesh the enmity...that in Himself He might make of the two one new man, so making peace; and that He might reconcile both unto God in one body through the cross, having slain the enmity thereby" (Eph. 2:14–16).

It may well be that Irenaeus was crying out in despair over what he already had seen as the beginnings of a second wall of separation between Jews and Gentiles, which was well in progress at the time of this writing and continued later in full force during and following the Council of Nicea in 325.

The Way understood that Yeshua restores unity in a twofold sense: He destroys both the vertical wall which separates the two people and the horizontal one which separates man from God; and He does this by the cross, which now seems to represent the double operation of Yeshua extending both vertically and horizontally to form a cross.[11]

Irenaeus speaks of receiving this theology from a predecessor who very likely was a first-generation member of The Way. He develops this understanding further in his writing *Demonstratio*, written just before the second century:

> By the obedience which He practiced unto death hanging on the tree, He undid the old disobedience occasioned by the tree. And because He Himself the Word of God Almighty, whose invisible presence is spread abroad in us and fills the whole world, He extends His influence in the world through its whole length, breadth, height and depth. For by the Word of God all things are subject to the influence of the economy of redemption, and the Son of God has been crucified for all having traced the sign of the Cross on all things. For it was right and necessary that He made Himself visible, should lead all visible things to participate in His Cross; and it is in this way that, in a form that can be perceived, His own special influence has had its own special effect on visible things: for it is He that illuminates the heights, that is the heavens; it is He that penetrates that which is beneath; He that traverses the whole vast extent from East to West, and He that covers the immense distance from North to South,[12] summoning to the knowledge of His Father those scattered in everyplace.[13]

The Way understood the cross of Yeshua as something far more than just the tree He was hung on. They saw it in a much more elaborate way, as something that went down into hell with Yeshua, as a living entity unto itself that speaks and was intimately involved in Yeshua's glorification.

The apocryphal Gospel of Peter (circa A.D. 70–100) offers the following account:

> Early in the morning, as the Sabbath dawned, there came a large crowd from Jerusalem and the surrounding areas to see the sealed tomb. But during the night before the Lord's day dawned, as the soldiers were keeping guard two by two in every watch, there came a great sound in the sky, and they saw the heavens opened and two men descend shining with a great light, and they drew near to the tomb. The stone which had been set on the door rolled away by itself and moved to one side, and the tomb was opened and both of the young men went in.
>
> Now when these soldiers saw that, they woke up the centurion and the elders (for they also were there keeping watch). While they were yet telling them the things which they had seen, they saw three men come out of the tomb, two of them sustaining the other one, and a cross following after them. The heads of the two they saw had heads that reached up to heaven, but the head of him that was led by them went beyond heaven. And they heard a voice out of the heavens saying, "Have you preached unto them that sleep?" The answer that was heard from the cross was, "Yes!"[14]

Moreover, The Way held that the cross will precede Yeshua at His second coming. The apostle Matthew recorded this understanding in his Gospel, which was, according to Woodard, completed circa A.D. 37, just seven years after Yeshua's ascension.

> Then the sign of the Son of Man [the cross] will appear in heaven, and then all the tribes of the earth will mourn, and they will see the Son of Man coming on the clouds of heaven with power and great glory.
>
> —Matthew 24:30

The Apocalypse of Peter (circa A.D. 100–150) makes it clear that the sign spoken of in the canonized gospel is indeed the cross of Yeshua.

> For the coming of the Son of God shall not be plain (i.e. foreseen); but as the lightning that shineth from the east unto the west, so will I come upon the clouds of heaven with a great host in my majesty; with my cross going before my face will I come in my majesty, shining sevenfold more than the sun will I come in my majesty with all my saints, mine angels (mine holy angels). And my Father shall set a crown upon mine head, that I may judge the quick and the dead and recompense every man according to his works.[15]

Another confirmation of this understanding is found in the Epistle of the Apostles (circa 140–150):

> Then said we to him: Lord, that which thou hast revealed unto us is great. Wilt thou come in the power of any creature or in an appearance of any kind? He answered and said unto us: Verily I say unto you, I shall come like the sun when it is risen, and my brightness will be seven times the brightness thereof! The wings of the clouds shall bear me in brightness, and the sign of the cross shall go before me, and I shall come upon earth to judge the quick and the dead.[16]

There is a fascinating historical account regarding early visions of the cross as they were seen in the sky. In the first instance, as you will remember, the Roman Emperor Constantine declared Christianity to be the state religion in A.D. 313 purportedly on the basis of a vision he had seen of the cross in the sky over Rome. According to tradition, what he saw was actually the cross of the sun god Mithra, whom he worshiped. The presence of a figure of Satan in a fresco on display in the Vatican speaks to the unholy nature of this vision.[17]

In the next instance, Cyril, who became bishop of Jerusalem in 349, wrote a letter to this self-same Constantine reporting a much more credible counter-vision of the cross of Yeshua that appeared in the sky over Jerusalem.

> . . . a gigantic cross formed of light appeared in the sky above holy Golgotha stretching out as far as the holy Mt. of Olives. It was not seen by just one or two but was most clearly displayed before the whole population of the city. Nor did it as one might have supposed pass away quickly like something imagined. But was visible to sight above the earth for some hours, while it sparkled with a light brighter than the sun's rays.[18]

It also seems quite remarkable that there are a number of types of Yeshua's cross within the pages of the Old Testament that are confirmed in the writings of The Way. For example, consider the account of Moses's seesawing battle with Amalek, where he literally wins favor by making himself into the sign of the cross.

> And Moses said to Joshua, "Choose us some men and go out, fight with Amalek. Tomorrow I will stand on the top of the hill with the rod of God in my hand." So Joshua did as Moses said to him, and fought with Amalek. And Moses, Aaron, and Hur went up to the top of the hill. And so it was, when Moses held up his hand, that Israel prevailed; and when he let down his hand, Amalek prevailed. But Moses' hands became heavy; so they took a stone and put it under him, and he sat on it. And Aaron and Hur supported his hands, one on one side, and the other on the other side; and his hands were steady until the going down of the sun.
>
> —Exodus 17:9–12

In summary, The Way's understanding of the cross has a rich diversity. It is a sign of Yeshua's victory; and thus it represents the very essence of glory. It is Yeshua's companion in His works of power, in hell, and at His second coming. It is the instrument by which the incarnate Word accomplishes His work of salvation. Its shape symbolizes the universality of redemptive action, unifying all things and consolidating the new creation. Finally, the cross represents the whole plan of redemption as this action is spread over the breadth of space and the length of time.[19]

Yeshua's Ascension into Heaven

The Way's theology of Yeshua's ascension can most simply be understood as the flip side of their understanding of His descent through the heavens, after which, by the power of the Holy Spirit, He first entered His mother's womb. Both of these transits of Yeshua through the angelic spheres, as they were first understood by The Way, carried over into several New Testament references. (See Ephesians 4:9, Philippians 2:5–10, and John 16:28.)

There are, of course, some differences between the early Jewish and contemporary Christian expressions of these two heavenly journeys, the first being a matter of relative emphasis. While a central, if not *the* central emphasis of contemporary Christian theology is upon the glory of Yeshua's resurrection from the dead, The Way, while giving this cardinal understanding of our faith due attention, nevertheless gives even more attention in their writings to the wonder of Yeshua's divine ascension through the six heavens. There, in the climax of His glory, He seated Himself on the heavenly throne in the seventh at the right hand of His Father.

The Testament of Benjamin (A.D. 70) speaks to this point: "And He shall ascend from Hades and pass from earth to heaven. I know how lowly He shall be upon the earth, and how glorious in heaven."[20] Please note in this writing that Yeshua's resurrection is not mentioned as such, while His glorification is connected directly with His ascension. There is no interceding event here; Yeshua goes directly from the tomb to His Father's throne.

It is important to understand here that The Way isn't saying that there wasn't a resurrection. Rather, they simply skip over this event in these example writings to underscore what to them was the greater importance of the Ascension.

The Gospel of Peter echoes this emphasis upon the Ascension in its description of the dialogue between the angels and the women who are seeking His body: "He is not there for He is risen and departed to the place from which He had been sent."[21] Again, Yeshua ascends directly, without delay into His glorification.

Johannine theology, that of the apostle John, is closer to Paul's theology on this point. John distinguishes the Resurrection from the Ascension but places the latter on the eighth day. When Yeshua manifests Himself before His Ascension, not wanting to be delayed, He protests, "I have not yet ascended to my Father."[22]

While The Way's focus is upon exalting Yeshua during His Ascension rather than His Resurrection, they also attribute great importance to the length of Yeshua's stay on earth between these two monumental events.

The Ascension of Isaiah speaks specifically regarding this interval: "...He will ascend [from the grave] on the third day and He will remain in this world for 545 days...."[23] Here there is first Yeshua's descent into hell, and then three days later His ascent from the grave, which is His resurrection. Then, following this "ascent" (His resurrection), there is an interval of 545 days before His ascension to the seventh heaven.[24]

As a final note regarding The Way's understanding of Yeshua's descent from and ascent into heaven, we read in the Ascension of Isaiah that Yeshua ascended through the seven heavens and that this ascent was made to balance His descent. In His descent, the angels had not recognized Him because He purposefully hid His glory from them by changing His appearance. If He had not done so, they would have made every effort to stop Him from fulfilling His divine appointment with the cross. However, in the ascent Yeshua reveals His glory, and the angels recognize and adore Him. This text was to have a great influence on what was to emerge as generally agreed-upon Christian theology.[25]

Chapter 19
The Way's Understanding of Predestination

Did our Creator predetermine those who were to be saved and those who were not before they were born, even before the beginning of time?

> For whom He foreknew, He also predestined to be conformed to the image of His Son, that He might be the firstborn among many brethren. Moreover whom He predestined, these He also called; whom He called, these He also justified; and whom He justified, these He also glorified.
>
> —Romans 8:29–30

Or, does each of us enter this world as free and equal creations, able to use our own individual, God-given free will to either accept or reject salvation through Yeshua by His grace through our faith in Him?

> For by grace you have been saved through faith, and that not of yourselves; it is the gift of God, not of works, lest anyone should boast.
>
> —Ephesians 2:8–9

> That if you confess with your mouth the Lord Jesus and believe in your heart that God has raised Him from the dead, you will be saved.
>
> —Romans 10:9

This issue of predestination versus free will is perhaps the most divisive of all the many issues that continue to divide the body of Christ, the church, along denominational lines in such a way as to strike at the very heart of unity.

As we have seen thus far, the Nazarenes of The Way directly transferred much of their belief system from that of the Essenes, from whom a growing body of scholarship believes they directly evolved. Thus, in attempting to determine The Way's position on this central issue of theology it seems reasonable to look first to the Essene position, as it is well recorded in multiple places in the Dead Sea Scrolls.

The Manual of Discipline (4Q260–366) is regarded by many Dead Sea Scroll scholars to be the most important of the more than fifteen thousand scrolls and fragments found in Cave Four at Qumran. Soon after this document was translated and studied, it became clear that its central subject spoke to the Essenes' in-depth understanding and approbation of the doctrine of predestination, more precisely double predestination.

Simple predestination is the understanding that God has preelected those who are to be saved, and that this election is inalterable. At the same time, simple predestination understands that God had not preelected those who are not to be saved, allowing for the possibility that those not so elected in the first place may eventually be saved. Double predestination, on the other hand, is the understanding that God preelects both those who are and who are not to be saved. Moreover, in this understanding there is no opportunity to move from one of these groups to the other.[1]

The Essene approbation of double predestination is also seemingly evident in three other major scroll documents: the Thanksgiving Scroll, the War Scroll, and the Habakkuk Commentary.[2]

The Manual of Discipline was also found in Cave One (1QS 3.13–4.26), which in part is translated as:

> From the God of Knowledge comes all that is occurring and shall occur. Before they came into being He established all their design; and when they come into existence in their fixed times they carry through their task according to His glorious design. Nothing can be changed.[3]

The Thanksgiving Scroll, a collection of psalm-like hymns that were sung regularly by the Essenes, contains multiple references to their understanding of God's glory versus man's lowliness. The author of these hymns and the celebrants whom he inspired cry out their thanks to God for having saved them. One such ancient song of praise includes:

> In the wisdom of thy knowledge
> Thou didst establish their destiny before ever they were.
> All things exist according to Thy will,
> And without Thee, nothing is done.[4]

Two other striking examples of the Essenes' adherence to double predestination were also found at Cave One.

> I have known, thanks to your intellect, that it is not by a hand of flesh that the path of a man is straightened out, nor can a human being establish his steps. I know that every spirit is fashioned by your hand, and all its travail

> you have established even before creating him. How can anyone change your words? You, you alone have created the just man. For him, from the womb, you determined the period of approval, so that he will keep your covenant and walk on all your paths, to empty upon him your plentiful compassion, to open all the narrowness of his soul to eternal salvation and endless peace, without want. Upon flesh you have raised his glory. But the wicked you have created for the time of wrath, from the womb you have predestined them for the day of annihilation. For they walk on paths that are not good, they reject your covenant, their soul loathes your decrees, they take no pleasure in what you command, instead they choose what you hate. You have established all those who hate your law to carry out great judgments against them in the eyes of all your creatures, so they will be a sign and an omen for all eternal generations so that all will know your glory and your great might.
>
> —1QH VII 16–25

> From the God of Knowledge comes all that is and shall be. Before ever they existed He established their whole design, and when, as ordained for them, they come into being, it is in accord with His glorious design that they accomplish their task without change. The laws of all things are in His hand and He provides them with all their needs. He has created man to govern the world, and has appointed for him two spirits in which to walk until the time of His visitation: the spirits of truth and injustice. Those born of truth spring from a fountain of light, but those born of injustice sprint from a source of darkness. All the children of righteousness are ruled by the Prince of Light and walk in the way of light, but all the children of injustice are ruled by the Angel of Darkness and walk in the ways of darkness.
>
> —1QS 3:15–21

Again, to this point we have seen how The Way's systematic theology was very much influenced if not a mirror image of the parallel understandings of their predecessors, the Essenes. It should therefore not be surprising that the Essene understanding of double predestination was also seemingly fully appropriated by these early orthodox Jewish believers on Mount Zion.

Moreover, contemporary traditional Jewish understanding supports the notion that history is entirely determined in advance and men have only to wait for it to unfold. Let us turn to some examples of this understanding, as they were written by members of The Way, that were later included in the Canon of Scripture. The apostle Luke wrote in his gospel, telling the Seventy, "Rejoice that your names are written in heaven" (Luke 10:20, NIV). The same idea appears in

Philippians 4:3, where Paul points out that our "names are in the book of life." John's Revelation has similar references. Those who worship the Beast are those "whose names have not been written in the book of life of belonging to the Lamb that was slain from the creation of the world" (Rev. 13:8). Only those are to enter the heavenly city "who are written in the Lamb's book of life" (Rev. 21:27).

Some of what may or may not have been the Nazarenes of The Way's apocryphal writings exhibit this same imagery:

> Rejoice...that through the good pleasure of God your names, as of the ever-living, are written in heaven.[5]

> And we prayed and went down from the mountain, glorifying God, which hath written the names of the righteous in heaven in the book of life.[6]

Certainly, these two nebulous sources are anything but sufficient to determine that the Nazarenes of The Way wrote them, much less that they did indeed embrace double predestination as it was clearly understood by the Essenes. Moreover, some other of their apocryphal writings would suggest that they might have been inclined to a more pragmatic or liberal simple predestination understanding than that held by their more conservative Essene and traditional Jewish predecessors.

> If they (Thy children) shall repent with all their heart, they shall be written in the Book of Life with the saints.[7]

> All those who overcome shall be written in the Book; for their book is the victory which is yours.[8]

While these two writings would support either the doctrine of simple predestination or free will, they are, standing alone, still insufficient to make a definitive statement as to The Way's position on this issue.

Again, as we saw earlier, the apostle Paul seems to speak to both sides of this understanding. Thus, whatever our denomination's position may be, in the end, for me the apostle John has the most acceptable "final take" on this matter until we meet our Lord face to face in glory.

> And I saw in the right hand of him that sat on the throne a book written within and on the back, close sealed with seven seals. And I saw a strong angel proclaiming with a great voice, Who is worthy to open the book, and to loose the seals thereof? And no one in the heaven, or on the earth, or under the earth, was able to open the book, or to look thereon.
>
> —Revelation 5:1–3, asv

The seeming unclear position of the Nazarenes of The Way on the matter of predestination may well have been the early springboard from which arose the modern day church's continuing argument concerning this same core theological understanding—predestination versus free will.

This persistent, denominationally oriented division no doubt long preceded the Protestant Reformation (1517–1648). Even now the multifarious advocates, ranging from total free will to rigid double predestination, can be found holding their ground, firmly entrenched across the entire denominational spectrum.

At one extreme, the Roman Catholics assert:

> God predestines no one to go to hell; for this, a willful turning away from God (a mortal sin) is necessary, and persistence in it until the end. In the Eucharistic liturgy and in the daily prayers of her faithful, the Church implores the mercy of God, who does not want "any to perish, but all to come to repentance": Father, accept this offering from your whole family. Grant us your peace in this life, save us from final damnation, and count us among those you have chosen.[9]

At the other end of the theological spectrum stand the seventy-five million adherents in the one hundred denominations of the World Alliance of Reformed Churches who embrace the most rigid understanding of double predestination. And, between these two can be found all manner of theological permutations and combinations among the more than nine thousand Christian denominations that comprise the universal body of the church.[10]

Chapter 20
The Way's Understanding of the Body of Yeshua, the Church

As earlier noted, many modern day Jews, believers and non-believers alike, are predisposed to react negatively at the very mention of the cross, which they see as a symbol of the horrendous things that have been perpetrated by Christians against the Jewish people from the very inception of Christianity. Sadly, as with the cross, some Jewish believers, mostly those who remain close to their traditional rabbinical backgrounds, perceive church as something exclusively Christian and thus to be avoided. Herein lies perhaps the greatest of several stumbling blocks along the pathway to the salvation of my people, the Jews. Here also, I believe, can be found the primary cause and sustainer of the them-and-us perception of many Jewish believers toward Gentile Christians. It is this perception that has driven many believing Jews into a self-imposed isolation from which they distance themselves as much as possible from what they see as an alien Gentile church.

It is these self-isolated individuals of my born-again Jewish brethren who I believe have sadly missed the meaning of the apostle Paul's clarion call, first to the Ephesians but also to the entire body:

> For He Himself is our peace, who has made both one, and has broken down the middle wall of separation, having abolished in His flesh the enmity, that is, the law of commandments contained in ordinances, so as to create in Himself one new man from the two, thus making peace, and that He might reconcile them both to God in one body through the cross, thereby putting to death the enmity. And He came and preached peace to you who were afar off and to those who were near. For through Him we both have access by one Spirit to the Father.
>
> —Ephesians 2:14–18

As it was with their theologically elaborate perception of the cross, there is also an enormous irony in the fact that The Way had a deep and rich theological understanding of the body of Yeshua, the Church—far deeper and richer than that of their successors in the Gentile body. Over the ensuing centuries, several seemingly unrelenting realities have been at play: discrimination and persecution by the world's various secular governments; "replacement" by large segments of an often anti-Semitic church; and frequent, sometimes militant opposition from their Rabbinical Jewish brethren. All of this has, understandably, driven many of the miniscule minority body of modern day Jewish believers to aggressively distance themselves from any and all things that would identify them with the church. Ironically, this selfsame body of all believers was a central understanding and focus of the systematic theology of their first-century Jewish fathers on Mount Zion.

Perhaps some of this contemporary negative perception of the church by Jewish believers is simply a matter of semantics. There is no evidence the Jewish believers on Mount Zion or those widely dispersed congregations that developed after the martyrdom of Stephen in A.D. 35 identified themselves by the early Greek label *domus ecclesia*, which interestingly translates in English as "house of the church."[1] While these early ethnically Jewish congregations may have thought of themselves separately or even collectively as the *kneeseea*, or "places of meeting,"[2] it is certain that they had an even more well developed understanding of the great significance of what can in its early predominately Jewish context be labeled as "the body of Yeshua," as opposed to "church."

The Way's theological understanding of the body of Yeshua is well rooted in traditional Judaism and in the Qumran writings. The prophets in particular constructed an entire theology of Israel as "the bride of YHWH," the "vine of the Lord," and as "the city of the Most High."[3] The Dead Sea Scrolls speak of the Essene community's understanding of its own eschatological significance as an entity unto itself, describing it as "an eternal plant" and "a sanctuary for Israel."[4] The Way picked up on these understandings, as can be found in their writings, where the body of Yeshua is seen as the "plantation planted by the Apostles of the beloved"[5] and "the sanctuary built upon the foundation of the Apostles and the Prophets" (Eph. 2:20).

Moreover, The Way held that the body of Yeshua was a pre-existent reality. Hermas, for example, asserts, "She was created before all things...and for her sake the world was framed."[6] Clement of Rome (circa A.D. 88) confirms this understanding of pre-existence by asserting that the church was "created before the sun and the moon."[7]

Chapter 21
Angelology: The Way's Understanding of the Angels

The Way had a highly developed understanding of the angels that portrayed these heavenly creatures as being intimately involved in their everyday lives. Accordingly, angelology was a key component of their theology, doctrine, and worship practice.

While this angelic involvement was a major aspect of their systematic theology, even the most negatively disposed of their detractors focused their objections entirely upon The Way's continued compliance with the Torah and their persistent embrace of long-held and practiced Jewish tradition. Nothing I have found in any of the specifically "anti-heresy" and other church history writings from the likes of Hegesipus (110–180), Eusebius (263–339), and Irenaeus point to the Nazarene of The Way's emphasis on angels as detracting from their acceptance as fully orthodox believers who were to be fully accredited as fellow members of the body of Christ. To the contrary, The Way's understanding of the angels is mirrored in the angelology of both biblical testaments. Although the angels are less emphasized in practice by Christianity in general, the church's understanding of angelology is, nevertheless, still quite elaborate. The fact is, the terms *angel*, *angels*, and *host of heaven* or *heavenly host* are mentioned in varying appearances or functions 134 times in the Old Testament and 185 times in the New Testament.

The very close, daily involvement of the angels in their lives as it was understood by these first orthodox Nazarene Jewish believers would be an appropriate subject for a separate writing and by no means can be fully addressed in this current context. Thus, a discussion of some of The Way's more striking theological understandings of the presence and functions of angels follows.

Angels and the Name of Yeshua

"Angel" was one of the names given to Yeshua up through the fourth century by both The Way and the emerging church. This usage still carries over into our modern translations in the Old Testament expression "Angel of the Lord." It is generally agreed upon by biblical scholars that in each of its fifty-six uses, this term makes reference to Yeshua. It seems certain that the use of this term in no way implies that Yeshua, by His nature, is an angel.

Hermas, a second-century writer of the early Church of Rome, calls Yeshua "glorious angel" and "most venerable angel." In his famous writing, the Shepherd of Hermas, the shepherd, who is a lesser angel, is sent to Hermas by the "Glorious Angel." In this connection, the "Glorious Angel of the Lord" distributes the traditional branches to the people on the first day of the Feast of Tabernacles; he distinguishes between the just and sinners; he crowns the just; and he ushers the people into the tower, an allegorical expression of the body of Yeshua.

A second point to consider from the writings of Hermas and others is the presumed colossal stature of the "Glorious Angel." His enormous size is specifically characteristic of The Way's representation of angels. It serves precisely to establish the transcendence of the "Glorious Angel" by showing that he, Yeshua, infinitely surpasses the angels.[1]

Beyond the identification of Yeshua as the "Glorious Angel," The Way's angelology uses other angelic names and identities for Yeshua as a means to ascribe the particular attributes of these specific angels or groups of angels to Yeshua as He interfaces with given situations or events. In each of these cases, Yeshua is portrayed as in every way surpassing those who are genuine angels. For example, Yeshua is shown to be surrounded protectively by six archangels, with the implication that in every way He greatly surpasses them all. Hermas writes:

> Didst thou see the six men and the glorious and mighty man in the midst of them, him that walked about the tower and rejected the stones from the building?...The glorious man is the Son of God, and those six are the glorious angels who guard him on the right and on the left. Of these glorious angels not one shall enter in unto God without him; whosoever shall not receive His name, shall not enter into the Kingdom of God.[2]

Created Before All Other Creatures

While canonized Scripture offers no clear-cut statement regarding when the angels were created, The Way, being very concerned with all creatures that inhabit the cosmos, thoroughly addressed this interesting point in their writings. According to their understanding, when God created the cosmos, and in particular the heavens, He created the angels before making the other creatures. An early writing of The Way, 2 Enoch, written around the late first century A.D., quotes the Creator: "From the rocks I made a great fire break out, and from the fire I made all the incorporeal host and all the host of the stars, and the Cherubim and Seraphim and the Ophanim."[3] Hermas and Clement of Alexandria echo this conception that the Angels were the first of the created creatures. They comment further on the creation account of Genesis, pointing out that in the expression "God created the heaven and the earth," heaven was understood by some as referring to or including the angels, while others identified them with the "waters above the firmament."[4]

Their Appearance, Orders, and the Seven Heavens

As previously noted, The Way understood that the angels were enormous in stature. This understanding appears in several of their texts, for example: "Two men, very tall, such as I have never seen on earth."[5] In the Gospel of Peter, the heads of the two angels who carry the risen Yeshua "touch the sky."[6]

The Way held that there are many ranks of angels, the highest orders of which formed "the heavenly court," while the lower orders watched over and administered the affairs of this world. There were seven such angelic orders described, and they were arranged in parallel with The Way's understanding of the seven heavens. Irenaeus describes how this structure appeared at the beginning:

> "The earth is encompassed by seven heavens in which dwell Powers, Angels and Archangels giving homage to the Almighty God who created all things." He then compares the seven heavens to the seven branched candlestick (the menorah), a decidedly Nazarene and traditional Jewish understanding.[7]

The seventh heaven, the highest, is reserved for "the great Glory," God Almighty.

In the sixth heaven, as described by Enoch:

> The hosts, drawn up according to their rank, advancing and bowing before the Lord, then retiring and going to their places in joy and gladness...The Glorious serve Him, neither retiring from Him at night, nor leaving Him during the day, standing before the face of the Lord...All

> the Host of the Cherubim around His throne, singing before the face of the Lord.[8]

Enoch describes the fifth heaven as the "Realm of the Watchers," who are angels watching over and interceding in the affairs of men.[9]

For those who might not easily take to the notion that there are created beings watching over them from a fifth heaven, I offer my own personal testimony regarding three interventions of angels in my own life, though I am sure there have been many more.

The first deals with an amazing encounter I had while I was struggling to prepare for the position I had accepted in Israel as the director of marketing of an Israeli company. On the red-eye flight home from New Mexico to Seattle following my successful interview I prayed for guidance to a number of specific questions I had that were related to the mechanics my new position. As the plane, still darkened, began to descend for landing, a lovely young woman across the aisle from where I was seated literally began to glow with supernatural illumination as she turned toward me and with both of her hands extended an open book to me. "This is for you," she said gently, at which point the cabin lights came on, and she withdrew the book as she sat up straight in her seat. After we landed, I approached her, and she once again showed me the book, *Guerilla Marketing*. She repeated simply, "You need to read this book." As it turned out there was only one shop open at SEATAC airport very late that night. It was a Jewish-owned bookstore manned by one clerk in an otherwise totally darkened concourse where there were no other persons in sight. Amazingly, there was a single copy of that obscure book, *Guerilla Marketing*, on the shelf. I was amazed to see that the table of contents corresponded exactly in subject and order to my recently lifted-up prayer request for specific guidance. I feel certain that the young woman who vanished right after we exited the plane was an angel. In any event, this supernatural encounter was a thrilling and direct answer to prayer.

Next, several years ago when my wife, Donna, and I were driving back from Jerusalem to Tiberias on a very narrow and twisty section of the Jordan Valley highway, we rounded a blind turn to behold, to our horror, a seemingly imminent, unavoidable head-on collision with another car that was passing blindly from the other direction. I had no time to react; there was no shoulder, but only a sharp drop-off to our right. Suddenly I felt the steering wheel move sharply in my hands, and instantly we were beyond the situation and back on the road heading for Tiberias. Neither of us even made a comment but went on with what we had previously been discussing. It took me a few moments to recall what had just occurred, and then in amazement we were able to communicate about the supernatural intervention that had saved us from what would most likely have been a disastrous collision.

I know that I was to offer these examples of angelic intervention in this writing because of what occurred just yesterday morning as I was beginning to prepare my breakfast before taking up my day's writing. I put two slices of bread in our toaster oven, and then the phone rang. It was Donna, on a first break from her all-day Hebrew lessons, just wanting to chat. I left the kitchen and forgot all about my toast. A good ten minutes later, after we concluded our conversation, I suddenly remembered my toast. I ran to the kitchen, expecting at best a cloud of smoke. Instead, to my amazement, "someone" had turned the rather stiff rotary switch of the toaster oven not only to the off position but two settings beyond "off," evidently just to make the point that I was indeed being looked after.

Enoch describes the fourth heaven as the realm of the sun and the moon and the angels who preside over them. The third heaven contains paradise, where the souls of the just await the resurrection, and Sheol, where the souls of the impious await punishment. The second heaven is the prison of the apostate angels who fell from the fifth heaven, and the first heaven, the lowest of them all, contains the higher waters, the reservoirs of snow and rain, with the angels in charge of them, the stars, and the angels who control their courses.[10]

Guardians of Communities

While we have seen how the angels preside over natural phenomena and individual human affairs, according to The Way's understanding there are also angels who are responsible to watch over and protect human communities. There are multiple apocryphal writings that state, "The governments by the angels have been distributed over nations and cities."[11]

It is interesting that Daniel shows that this governmental authority has been given to Yeshua. Evidently, in The Way's understanding, His authority in this respect is implemented by the angels.

> Then to Him was given dominion and glory and a kingdom, That all peoples, nations, and languages should serve Him. His dominion is an everlasting dominion, Which shall not pass away, And His kingdom the one Which shall not be destroyed.
>
> —Daniel 7:14

I can certainly testify to the truth of this understanding. During the August 2006 War with Hezbollah, our city of Tiberias was within easy range of almost countless waves of *katyusha* rockets, which were rained down daily for five weeks upon us and the other cities of northern Israel. During this period, more than six hundred of these vicious weapons fell within our quite crowded city of some forty thousand souls. On the first evening of the war, one of these exploded only some fifty meters from our apartment building, sending us scurrying down five flights of stairs to our bomb shelter. We repeated this terrifying exercise several times each day for the next five weeks, counting the sound of exploding "incoming" as we hurried downward toward safety. When the conflict finally ground to its terrible conclusion, with Israel losing the first war in its sixty-year history, some six hundred *katyushas* had landed within our city.

All but a handful of these impacted in vacant areas between our crowded buildings, struck empty buildings, or landed in vacant fields. There were no fatalities and only a very few personal injuries, all of which were minor. There were no direct hits to buildings and only minimum property damage. Obviously, there was at least one angel overlooking our city whose loving hands skillfully diverted the hundreds of potentially devastating "fiery darts" the wicked one had been hurling our way.

An ancient unknown theologian of The Way provides us with a detailed view of The Way's doctrine regarding the angelic protection of the nations. He writes:

> There is an angel for every nation, to whom God has confided its care. God in fact has divided the nations and the whole world into 72 portions, giving them angels as princes. But only one of these, the first among all the archangels, Michael, was given the lot of caring for those who received the understanding and knowledge of God before all the rest.[12]

The nation that in this respect, in the eyes of God, stands above all the other nations is confirmed to be Israel in the Book of Daniel. (See Daniel 10:13 and 12:1.) For those believers who, like me, are convinced we are now in the End of Days, Daniel speaks out a special comfort:

> At that time [the End of Days] Michael shall stand up, The great prince who stands watch over the sons of your people; And there shall be a time of trouble, Such as never was since there was a nation, Even to that time. And at that time your people shall be delivered, Every one who is found written in the book. And many of those who sleep in the dust of

> the earth shall awake, Some to everlasting life, Some to shame and everlasting contempt. Those who are wise shall shine Like the brightness of the firmament, And those who turn many to righteousness Like the stars forever and ever.
>
> —Daniel 12:1–3

The Way's rather elaborate angelology is well rooted in the Essenes' very similar understanding as they recorded its elements in their scrolls. One such direct carryover from Qumran to Mount Zion is the doctrine of the individual guardian angel. Both the Epistle of Barnabas and the Shepherd of Hermas point out that every human is assigned a guardian angel; but, unfortunately, they teach that everyone is also burdened with his or her own individually assigned personal demon. This doctrine of opposing individual supernatural beings is directly rooted in the Essene doctrine of the "two spirits" (light and darkness).[13]

The Essene scroll Rule of the Community speaks directly to The Way's doctrine on the opposing forces of angels and demons as this understanding was taken from Qumran:

> From the God of knowledge stems all there is and all there shall be. Before they existed he made all their plans and when they come into being they will execute all their works in compliance with his instructions, according to his glorious design without altering anything. In his hand are the laws of all things and he supports them in all their needs. He created man to rule the world and he placed within him two spirits so that he would walk with them until the moment of his visitation: they are the spirits of truth and deceit. In the hand of the Prince of Lights is dominion over all the sons of justice; they walk on paths of light. And in the hand of the Angel of Darkness is total dominion over the sons of deceit; they walk on paths of darkness. Due to the Angel of Darkness, all the sons of justice stray, and all their sins, all their iniquities, their failings and their mutinous deeds are under his dominion in compliance with the mysteries of God until his moment; and all their punishments and periods of grief are caused by the dominion of his enmity; and all the spirits of their lot cause the sons of light to fall. However, the God of Israel and the angel of his truth assist all the sons of light. He created the spirits of light and darkness and on them established all his deeds and on their paths all of their labors.[14]

There is another particularly comforting, angelologic understanding of The Way holding that "aborted infants are entrusted to a guardian angel, so that having obtained a share in the gnosis [knowledge of God] they may arrive at a better destiny."[15]

Our Heavenly Intermediaries and Guides: Angels as Intermediaries

Another major development in the angelology of both The Way and later Christianity is the understanding that angels constitute a supernatural world of intermediaries between God and men. For The Way, many of the functions attributed by traditional Judaism to God were ceded to the angels.

As noted earlier in Chapter 5, water baptism was the second of The Way's three-part initiation of new members. Those to be baptized descended down a "cosmic ladder" consisting of seven steps, at the end of which they stood chest-deep in the running water of the *mikvah*, where they were met by their baptizers. According to Testa, the deacons (*mebaqqerim*) who supervised this triple immersion represented the angels who were given charge of material creation and spiritual recreation, both of which were accomplished through water that had been touched by the Holy Spirit.[16]

After this three-part self-immersion ceremony was complete, they ascended up the seven stairs of the "cosmic ladder," thus symbolically making their way up a spiritualized continuation of the ladder all the way through the six heavens until they were, in the spirit, seated with Yeshua at the right hand of the Father.

This rather elaborate process was spiritually loaded from its beginning to its conclusion. First, the descent of the initiates down the ladder into the water was held by The Way to be an imitation of Yeshua's descent into the womb of Mary, into the tomb, and then into Sheol. Next, their ascent up the ladder following their three-immersion baptism in the water of the *mikvah* was held to be an imitation of Yeshua's own resurrection, followed by His ascension. In this manner these who were newly baptized would join Yeshua in the spirit, as He is seated by His Father in the seventh heaven. Moreover, the archangel Michael, who was thought to be present, conveyed the gifts of the Holy Spirit (1 Cor. 12:4–11) upon those who had thus been immersed as they climbed out of the *mikvah* up the seven steps of the cosmic ladder.[17]

Surely, this arduous passage first into and out of the *mikvah*, then up the perilous climb through all of the heavens was simply too much for these just born again believers to undertake without some very special assistance. It was The Way's understanding that the archangel Michael, who served also as the "angel of baptism," chose to be present as the personal guide of each of them as they made their way throughout this entire ceremonial process.[18]

The theologians of The Way offer us yet another comforting thought from their understanding that near the hour of our death "the angel of repentance" manifests himself to us, begging us to mend our ways. Both Origen and Clement of Alexandria picked up on this doctrine as it was presented in the Shepherd of Hermas, and the call to repent still echoes throughout the hallowed halls of the church. The Way also held that "the angel of peace" would appear to us at the hour of our death to receive our soul as it departs our body and then lead it to paradise. However, those sad souls who go to their death unrepentant and unsaved will be met by their personally assigned demon, who will guide them to Sheol. We read in the Testament of Asher (circa A.D. 70):

> Keep the law of the Lord, and give not heed unto evil as unto good; but look unto the thing that is good indeed, and keep it in all commandments of the Lord, having your conversation unto Him, and resting in Him: for the ends at which men aim to show their righteousness, and know the angels of the Lord from the angels of Satan. For if the soul departs troubled, it is tormented by the evil spirit which also it served in lusts and evil works; but if quietly and with joy it hath known the angel of peace, it shall comfort him in life.[19]

A confirmation of this Essene-doctrine-*cum*-doctrine-of-the-Nazarenes carried over into the New Testament.

> Yet Michael the archangel, in contending with the devil, when he disputed about the body of Moses, dared not bring against him a reviling accusation, but said, "The Lord rebuke you!"
>
> —JUDE 9

Chapter 22
DEMONOLOGY: THE WAY'S UNDERSTANDING OF THE FALLEN ANGELS

As with the modern day church's general lack of attention to the realm of the angels, their evil counterparts, the demons, seem to receive even less serious emphasis. Instead, these very real agents of darkness are often consigned to the world of secular tradition, where their malicious efforts may often be acknowledged with the quip, "The devil made me do it." One can only speculate how often children from Christian homes are introduced to angels or demons at Halloween parties rather than in their churches or under watchful care in their homes.

There is a local tradition here in the Galilee arising from Yeshua's miracle of the swine, which he performed on the northeast side of the Sea of Galilee at Kursi.

> Now a large herd of swine was feeding there near the mountains. So all the demons begged Him, saying, "Send us to the swine, that we may enter them." And at once Jesus gave them permission. Then the unclean spirits went out and entered the swine (there were about two thousand); and the herd ran violently down the steep place into the sea, and drowned in the sea.
>
> —Mark 5:11–13

This local tradition has it that since demons cannot drown, they swam across the lake to Tiberias after their former hosts, the swine, thus perished, and there they have ever since plagued its many successive generations of human inhabitants.

Be that as it may, as with the angels, I can personally attest to the very real presence of demons in our day-to-day walk here in the land of our inheritance. As an example of the many such encounters we have endured during the past sixteen years, one spring morning while I was enjoying the lovely view of the lake with the wildflower-decorated Golan Heights as its backdrop, suddenly I saw a viper slithering on our balcony, just a few feet away from where I was sitting. I simply couldn't believe my eyes. "How could this deadly creature have made its way up five stories to this secluded place?" I pondered as I frantically called to Donna to come and give me a sanity check. It took only a moment after she arrived on the scene to give me the confirmation I sought, which she delivered in a terrified voice from the relative safety of her just-assumed perch on a nearby chair.

We just happened to have a garden spade nearby, and I began a somewhat prolonged battle with the two-foot-long, quickly moving snake, which began to strike at me in earnest as I countered with thrusts with the spade. My guardian angel was evidently also on the scene since—although it took several minutes—I managed to connect with my deadly adversary before it connected with me. So ended this bizarre incident. On reflection, I have little doubt that this was a spiritually loaded encounter and that this viper was in fact a demonic manifestation.

Why me? I was in the midst of writing my fourth book, *Full Circle*, at the time, and the enemy obviously was perturbed that I was determined to confront him head-on in that writing.

As with the angels who dwell on the side of the light, their counterpart, the demons, who inhabit the side of darkness, also found a place in The Way's doctrine. The Way understood that demons were constantly active in doing evil to humanity. They did so by inhabiting individuals, where they were better able to draw their hosts away from God. It was further understood that these demons could produce sickness and inflamed parts of the body, make them cold, or excite anger, hatred, lust, etc.[1]

The Testament of Solomon (circa A.D. 70), an early writing of The Way, recounts how Solomon was able to build the temple by defeating demons and employing their skills by means of a ring and its seal, which was given to him by the archangel Michael.[2]

The Way had two different understandings of the origin of demons, which both surface independently and converge in their writings. Most often, the demons were regarded as fallen angels. The pseudepigraphic 1 Enoch describes these angels as the "watchers," smitten with the desire for the daughters of men, who came down into the world under the direction of their leader, Satan, and brought forth giants from their illicit unions.[3] Papias (circa A.D. 110–140) echoed 1 Enoch's description of these demons as watchmen, writing, "God had given to certain angels the task of presiding over the government of earth."[4] Second Enoch names these two angels, Arioch and Marioch, whom God appointed to keep the earth and to govern temporal things.[5]

The second understanding of The Way regarding the origin of the demons is derived from the Essenes and presents an alternative to the various conceptions that associate the existence of evil angels with a fall. According to the Rule of the Community, the spirits of truth and injustice feuded in the hearts of men and were established from the beginning by God Himself. It explains, "For God has sorted them into equal parts until the appointed end and the new creation."[6]

The theologians of The Way were especially concerned with the "lower" demons, which they understood to be the souls of the giants who had been born from the union of the watchers and the daughters of men. Whatever their origin, these demons were held to have fallen from heaven and haunt the air and the earth.[7] The Way further held, as recorded in the *Testament of Reuben*, that there was a lower demon associated with each of the seven great vices: lust, gluttony, greed, sloth, wrath, envy, and pride.[8] The Way further held that these lower demons entered into bodies, which then became the objects of genuine possession. This doctrine continues in contemporary theological understanding. An example is seen in Mark 16:9, where the seven demons driven out of the sinful Mary Magdalene may be these same seven demons with their associated vices cited in the *Testament of Reuben*.[9]

Three of the most recently translated and studied Dead Sea Scrolls are psalms written to challenge these armies of demons head-on. The following passage is part of Psalm 2, a hiterhto unknown psalm of David from Cave Eleven:

> Concerning the words of Solomon, uttered in the name of YHWH: He will invoke the name of YHWH to set him free from every affliction of the spirits, of the devils [demons]. These are the devils, and the prince of enmity is Belial who rules over the abyss of darkness. And to magnify the God of wonders, the sons of his people have completed the cure; those who have relied on your name invoke the guardian of Israel, lean on him with all that is in them, he who separated light from darkness. . . . And He, YHWH, will send a powerful angel who will evict you [demons] from the whole earth. YHWH is to strike a mighty blow which is to destroy you forever and in the fury of his anger he will send a powerful angel against you to carry out all his commands, one who will not show you mercy, who above all these will hurl you into the great abyss, to the deepest Sheol. Far from the home of light shall you live, for the great abyss is utterly dark. You shall no longer rule over the earth but instead you

> shall be shut in forever. You shall be cursed with the curses of Abaddon[10] and punished by the fury of YHWH's anger.[11]

A final observation regarding the demonology of the Nazarenes of The Way concerns the fate shared by all departed souls with their crucified Lord, Yeshua. In the same way that Yeshua was required, after His resurrection, to ascend through the six heavens to sit beside His Father in the seventh, the Nazarenes held that all departing human souls, in imitation of Yeshua, must make the same perilous ascension through the territory of the enemy, where demon sentinels await their upward passage. Fortunately, angels as well as demons are on duty at every level, and for those souls who have nothing upon them that can be easily grasped by a demon, the passage upward is not problematic. In any event, this doctrine holds that both evil and good angels in their role as guardians of the cosmos have a type of prejudgment function of human souls as they proceed through the successive heavens on the way to be judged by their Maker.[12]

Chapter 23
Millenarianism: The Way's Understanding of Eschatology, the End of Days

I have watched a dear brother in the Lord over the past nearly thirty years as he, totally captivated, has meticulously calculated and fine-tuned what he ever-confidently calls his "chronology," an amazingly detailed, passionately studied attempt to predict the day and the hour of Yeshua's second coming. First, there were the successive dates he predicted in the 1990s when this momentous event would occur. Then when these dates came and went to no avail, he made yet more recalculations to select the next round of "sure to happen" dates following the turn of the century. And so he has persisted with the unabated encouragement and applause of a growing number of fascinated, steadfast, and undaunted devotees who can hardly wait to hear his latest prediction, presumably in order that they might be able to once again pack their spiritual luggage for the next soon-expected beaming up into the heavenlies.

Certainly, this dear brother and his devotees aren't alone in what, according to Matthew 24:36–37, seems to be a biblically unsound and hopeless quest: "But of that day and hour no one knows, not even the angels of heaven, but My Father only."

The theological understandings of the modern day church often stand in stark disunity over various matters of key doctrine and other important biblical issues. Of these, perhaps none is more passionately troubling and enduring than those loyal adherents who attach themselves to the various conflicting eschatological positions, each of which claims to predict, relative to the promised tribulation, when the Father will call His Son's spotless bride home in fulfillment of the much-anticipated Rapture. Some may find it surprising that while these passionately held understandings of the End of Days can be argued, often convincingly, through exegeses of selected scriptures, the word *rapture* is not to be found in the New Testament.

According to the Christian History Institute (CHI),[1] the Reverend C. I. Scofield, a Congregationalist preacher, became a strong proponent and promoter of the pre-Tribulation Rapture teaching, which he incorporated in his *Scofield Reference Bible*, first published in 1909. Moreover, CHI concludes that the *Scofield Bible* had an immediate impact on what the average Christian believed. Due in large part to Scofield, vast numbers of Christians now hold the view that Yeshua will return for Christians before the Great Tribulation, a teaching not held by any significant segment of the church before the mid-1800s.[2]

Given the intensity of this seemingly irresolvable issue in the modern day church, it is edifying to once again examine the understanding of the very first Jewish believers, who physically walked with Yeshua and took in face-to-face the wonder of His teachings. Interestingly, The Way had a much more developed but in some ways considerably different understanding of the End of Days than does the modern day church.

Central to The Way's understanding was the anticipated one-thousand-year earthly reign of Yeshua before the End of Time. This core doctrine, which originated on Mount Zion, is elaborately expressed by John in his Revelation. (See Revelation 20:1–6.) According to The Way's understanding, the Parousia, Yeshua's return to Earth to set up his kingdom, will occur at some unspecified time in the last days and will cover Yeshua's return, the resurrection of the saints, the general judgment, and the inauguration of the new creation.

The Ascension of Isaiah describes The Way's understanding of the Parousia in some detail.

> [Following the reign of the Antichrist] after 1,332 days, the Lord will come with His angels and with the armies of the holy ones from the seventh heaven, with the glory of the seventh heaven, and He will drag Belial and his armies into Gehenna.
>
> And he will give rest to the godly whom he shall find in the body in this world.... But the saints will come with the Lord with their garments which are stored up on high in the seventh heaven: with the Lord they will come, those whose spirits have been reclothed; they will descend and be present in the world; and He will establish those who have been found in the body, with the saints, in the garments of the saints; and the Lord will minister to those who have kept watch in this world. And afterwards they will be transformed in their garments on high, and their bodies will be left in the world.[3]

The following chart describes several key points of connection between The Way's understanding as it is recorded in the Ascension of Isaiah and in the New Testament account.

ASCENSION OF ISAIAH	NEW TESTAMENT PARALLEL
Victory over the Antichrist	Revelation 19:19
Belial cast into the lake of fire	Revelation 19:20; 20:10
Resurrection of the already dead saints	Revelation 20:4; 1 Corinthians 15:21
Transfiguration of the saints who are still living	1 Corinthians 15:23; 1 Thessalonians 4:17
All will reign on Earth with Yeshua	Revelation 20:4
This is called "the time of rest"	2 Thessalonians 1:7
It is also called the Millennium	Revelation 20:4
The Last Judgment	Revelation 20:12–15
The resurrection of the wicked for punishment	Revelation 20:12–15
The transfiguration of the righteous, which is a second resurrection and entry into incorruptible life	Matthew 22:23–32; Mark 12:18–27; Luke 20:27–40

This orthodox view of the Nazarenes of The Way, which migrated intact into the New Testament, presumably originated in the "region of Damascus" after the martyrdom of Stephen. This end-of-days understanding of The Way, however, was soundly rejected by the Ebionites and the other heterodox groups who, instead of emphasizing Yeshua's return and reign, focused on the material aspects they saw coming to the righteous, such as wonderful food, endless sex, and greatly increased procreation.[4]

The Way's orthodox view is richly developed in various early writings. For example, Irenaeus writes:

> ...the Creation, having been renovated and set free, shall bring forth an abundance of all kinds of food simply from the dew of heaven, and from the fertility of the earth.... The days will come in which vines shall grow each having ten thousand branches, and in each branch ten thousand twigs, and in each twig ten thousand shoots, and in each one of the shoots ten thousand clusters, and on every one of the clusters the thousand grapes, and every grape when pressed will give five and twenty measures of wine. And when any one of the saints shall lay hold of a cluster, another shall cry out: "I am a better cluster, take me; bless the Lord through me."[5]

This same conception is found in the Book of Amos:

> "Behold, the days are coming," says the LORD, "When the plowman shall overtake the reaper, And the treader of grapes him who sows seed; The mountains shall drip with sweet wine, And all the hills shall flow with it."
>
> —AMOS 9:13

Irenaeus goes on to describe similar abundance of all the other vegetables and fruits on the earth during the Millennium, and he adds:

> All the animals, feeding lonely on the produce of the earth, shall in those days live in peaceful harmony together, and in perfect subjection to Man.[6]

The new element introduced here is the perpetual renewal of the earth, which will bring forth its abundance without the need of tilling or other intervention of man. The more important implication is that during Yeshua's thousand-year reign, those who reign with Him on the earth will continue to take material nourishment.

Methodius of Olympus, a late-first-century historian, offers further insight into The Way's understanding of this era. He says there will be a first resurrection in which the just will have a transfigured body, but it will still be earthly and will be followed by a second, more complete transformation.

Moreover, Methodius sees the time spent by the Jews in the tabernacle in the desert before they entered into the land of their inheritance as a type of what he had earlier called "the thousand years of rest" and "the resurrection." Here, the tabernacle represented the bodies of the risen men who still keep their earthly form during the Millennium. He writes:

> Just as the Jews, after the repose of the Feast of Tabernacles, arrived at the Promised Land, so I too, following Christ who has passed into the heavens, shall attain to Heaven, no longer living in tabernacles, or rather my own tabernacle no longer remaining as it was but being transformed after the millennium from a human and corruptible form into angelic greatness and beauty.[7]

Yeshua Himself seemed to be speaking to the nature of the first resurrected human body during the Millennium when at His Last Supper He proclaimed, "I shall not drink henceforth of this fruit of the vine, until that day when I drink it new with you in my Father's kingdom" (Matt. 26:29, ASV).

Irenaeus writes:

> He promised to drink of the fruit of the vine with His disciples, thus indicating both these points: the inheritance of the earth in which the new fruit of the vine is drunk, and the resurrection of His disciples in the flesh. For the new flesh which rises again is the same which also received the new cup. And He cannot by any means be understood as drinking of the fruit of the vine when settled down with his [disciples] above in a super-celestial place; nor, again, are they who drink it devoid of flesh, for to drink of that which flows from the vine pertains to flesh, and not spirit.[8]

The Way's Understanding of Yeshua's Earthly Reign of One Thousand Years

In keeping with their rather elaborate understanding of the End of Days, the Nazarenes of The Way developed and embraced a variety of teachings that speak to several key aspects of how life will progress during Yeshua's kingdom reign.

First, the very idea of the earthly reign being for one thousand years has its roots in traditional Judaism. In the Book of Jubilees we are told that "Adam, because of his sin, died seventy years before attaining the one thousand-year span promised to men in paradisal times:

> And at the close of the nineteenth jubilee, in the seventh week in the sixth year thereof, Adam died, and all his sons buried him in the land of his creation, and he was the first to be buried in the earth. And he lacked seventy years of one thousand years; for one thousand years are as one day in the testimony of the heavens and therefore was it written concerning the tree of knowledge: 'On the day that ye eat thereof ye shall die.' For this reason he did not complete the years of this day; for he died during it.[9]

The prophet Isaiah speaks to the extraordinary life expectancy of humans who live during the Millennium:

> Neither shall there be anymore a child that dies untimely, or an old man who shall not complete his time; for the youth shall be a hundred years old.... For as the days of the tree of life shall be the days of my people.[10]

The Nazarenes of The Way developed a doctrine wherein the time from the Creation to the end of the millennial reign of Yeshua was described as a "cosmic week" consisting of seven millennia. Irenaeus speaks to this understanding:

> The Lord, therefore, recapitulating in Himself this day, underwent His sufferings on the day preceding the Sabbath, that is, the sixth day on which man was created.... Some, again link the death of Adam with the

> period of a thousand years, and therefore Adam dies before completing a thousand years; for since they say, A day with the Lord is as a thousand years, he did not exceed the thousand years, but died within them, thus fulfilling the sentence passed on his transgression.[11]

The concept of a one-thousand-year reign is carried forward into the writings of the church fathers. For example, Justin Martyr, writing circa 150, explains:

> Now we are of the opinion...that by these words: For according to the days of the tree shall be the days of my people....he signifies a thousand years in a mystery, for in accordance to that which was said to Adam, that in the day in which he should eat of the tree, in that day he should die (Gen. 2:17), we know that he did not fill up a thousand years. We understand that the saying: A day of the Lord is as a thousand years, accords with this. And, further, a man among us named John, one of the Apostles of Christ, prophesied in the Revelation that they who have believed on our Christ will spend a thousand years in Jerusalem, after which will come to pass the universal, and, in a word, eternal resurrection of all at once, followed by the judgment. And this too our Lord said: They shall neither marry, nor be given in marriage, but shall be as the angels, being children of the God of the resurrection.[12]

Justin shows here that life in the millennial paradise is for a thousand years; and since Isaiah makes the span of life in messianic times equal to that of life in paradise, it is clear that the length of life in the messianic kingdom will be a thousand years.[13]

The Way parts company with their traditional Jewish brethren in their very different understandings of procreation during the millennial reign. The traditional Jewish understanding is that procreation will continue: "The righteous shall live until they have begotten one thousand children."[14] None of the elders of The Way or the early Gentile Church fathers who followed them—Papias, Irenaeus, and Montanus—make any reference to procreation during the Millennium. This understanding is consistent with the application of the Adamic millennium to messianic times, which would apply to a single generation covering a thousand years and thus not allow for the birth of children.[15]

The Jewish-Christian Sibylline Oracles affirm this understanding of The Way:

> Then thy race shall cease to be as it was before; none shall cut the deep furrow with the rounded plough; there shall be neither vine-branch nor ear of corn, but all alike shall eat from the manna of heaven with their white teeth.[16]

The Seventh Millennium

The Millennium, the thousand-year reign of Yeshua, was taken by The Way to be the last of seven millennia. Barnabas writes:

> Of the Sabbath he speaketh of the beginning of creation: and God made the works of His hands in six days, and He ended on the seventh day, and rested in it. Give heed children to these words: He ended in six days. He meaneth this, that in six thousand years the Lord will bring all things to an end, for to Him a day is as a thousand years; and this He Himself beareth me witness, saying: Behold, the day of the Lord shall be as a thousand years. Therefore children, in six days, that is in six thousand years, everything shall come to an end. And He rested on the seventh day meaneth this; when His Son shall come and abolish the time of the Lawless One, and shall judge the ungodly, and shall change the sun and the moon and the stars, meaning; He says to the Jews, It is not your present Sabbaths that are acceptable unto Me, but the Sabbath which I have made, in the which, when I have set all things at rest, I will make the beginning of the eighth day which is the beginning of another world.[17]

Barnabas introduces a new element here: the "eighth day." The eighth day is referenced in both the Old and New Testaments as the day of circumcision of the flesh, but I can find no biblical reference to it as being a replacement for Sunday, historically understood by Jews as the first day of the week (Acts 20:7–8). The Way congregated on *Shabbat* evening after the sun went down, as do most modern day observant Jews. This is considered the beginning of the first day of the next week, for what has come to be known as the *Motzei Shabbat* or *Havdalah* service. For all Jews, the first purpose of these weekly congregational gatherings was and remains to say farewell to the just-ended week and to prayerfully welcome in and bless the next.

The Emperor Constantine, in a milestone de-Judaizing edict in March of A.D. 321, declared that "Sun-day," the birthday of Mithra, the pagan sun god whom he continued to embrace, was to be a day of rest throughout the Roman Empire.

> On the venerable day of the Sun let the magistrates and people residing in cities rest, and let all workshops be closed. In the country however persons engaged in agriculture may freely and lawfully continue their pursuits because it often happens that another day is not suitable for gain-sowing or vine planting; lest by neglecting the proper moment for such operations the bounty of heaven should be lost.[18]

The Church Council of Laodicea circa A.D. 364 then carried this process of the de-Judaizing of Christianity to its inevitable conclusion by declaring that religious observances were to be conducted on Sunday, not Saturday.

> Christians must not Judaize by resting on the Sabbath, but must work on that day, rather honoring the Lord's Day; and, if they can, resting then as Christians. But if any shall be found to be Judaizers, let them be anathema from Christ.[19]

Thus Sunday, "the Lord's day," replaced *Shabbat* as the Sabbath.

Conclusion

Finally, while the modern day church speaks variously of a pre-, mid-, and post-Tribulation Rapture, these terms and the understandings they represent are not to be found in the writings nor apparently in the thinking of the Nazarenes of The Way.

One thing does seem clear regarding their understanding of just how these momentous events of Yeshua's second coming will unfold. The key to this understanding, which amazingly managed to survive the onslaught of pre- and post-Nicea de-Judaization and found its way into the New Testament, is to be found in 1 Thessalonians 4:17:

> Then we who are alive and remain shall be caught up together with them in the clouds to meet the Lord in the air. *And thus we shall always be with the Lord.* (emphasis added)

For The Way, the timing of this most holy event that will usher in the millennial reign was not of primary concern, but rather it was the spiritual and material substance of this event that gave rise to their prophetic end-times doctrine. Simply stated, the scenario envisioned by The Way would seem to be that when Yeshua appears in the clouds, accompanied by the saints who have already risen, those saints who remain alive on Earth will rise up to greet Him and will then accompany Him and the others back to Earth, at which point the millennial reign will commence.

Part IV

The Sacred Writings of The Way

***There is a supreme injustice in opposing Christianity to Judaism by way of reproach, since all primitive Christianity possesses came bodily from Judaism.*[1]**
—ERNEST RENAN, CHURCH HISTORIAN

IT TAKES LITTLE MORE than a cursory examination to see the truth of Ernest Renan's understanding of the foundational relationship of Judaism to Christianity, a truth that can also readily be seen in the parent-child relationship between The Way and the church. This relationship is especially evident in the vast body of The Way's sacred writings, which formed a vital part of their great legacy to the church. One need only pick up the Bible and review its table of contents. For starters, all sixty-six sacred books, with the possible exception of the Gospel According to Luke and the Book of Acts, were authored by ethnic Jews, and Luke is thought by some scholars to have been a convert to Judaism.

I strongly stand with the shrinking minority who hold that the canonized Bible is the inerrant Word of God, as it was originally written down and assembled over many years by numerous Jewish authors. However, I also believe that the many other writings of The Way that did not find their way into the Canon are also worthy of our careful study and consideration. By selectively studying the apocryphal and pseudepigraphic (not canonized) literature that was written concurrently with the biblical writings, we can often gain a better insight into the intended meaning of the related canonized writing.

Much of this apocryphal and pseudepigraphic literature is deeply rich and apparently written to supplement canonical Scripture. For example, many of the apocryphal Gospels offer interesting suggestions as to what occurred during the so-called "missing years" during Yeshua's childhood. Others attempt to provide support for later theological convictions—both orthodox and heretical.

Included in this enormous collection of the non-canonical writings of The Way are: sixteen Gospels, twenty-seven Books of Acts, thirteen New Testament apocalypses, and many other related writings.[2] The size and scope of this collection is enormous, and a detailed discussion of them all would require several large volumes. However, in the following chapters of Part 4, I will briefly discuss the most important of these writings in each of the mentioned categories.

Chapter 24
The Canonical Gospels of The Way and the Rediscovered Codex Washington

While researching for this writing, I encountered the work of the Reverend Dr. Lee W. Woodard, a pastor and unique biblical scholar with particular expertise in the study of ancient manuscripts using forensic paleography, a new discipline that he began developing during his doctoral studies more than twenty-four years ago.

Forensic paleography is, according to Dr. Woodard, an exciting new scholarly tool with enormous potential. He writes:

> Forensic paleography is the use of modern photographic and other applicable technology, along with a knowledge of applicable linguistics, history, philosophy, theology and art, applied intensively to actual ancient manuscript pages, margins and covers, to better see and interpret all (regardless of how small or seemingly insignificant) manuscript markings, linguistic or alpha numeric entries, symbolic art, and any erasures or modifications of original entries, or changes in scribal techniques, including deletions of or insertions into previous lines or pages of text, in order to better understand, when, where and by whom specific manuscripts were penned and used.[1]

While pursuing his doctorate, Dr. Woodard was encouraged by one of his professors to find and carefully study the calligraphy of the most ancient manuscript to which he could gain access. This quest led him to the Freer Gallery of the Smithsonian Institution in Washington, DC, where he encountered a long, mostly ignored, and misidentified codex of the four New Testament Gospels. The documents were previously thought to have been interesting but unremarkable, undated duplicates of some earlier copies of the original manuscripts.

The codex and its acquisition by the Smithsonian Institute is an extraordinary story by itself. The Freer Galleries of the Smithsonian Institute where these ancient manuscripts, known officially as Codex Washington, or Codex W, are on display writes:

> During his first visit to Egypt in 1906, Charles Lang Freer was offered a small group of biblical manuscripts for purchase. Freer was intrigued enough to venture outside his usual collecting interests and, despite knowing little of their value or significance, he acquired the manuscripts. His instincts were good. In subsequent years he obtained additional manuscripts from Egypt, some in fragmentary condition and written in Greek and Coptic, the Egyptian language used from the third century. The manuscripts are written on sheets made of parchment or papyrus and are in codex form, with folded sheets forming leaves like the modern book. As a group, these manuscripts form one of the most important collections of biblical manuscripts outside Europe.[2]

According to Dr. Woodard, following this exciting acquisition, Freer had the best scholars available study these ancient manuscripts to both identify and date its pages. However, those who undertook this evaluation were only able to speculate that the undated manuscripts were fourth- or fifth-century *copies of copies* of the original Gospels—by no means original versions, nor even likely to be first-generation copies of the original writings.

Hence, Charles Freer, having finally run this course to no satisfying conclusion, later donated the codex to the Smithsonian Institution, where it has remained on exhibition to this day in his namesake Freer Galleries.

The new owners of Codex W, not satisfied, undertook studies of their own to better ascertain the contents and date of their fascinating new acquisition. The results of these efforts, as quoted above from their Web site, have remained the library's official position since soon after the codex went on display.

Dr. Woodard, however, strongly disagrees with these findings, and having spent most of the twenty-four years applying his new discipline, forensic paleography, he has reached potentially very important new conclusions about their identification, importance, and dating. From the outset, he became absolutely determined to share the truth of his important discoveries with the church and the world beyond.

Following are excerpts from my extensive personal e-mail exchange with Dr. Woodard from December 2007 to June 2008.

Most of Dr. Woodard's personal e-mail comments shared here and a great wealth of additional scholarly detail are included in his just-completed, limited edition book with over 150 full-color illustrations, *First Century Gospels*

Found! by Lee W. Woodard with James Rutz. Dr. Woodard has been kind enough to share his book with me in a prepublication copy. He writes:

> Codex W is composed of Gospel Namesake Hebraic signed, Gospel Namesake Sealed manuscripts.[3] It was incredibly misdated by earliest analysts. Various pages within it date to 37–67 A.D. (for Matthew), 67–97 (for John), 60's–73 (for Mark), and 74 (for Luke). Some pages even though dated thus were copied from earlier pages, but quite a few pages are probably the Greek originals, including [the] genealogy of Matthew, which has what is purported to be the Hebraic signature of "Matthew." There are exceedingly powerful evidences that John Mark and his Cousin Barnabas carried these manuscripts to Egypt. Barnabas was [the] primary scribe and artist. He painted wooden covers that feature actual images of the Gospel Namesakes.
>
> There are many indications among the numerous tiny Hebraic entries upon [the] pages of Codex W that suggest that Barnabas (the scribe) and other earliest of Codex W manuscript users were Bi-Lingual Hebraic-Greek, but that they most often thought in Hebrew.
>
> Additionally, especially the earlier pages of Matthew's and John's manuscripts, and some within Mark, have evidences that they (most often Barnabas) probably were using some sort of written Hebrew sources.
>
> The Infrared and Ultraviolet [scans] also seem to show that the Genealogy of Matthew (which absolutely has to be the Greek first draft original) probably was written over the equivalent data in Hebrew. However, they had the means of erasing and re-entering so well upon parchment pages that even with Infrared and Ultraviolet it is difficult to tell what was within the initial writings or annotations. I can see enough, however, to tell that there was an underlying Hebrew Genealogy or notes for Genealogy, but I can only recognize a few bits and pieces here and there. For instance, in the margin near "Roboam" in the Genealogy, there is "Like Jeroboam"....Which is one of those tell-tale signs of them being most at home using Hebrew. That Genealogy looks to me like Barnabas may have been entering Greek translations of Hebrew written sentences above them, while carefully erasing beneath that line what had been earlier written in Hebrew. It is like an Interlinear, but with the older source being erased.
>
> They (Scholars) can now use Mass Spectrometry to recover much better some of those underlying entries. We are trying to persuade Freer Gallery of Art to use that technology. We even have had an offer from Stanford University Graduate School to do some of it without cost, as

> part of their research programs. But, so far Freer Gallery has been very zealously not allowing others to handle the Codex.[4]
>
> ...each of those Gospels within that Old and Holy Book is dated as to date of actual penmanship, with some very important implications for what is known as "The Synoptic Problem"....Additionally...these Gospels tell the dates of the Birth and Ascension of Jesus as 4 B.C. and 31 A.D., respectively. Some may want to quarrel with those dates, but I'm just announcing what a scribe named Barnabas wrote during A.D. 65–74 on penned manuscripts, after having had relationships with James, "brother of the Lord" and the actual Apostles of Jesus. That Scribe-Artist, Barnabas, who recorded these dates signed Codex W in 73 A.D.
>
> One other very surprising matter that will be of much interest to many is that the first segment of the First Edition of the Gospel of John is within this Codex and is dated and ostensibly covertly signed by Apostle-Elder John in our A.D. 65, even though some later pages within John's Codex W manuscript are dated in 67 and 97 A.D.[5]

The many implications of Dr. Woodard's discoveries relative to the dating of the Gospels and his amazing conclusion that there are surviving copies of these precious New Testament scriptures—authored and signed by their namesake apostles of The Way and authenticated by Barnabas of the New Testament—are potentially profound and far-reaching. Nonetheless, wide acceptance of any new, much less revolutionary understanding, such as those proposed by Dr. Woodard, by the large and diverse body of biblical scholarship is a formidable undertaking that can span many years. I have personally found that the precise dating Dr. Woodard assigns to each of the four Gospels fits perfectly with my own considerable research on the early writings and other related subjects concerning The Way during the first century.

This brief introduction to Dr. Woodard's work and Codex W is necessarily constrained by the limitations of the present context. I thus urge all interested readers to visit Dr. Woodard's Web site, www.washington-codex.org. And, for those interested in exploring this work in much greater depth, I recommend Dr. Woodard's soon-to-be-available scholarly and meticulously illustrated and documented book.

For any believer in Yeshua, it should go without saying that the four Gospels are the very heart and substance of New Testament Scripture, as they were presumably authored by their namesake apostles, who, with the exception of Luke, were on hand to witness the miraculous acts of Yeshua and to hear His words firsthand. Luke did not personally walk with Yeshua while

He appeared among them in the flesh, but he certainly heard, then recorded in his Gospel, these wondrous words and events through the secondhand, meticulously reliable, Holy Spirit-inspired accounts of his brother apostles and other firsthand witnesses.

As remarkable and exciting as their very existence may be, Dr. Woodard's precise dating of the four canonized Gospels lends a particularly important potential confirmation of the history and movement of The Way during the first century, when previously the chronology of these historical events could only be conjectured by reference to other, most often entirely speculative sources.

Of particular interest in this regard is Dr. Woodard's dating from Codex W of the first edition of the Gospel of Matthew to A.D. 37 and the fact that this initial draft of the first canonized Gospel was completed in Damascus.[6] Dr. Woodard's dating suggests that this first edition of Matthew was distributed from Damascus to other emerging churches by the scribe Barnabas in the company of John-Mark, the author of the Gospel of Mark, during the period 37 to 43.[7] The importance of this precise dating suggested by Dr. Woodard's forensic analysis is that it validates the theory of the persecution-driven dispersal of The Way from Mount Zion, which previously had been only speculatively dated. We can now say with increased confidence that this dispersal to the Galilee, "the region of Damascus," and to other locations most likely began no more than just five years following Yeshua's ascension.

Herein we have a potentially significant revision of early church history. Most biblical scholars up to now have assumed that this dispersion from Mount Zion did not begin in earnest until just prior to the first Jewish revolt around A.D. 62, when the majority of those who fled were understood to have made their way to Pella, a city in the Decapolis. While this earlier flight of The Way from Jerusalem is not mentioned in the New Testament, it was otherwise documented by Eusebius[8] and in other historical sources. When Dr. Woodard's assessment that the Gospel of Matthew was completed in Damascus in A.D. 37 is added to other historical sources,[9] it seems plausible that many of The Way had already dispersed from Jerusalem before A.D. 62.

The Way's sojourn in Pella may have been of short duration since there is also now other both anecdotal and material evidence strongly suggesting that there was a concurrent ongoing migration of The Way to the Galilee, specifically, for example, to Tiberias, where very recently the remains of the Tiberias synagogue of The Way have been partially excavated and reliably dated to circa A.D. 150.

Chapter 25
Old Testament Pseudepigraphic Writings Pertinent to The Way

The pseudepigrapha writings (literally, "falsely titled") are a large body[1] of uncanonized, biblically oriented texts written between 200 B.C. and A.D. 200 whose authorship is spuriously ascribed to various biblical prophets and kings. For example, principal among these as they apply to our present context is the Ascension of Isaiah, which purports by its title to have been written by the major prophet himself. In its present form, this work is Christian in its orientation, and it was assembled by some unknown writer in the second half of the second century, at the earliest.

This specific writing, as well as the pseudepigrapha and the apocryphal writings in general, should not be rejected out of hand simply because of their unknown or spurious authorship, or by their omission from the body of the Canon. Certainly, all believers, like the biblical Bereans, must be fair-minded and receive these inputs with all readiness but carefully search the Scriptures daily to find out whether these things are so (Acts 17:11).

While each of these writings was apparently undertaken to address a specific purpose and need within the body at the time it was written, many offer further insight into the theological understandings of their mostly Jewish-believer authors.

Again, turning to our earlier example, The Ascension of Isaiah was written in the manner of an ancient apocalypse to combat certain then-contemporary evils and the lack of discipline and divisions in the church. However, in a broader sense, this writing is replete with deep theological insights that provide a unique window into The Way's systematic theology.

While it would take a separate volume to thoroughly discuss all such pseudepigraphic writings as they pertain to the development of The Way's systematic theology, a brief exposition of the writings that are most germane to our present context will hopefully provide a sound introduction to the usefulness of both this body of non-canonical writings and to the apocryphal writings in general.

The Ascension of Isaiah

To continue with our example, the Ascension of Isaiah, a relatively well-known pseudepigraphic work, was written in Aramaic in Antioch circa A.D. 80–90. This writing, presented in an easy-to-read storytelling format, is one of the primary pseudepigraphic sources used by church historians for information and insight concerning The Way's theological understandings. Specifically, this work addresses such core subjects as the triune Godhead, the nativity of Yeshua, His death and resurrection, and His descent into hell.[2]

In its present Christian form, the Ascension of Isaiah narrates the prophet's vision, which has him taking an angel-guided tour through the seven heavens. During this tour, Isaiah becomes privy to God's plan to send His Son, Yeshua, into the world to do away with all evil. Satan, unfortunately, becomes aware of Isaiah's newfound knowledge, and he thus proceeds to have him martyred by being sawn in half.[3]

Before the prophet comes to this sad end, his travels through the seven heavens are described in great and vivid detail. He beholds in each of them a throne surrounded by angels, with the glory of each growing ever more glorious as he comes nearer to the final, seventh heaven. When he finally reaches this highest heaven, he finds it to be the dwelling place of the Most High God and his Beloved, Lord Yeshua. There Isaiah sees all of the most prominent saints who have been appointed to dwell in this exalted place, including Adam, Abel, and Enoch. The prophet is especially taken by the appearance of all the saints who dwell in this place, who are each gloriously appearing in their new bodies and look like angels.[4]

Isaiah is then given a vision of what will occur in the End of Days, when the Most High will once again send Yeshua down through the seven heavens for His final dealing with Satan. After he has successfully accomplished His assigned task of defeating Satan, Yeshua once more ascends up the cosmic ladder, freely passing through each level, until He once more resumes His place at the right hand of His Father.[5]

The writer of this saga then interjects a dramatic flashback. Satan, it seems, witnessed this impending descent of Yeshua into the world to bring about his end, so he reacts accordingly. He takes up the role of the Antichrist, doing as he pleases and causing all manner of sorrows everywhere, including causing one of the Twelve to betray Yeshua at the Last Supper. All the while, many of the people believe his declaration that he alone is the Lord God and there is no other.

This Satanic attack upon the body continues for 1,332 days until the Father sends Yeshua down into the world for the final battle, which ends with Satan and his demons being cast into hell.

2 Enoch

The Book of Enoch is an ancient composition known from two sets, an Ethiopic version known as 1 Enoch and a Slavonic version known as 2 Enoch or the Book of the Secrets of Enoch. Both versions are based on early sources that enlarged upon the short biblical account of Enoch, the seventh patriarch after Adam, who, because "he walked with God," was taken up into heaven. (See Genesis 5:4–23 and Hebrews 11:5.)

Second Enoch, or the Slavonic Apocalypse of Enoch, was written in the late first century A.D. in Syria by a Jew who was, presumably, a member of The Way. This text survives only in late Old Slavonic manuscripts. It most likely was composed originally in Aramaic or Hebrew, later translated into Greek, and later still translated into Old Slavonic. Functionally, this work is a commentary and amplification of Genesis 5:21–32 (from Enoch to the Flood). Its major theological themes include:

- God created the world out of nothing.
- There are seven heavens populated with angelic hosts.
- God created the souls of men before the foundation of the earth.
- The abodes of heaven and hell are already prepared for the righteous and sinners.
- Ethical teachings are presented that at times closely parallel those of the New Testament and the Book of Proverbs.
- Corporeal resurrection of the dead is introduced.
- Yeshua and the Holy Spirit, for various purposes, are seen taking the form of angels.[6]

One of the most fascinating passages of the Slavonic Enoch is the account of the dramatization of eternity found in chapter 33. As the world was made in six days, so its history would be accomplished in six thousand years, and this would be followed by one thousand years of rest, when the balance of conflicting moral forces has been struck and human life has reached the ideal state. (A reference to this conflict is also found in "the War Scroll," which describes a future battle between the sons of light and the sons of darkness. These writings were recently discovered in Qumran Cave 1).[7]

Testaments of the Twelve Patriarchs

The Testaments of the Twelve Patriarchs are purported to be the deathbed bequests of the twelve sons of Jacob. While the origin of this work, written circa the first century B.C., is regarded by most scholars to be Jewish in its original form, it was later revised by early Jewish believers in Yeshua and then revised again by later Christian writers, who added their own interpretations. Of particular note are the clearly Essenic doctrines, such as "the two spirits," and "the two visitations of the Messiah," that are included in the later redaction.

While the original Jewish version of the Testaments of the Twelve Patriarchs was most likely presented as twelve separate writings, it seems apparent that their combination into one volume with the addition of clearly pointed Messianic Jewish theological and doctrinal understandings was the concerted work of The Way.

The Way's systematic theology can also be seen embedded in these testaments in two further examples: The first of these is the frequent reference to The Way's doctrine of the seven heavens, as opposed to the earlier traditional Jewish understanding of three heavens. The second example comes from the Testament of Levi, which contains a detailed description of The Way's ceremony of initiation, which includes full-body anointing with oil preceding a three-immersion water baptism. This form of water baptism reappeared in the Syrian Church, where it remains in practice.[8]

M. de Jonge speaks to the difficulty scholars continue to encounter when attempting to precisely determine the origin, content, and purposes of this nevertheless important collection of apocryphal writings. He writes in his book *The Testaments of the Twelve Patriarchs*:

> There is no doubt that the present version of these writings is very early Christian in their present form and must have received that form sometime in the second half of the 2nd century A.D. One first has to establish the meaning of the present version, allowing, of course, for possible alterations in the period between their origin and the origin of the archetype of our manuscript tradition for a Christian audience around A.D. 200. Because the Christian passages cannot be removed without damaging the fabric of large sections of the work, we must assume at least a thoroughgoing Christian redaction. It is very difficult, if not impossible, to establish the exact contents of this "original" (pre-Christian) Jewish document, let alone to detect different stages in the redaction of that document. It is, in fact, uncertain whether one should speak of a Christian redaction of an existing Jewish original version, or of a Christian composition.[9]

The Sibylline Oracles attributed to The Way

The Sibylline Oracles bear a marked similarity to the Testaments of the Patriarchs in that both are either a Christian remodeling of earlier Jewish works or writings of The Way that were inspired by Jewish prototypes. With the Oracles, however, it is possible to trace the development of The Way's contributions without speculation.

The Sibylline Oracles are preserved in a voluminous collection of twelve "books" consisting, collectively, of over four thousand verses. This collection came into being over an extended period, from 180 B.C. to the third century *A.D.* Book Three was probably the first to be composed in Alexandria. Book Six, clearly a writing of The Way, certainly came into being later, while Books Seven and Eight are predominantly writings of The Way. Sibyl, the narrator, always speaks in the first person and almost always in the future tense.

The famous acrostic *IXTHYS*, meaning "Jesus Christ, Son of God, Savior," is found in Book Eight.[10] According to Eusebius, Emperor Constantine, by quoting this acrostic, made it instantly popular. Subsequently, it can be widely seen in contemporary use as a Christian logo consisting of the aforementioned acrostic in Greek letters inside a simple outline of a fish.

As a matter of related interest, during the 2004 dig season at Hippos/Sussita in the nearby Golan Heights, this acrostic was found scribed on a marble pillar of the northwest church, which has been dated to circa the fifth century.[11]

Book Four of the Oracles is particularly rich in the theological understandings and tell-tale stylistic traditions of The Way. For example, this text begins with an elaborate description of the baptism of Yeshua, much like that in the opening verses of the Gospel of Mark. Interestingly, this same holy baptismal recounting was adopted by the heterodox Ebionites, and it appears in several of their writings, including The Gospel of the Ebionites. The book ends with an account of the heavenly ascension of the cross, which, as we discussed earlier in chapter 18, is a distinct and unique theological understanding of The Way.

Book Seven describes horrendous eschatological plagues that will, at the End of Days, consume the world by fire, cause global social chaos through the utter confusing of the nations, and destroy the morality of mankind through illicit unions.

I can only take pause that this ancient prophecy is seemingly being fulfilled before our very eyes, as seen on Fox News here in Israel, which regularly offers us frightening coverage of vast areas of northern California that are ablaze with out of control, "consuming" fires. Could these fires, along with unprecedented floods in middle America and the myriad other natural disasters that have occurred in recent times, be the beginnings of God's judgment on America? It is hard to imagine that America and the other nations could be in a more confused state than they are at the moment, what with the ongoing collapse of the petroleum-centered world economic system, wars and the rumor or wars, etc. Certainly, there has been a terrible breaking down of morality at all levels of the American society.

Book Seven continues at the end of this travail with an exciting description of the coming of the Messianic Age.

Interestingly, this same cosmic eschatological scenario appears in the apocryphal Apocalypse of Peter as well as in the canonized Second Epistle of Peter.[12] It is also to be found in the Dead Sea Scrolls, where it appears in the Psalms of Thanksgiving.[13]

Chapter 26
The New Testament Apocryphal Writings of The Way

The writers of The Way were highly prolific. Included in their very large portfolio of religious texts are six Gospels, a variety of epistles, apocalypses, and other writings. Taken together as a special collection, this very large portfolio provides us with an enlightening insight into The Way's orthodox theological understandings. They also give us better insight into precisely how the understandings of the Ebionites and other heterodox groups deviated from those of The Way.

Let us begin our exploration of these New Testament writings of The Way with a brief overview of the four apocryphal Gospels that are generally considered to be orthodox in their orientation.

The Gospel of Peter

Like the other apocryphal gospels of The Way, it is highly unlikely, though possible, that the Gospel of Peter was actually written by its namesake author. Most biblical scholars have dated this work to between A.D. 70 and 160.

The Gospel of Peter has been a source of much controversy concerning both its validity and origin. Principal among the objections of those who would discount its validity is its docetic[1] tendency in disclaiming that Yeshua suffered physically on the cross, thus denying His humanity. Further they offer the objection that after His death Yeshua was immediately taken up into heaven, thus discounting the canonized accounts of His burial and resurrection.

F. F. Bruce, longtime professor of biblical criticism and exegesis at the University of Manchester, points out other serious deviations from orthodox understandings, including the complete exoneration of Pilate from responsibility for Yeshua's crucifixion, the diminishing of the Roman soldiers' role to that of only guarding the tomb, and the assignment of all blame for His death to the Jews, especially to the chief priests and the scribes.[2]

However, Ron Cameron, noted theologian and professor of religion at

Wesleyan University, takes a much different position on this apocryphal gospel, which underscores both its authenticity and its seminal importance. He does so in part by pointing out his understanding that the previously noted heretical positions were actually much later additions to the original orthodox writing.[3]

Three fragments of the Gospel of Peter have been preserved: an eighth-century text discovered in a monk's grave in the modern Egyptian city of Akhmim, Egypt, and two small papyri unearthed at Oxyrhynchus, Egypt, dating from the sixth century and first published in 1972.

Eusebius wrote that the leadership of the Antioch Church did not object to the Gospel being read in the churches of Western Syria, thus underscoring its very early acceptance by the church of that time. He no doubt based this conclusion on a publicly circulated letter from Serapion, Bishop of Antioch, in 190–203. Serapion had found upon examining the Gospel that "most of it belonged to the right teaching of the Savior."[4] Professor H. B. Swete, Cambridge University Bible and patristic scholar, was convinced that the Gospel of Peter originated in some community of The Way in western Syria, where it was read with authority. Swete dated the work between 150 and 165.[5]

The Gospel of Peter underscores several recurrent and uniquely emphasized theological understandings of The Way, including: a strong focus on the divinity of Yeshua, the great importance and functions of angels, and the exaltation of Yeshua's humanity above all the created beings.

Moreover, there is a close relationship between this apocryphal gospel and the Dead Sea Scrolls' Damascus Document, in which Yeshua is portrayed as having an immense size so as to underscore His divine nature.[6]

Which Was the First of the Gospels: The Gospel of the Nazarenes, the Gospel of the Hebrews, or the Gospel of Matthew?

Dr. Woodard's life's work properly dating the four canonized Gospels has also gone a long way toward our understanding of the historicity of the apocryphal writings, which hitherto has been entirely speculative.

Up to now there have been three principal views regarding which of the various Gospel writings of The Way was the first to emerge. Setting aside the long and still ongoing scholarly arguments concerning the completion order of the four canonical Gospels, most biblical scholarship has held that there was another, very early apocryphal Gospel that preceded the three synoptics and the Gospel of John.

Some have understood this first Gospel to be the Gospel of the Hebrews. Another consensus has understood this earliest Gospel to be the Gospel of the Nazarenes. If Woodard's findings are correct, then neither of these apocryphal works came first. Rather, it was a very early version of Mathew that was completed and distributed in A.D. 37.[7] It is virtually certain that the Gospel of the Hebrews and the Hebrew Gospel of Mathew were the same text, and probably all three were called by different names at different times and in different places by different commentators.

The Gospel of the Hebrews survives as a small number of fragment remnants from the writings of the church fathers. Following are the several surviving fragments of the Gospel of the Hebrews: [8]

> When Christ wished to come upon the earth to men, the good Father summoned a mighty power in heaven, which was called Michael, and entrusted Christ to the care thereof. And the power came into the world and it was called Mary, and Christ was in her womb seven months.[9]

According to the Gospel written in the Hebrew speech, which the Nazarenes read, "the whole fount of the Holy Spirit shall descend upon him." Further in the Gospel which we have just mentioned, we find the following:

> And it came to pass when the Lord was come up out of the water, the whole fount of the Holy Spirit descended upon him and rested on him and said to him: My son, in all the prophets was I waiting for thee that thou shouldest come and I might rest in thee. For thou art my rest; thou art my first-begotten Son that reignest for ever.[10]

And if any accept the Gospel of the Hebrews, here the Savior says:

> Even so did my mother, the Holy Spirit, take me by one of my hairs and carry me away on to the great mountain Tabor.[11]

It also stands written in the Gospel of the Hebrews:

> He that marvels shall reign, and he that has reigned shall rest.[12]

To those words (from Plato, Timaeus 90) this is equivalent:

> He that seeks will not rest until he finds; and he that has found shall marvel; and he that has marvelled shall reign; and he that has reigned shall rest.[13]

As we have read in the Hebrew Gospel, the Lord says to His disciples:

> And never be ye joyful, save when ye behold your brother with love.[14]

In the Gospel According to the Hebrews, which the Nazarenes were wont to read, there is counted among the most grievous offenses:

> He that has grieved the spirit of his brother.[15]

The Gospel According to the Hebrews, which was recently translated by me (Jerome) into Greek and Latin, which Origen frequently uses, records after the resurrection of the Savior:

> And when the Lord had given the linen cloth to the servant of the priest, he went to James and appeared to him. For James had sworn that he would not eat bread from that hour in which he had drunk the cup of the Lord until he should see him risen from among them that sleep. And shortly thereafter the Lord said: Bring a table and bread! And immediately it added: he took the bread, blessed it and brake it and gave it to James the Just and said to him: My brother, eat thy bread, for the Son of man is risen from among them that sleep.[16]

There is considerable doubt that this Gospel of the Hebrews was the first Gospel to appear. Danielou suggests that it may have been one of the sources for the Gnostic Gospel of Thomas, which would place its writing at the beginning of the second century and most likely associate it with a Nazarene Jewish community in Egypt, suggesting that it too is a Gnostic work.[17]

Hence, while the Gospel of the Hebrews, like the Gospel of Thomas, was decidedly Gnostic (if not heterodox) in its character, content, and form, the four later to be canonized Gospels constituted what the church regarded as an entirely orthodox baseline.

The Gospel of the Nazarenes, on the other hand, was first mentioned by Hegesippus and later by Jerome. Both of these respected church fathers taught that this orthodox Gospel was an early Aramaic version of the later canonized Gospel of Matthew. The mention of Hegesippus, however, puts the writing of this Gospel back to the first half of the second century.[18] The Gospel of the Nazarenes, like the Gospel of the Hebrews, also survives only in fragments found in the writings of various church fathers. I have quoted these twenty-one fragments in Appendix One.

Let us now consider these fragmented remnants of the two apocryphal Gospels against the backdrop of known historical events, the most central of which was the martyrdom of Stephen, which took place at some point between A.D. 32 and 35. Consider next that Yeshua's ascension and thus, contemporaneously, the founding of The Way most likely occurred in A.D. 30.

As earlier discussed, driven by multi-faceted persecution, adherents of The

Way began to disperse from Jerusalem in considerable numbers immediately following Stephen's tragic death. Thus at the very most, from its very beginning The Way had no more than five years, most likely less, before this original, core orthodox group began to flee from Jerusalem to various locations, many of which were in the Galilee and throughout western Syria, most notably Damascus, and "the region of Damascus."

As a starting point, let us assume that Woodard's suggested dating and place of completion of the four Gospels of Codex W are correct. Then using these findings as a baseline alongside the previously noted documented historical events, we can at long last put the matter of the order of the Gospels to rest. As earlier noted, Woodard proposes based upon his forensic analysis of Codex W that the first edition of Matthew was completed in A.D. 37,[19] not in Jerusalem but rather in Damascus. Hence, in keeping with the conclusions of Hegesippus and Jerome, it is most likely that the Gospel of the Nazarenes was an early draft of Matthew, the first synoptic Gospel, which was completed no more than five years nor less than two years following the ascension of Yeshua.

The Gospel of Thomas

The Gospel of Thomas was a product of The Way written in Adiabene (modern day Iraq). The dating of this apocryphal Gospel is highly conjectural, and scholarly opinion varies widely. The Nag Hammadi text dates from around A.D. 340. The Oxyrhynchus fragments are dated at around A.D. 140, maybe earlier. The consensus of scholars, however, because of its genre and content, is that it originated in the first century.[20]

The Gospel of Thomas is not written in the form or general content of the four canonized Gospels. Rather, it is a seemingly random collection of 114 sayings, which are attributed to Yeshua. The author of this writing may indeed have been the biblical Didymos Judas Thomas, but the scholarly consensus is that it is pseudepigraphic (i.e., that it was written by some one other than its namesake author).

In its original form, the Gospel of Thomas, widely understood to have been entirely orthodox, underwent later significant gnostic redaction. Helmut Koester, in the introduction to the Gospel of Thomas found in James Robinson's edition of the Nag Hammadi Library opinions that neither the Coptic translation nor the Greek fragments have preserved the Gospel as it was originally written. Koester points out that there were even changes made between the two versions during the process of transmission from one version to the other.[21]

Representative examples from the Gospel of Thomas's 114 sayings follow in two groupings: those that parallel passages in the canonized Gospels and those that are entirely new and independent of the Canon.

Example Sayings Parallel to the Canonized Gospels:

Saying 9 (cf. Matthew 13:3–9)

Jesus said, Look, the sower went out, took a handful [of seeds], and scattered [them]. Some fell on the road, and the birds came and gathered them. Others fell on rock, and they didn't take root in the soil and didn't produce heads of grain. Others fell on thorns, and they choked the seeds and worms ate them. And others fell on good soil, and it produced a good crop: it yielded sixty per measure and one hundred twenty per measure.

Saying 20 (cf. Matthew 13:31–32)

The disciples said to Jesus, "Tell us what Heaven's imperial rule is like." He said to them, It's like a mustard seed. [It's] the smallest of all seeds, but when it falls on prepared soil, it produces a large branch and becomes a shelter for birds of the sky.

Saying 26 (cf. Matthew 7:3–5)

Jesus said, "You see the sliver in your friend's eye, but you don't see the timber in your own eye. When you take the timber out of your own eye, then you will see well enough to remove the sliver from your friend's eye.

Saying 36 (cf. Matthew 6:31)

Jesus said, "Don't fret, from morning to evening and from evening to morning, about what you're going to wear."

Saying 44 (cf. Luke 12:10)

Jesus said, "Whoever blasphemes against the Father will be forgiven, and whoever blasphemes against the son will be forgiven, but whoever blasphemes against the holy spirit will not be forgiven, either on earth or in heaven."

Example Sayings New and Independent of the Canonized Gospels:

Saying 3

Jesus said, "If your leaders say to you, 'Look, the (Father's) imperial rule is in the sky,' then the birds of the sky will precede you. If they say to you, 'It is in the sea,' then the fish will precede you. Rather, the (Father's) imperial rule is inside you and outside you. When you know yourselves, then you will be known, and you will understand that you are children of the living Father. But if you do not know yourselves, then you live in poverty, and you are the poverty."

Saying 8

And he said, "The human one is like a wise fisherman who cast his net into the sea and drew it up from the sea full of little fish. Among them the wise fisherman discovered a fine large fish. He threw all the little fish back into the sea, and easily chose the large fish. Anyone here with two good ears had better listen!"

Saying 12

The disciples said to Jesus, "We know that you are going to leave us. Who will be our leader?" Jesus said to them, "No matter where you are, you are to go to James the just, for whose sake heaven and earth came into being."

Saying 21

Mary said to Jesus, "What are your disciples like?" He said, They are like little children living in a field that is not theirs. When the owners of the field come, they will say, "Give us back our field." They take off their clothes in front of them in order to give it back to them, and they return their field to them. For this reason I say, if the owners of a house know that a thief is coming, they will be on guard before the thief arrives, and will not let the thief break into their house (their domain) and steal their possessions. As for you, then, be on guard against the world. Prepare yourselves with great strength, so the robbers can't find a way to get to you, for the trouble you expect will come. Let there be among you a person who understands. When the crop ripened, he came quickly carrying a sickle and harvested it. Anyone here with two good ears had better listen!

Saying 39

> Jesus said, "The Pharisees and the scholars have taken the keys of knowledge and have hidden them. They have not entered, nor have they allowed those who want to enter to do so. As for you, be as sly as snakes and as simple as doves."

In summary, today most scholars would agree that the Gospel of Thomas has opened a new perspective on the earliest Christian tradition. Recent studies centered on this Gospel have led to a reappraisal of the forces and events that define orthodoxy during the second and third centuries. The *incipit*, or beginning words, of Thomas invite each of us "who has ears to hear" to join in a unique quest:

> These are the hidden words that the living Jesus spoke, and that Didymos Judas Thomas wrote down. And He said: "Whoever finds the meaning of these words will not taste death."[22]

The Apocalypses of The Way

We now turn to the apocalypses, a group of writings that are related to the Gospels but nevertheless differ from them in form and purpose. With respect to our current context, an *apocalypse* is defined as any of a class of Jewish or Christian writing that appeared from about 200 B.C. to A.D. 350 and were assumed to make revelations of the ultimate divine purpose. The two apocalypses produced by writers of The Way that have been considered orthodox are briefly summarized in this section.

The Apocalypse of Peter

The Apocalypse of Peter, written in Syria toward the end of the first century, was included in the canon of Scripture in the Muratorian Fragment of the late second century and was then again included in Clement's list of canonized writings in A.D. 208. It was, however, not included in later canonical listings.[23]

Given its recognition by Clement of Alexandria, the Apocalypse of Peter presumably came into being in Egypt under the auspices of the very early church that thrived there, as suggested by Phillip's encounter with and baptism of the Ethiopian eunuch during his regional pastoral visits (Acts 8:27–40).

The vivid scene of Yeshua's transfiguration and with it Peter's firsthand description of heaven and hell are a striking example of The Way's writing style and substance.

The surviving fragment is quoted here in its entirety.

…many of them will be false prophets, and will teach divers ways and doctrines of perdition: but these will become sons of perdition. And then God will come unto my faithful ones who hunger and thirst and are afflicted and purify their souls in this life; and he will judge the sons of lawlessness. And furthermore the Lord said: Let us go into the mountain: Let us pray. And going with him, we, the twelve disciples, begged that he would show us one of our brethren, the righteous who are gone forth out of the world, in order that we might see of what manner of form they are, and having taken courage, might also encourage the men who hear us. And as we prayed, suddenly there appeared two men standing before the Lord towards the East, on whom we were not able to look; for there came forth from their countenance a ray as of the sun, and their raiment was shining, such as eye of man never saw; for no mouth is able to express or heart to conceive the glory with which they were endued, and the beauty of their appearance. And as we looked upon them, we were astounded; for their bodies were whiter than any snow and ruddier than any rose; and the red thereof was mingled with the white, and I am utterly unable to express their beauty; for their hair was curly and bright and seemly both on their face and shoulders, as it were a wreath woven of spikenard and divers-colored flowers, or like a rainbow in the sky, such was their seemliness. Seeing therefore their beauty we became astounded at them, since they appeared suddenly. And I approached the Lord and said: Who are these? He saith to me: These are your brethren the righteous, whose forms ye desired to see. And I said to him: And where are all the righteous ones and what is the aeon in which they are and have this glory? And the Lord showed me a very great country outside of this world, exceeding bright with light, and the air there lighted with the rays of the sun, and the earth itself blooming with unfading flowers and full of spices and plants, fair-flowering and incorruptible and bearing blessed fruit. And so great was the perfume that it was borne thence even unto us. And the dwellers in that place were clad in the raiment of shining angels and their raiment was like unto their country; and angels hovered about them there. And the glory of the dwellers there was equal, and with one voice they sang praises alternately to the Lord God, rejoicing in that place. The Lord saith to us: This is the place of your high-priests, the righteous men. And over against that place I saw another, squalid, and it was the place of punishment; and those who were punished there and the punishing angels had their raiment dark like the air of the place. And there were certain there hanging by the tongue: and these were the blasphemers of the way of righteousness; and under them lay fire, burning and punishing them. And there was a great lake, full of flaming mire, in which were certain men that pervert righteousness, and tormenting angels afflicted them. And there were also others, women, hanged by their hair over that mire that bubbled up: and these were they who adorned themselves for adultery; and the men who mingled with them in the defilement of adultery, were hanging by the feet and their heads in that mire. And I said: I did not believe that I should come into this place. And I saw the murderers and those who conspired with them, cast into a certain strait place, full of evil snakes, and smitten by those beasts, and thus turning to and fro in that punishment; and worms, as it were clouds of darkness, afflicted them. And the souls of the murdered stood and looked upon the punishment of those murderers and said: O God, thy judgment is just. And near that place I saw another strait place into which the gore and the filth of those who were being punished ran down and became there as it were a lake: and there sat women having the gore up to their necks, and over against them sat many children who were born to them out of due time, crying; and there came forth from them sparks of fire and smote the women in the eyes: and these were the accursed who conceived and caused abortion. And other men and women were burning up to the middle and were cast into a dark place and were beaten by evil spirits, and their inwards were eaten by restless worms: and these were they who persecuted the righteous and delivered them up. And near those there were again women and men gnawing their own lips, and being punished and receiving a red-hot iron in their eyes: and these were they who blasphemed and slandered the way of righteousness. And over against these again other men and women gnawing their tongues and having flaming fire in their mouths: and these were the false witnesses. And in a certain other place there were pebbles sharper than swords or any spit, red-hot, and women and men in tattered and filthy raiment rolled about on them in punishment: and these were the rich who trusted in their riches and had no pity for orphans and widows, and despised the commandment of God. And in another great lake, full of pitch and blood and mire bubbling up, there stood men and women up to their knees: and these were the usurers and those who take interest on interest. And other men and women were being hurled down from a great cliff and reached the bottom, and again were driven by those who were set over them to climb up upon the cliff, and thence were hurled down again, and had no rest from this punishment: and these were they who defiled their bodies acting as women; and the women who were with them were those who lay with one another as a man with a woman. And alongside of that cliff there was a place full of much fire, and there stood men who with their own hands had made for themselves carven images instead of God.

> And alongside of these were other men and women, having rods and striking each other and never ceasing from such punishment. And others again near them, women and men, burning and turning themselves and roasting: and these were they that leaving the way of God...[24]

The Apocalypse of Peter as an important witness of the Petrine literature is considered by many biblical scholars to be of great importance. Peter's vivid view of eschatological events in this apocryphal account adds depth and richness to the canonical descriptions. In his recounting here of the Transfiguration, heaven, and hell, Peter draws upon the beautiful eastern imagery of the early Egyptian Church. His description of the river of fire is an enlightening eschatological vision extending back to at least the very early Egyptian Christians.

The Epistle of the Apostles

The Epistle of the Apostles, like the Gospel of Thomas, takes the form of various sayings attributed to Yeshua that were purportedly spoken directly to the twelve apostles. It opens with the second "leaf" of the Ethiopic version:

> *We*, John, Thomas, Peter, Andrew, James, Philip, Bartholomew, Matthew, Nathanael, Judas Zelotes, and Cephas, write unto the churches of the east and the west, of the north and the south, the declaring and imparting unto you that which concerneth our Lord Jesus Christ: we do write according as we have seen and heard and touched him, after that he was risen from the dead: and how that he revealed unto us things mighty and wonderful and true.[25]

The form, style, and content of The Epistle of the Apostles are strikingly similar to other apocryphal writings. The work is a blend of details also found in the canonical Gospels, along with expanded information concerning Yeshua's instruction relative to His resurrection and His second coming. They are presented in fifty-one "leaves" (short chapters), making up a relatively long and impressive writing. The words of Yeshua are frequently documented with references to Scripture, helping to promote this writing as a legitimate extension of the gospel tradition for the early body of Yeshua and the emerging Christian Church.

The earliest text is a fourth- or fifth-century Coptic-language manuscript translated from the original Greek, which is dated to the mid second century because of similarities in its style and content to other documents of that period, especially to those that came from the early Egyptian branch of The Way.

There is a striking resemblance in both theme and substance between this writing and the Apocalypse of Peter. Both reveal the most secret mysteries and throw light on matters that the Gospels left unrevealed. The work is also certainly Nazarene Jewish in its style and character. Yeshua's descent into hell, as in the Gospel of Peter, is concerned with the salvation of the saints of the Old Testament. As He did in the Ascension of Isaiah, during His descent into His mother's womb, Yeshua takes on the form of the angels as He passes through the seven heavens. His second coming to reign on Earth for one thousand years is preceded by cosmic signs and is accompanied by the glorious cross.[26]

Examples both of Gospel-derived "leaves" and expanded revelation and instruction follow. First, several miracles of Yeshua are recounted from the canonical Gospels.

> Thereafter was there a marriage in Cana of Galilee; and they bade him with his mother and his brethren, and he changed water into wine. He raised the dead, he caused the lame to walk: him whose hand was withered he caused to stretch it out, and the woman which had suffered an issue of blood twelve years touched the hem of his garment and was healed in the same hour. And when we marveled at the miracle which was done, he said: Who touched me? Then said we: Lord, the press of men hath touched thee. But he answered and said unto us: I perceive that a virtue is gone out of me. Straightway that woman came before him, and answered and said unto him: Lord, I touched thee. And he answered and said unto her: Go, thy faith hath made thee whole. Thereafter he made the deaf to hear and the blind to see; out of them that were possessed he cast out the unclean spirits, and cleansed the lepers. The spirit which dwelt in a man, whereof the name was Legion, cried out against Jesus, saying: Before the time of our destruction is come, thou art come to drive us out. But the Lord Jesus rebuked him, saying: Go out of this man and do him no hurt. And he entered into the swine and drowned them in the water and they were choked.[27]

Example amplifications of the canonical Gospel text:

> Then said the Lord unto Mary and her sisters: Let us go unto them. And he came and found us within, and called us out; but we thought that it was a phantom and believed not that it was the Lord. Then said he unto us: Come, fear ye not. I am your master, even he, O Peter, whom thou didst deny thrice; and dost thou now deny again? And we came unto him, doubting in our hearts whether it were he. Then said he unto us: Wherefore doubt ye still, and are unbelieving? I am he that spake unto you of my flesh and my death and my resurrection. But that ye may know that I am he, do thou, Peter, put thy finger into the print of the nails in mine hands, and thou also, Thomas, put thy finger into the wound of

the spear in my side; but thou, Andrew, look on my feet and see whether they press the earth; for it is written in the prophet: A phantom of a devil makes no footprint on the earth.

And we touched him, that we might learn of a truth whether he were risen in the flesh; and we fell on our faces (and worshipped him) confessing our sin, that we had been unbelieving. Then said our Lord and Savior unto us: Rise up, and I will reveal unto you that which is above the heaven and in the heaven, and your rest which is in the kingdom of heaven. For my Father hath given me power to take you up thither, and them also that believe on me.[28]

Examples of the dialogue between Yeshua and the apostles:

Then said we to him: Lord, that which thou hast revealed unto us is great. Wilt thou come in the power of any creature or in an appearance of any kind? He answered and said unto us: Verily I say unto you, I shall come like the sun when it is risen, and my brightness will be seven times the brightness thereof! The wings of the clouds shall bear me in brightness, and the sign of the cross shall go before me, and I shall come upon earth to judge the quick and the dead.[29]

And this preach ye also and teach them that believe on me, and preach the kingdom of heaven of my Father, and how my Father hath given me the power, that ye may bring near the children of my heavenly Father. Preach ye, and they shall obtain faith, that ye may be they for whom it is ordained that they shall bring his children unto heaven.

And we said unto him: Lord, unto thee it is possible to accomplish that whereof thou tellest us; but how shall we be able to do it? He said to us: Verily I say unto you, preach and proclaim as I command you, for I will be with you, for it is my good pleasure to be with you, that ye may be heirs with me in the kingdom of heaven, even the kingdom of him that sent me. Verily I say unto you, ye shall be my brethren and my friends, for my Father hath found pleasure in you: and so also shall they be that believe on me by your means. Verily I say unto you, such and so great joy hath my Father prepared for you that the angels and the powers desired and do desire to see it and look upon it; but it is not given unto them to behold the glory of my Father. We said unto him: Lord, what is this whereof thou speakest to us?[30]

Chapter 27
The Didache: The Lord's Teaching Through the Twelve Apostles to the Nations

The Way's writings we have so far examined reflect the theological and doctrinal wellspring of all New Testament understanding. This next group, their liturgical writings, were the divinely inspired font from which came forth, in uniquely Jewish expression, their formal teachings, worship system, morality, and ascetism (self-denial).

The two principal writings of The Way among these liturgical offerings are the Didache and the Odes of Solomon. The Didache is perhaps the most important of these in that it provides an open window into the liturgy, sacraments, and worship practices of the very first orthodox Jewish believers, some of which still endure in today's church and others that long ago faded into obscurity.

As aforementioned, the underlying purpose of the book you hold in your hands is to provide detailed, specific guidance to modern day home congregations that are seeking to return to the Jewish roots of our faith through an exposition of the theology, doctrine, writings, and worship system as they were understood and first practiced by The Way. It is thus after many centuries of obscurity that the Didache is once again brought forth into the light of day as a major, still foundationally relevant source for this greatly important and even urgently needed guidance.

The apostle Paul invariably comes to the forefront of any discussion concerning evangelistic outreach during the several decades following the ascension of Yeshua, and deservedly so. Known throughout the church as the first great evangelist, Paul was not only the author of much of the foundational corpus of Christian theology and doctrine, but he was also enormously successful in sowing this newly codified holy seed in rich, anointed soil, from which came forth a large array of new congregations along the widely spread pathways of his four legendary missionary journeys. It is historically clear that Paul's great harvest contributed mightily to the eventual rise of the Western and Eastern Churches and, thereafter, all of the ecclesiastical progeny that emerged from them over the ensuing centuries into what has become the modern day church.

Even so, as heroically foundational as Paul's evangelical harvest may have been, by no means did he stand alone in laying this God-ordained foundation upon which the future church was to arise. The great things the original twelve apostles who had actually walked with Yeshua did in His name are often overlooked in the shadow of Paul's triumphs. Even so, it is clear that they took His great commission very much to their own hearts and through their extensive travel had already brought a great soul harvest of their own into the kingdom long before Paul departed on his first evangelical journey to Antioch and beyond circa A.D. 46–48.

The fact is, along with the thousands who were embracing Yeshua in Jerusalem (Acts 2:41), by the year 38, only eight years after His ascension and little more than one year after the martyrdom of Stephen, the gospel message had been preached to the entire population on the western side of the Jordan. The apostles and other Jewish believers in the Galilee had also, during this time, evangelized "the region of Damascus," where a thriving church had already been established.[1]

Moreover, there is considerable evidence that the predominately Gentile church had its beginnings even before Yeshua's death on the cross. This was a consequence of His second feeding of the mostly pagan multitude at Tel Hadar circa A.D. 29 (Mark 8:1–21) and the presumed subsequent establishment of the first Gentile Christian church at nearby Hippos (modern day Sussita), a city of the Decapolis.[2]

Take Philip for example, a *mebaqqer* (deacon) of the Mount Zion mother congregation. He, along with many other second-tier evangelists, worked separately from or side by side with the twelve apostles as they responded to the Great Commission by energetically sharing the gospel with both Jews and non-Jews. While Phillip is perhaps best remembered for his evangelical encounter with the Ethiopian eunuch (Acts 8:26–37), this *mebaqqer*-turned-anointed-evangelist was also responsible for the conversion of many other Jews and non-Jews throughout Samaria, Judea, and along the Mediterranean basin east of Jerusalem.[3]

Eusebius speaks of the "vast numbers of the circumcision who by then [the appointment of Justus as third bishop of Jerusalem] believed in Christ."[4] He also points out that the apostles and others were hard at work evangelizing non-Jews in many different locations, well removed from Jerusalem. Eusebius writes:

> Meanwhile, the holy apostles and the disciples of our Savior were scattered over the whole world. Thomas, tradition tells us, was chosen for Parthia,[5] Andrew for Scythia,[6] John for Asia, where he remained until his death at Ephesus. Peter seems to have preached in Pontus, Galatia, Bithynia, Cappadocia,[7] and Asia.... Finally, he came to Rome...[8]

Hence, James and the apostles over whom he presided, who together made up the Council of Jerusalem, were faced with the enormous task of providing instruction to a huge, rapidly emerging new majority of non-Jews who were swelling the ranks and stretching the boundaries of the no longer nascent church.

Consider the depth and the breadth of the enormous challenge laid at the doorstep of the mother congregation on Mount Zion. Until the very moment of their miraculous salvation, these untold thousands of non-Jewish new converts had been uncircumcised, idol worshipping pagans. Now, suddenly, by the power of the Holy Spirit, they had miraculously become born-again participants in an entirely Jewish-based religious infrastructure in which they had absolutely no background or understanding. Moreover, they had no knowledge or understanding of the Torah and the rest of the Tenach, which formed the basis of the salvation in Yeshua with which they had just been divinely blessed. Certainly, when they listened to the gospel, most likely preached to them from the pages of the newly produced first edition of Matthew, they were among those very blessed who were "drawn" by the Father after they had "heard" (John 6:44–45). But then, most likely soon after the local church had been planted, the anointed evangelist from Mount Zion moved on to plow other still-waiting, spiritually starved new ground. And what, if anything, was he able to leave behind?

As previously suggested by Woodard, around A.D. 37 Barnabas and John-Mark traveled widely among the newly planted churches to deliver copies of the first version of the Gospel of Matthew. Praise God for His provision of this Gospel to these many Gentile new believers. But, was this by itself sufficient spiritual food to fully satisfy the enormous appetites of these just-converted pagans?

The teachings of Yeshua in this wonderful first Gospel are drawn almost entirely from the earlier teachings from the Old Covenant. While the Gospel of Matthew, in its some 48 pages, conveys the very essence of the entire Bible, it can only begin to share the full richness and depth of God's Holy Word as it was first given and elaborated in the some 1,423 pages of the 39 books of the Old Testament. Moreover, so very much of ancient Jewish tradition is irrevocably woven into the very fabric of this "new understanding" of The Way and could not be included in even all of the some 500 pages of the relatively succinct New Testament.

Herein we find two serious congenital birth defects that I believe still plague the body of Christ, the church, today. First is the quite understandable conception held by much of the church that the Bible begins in Matthew, not Genesis. Hence, this so-called New Testament church is understood as having replaced Israel, and the Jews are no longer relevant. Second, just as understandably, was the widespread inculcation of long-held pagan traditions, holidays, and practices with which Paul and others later grappled during their follow-up outreaches to the newly planted Gentile congregations. But, this was only part of a bigger problem.

Back on Mount Zion, Peter and Paul had argued passionately regarding to what extent non-Jews would be required to comply with the Torah in order to join their movement. This fundamental question went far beyond the core issues of circumcision of the flesh, compliance with the biblical dietary laws, etc. After a debate before the council, Paul won the day with James on these issues. Thus, new Gentile members were henceforth required to comply with only four things:

> We have therefore sent Judas and Silas, who will also report the same things by word of mouth. For it seemed good to the Holy Spirit, and to us, to lay upon you no greater burden than these necessary things: that you abstain from things offered to idols, from blood, from things strangled, and from sexual immorality. If you keep yourselves from these, you will do well. Farewell.
>
> —Acts 15:27–29

Be that as it may, the simple "farewell" with which these instructions were sealed may have been the end of the immediate open disagreement between Peter and Paul. This was, however, only the beginning of a now well-defined training problem that the council had created for itself. With this "farewell" came an enormous, unprecedented need for The Way to teach their former-pagan brothers in Yeshua the very basics of their newly embraced Jewish-centered faith. Without an understanding of the Torah-centered foundation of their new faith, they could hardly be expected to successfully function within what was for them its complex and entirely foreign list of boundaries and requirements.

It was toward this end, probably soon after it published these quite liberal "entrance requirements" for non-Jewish members, that the Council of Jerusalem wrote and disseminated the Didache, "The Doctrine of the Lord Brought to the Nations by the Twelve Apostles." First mentioned in the list of canon attributed to Hippolytus in A.D. 200, formally canonized in Clement's list in 208, and then again included as canon by Origen in 250, the Didache was not included in the final list of canon in the fifth century that stands today.[9]

Still, I believe that even the most liberal biblical scholar would readily agree that the Didache was a brilliant guidepost for the emerging church. In what surely must have been by God's providence, the apostles managed to include in its sixteen relatively short chapters the very essence and practical application of virtually all of The Way's most important understandings and practices.

The Didache served as the inspired guidepost of the emerging body of Yeshua until the Council of Nicea in 325 and the anti-Semitic councils that followed. It was then, perforce, that The Way itself was quickly replaced by the church. Then, no longer having any acknowledged purpose, the Didache was soon relegated to an obscurity of its own.

In November 2002, Dr. Alan J. P. Garrow, recognizing the importance of the Didache, wrote as his doctoral thesis at Oxford "The Gospel of Matthew's Dependence on the Didache." In it he cited numerous points of contact between the Gospel of Matthew and the Didache, convincingly demonstrating that there is a direct contact between the two works and concluding that Matthew most likely used the Didache as a primary source for his Gospel.

Since, however, Dr. Woodard concludes the Gospel of Matthew came forth in its first edition in A.D. 37, and since other historical sources indicate that the Didache was written and distributed no earlier than A.D. 50, it is likewise reasonable to further suggest that Garrow had a reverse understanding of the relation between these two documents. It now seems clear that the Didache relied very heavily on not only Matthew—instead of vice versa—but also upon the two other synoptics, Mark and especially Luke. Moreover, it can be demonstrated that the Didache also relied upon the then already written Epistles of James, 1 Peter, and 1 John. (See Appendix Two.)

Even more to the point, the Didache contained well-considered additional information for the emerging church regarding its purpose, operation, and understandings that were not necessarily within the purview of these soon-to-be-canonized writings. Perhaps this was why, as history records, The Way distributed a copy of the Didache to each of the new Christian synagogues they visited.[10]

Putting all of this together, we can now reasonably conclude that the Didache can best be described as a highly instructive commentary derived from New Testament Scriptures with heavy dependence upon the Gospels of Matthew and Luke. Further, it was distributed to the churches to supplement the canonized Scriptures that they already had in their keeping.

From its first chapter, the Didache's dependence upon two connected yet distinctly separate sources is both self-evident and striking. First, as earlier noted, much of The Way's theology, doctrine, and worship practice came to them as a direct transfer of earlier parallel holdings and practices of the Essenes at Qumran. Moreover, this transference can be found, as a substantial matter of record, within the vast collection of the Dead Sea Scrolls. Second, as was also earlier noted, there are often direct parallels between the Didache and the teachings of Yeshua as they are set forth in the synoptic Gospels, especially Matthew and Luke. These parallels are frequent, complimentary, and instructive enough to suggest that the Didache is highly dependent upon these and other New Testament Scriptures.

The principal points of contact between the Didache and New Testament writings are detailed in Appendix Two.

What follows is a brief commentary on each of the Didache's sixteen chapters. For your further study, the entire work is presented as Appendix Three.

The Didache: The Lord's Teaching Through the Twelve Apostles to the Nations

Chapter 1: The Two Ways and the First Commandment

The Didache begins with a clear statement of the only two options for how we may live our human lives: we may choose either good or evil. Hence we encounter the doctrine of the "two ways" (light vs. darkness, good vs. evil, etc.) as it is first found in the Dead Sea Scrolls. According to James H. Charlesworth, John 3:16–21 draws its references to light versus darkness in the context of the End of Days from the Qumran Scrolls, specifically from the Rule of the Community, where those who are not the "sons of light" will receive "eternal perdition by the fury of God's vengeful wrath, everlasting terror and endless shame, along with disgrace of annihilation in the fire of murky Hell" (1QS 4:12).[11]

Below are further examples of this Essenic dualism as seen in their scrolls.

> In the hand of the Prince of Lights is the dominion of all the Sons of Righteousness; in The Ways of light they walk. But in the hand of the Angel of Darkness is the dominion of the Sons of Deceit; and in The Ways of darkness they walk.
>
> —1QS 3:20-21

> Until now the spirits of truth and of injustice feud in the heart of man and they walk in wisdom or in folly. In agreement with man's birthright in justice and in truth, so he abhors injustice; and according to his share of the lot of injustice he acts irreverently in it and so abhors the truth. For God has sorted them into equal parts until the appointed end and the new creation.
>
> —1QS 4:23–24

While the synoptic Gospels frequently echo this Essenic dualism, their connectivity is particularly clear between the scrolls and the writings of the apostle John.

> Then Jesus said to them, "A little while longer the light is with you. Walk while you have the light, lest darkness overtake you; he who walks in darkness does not know where he is going. While you have the light, believe in the light, that you may become sons of light." These things Jesus spoke, and departed, and was hidden from them.
>
> —John 12:35–36

The Essenes also transferred to The Way their doctrine of striving to seek godly perfection. Consider the similarity of the message of the two passages below, the first from the Bible and the second from one of the scrolls.

> Therefore you shall be perfect, just as your Father in heaven is perfect.
>
> —Matthew 5:48

> ...in order to seek God with all one's heart and with all one's soul...in order to welcome into the covenant of kindness all those who freely volunteer to carry out God's decrees, so as to be united in the counsel of God and walk in perfection in his sight...
>
> —1QS I 1, 6–8

Chapter 2: The Second Commandment—Grave Sin Forbidden

The Didache includes a strong prohibition against "murdering a child by abortion." This same prohibition is included in the Epistle of Barnabas.

The Didache also includes in this chapter a specific denunciation of male homosexual relations, particularly with minors.

Chapter 3: Other Sins Forbidden

Yeshua's further development of Old Testament imperatives is very evident in the Didache, Chapter 3. For example, He teaches that to think lustfully is to already have committed adultery. (See Matthew 5:28.) Also, He teaches that anger against another person is from the same source as murder and places one in danger of judgment. (See Matthew 5:21–22.)

The Didache's amplification of the basic teachings and commandments of Scripture is especially evident in this excerpt:

> Be neither a filthy talker, nor of lofty eye, for out of all these adulteries are engendered. My child, be not an observer of omens, since it leads to idolatry. Be neither an enchanter, nor an astrologer, nor a purifier, nor be willing to look at these things, for out of all these idolatry is engendered.
>
> —Didache 3:3–4

Chapter 4: Various Precepts

This entire chapter could well be a concise summary of the "way to life" side of the Essene teaching of the "two ways" as it is specifically recorded in a number of references throughout the Dead Sea Scrolls. Moreover, while there are no specific points of contact in this chapter with the Gospel of Matthew, there are thematic and often specific connections between these teachings of the Didache elsewhere within the Scriptures.

Chapter 4 begins with a call for believers to fellowship with those who are like-minded and to work against division in the body.

> My child, remember night and day him who speaks the word of God to you, and honor him as you do the Lord. For wherever the lordly rule is uttered, there is the Lord. And seek out day by day the faces of the saints, in order that you may rest upon their words.
>
> —Didache 4:1–3

This chapter, which maintains the same amplification of Scripture throughout, ends on the same strong note, underscoring the Word with fatherly, authoritative entreaty:

> You shall hate all hypocrisy and everything which is not pleasing to the Lord. Do not in any way forsake the commandments of the Lord; but keep what you have received, neither adding thereto nor taking away therefrom. In the church you shall acknowledge your transgressions, and you shall not come near for your prayer with an evil conscience. This is the way of life.
>
> —Didache 4:12–14

Chapter 5: The Way of Death

This chapter could well be the flip side of Chapter 4, as it presents a concise summary of "the way to death" or the dark side of the Essene doctrine of the "two ways."

This chapter is a microcosm of the forthright, solidly biblical message I am calling for to be restored to the pulpits of the church. This short but powerful chapter follows in its entirety:

> And the way of death is this: First of all it is evil and accursed: murders, adultery, lust, fornication, thefts, idolatries, magic arts, witchcrafts, rape, false witness, hypocrisy, double-heartedness, deceit, haughtiness, depravity, self-will, greediness, filthy talking, jealousy, over-confidence, loftiness, boastfulness; persecutors of the good, hating truth, loving a lie, not knowing a reward for righteousness, not cleaving to good nor to righteous judgment, watching not for that which is good, but for that which is evil; from whom meekness and endurance are far, loving vanities, pursuing revenge, not pitying a poor man, not laboring for the afflicted, not knowing Him Who made them, murderers of children, destroyers of the handiwork of God, turning away from him who is in want, afflicting him who is distressed, advocates of the rich, lawless judges of the poor, utter sinners. Be delivered, children, from all these.

Chapter 6: Against False Teachers and Food Offered to Idols

> See that no one causes you to err from this way of the Teaching, since apart from God it teaches you. For if you are able to bear the entire yoke of the Lord, you will be perfect; but if you are not able to do this, do what you are able. And concerning food, bear what you are able; but against that which is sacrificed to idols be exceedingly careful; for it is the service of dead gods.
>
> —Didache 6:1–3

While there are no direct points of contact between this chapter and the Gospel of Matthew, there are two interesting observations. First, once again the Essenic theme of striving toward godly perfection is repeated. The second interesting point is raised by the Didache's instructions regarding dietary restrictions. The more comprehensive dietary restrictions, namely prohibitions against eating blood and things strangled, which were set forth by the Council of Jerusalem (Acts 15:29) were presumably distributed immediately to the emerging Gentile Christian Church circa A.D. 49, while the Didache was likely distributed at least twenty-five years later. Even so, the Didache only requires its recipients to abstain from things "sacrificed to idols," accompanied by a seeming disclaimer—"do the best that you are able"—regarding any other biblical, expressed, or implied dietary matters.

It seems to me that the Didache is echoing here what Paul wrote circa A.D. 51–57 to the emerging church in Galatia.

> What purpose then does the law serve? It was added because of transgressions, till the Seed should come to whom the promise was made; and it was appointed through angels by the hand of a mediator.
>
> —Galatians 3:19

Yeshua, the promised Seed, had come! He came as and remained a fully Torah-observant Jew. Moreover, He taught what had to have been an almost exclusively Jewish gathering on Mount Ermos:

> Do not think that I came to destroy the Law [Torah, instructions] or the Prophets. I did not come to destroy but to fulfill. For assuredly, I say to you, till heaven and earth pass away, one jot or one tittle will by no means pass from the law [the Torah] till all is fulfilled.
>
> —Matthew 5:17–18

Heaven and earth have not yet passed away, and the "new heaven and new earth" John told us about in Revelation 21:1 have not yet appeared, nor do I believe they will any time soon. The Way understood that this passing away would not occur until the end of Yeshua's one-thousand-year reign on Earth following His second coming (see Chapter 23). God's plan for the redemption of His people, which began in the Garden of Eden, will not be completed until all is fulfilled. This will not occur until the end of Yeshua's millennial reign.

I believe that the dietary restrictions as they are set forth in the Torah still apply to me as a Jew, and I will do my best to observe them; however, Paul was speaking directly to Gentiles in Galatians 3:19. Thus, it seems clear that Gentiles are not specifically required to keep biblical kosher. Even so, I believe they should strive to do so, if for no other reason than for their good health.

Chapter 7: Concerning Baptism

The Way rigorously complied with the baptismal instructions set forth in this chapter of the Didache. Those instructions are, in part, rooted in the initiation practices of the Essenes. Sadly, virtually all of The Way's lovely, deeply meaningful, and elaborate process of initiating new members into their fellowship has been lost to the modern day church and begs restoration.

(The initiation practice that The Way adapted from this Essene foundation is discussed in some detail elsewhere in this current writing.)

Chapter 8: Fasting and Prayer (The Lord's Prayer)

This very important chapter follows in its entirety:

> But let not your fasts be with the hypocrites, for they fast on the second and fifth day of the week. Rather, fast on the fourth day and the Preparation [Friday]. Do not pray like the hypocrites but rather as the Lord commanded in His Gospel, like this: Our Father who art in heaven, hallowed be Thy name. Thy kingdom come. Thy will be done on earth, as it is in heaven. Give us today our daily (needful) bread, and forgive us our debt as we also forgive our debtors. And bring us not into temptation, but deliver us from the evil one (or, evil); for Thine is the power and the glory forever. Pray this three times each day.

Fasting was in integral part of The Way's worship practice and one that has for the most part been lost to the modern day church. All early believers were instructed, as a matter of practice, to fast each Wednesday and Friday and pointedly told not to fast on Mondays and Thursdays, as was the practice of the Pharisees, who were pointed to by The Way in this context as hypocrites.

Prayer, in particular the Lord's Prayer, was centrally important to The Way, who instructed all believers to lift up this special prayer three times each day. This anointed, all-encompassing prayer, given to us by Yeshua Himself, has fallen into almost universal disuse within the Protestant churches, much less its mandated thrice-each-day repetition. The doxology at the end of this prayer, "For thine is the kingdom, and the power, and the glory, for ever; amen," is found in the majority of Greek manuscripts, the Greek Textus Receptus, and Majority Text; and is included in the early English versions, the King James Version and the New King James Version.

The Lord's Prayer is likewise found in several ancient translations, such as some Old Latin manuscripts, the Old Syrian, and some Coptic versions. The Syriac Peshitta from the second or third century reads, "And bring us not into temptation, but deliver us from evil: For Thine is the kingdom, and the power, and the glory, for ever and ever: Amen." It therefore seems clear that the version ending in the doxology was both very early and widespread.

Chapter 9: The Lord's Supper and Chapter 10: Prayer After the Lord's Supper

The Didache teaching on the Lord's Supper is reviewed in some detail in Chapters 4, 5, and 34 of this writing.

The Didache preserves for us the richness of the original liturgical prayers offered by The Way each time they partook of the Lord's Supper and underscores the seminal importance of this sacrament, in that it is meant for only baptized believers. Moreover, the *Didache* speaks to the reality that God provides bread and wine (all food) to all men (the saved and unsaved alike) but that He provides this "spiritual food" only to born-again believers.

> You gavest food and drink to men for enjoyment, that they might give thanks to Thee; but to us You didst freely give spiritual food and drink and life eternal through Thy Servant [Yeshua].
>
> —Didache 10:3

The apostle Matthew writes in his Gospel:

> And as they were eating, Jesus took bread, blessed and broke it, and gave it to the disciples and said, "Take, eat; this is My body." Then He took the cup, and gave thanks, and gave it to them, saying, "Drink from it, all of you. For this is My blood of the new covenant, which is shed for many for the remission of sins.
>
> —Matthew 26:26–28

With respect to the Lord's Supper, there are no direct points of contact between the Gospel of Matthew and the Didache. Yeshua, in the Gospel of Matthew, simply instructs believers to partake of the Lord's Supper. The Didache provides important guidance on the meaning and purpose of this sacrament as well as how it should be celebrated.

There is an important point to be made here that affects the dating of the Didache. The Gospels of Matthew and Mark both put the taking of the bread of the Lord's Supper before the taking of the wine. (See Matthew 26:26–28; Mark 14:22–26.) Moreover, the Gospel of John, although it does not have a Lord's Supper scenario as such, records the words of Yeshua twice putting the bread before the wine with respect to their necessity to achieve eternal life in Him. (See John 6:53–54.) Only the Gospel of Luke places the taking of the wine before the taking of the bread. (See Luke 22:17–19.)

Biblical scholars generally agree that the Didache was an early writing of The Way. However, prior to Dr. Woodard's proposed dating of the Codex W Gospel manuscripts, both their dating and the dating of the Didache could only have been speculative. As earlier noted, Woodard puts the dating of the Gospels as: Matthew (37–67), Mark (60–73), John (67–97), and Luke (74).[12] Thus, based upon the "wine before bread" uniqueness of the Gospel of Luke, it seems reasonable to conclude that the Didache was not completed before 74, the year that, according to Woodard, the Gospel of Luke was completed.

As earlier discussed, given that all but a handful of The Way had dispersed from Jerusalem before the early seventh decade to Pella, the Galilee, Syria, and Egypt, among other locales, I believe it is also reasonable to conclude that the Didache was written in one of these locations, most likely at their largest and most important community in "the region of Damascus."

Danielou calls the Didache "the most venerable surviving document of Jewish Christian (Nazarene Jewish) literature" and agrees with its dating circa A.D. 70. However, he also conjectures that it was most likely further developed in a Syrian community after 70.[13]

Chapter 11: Concerning Teachers, Apostles, and Prophets

(The next two sections provide the text of the Didache, Chapters 11–12. Commentary about these chapters may be found in the section entitled, "Chapter 13: Support of Prophets.")

> Whosoever, therefore, comes and teaches you all these things that have been said before, receive him. But if the teacher himself turns and teaches another doctrine to the destruction of this, hear him not. But if he teaches so as to increase righteousness and the knowledge of the Lord, receive him as the Lord. But concerning the apostles and prophets, act according to the decree of the Gospel. Let every apostle who comes to you be received as the Lord. But he shall not remain more than one day; or two days, if there's a need. But if he remains three days, he is a false prophet. And when the apostle goes away, let him take nothing but bread until he lodges. If he asks for money, he is a false prophet. And every prophet who speaks in the Spirit you shall neither try nor judge; for every sin shall be forgiven, but this sin shall not be forgiven. But not every one who speaks in the Spirit is a prophet; but only if he holds the ways of the Lord. Therefore from their ways shall the false prophet and the prophet be known. And every prophet who orders a meal in the Spirit does not eat it, unless he is indeed a false prophet. And every prophet who teaches the truth, but does not do what he teaches, is a false prophet. And every prophet, proved true, working unto the mystery of the church in the world, yet not teaching others to do what he himself does, shall not be judged among you, for with God he has his judgment; for so did also

> the ancient prophets. But whoever says in the Spirit, Give me money, or something else, you shall not listen to him. But if he tells you to give for others' sake who are in need, let no one judge him.

Chapter 12: Reception of Christians

> But receive everyone who comes in the name of the Lord, and prove and know him afterward; for you shall have understanding right and left. If he who comes is a wayfarer, assist him as far as you are able; but he shall not remain with you more than two or three days, if need be. But if he wants to stay with you, and is an artisan, let him work and eat. But if he has no trade, according to your understanding, see to it that, as a Christian, he shall not live with you idle. But if he wills not to do, he is a Christ-monger. Watch that you keep away from such.

Chapter 13: Support of Prophets

> But every true prophet who wants to live among you is worthy of his support. So also a true teacher is himself worthy, as the workman, of his support. Every first-fruit, therefore, of the products of wine-press and threshing-floor, of oxen and of sheep, you shall take and give to the prophets, for they are your high priests. But if you have no prophet, give it to the poor. If you make a batch of dough, take the first-fruit and give according to the commandment. So also when you open a jar of wine or of oil, take the first-fruit and give it to the prophets; and of money (silver) and clothing and every possession, take the first-fruit, as it may seem good to you, and give according to the commandment.

Nothing seems to have changed much here in Israel with respect to the subjects addressed in the foregoing three chapters of the Didache since the apostles penned them more than two thousand years ago. According to our own personal experience and the testimony of our closest friends, the miniscule and often marginally surviving body of believers in Israel is frequently beset by presumably well-meaning friends and "friends of friends" often several times removed who express their desire to come "minister" here in the Land. The majority of these dear ones, I believe, have indeed been called by God to come and pray for and with us and to otherwise participate in a number of anointed ways in our worship and outreach. These are those who come with a clear mission and sufficient financial resources to see to their own support while they are with us. However, some come with neither clear callings nor adequate self-support. Thus, when their limited funds run out, having no other alternative, they often turn to the already struggling-to-survive body here in the Land to see them through their desperate situations.

Chapter 14: Christian Assembly on the Lord's Day

> But every Lord's day gather yourselves together, and break bread, and give thanksgiving after having confessed your transgressions, that your sacrifice may be pure. But let no one who is at odds with his fellow come together with you, until they be reconciled, that your sacrifice may not be profaned. For this is that which was spoken by the Lord: "In every place and time offer to me a pure sacrifice; for I am a great King, says the Lord, and my name is wonderful among the nations."
>
> —Didache 14:1–3

The Didache, as we have previously suggested, was most likely written and distributed circa 74. At this time *Shabbat*, the biblically ordained Sabbath, had not yet been replaced by "the day of the Sun," which it was much later by the Church Council of Laodicea. Thus, the "Day of the Lord," referred to in other translations as "the Lord's Day" and "the Lord's Own Day," could not in the understanding of The Way have referred to *Shabbat*, which to them was a day set aside for rest rather than for congregational gatherings.

The Way met on the first day of the week, Sunday, which commenced *Shabbat* evening after sunset, which was technically, as determined by Jewish tradition, the moment when the third star became visible in the heavens. Hence, The Way conducted their main gathering of the week at this time in a service known as *Motzei Shabbat,* meaning "farewell to the Sabbath." *Motzei Shabbat* was and remains for some groups today a full congregational worship service centered on the Lord's Supper, which is served from a centrally located table, as it was during the time of The Way.

Chapter 15: Bishops and Deacons; Christian Reproof

> Appoint, therefore, for yourselves, bishops and deacons worthy of the Lord, men meek, and not lovers of money, and truthful and proved; for they also render to you the service of prophets and teachers. Therefore do not despise them, for they are your honored ones, together with the prophets and teachers. And reprove one another, not in anger, but in peace, as you have it in the Gospel. But to anyone that acts amiss against another, let no one speak, nor let him hear anything from you until he repents. But your prayers and alms and all your deeds so do, as you have it in the Gospel of our Lord.

The following table shows the great similarity—if not a dependency relationship—of the Didache 15 and Titus 1:7–9, written by Paul circa 63–65.

DIDACHE 15:1	TITUS 1
"worthy of the Lord"	"blameless…steward of God" (v. 7)
"not lovers of money"	"not greedy for money" (v. 7)
"true who have proven themselves"	"holding fast the faithful word as he has been taught" (v. 9)
"perform the functions of prophets and teachers"	"be able, by sound doctrine, both to exhort and convict" (v. 9)

Chapter 16: Watchfulness; the Coming of the Lord

> Watch for your life's sake. Let not your lamps be quenched, nor your loins unloosed; but be ready, for you know not the hour in which our Lord will come. But come together often, seeking the things which are befitting to your souls: for the whole time of your faith will not profit you, if you are not made perfect in the last time. For in the last days false prophets and corrupters shall be multiplied, and the sheep shall be turned into wolves, and love shall be turned into hate; for when lawlessness increases, they shall hate and persecute and betray one another, and then shall appear the world-deceiver as Son of God, and shall do signs and wonders, and the earth shall be delivered into his hands, and he shall do iniquitous things which have never yet come to pass since the beginning. Then shall the creation of men come into the fire of trial, and many shall be made to stumble and shall perish; but those who endure in their faith shall be saved from under the curse itself. And then shall appear the signs of the truth: first, the sign of an outspreading in heaven, then the sign of the sound of the trumpet. And third, the resurrection of the dead…yet not of all, but as it is said: "The Lord shall come and all His saints with Him." Then shall the world see the Lord coming upon the clouds of heaven.
>
> —Didache 16:1–8

There are many points of contact between the three synoptic Gospels and Chapter 16 of the Didache, as demonstrated in the following table.

DIDACHE 16	MATTHEW	MARK	LUKE
"watch over your life…you do not know the hour" (v. 1)	24:42; 25:13	13:33–37	12:35–40
"multiplied false prophets" (v. 3)	24:11–12	13:22	21:8

DIDACHE 16	MATTHEW	MARK	LUKE
"increase of lawlessness" (v. 4)	24:10	13:12	21:16
"many shall be caused to stumble" (v. 5)	24:10	13:12	21:16
"then shall appear signs in heaven" (v. 6)	24:30	13:26	21:27
"coming upon the clouds of heaven" (v. 8)	24:30	13:26	21:27
"His holy ones with Him on His royal throne" (v. 8)	16:27; 25:31	8:38; 14:62	9:26; 22:69
"evil into eternal punishment, righteous into life eternal" (v. 9)	25:34, 46	9:44	16:26

I find it particularly interesting that there is no mention of a rapture of the righteous in this chapter, elsewhere in the Didache, or in any of the other writings of The Way. (See Chapter 23.)

Part V

The Praise and Worship of The Way

With the offering of the lips I will praise Him according to a statute
engraved forever:
At the head of years and at the turning point of the seasons,
By the completion of the statute of their norm...
Each day having its precept...
One after the other;
From the season for harvest until the summer;
From the season for sowing until the season of grass;
From the seasons for the years until their seven year periods;
At the beginning of their seven year period until the Jubilee.

—DEAD SEA SCROLLS: 4QS MS D FRAG. 4 LINE 3–6

Be filled with the Spirit, speaking to one another in psalms and hymns and spiritual songs, singing and making melody in your heart to the Lord, giving thanks always for all things to God the Father in the name of our Lord Jesus Christ, submitting to one another in the fear of God.

—EPHESIANS 5:18–21

PRAISE AND WORSHIP ARE the very fabric of Jewish expression, woven from a holy thread and set before the Master's throne as a glorious carpet of unbounded joy and unceasing adoration. Blessed be His name.

Every Jew, born again or not, even the least reverent among us, has from time to time cried out the holy words of the *Sh'ma,* the very essence of what it is to be Jewish:

Hear, O Israel: The LORD our God, the LORD is one! You shall love the LORD your God with all your heart, with all your soul, and with all your strength.

—DEUTERONOMY 6:4–5

While He clearly commanded us to love Him completely and without ceasing, by His grace, through David, the Lord our God also showed us how to do so.

Oh, worship the LORD in the beauty of holiness!

—PSALM 96:9

Let Israel rejoice in their Maker;
Let the children of Zion be joyful in their King.

> Let them praise His name with the dance;
> Let them sing praises to Him with the timbrel and harp.
> For the LORD takes pleasure in His people;
> He will beautify the humble with salvation.
>
> —PSALM 149:2–4

How precious it is that the Lord our God equipped His people to worship Him in spirit and in truth, to lift up His holy Name in praise, song, and dance. Is it any wonder that *praise* appears in the Old Testament 245 times and *worship* 149 times?

What a joy it is for me each year on Simchat Torah, the last day of the Feast of Tabernacles, to sit in the perch of my office looking out over the streets of the Orthodox section of this ancient city. It is on that day that I rejoice as I behold the totally enraptured men, women, and children nearly bursting with joy as they dance about with Torah scrolls clutched to their breasts, singing out their praises to the Lord our God, who gave them this His Holy Word for yet another year. How much more, I then reflect, should we believers—Jewish and Gentile alike—sing out our joy to the Lord our God, who has given us eternal life through Him, the Living Word!

While Simchat Torah may be one of the annual high points of praise and worship for modern day Jews, such praise and worship of the Lord our God has been at the very center of all forms of Jewish expression from its very beginning. Immediately after he departed from the ark, Noah built an altar and worshiped God. (See Genesis 8:20.) Abraham worshiped the Lord our God as he obediently prepared to sacrifice Isaac, his only son. (See Genesis 22:5.) The host of angels and the shepherds who beheld Yeshua at His birth praised the Lord our God for the amazing things He had done. (See Luke 2:8–13.) After Yeshua's resurrection, when He appeared among His disciples in the Upper Room, they were filled with amazement and joy. Then, when He ascended into heaven, they worshipped Him with great joy (Luke 24:36–52).

This joyful post-Ascension celebration was by no means the beginning of praise and worship of our Messiah, Yeshua. The Essenes understood and wrote about His imminent coming. They worshipped Him whom they understood to be triune in nature[1] through an enormous body of beautiful, divinely inspired psalms, hymns, and odes, which they recorded in their scrolls as a precious legacy.

Sadly, much of this remarkable inheritance of ancient praise and worship has been long forgotten by the church, whose most recent generations have found new avenues of expression in electronically amplified outpourings of computer-enhanced keyboards, electric guitars, and acoustic drum sets. Just as sadly, the musical accompaniment to this wonderful collection of the Essenes and, later, of The Way's praise and worship did not survive the multiple millennia that separate them from our modern day worship teams.

Not one single song sheet, recognizable or not, has come down to us from traditional Judaism, the Essenes, or The Way to enable us to use or fully appreciate this lyrical treasure-hoard in its original form. Written musical notation was not introduced until A.D. 524 and did not come into its now recognizable form as an eight-note modern day scale until after 1000,[2] and Thomas Edison would not invent the cylinder phonograph for another nearly two thousand years. Moreover, electronic recording—much less man's mastery over electricity itself—had yet to be conceived.

While The Way were heirs to this massive collection of Old Testament oriented Essene praise and worship writings, which continued to be highly relevant in both content and timeliness, they also created an impressive new collection of praise and worship songs of their own, known as the Odes of Solomon. I feel certain that these lovely and obviously anointed Odes were inspired by The Way's firsthand and secondhand association with and direct knowledge of the life and teachings of Yeshua.

One might reasonably compare the relationship of the Qumran Psalter and the Odes of Solomon to that of the old hymns of the church and modern day praise and worship songs. In each of these comparisons, the former provides a solid foundation for the latter while continuing to stand up well on its own merit, relevance, and importance.

Speaking to the relationship between the *Hodayoth* and the Odes of Solomon, James H. Charlesworth suggests that those who composed the Odes were probably influenced by the images and thoughts contained in the Dead Sea Scrolls, especially the *Hodayoth*.[3]

Chapter 28
The Essene Psalter of Old Testament and Apocryphal Psalms

The canonized Book of Psalms is actually a collection of collections of lesser psalters, the beginnings of which can be traced back to the time of King Solomon (circa 1020 B.C.). Within its holy pages are 150 sacred songs that were regularly offered up in praise and worship with and without the accompaniment of ancient musical instruments. Speaking of the schools of the prophets, which came into prominence during the time of the prophet Samuel (circa 930 B.C.), Arthur Penrhyn Stanley, dean of Westminster, wrote:

> Whatever be the precise meaning of the peculiar word, which now came first into use as the designation of these companies, it is evident that their immediate mission consisted in uttering religious hymns or songs, accompanied by musical instruments, psaltery, tabret, pipe, and harp, and cymbals. In them, as in the few solitary instances of their predecessors, the characteristic element was that the silent seer of visions found an articulate voice, gushing forth in a rhythmical flow, which at once riveted the attention of the hearer.[1]

In earlier chapters I have pointed to the Essenes as the principal originators of the theology, doctrine, and other religious aspects from which Christianity, as a fulfillment of Judaism, arose as the very foundation of the modern day church. However, we must not forget that these same Essenes were first a sect comprised of very ascetic, Torah-centric, orthodox Jews. Indeed, those who fled from Jerusalem to the monastic caves of Qumran were even more rigorously puristic in every sense than the Pharisees and Sadducees they left behind, who remained content to continue their worship in the temple, even though their Essene brothers considered it to be polluted.

Is it, then, any wonder that the Dead Sea Scrolls at one time contained all 150 of the psalms that also found their way into the psalter of the Old Testament? Moreover, even beyond the 150 canonized psalms of the Old Testament, the Essenes included in their Qumran Psalter additional psalms that were known by traditional Judaism of the time as apocryphal and still other psalms that were previously unknown and did not resurface until modern times with the discovery of the Dead Sea Scrolls.

But there was even more than all of this in the Essenes' evidently enormous repertoire of sacred praise and worship material. In addition to their already noted psalms, the apparently steadfast worshiping community of Qumran and, presumably, the widely scattered communities of their diaspora in the Galilee and beyond could also call upon a large, separate collection of *Hodayoth* (Hymns of Thanksgiving), which is the subject of the next chapter.

The Canonized Psalms in the Dead Sea Scrolls

The psalms are the most highly represented biblical writings within the massive collection of almost nine hundred Dead Sea Scroll manuscripts that have been recovered from eight different locations in and near Qumran. Among the collection are forty psalm scrolls or other scrolls that include psalms.

Contained within these 40 psalm and psalm-containing scrolls are 126 at least partially preserved psalms from the canonized psalter, which is made up of 150 psalms. The missing 24 psalms, while mentioned elsewhere as having once been a part of the collection, no longer survive and are believed to have been turned to dust or buried in mudslides over the ensuing centuries. In addition to these canonized psalms, there are another at least fifteen hitherto known but not widely published apocryphal psalms distributed among four scrolls found in Caves Four and Eleven.[2]

Underscoring the presumption that the Essenes sung these psalms as a mainstay of their regular praise and worship, at least ten of the forty psalms scrolls are scribed stichometrically, i.e., they are written as prose text in lines of often slightly differing lengths that correspond to units of sense and indicate phrasal rhythms, showing that they were written to be sung or read as a poem.

The Apocryphal Psalms in the Dead Sea Scrolls

I must confess my own complete ignorance of the existence of any apocryphal psalms before I "discovered" them during the course of my research for this current writing. Given that most readers will likely share my own previous unfamiliarity with these apocryphal writings and because of the beauty and applicability of these particular works as potential additions to our contemporary bodies of praise and worship, I would like to share two of these six compositions. While these lovely works have previously been scarcely known to the modern day church, they, like so many other Essene writings, most likely were known to The Way.

A Hallelujah of David, Son of Jesse

Smaller was I than my brothers and the youngest of the sons of my father,
so he made me shepherd of his flock and ruler over his kids.
My hands have made an instrument and my fingers a lyre; and so have
I rendered glory to the Lord, thought I, within my soul.
The mountains do not witness to Him, nor do the hills proclaim; the trees
have cherished my words and the flock my works.
For who can proclaim and who can bespeak and who can recount the
deeds of the Lord? Everything has God seen, everything has He
heard and He has heeded.
He sent His prophet to anoint me, Samuel to make me great; my brothers
went out to meet him, handsome of figure and appearance.
Though they were tall of stature and handsome by their hair, the Lord
God chose them not.
But He sent and took me from behind the flock and anointed me with
holy
oil, and He made me leader of His people and ruler over the sons of
His covenant.[3]

Untitled

O Lord, I called unto Thee, give heed to me.
I spread forth my palms towards Thy Holy dwelling.
Incline Thy ear and grant me my plea,
And my request withhold not from me.
Edify my soul and do not cast it down,
And abandon it not in the presence of the wicked.
May the Judge of Truth remove from me the rewards of evil.
O Lord, judge me not according to my sins; for no man living is righteous
Before Thee.
Grant me understanding, O Lord, in Thy law and teach me Thine
ordinances.
That many may hear of Thy deeds and peoples may honor Thy glory.
Remember me and forget me not, and lead me not into situations too hard
for me.

The sins of my youth cast far from me, and may my transgressions not be
remembered against me.
Purify me, O Lord, from the evil scourge and let it not turn again upon
me.
Dry up its roots from me, and let its leaves not flourish within me.
Thou art my glory, O Lord.
Therefore is my request fulfilled before Thee.
To whom may I cry and He would grant it me?
And the sons of man... what more can their power do?
My trust, O Lord, is before Thee.
I cried "O Lord," and He answered me, and He healed my broken heart.
I slumbered and slept, I dreamt; indeed I woke.[4]

Previously Unknown Apocryphal Psalms in the Dead Sea Scrolls

Ten previously unknown psalms of the Essenes, having been literally buried in the caves of Qumran for nearly two centuries, again saw the light of day with the relatively recent discovery and translation of the Dead Sea Scrolls. The theological soundness, continued timeliness, and general loveliness of these writings would seem to underscore the reasonableness of once again reopening the canonized psalter for their potential inclusion.

Four samplings of these very special, long-buried psalms, which seem especially adaptable for contemporary use, are presented as follows.

Against Demons

(Of David. Concerning the words of a spell in the name of YHWH.)

Call on the heavens at any time.
When Belial comes upon you, you shall say to him:
Who are you accursed amongst men and amongst the seed of the Holy
ones?
Your face is a face of futility, and your horns are horns of a wretch.
You are darkness and not light, sin and not justice.
Against you [is] the Chief of the Army.
YHWH will shut you in the deepest Sheol.
He will shut the two bronze gates through which no light penetrates.
On you there shall not shine the light of the sun, which rises upon the just
man to illuminate his face.
You shall say to him: Is there not perhaps an angel with the just man,
to go to the judgment when Satan mistreats him?

And he will be freed from darkness by the Spirit of Truth,
because justice is with him to uphold him at the judgment.[5]

Catena

O give thanks to the LORD for he is good; for His steadfast love endures for ever!
Hark, glad songs of victory in the tents of the righteous: "The right hand of the LORD does valiantly.
The right hand of the LORD is exalted, the right hand of the LORD has wrought strength!"
It is better to trust in the Lord than to put confidence in man.
It is better to take refuge in the Lord than to put confidence in princes.
It is better to trust in the Lord than to put confidence in a thousand people.
O give thanks to the LORD for He is good; for His steadfast love endures
for ever! Praise the LORD![6]

David's Compositions

And David, the son of Jesse, was wise, and a light like the light of the sun,
and literate, and discerning in all his ways before God and men.
And the Lord gave him a discerning and enlightened spirit.
And he wrote 3,600 psalms; and songs to sing before the altar over the whole-burnt
perpetual offering every day, for all the days of the year, 364;
and for the offering of the Sabbaths, 52 songs;
and for the offering of the New Moons,
and for all the Solemn Assemblies and for the Day of Atonement, 30 songs.
And all the songs that he spoke were 446, and songs
for making music over the stricken, 4.
And the total was 4,050.
All these he composed through prophecy which was given him from
Before the Most High.[7]

Hymn to the Creator

Great and holy is the LORD, the holiest of the holy ones for every generation.
Majesty precedes him and following him is the rush of many waters.
Grace and truth surround his presence; truth and justice and righteousness are the foundation of his throne.

Separating light from deep darkness, he established the dawn by the knowledge of his mind.
When all his angels had witnessed it they sang aloud; for he showed them
what they had not known:
Crowning the hills with fruit, good food for every living being.
Blessed be he who makes the earth by his power, establishing the world in his wisdom.
In his understanding he stretched out the heavens, and brought forth wind from his storehouses.
He made lightning for the rain, and caused mist to rise from the end of the earth.[8]

Chapter 29
The *Hodayoth* (Hymns of Thanksgiving)

The Thanksgiving Hymns, called the *Hodayoth,* are recorded on one of seven major scrolls found in Cave One. The Essenes' ancient hymns are meticulously scribed using an unusually large format that points out the normative and revered position they held in the community. They are highly emotive, conceptually rich, steeped in Scripture, and are closely related to the writings of the Qumran Psalter, with a particular emphasis on intermittingly expressing the deepest thoughts and ideas of their author.[1]

These hymns are greatly different in form from their psalms. While the psalms are presented in a regular form and meter, with consistent length of lines so as to suggest that they were easily accompanied by music and sung, the structure and form of the hymns are consistently irregular, suggesting that they might have been recited, perhaps with a musical background. This irregular structure can be seen in the following example.

> I give you thanks, Lord,
> for your eye keeps watch over me.
> You have freed me from the zeal of the sowers of deceit.
> From the congregation of the interpreters of flattering things.
> You have freed the life of the poor person
> which they thought to finish off,
> pouring out his blood while he was at your service.
> But they did not know that my steps come from You.
> Then to Him was given dominion and glory and a kingdom,
> That all peoples, nations, and languages should serve Him.
> His dominion is an everlasting dominion,
> Which shall not pass away,
> And His kingdom the one
> Which shall not be destroyed.
> They have put me as a mockery and a reproof
> in the mount of all the interpreters of trickery.

> But you, O God, have freed the soul of the poor and needy
> from the hand of someone stronger than him;
> from the hand of the powerful you have saved my soul.[2]

It can be reasonably surmised that these hymns were composed during the lifetime of "the teacher of righteousness," the revered leader of the Essenes, whose true identity has long been the subject of scholarly debate. For example, the teacher has been variously identified as a prototype of Yeshua, James the Just, or, more reasonably, as a special, ordained priest of Zadok.

In any event, the scrolls speak of the origins of the sect that wrote them as being 390 years after the exile, and then after 20 years of "groping" blindly for the way, "God... raised for them a Teacher of Righteousness to guide them in the way of His heart."[3] The teacher claimed to have the proper understanding of the Torah since he was the anointed one of God who had been called to reveal to the community "the hidden things in which Israel had gone astray"[4] and also the one "to whom God made known all the mysteries of the words of his servants the prophets."[5]

Is it not surprising, therefore, that there is considerable scholarly support that the teacher himself was the author of the Hymns of Thanksgiving. Many have discerned in these hymns something significantly personal about the life and times of the teacher.[6] Some scholars look to the following hymn as an autobiographical writing of the teacher.

> And I, when I lean on you, I remain resolute and rise above those who scorn me and my hands succeed against all those who mock me; for they do not value me, even though you exhibit your power in me and reveal yourself in me through Your strength to enlighten them.[7]

The teacher seems to use the hymns as a platform from which to sing out the sect's foundational theological understandings. For example, He clearly proclaims their holding of double predestination[8] in the following:

> And I, the Instructor, have known you, my God,
> through the Spirit which you gave in me,
> and I have listened loyally to your wonderful secret
> through your Holy Spirit.[9]

> I know that the impulse of every spirit is in your hand,
> and all its tasks you have established even before creating him.
> You have fashioned the spirit and organized its task before the centuries.[10]

The hymns also encompass a collective sense of Essenic eschatology that, at the End of Days, culminates in a universal conflagration that renews the universe. The hymns show the understanding that this explosive conflagration in the deepest Sheol is linked to God's pardon and purification of the faithful, to whom He bequeaths all of the glory of Adam in an abundance of days.[11]

> And I know that there is hope for someone you fashioned out of clay
> to be an everlasting community.
> The corrupt spirit you have purified from the great sin [the sin of Adam] so that he can take his place with the host of the holy ones,
> and can enter into communion with the congregation of the sons of heaven.
> You cast eternal destiny for man with the spirits of knowledge,
> so that he praises your name together in celebration,
> and tells of your wonders before all of your works.
> And I a creature of clay, what am I?
> Mixed with water, with whom shall I be counted?
> What is my strength?
> For I find myself at the boundary of wickedness and with those doomed by lot.
> The soul of the poor person lived amongst great turmoil,
> and the calamities of hardship are with my footsteps.
> When the traps of the pit open all the snares of wickedness are spread
> and the nets of the doomed are upon the surface of the sea.
> When all the arrows of the pit fly without return
> they hit without hope.[12]

As I wrote at length in my earlier book, *Full Circle*, atonement in the shed blood of their anticipated Messiah was an underlying theme of Essenic theology that was immediately fulfilled in the appearance, sacrificial death, and resurrection of Yeshua, as these wondrous events were witnessed firsthand by the founding members of The Way.[13]

It isn't at all surprising that the Thanksgiving Hymns are loaded with outpourings of praise for this as yet unfulfilled but anticipated atonement.

> I said, for my sin I have been barred from your covenants.
> But when I remembered the strength of your hand and the abundance of your compassion
> I remained resolute and stood up; my spirit kept firmly in place in the face of my distress.

> For you have supported me by your kindness and by your abundant
> compassion.
> Because you atone for sin and cleanse man of his fault through your
> justice.[14]
>
> You do not take gifts for evil deeds;
> or accept a bribe for wicked acts.
> For you are God of truth
> and you destroy all sin.[15]
>
> You have purified your servant from all sins
> by the abundance of your compassion,
> as you said through the hand of Moses,
> forgiving rebellion, iniquity, sin,
> atoning for failings and disloyalty.[16]

Finally, the principal underpinning of all Christian theology, salvation by faith through grace, was written in the pages of the hymns and from there migrated to Mount Zion. From thence it has traveled over the centuries to the lips of every born-again believer in Yeshua, who in a mighty eternal chorus join the heavenly hosts echoing in song the praises of their forefathers at Qumran.

> I know that there is hope, thanks to your kindness, and trust in the greatness of your strength. For none is just in your judgment, or innocent at your trial. Only by your grace is man justified, and by the abundance of your compassion is he purified.[17]

Chapter 30
The Odes of Solomon

One of the great highlights of my walk of many years with Yeshua was the Sunday morning in the late 1980s when Donna and I had the wonderful blessing of meeting Father Dennis Bennett, founder of the Charismatic Renewal of the 1960s, just before he was about to begin a service in an Episcopal church in a suburb of Seattle. I was almost overcome with emotion when we approached this great man of God at the altar and had the opportunity to thank him for the profound influence he had on our lives: we had been baptized with the Holy Spirit after having read his several books on this central subject of his ministry. When not too long after we had met I heard the news that Father Bennett had gone to his heavenly reward, I was at first deeply saddened as I fondly remembered that very special moment at the altar when he had placed his arms around the two of us and blessed us in the name of Yeshua.

Shortly after Father Bennett's funeral in St. Mark's Episcopal Cathedral, which we were unable to attend, Rita, his widow, sent us a video of the event that we will always treasure. The video opens with a sweeping view inside the dark and cold-looking old sanctuary. The gut-wrenching sadness of the setting was exacerbated by the depressing strains of an ancient funeral dirge pouring out its sonorous gloom from the mammoth pipe organ that occupied the cathedral's entire back wall. My heart sank as the camera swept about the darkened interior, showing seemingly countless utterly silent mourners bowing down in row after row of full-to-overflowing wooden pews before it finally settled upon the coffin in its central place in front of the altar.

Thanks be to God, the utter despair of these opening moments was abruptly broken when the camera's view shifted to a pink Cadillac limousine as it delivered Rita and other family members and friends to the stoic old cathedral's main entrance. Rita was the first to emerge. She was wearing a lovely, brightly colored dress set off by a large Hawaiian floral lei. She was smiling joyfully, waving, greeting everyone as she and the rest of her similarly attired and florally adorned party entered the cathedral and proceeded toward their reserved place in the front pew.

As they did so, as if on cue, the dirge abruptly ceased, and without missing a beat the organist broke forth in a thrilling, modern praise song. In immediate response, the entire assemblage of mourners jumped to their feet, threw their hands into the air, and joined together in a spontaneous, nearly overwhelming, Holy Spirit-filled outpouring that in an instant transformed the entire cathedral and its proceedings from a time of horrific darkness and despair into a highly anointed, joyful celebration. This was Dennis Bennett's homecoming!

Some might reasonably wonder how and by what spiritual catalyst St. Mark's Cathedral had been so spontaneously and miraculously transformed that morning from a place of darkness to a pavilion of light. Surely, at least most of those who filled the overflowing pews were born-again believers who knew the gospel message of salvation and understood that their beloved Father Bennett was now with the Lord. Moreover, we can also reasonably conjecture that Johann Sebastian Bach, who had written the funeral dirge, and the brilliant organist who had rendered it were both Christians.

The Lord our God greatly used Dennis Bennett to renew and ignite the fire of His Holy Spirit throughout much of the worldwide church, where it had lain dormant for nearly two thousand years. It was this same Holy Spirit fire that had so amazingly touched legions of Christians through Father Bennett's ministry that also had, so appropriately, transformed St. Mark's Cathedral from the agony of an ending to the resounding joy of a new and glorious beginning.

The psalms of the Old Testament are adored by us all, Jews and Christians alike. They are filled with anointed praise of our heavenly Father and are overflowing with prophetic assurance of a salvational Messiah who was yet to come. Similarly, the psalms and hymns of the Essenes, which they added to this body of ancient praise, echoed the same messianic expectation of the canonized psalter. The Essenes, however, well understood what the Pharisees had altogether missed. The scribes of Qumran recorded their clear understanding of the soon-coming Messiah's divine nature and His atoning, salvational purpose.

St. Mark's Cathedral was filled with gloom that morning before the outpouring of the Holy Spirit enabled a spontaneous, joyful worship of Yeshua. In much the same way, though the Lord God of Israel was manifest in the psalms and hymns as they were offered up by the Pharisees in their first-century synagogues, their praise was incomplete. Moreover, He was also present in this same way in the psalms and hymns offered up by the Essenes at Qumran and in their congregational gatherings throughout their diaspora in the Galilee, Syria, and beyond; but, as at the outset of Father Bennett's funeral, the worship experience was spiritually incomplete.

It isn't that the Holy Spirit wasn't present with the Pharisees; it was simply that they recognized only the Father, who they understood to be a one-member, absolutely indivisible Godhead. Likewise, it isn't that the Essenes didn't understand the triune nature of God; they wrote about its members both separately and collectively in their scrolls. Quite simply, Yeshua had not yet appeared among them, and the outpouring of the Holy Spirit at Pentecost was also yet to come.

Therefore, it seems reasonable to liken the deeply unsatisfying funeral dirge that preceded Rita Bennett's entry into St. Mark's Cathedral that morning to the traditional psalms and hymns that preceded the outpouring of the Holy Spirit at Pentecost. In much the same way, the spontaneous outpouring of joyful praise that burst forth when Rita entered the cathedral can be well likened to the Odes of Solomon.

The Odes are a highly anointed, Holy Spirit-filled body of praise songs that were most likely written by a single member of The Way circa 70 in the "region of Damascus" after the dispersion from Mount Zion. By His grace, a collection of forty-one of these anointed, ancient praise songs have survived the ravages of time. While they were probably originally written in Aramaic, the surviving collection was scribed in Syriac.[1]

The rich Jewish heritage of the Odes' single poet/composer can be seen throughout his compositions, which reflect a clear influence of Jewish temple worship in their words, cadences, and imagery. However, the title, the "Odes of Solomon," is pseudepigraphic and does not in any material way connect the work to King Solomon. The Odes were most likely written by a Jewish believer who would have been familiar, at least to some extent, with the 1,005 songs attributed to King Solomon, who continued the anointed praise-song writing of his father David. (See 1 Kings 4:32.) It thus seems reasonable to conclude that this unknown Jewish believer was, like David and Solomon, anointed by the Holy Spirit to further continue the tradition by writing the first body of songs, the Odes of Solomon, in recognition, praise, and worship of the newly revealed Messiah, Yeshua.

The Odes were included throughout early church history in a wide variety of extra-biblical writings. Even so, despite their central importance to early believers, they, like the vast majority of the other apocryphal writings of The Way, eventually slipped into obscurity, only to be rediscovered in 1909 by a

Quaker scholar who, while cleaning out his study, came upon a dusty manuscript that contained the long-lost treasure.[2]

The Odes of Solomon exude the Holy Spirit-fired, joyful thanksgiving and praise that set apart the early Jewish believers of The Way. Individually and collectively as a body of praise, the Odes reflect the style and substance of the worship and praise of the just-emerging Eastern Church, which unlike most of the Western Church even unto this day, still clings relatively close to its Semitic rooting in The Way.

There is convincing evidence that the Odes of Solomon were being used as a body of praise and worship songs as early as A.D. 111 by a group of believers just north of Galatia in the province of Pontus/Bithynia, which is now a part of northern Turkey, bordering the Black Sea.

Pliny the Younger was governor of Pontus/Bithynia from 111–113. He was very close to the emperor, Trajan, who had appointed him, and he exchanged a series of letters with his mentor, seeking counsel on how to deal with a host of what were to him new and challenging issues. Not the least of these issues was Pliny's perplexity regarding how he should deal with Christians, whom he had just encountered for the first time. He wrote to Trajan:

> It is my practice, my lord, to refer to you all matters concerning which I am in doubt. For who can better give guidance to my hesitation or inform my ignorance? I have never participated in trials of Christians. I therefore do not know what offenses it is the practice to punish or investigate, and to what extent. And I have been not a little hesitant as to whether there should be any distinction on account of age or no difference between the very young and the more mature; whether pardon is to be granted for repentance, or, if a man has once been a Christian, it does him no good to have ceased to be one; whether the name itself, even without offenses, or only the offenses associated with the name are to be punished.
>
> Meanwhile, in the case of those who were denounced to me as Christians, I have observed the following procedure: I interrogated these as to whether they were Christians; those who confessed I interrogated a second and a third time, threatening them with punishment; those who persisted I ordered executed. For I had no doubt that, whatever the nature of their creed, stubbornness and inflexible obstinacy surely deserve to be punished. There were others possessed of the same folly; but because they were Roman citizens, I signed an order for them to be transferred to Rome.
>
> Soon accusations spread, as usually happens, because of the proceedings going on, and several incidents occurred. An anonymous document was published containing the names of many persons. Those who denied

that they were or had been Christians, when they invoked the gods in words dictated by me, offered prayer with incense and wine to your image, which I had ordered to be brought for this purpose together with statues of the gods, and moreover cursed Christ—none of which those who are really Christians, it is said, can be forced to do—these I thought should be discharged. Others named by the informer declared that they were Christians, but then denied it, asserting that they had been but had ceased to be, some three years before, others many years, some as much as twenty-five years. They all worshipped your image and the statues of the gods, and cursed Christ.

They asserted, however, that the sum and substance of their fault or error had been that they were accustomed to meet on a fixed day before dawn [*Motzei Shabbat*] and sing responsively a hymn to Christ as to a god, and to bind themselves by oath, not to some crime, but not to commit fraud, theft, or adultery, not falsify their trust, nor to refuse to return a trust when called upon to do so. When this was over, it was their custom to depart and to assemble again to partake of food—but ordinary and innocent food. Even this, they affirmed, they had ceased to do after my edict by which, in accordance with your instructions, I had forbidden political associations. Accordingly, I judged it all the more necessary to find out what the truth was by torturing two female slaves who were called deaconesses. But I discovered nothing else but depraved, excessive superstition.

I therefore postponed the investigation and hastened to consult you. For the matter seemed to me to warrant consulting you, especially because of the number involved. For many persons of every age, every rank, and also of both sexes are and will be endangered. For the contagion of this superstition has spread not only to the cities but also to the villages and farms. But it seems possible to check and cure it. It is certainly quite clear that the temples, which had been almost deserted, have begun to be frequented, that the established religious rites, long neglected, are being resumed, and that from everywhere sacrificial animals are coming, for which until now very few purchasers could be found. Hence it is easy to imagine what a multitude of people can be reformed if an opportunity for repentance is afforded.[3]

Emperor Trajan responded to Pliny with the following:

You observed proper procedure, my dear Pliny, in sifting the cases of those who had been denounced to you as Christians. For it is not possible to lay down any general rule to serve as a kind of fixed standard. They are not to be sought out; if they are denounced and proved guilty, they

> are to be punished, with this reservation, that whoever denies that he is a Christian and really proves it—that is, by worshiping our gods—even though he was under suspicion in the past, shall obtain pardon through repentance. But anonymously posted accusations ought to have no place in any prosecution. For this is both a dangerous kind of precedent and out of keeping with the spirit of our age.[4]

To summarize the historical gems revealed in this ancient exchange of letters:

- Believers in Yeshua, most likely all or most of whom were Gentiles, were meeting on *Motzei Shabbat*.
- They were meeting in Pontus/Bithynia, an area just north of Galatia where Paul had evangelized during his second missionary journey (A.D. 48–51) but had been stopped by the Holy Spirit from proceeding further north into this area. (See Acts 16:6–8.) Even so, in the ensuing sixty or so years, the gospel had spread north, and this congregation that so perplexed Pliny had been formed and was in full swing.
- From Pliny's testimony we learn that their Christology was orthodox in that they worshiped Yeshua as God, hence they were most likely a continuing part of or addition to the Diaspora of The Way that was finalized circa the mid seventh decade.
- We learn further from Pliny that they sang hymns to Yeshua "responsively."

The form of praise and worship singing in the early church was antiphonal, or what is commonly known as call-and-response; i.e., to use Pliny's description, they were sung "responsively." The Odes of Solomon were written in this antiphonal format.[5] It thus seems quite probable that in his description to Trajan, Pliny was referring to a very early rendition of the Odes of Solomon that he had heard offered up by this highly persecuted, grafted-in Gentile Christian congregation of The Way.

Interestingly, as we have seen earlier, some of the key writings of The Way, principally The Shepherd of Hermas and the Epistle of Barnabas, although not included in the final list of Canon, did appear in several earlier lists. One might reasonably ask why the Odes of Solomon, arguably at least as important as the Shepherd and Barnabas, were totally ignored through the many iterations of the Canon's development.

The answer, it seems to me, is quite apparent. The Odes of Solomon were all about the fire-filled ministry of the Holy Spirit. They were most likely written by a former Essene who was baptized with the Holy Spirit as the third part of his personal initiation into the fellowship of The Way. Moreover, the Odes were the principal body of praise and worship songs used by legions of born-again, Spirit-filled Jewish believers of The Way until the movement finally faded into obscurity in the fifth century. There is no compelling evidence that baptism in the Holy Spirit, as part of a sacramental initiation into the body of Christ, was carried over into the nascent Gentile Christian Church. Thus, this aspect of The Way's belief and worship systems presumably lay dormant in the hills of Syria until 1901—cited by most historians as the beginning of the Pentecostal movement—when Charles Parham, in a respected institutional setting in Topeka, Kansas, reintroduced baptism in the Holy Spirit and speaking in tongues.[6]

Subsequently, the Pentecostal churches emerged as the fastest growing branch of Christianity, continuing to flourish even now as the top liberal denominations precipitously continue to decline.[7]

Then, on a Sunday morning in 1959, Dennis Bennett announced to his congregation in Van Nuys, California, that he had been baptized with the Holy Spirit and had spoken in tongues. Thus began the world-wide Charismatic Renewal that restored the full ministry of the Holy Spirit to the mainline Christian Church.[8]

With the above historical setting as background, just weeks ago, when I was preparing the first draft of this chapter, I wrote, "I...earnestly pray and expect that the Lord our God will hopefully soon commission some modern day composers to resurrect or recreate this precious, long-lost legacy of the Essenes and The Way. In my spirit I can hear this ancient treasure of praise and worship crying out for our examination, restoration, and adaptation."

God is so good! Prior to this writing I had no way of knowing that He had already called forth John Schreiner and Eddy Duham, both of them brilliant composers, to this task just about the time He first called me to write this book. Then, most recently, the Lord led me to the Web site of The Odes Project,[9] where I made this incredible discovery. As I played the short samples of these reconstructed Odes, their incredible anointing fell upon me in a mighty way, and I greatly rejoiced in what the Lord had done and for what He is doing in restoring this wonderful first-century body of praise and worship to the modern day church. I immediately tried to order the two-CD collection of the twenty-eight Odes that have so far been beautifully reconstructed, orchestrated, and performed. To my great disappointment I found that The Odes Project itself does not ship outside North America. Never mind; the Lord, in His grace, immediately led me to another site, where not only much larger samples of the twenty-eight Odes are posted, but the CDs are also available to ship to Israel.[10] I stayed up most of the night basking in these amazingly anointed works.

The Lord has done a mighty work here. These reconstructed Odes were the missing link in the underlying calling of this book, *The Ways of The Way*. I am beyond thrilled to have found them and most pleased to highly recommend them to all who are seeking to return to the understandings and worship practices of the very first Jewish believers who embraced Yeshua on Mount Zion and beyond.

We have already begun to incorporate the Odes into the praise and worship of our home congregation here in Tiberias, where all have agreed that they are a highly anointed gift from the Lord.

By way of example, following are the original English-translation forms of four selected Odes of Solomon that have been reconstructed and are among the twenty-eight available at either of the two above-noted sources.

Ode 3

...I am putting on the love of the Lord.
And His members are with Him, and I am dependent on them; and He loves me.
For I should not have known how to love the Lord, if He had not continuously loved me.
Who is able to distinguish love, except him who is loved?
I love the Beloved and I myself love Him, and where His rest is, there also am I.
And I shall be no stranger, because there is no jealousy with the Lord Most High and Merciful.
I have been united to Him, because the lover has found the Beloved, because I love Him that is the Son, I shall become a son.
Indeed he who is joined to Him who is immortal, truly shall be immortal.
And he who delights in the Life will become living.
This is the Spirit of the Lord, which is not false, which teaches the sons of men to know His ways.
Be wise and understanding and awakened.
Hallelujah.[11]

Ode 7

As is the course of anger over wickedness, so is the course of joy over the Beloved; and brings in of its fruits unhindered.

My joy is the Lord and my course is towards Him, this path of mine is beautiful.

For there is a Helper for me, the Lord. He has generously shown Himself to me in His simplicity, because His kindness has diminished His dreadfulness.

He became like me, that I might receive Him. In form He was considered like me, that I might put Him on.

And I trembled not when I saw Him, because He was gracious to me. Like my nature He became, that I might understand Him. And like my form, that I might not turn away from Him.

The Father of knowledge is the Word of knowledge.

He who created wisdom is wiser than His works.

And He who created me when yet I was not knew what I would do when I came into being.

On account of this He was gracious to me in His abundant grace, and allowed me to ask from Him and to benefit from His sacrifice.

For He it is who is incorrupt, the perfection of the worlds and their Father.

He has allowed Him to appear to them that are His own; in order that they may recognize Him that made them, and not suppose that they came of themselves.

For towards knowledge He has set His way, he has widened it and lengthened it and brought it to complete perfection.

And has set over it the traces of His light, and it proceeded from the beginning until the end.

For by Him He was served, and He was pleased by the Son.

And because of his salvation He will possess everything. And the Most High will be known by His holy ones:

To announce to those who have songs of the coming of the Lord, that they may go forth to meet Him and may sing to Him, with joy and with the harp of many tones.

The Seers shall go before Him, and they shall be seen before Him.

And they shall praise the Lord in His love, because He is near and does see.

And hatred shall be removed from the earth, and with jealousy it shall be drowned.

For ignorance was destroyed upon it, because the knowledge of the Lord arrived upon it.

Let the singers sing the grace of the Lord Most High, and let them bring their songs.
And let their heart be like the day, and their gentle voices like the majestic beauty of the Lord.
And let there not be anyone who breathes that is without knowledge or voice.
For He gave a mouth to His creation: to open the voice of the mouth towards Him, and to praise Him.
Confess His power and declare His grace.
Hallelujah.[12]

Ode 9

Open your ears, and I shall speak to you.
Give me yourself, so that I may also give you myself.
The word of the Lord and His desires, the holy thought which He has thought concerning His Messiah.
For in the will of the Lord is your life, and His purpose is eternal life, and your perfection is incorruptible.
Be enriched in God the Father; and receive the purpose of the Most High. Be strong and redeemed by His grace.
For I announce peace to you, His holy ones, so that none of those who hear shall fall in the war.
And also that those who have known Him may not perish, and so that those who received Him may not be ashamed.
An everlasting crown is Truth; blessed are they who set it on their head. It is a precious stone, for the wars were on account of the crown.
But Righteousness has taken it, and has given it to you.
Put on the crown in the true covenant of the Lord, and all those who have conquered will be inscribed in His book.
For their book is the reward of victory which is for you, and she sees you before her and wills that you shall be saved.
Hallelujah.[13]

Ode 12

He has filled me with words of truth, that I may proclaim Him.
And like the flowing of waters, truth flows from my mouth, and my lips declare His fruits.
And He has caused His knowledge to abound in me, because the mouth of the Lord is the true Word, and the entrance of His light.

And the Most High has given Him to His generations, which are the interpreters of His beauty,
And the narrators of His glory,
And the confessors of His purpose,
And the preachers of His mind,
And the teachers of His works.
For the subtlety of the Word is inexpressible, and like His utterance so also is His swiftness and His acuteness, for limitless is His progression. He never falls but remains standing, and one cannot comprehend His descent or His way.
For as His work is, so is His expectation, for He is the light and dawning of thought.
And by Him the generations spoke to one another, and those that were silent acquired speech.
And from Him came love and equality, and they spoke one to another that which was theirs.
And they were stimulated by the Word, and knew Him who made them, because they were in harmony.
For the mouth of the Most High spoke to them, and His exposition prospered through Him.
For the dwelling place of the Word is man, and His truth is love. Blessed are they who by means of Him have perceived everything, and have known the Lord in His truth.
Hallelujah.[14]

Chapter 31
The Rich Jewish Heritage of Davidic Dance

Then David danced before the LORD with all his might.
—2 Samuel 6:14

King David [was] leaping and whirling before the LORD.
—2 Samuel 6:16

Now it had happened as they were coming home, when David was returning from the slaughter of the Philistine, that the women had come out of all the cities of Israel, singing and dancing, to meet King Saul, with tambourines, with joy, and with musical instruments. So the women sang as they danced.
—1 Samuel 18:6–7

Davidic dance takes its name from King David, who "leapt and whirled" before the Lord, dancing in praise and worship. It is as old as Judaism itself and is woven into the very fabric of its expression.

The Israelites danced on every occasion when there was a cause to celebrate: after each military victory; in thanksgiving for a successful harvest; after the birth of a child; and in conjunction with all manner of other family, religious, community, and national milestone events.[1]

Miriam, the sister of Aaron, led all the women in singing and dancing to celebrate the miracle when God opened up the Red Sea to let His people escape the Egyptians. (See Exodus 15:20–21.)

The psalmist, most likely David, called upon Israel some three thousand years ago to rejoice in their Maker by praising His name with dancing and music made with tambourine and harp. (See Psalm 149:2–3.)

Before and after every major battle, Israel gathered together for a celebratory feast where they ate, sang, and danced. For example, when David returned with King Saul from a battle, the two of them were greeted with joy, thanksgiving, singing, and dancing by women who had assembled for this purpose from all over the country. (See 1 Samuel 18:6.) The people also gathered together to dance when the ark of the covenant was carried back into Jerusalem. The Scriptures record that when the ark came into view, "David danced before the LORD with all his might...and all the house of Israel brought up the ark of the LORD with shouting and with the sound of the trumpet" (2 Sam. 6:14–15).

Through the ensuing centuries, dancing has accompanied the celebrations in Jerusalem as the faithful of traditional Judaism have joyfully and expectantly looked forward to the eventual construction of the third temple. For example, during Hanukkah in 2007, for the first time since the destruction of the second temple in A.D. 70, the Hanukkah menorah was lit in front of the southern Hulda gates of the Temple Mount. To further mark the occasion, members of the Faithful movement, carrying the Hanukkah menorah, marched along the streets of the Old City of Jerusalem, dancing in joyful expectation as they made their way to the holy Temple Mount.[2]

Davidic dancing is something far more than a physically expressed art form or even a uniquely Jewish form of worship and praise of the living God. It is, rather, an outward expression of the inward joy of those who have been touched in some very special way by the glory of their Creator.

While there is no direct mention of dancing in the writings of The Way, they were first Jews. Thus, they looked to the entire Tenach and Jewish tradition as the baseline upon which they modeled and lived out their lives. As previously noted, members of The Way regularly visited the temple courts, where there was continuous celebratory singing and dancing.[3] There is no reason to suspect that they may have discontinued dancing there as a part of their regular activity during these visits.

Yeshua, of course, was the singular salvational centerpiece of The Way's new understanding, which markedly differentiated them from the much larger body of their traditional Jewish brethren. But one must remember that Yeshua Himself was a fully observant orthodox Jew who remained steeped in Jewish tradition. The New Testament shows us that from the time He was presented at the temple as an infant and through several later incidents in His ministry He was by no means a stranger to the temple.

While there is no specific mention in Scripture that Yeshua danced, there is also no reason to suppose that He did not. More to the point, in His teachings He pointed to dancing as a positive expression of worship.

> But to what shall I liken this generation? It is like children sitting in the marketplaces and calling to their companions, and saying: "We played

> the flute for you, And you did not dance; We mourned to you, And you did not lament."
>
> —Matthew 11:16–17

Moreover, in His parable of the prodigal son, He used celebratory dancing in a positive context.

> Now his older son was in the field. And as he came and drew near to the house, he heard music and dancing. So he called one of the servants and asked what these things meant. And he said to him, "Your brother has come, and because he has received him safe and sound, your father has killed the fatted calf."
>
> —Luke 15:25–27

Since we have frequently looked to the Essenes as a model for much of The Way's understandings and practices, we can also look to them with respect to the matter of dancing as a form of worship.

While, as earlier noted, there are frequent references in the Qumran literature to the singing of psalms and hymns, there is no specific mention of dancing in this context. However, please remember that the Essenes were particularly ascetic orthodox Jews before they left the polluted temple in Jerusalem, and they remained so at Qumran. Hence, there is no reason to suppose that they left worship dancing behind in Jerusalem: so very much of their writings have been turned to dust or been absorbed in the mud of the Dead Sea.

Even so, we can look to the Theraputae, who were a well-known sect of the Essenes in Egypt and contemporaries of their brothers at Qumran. Jean Gould Bryant, et al., in researching the history of women through the Middle Ages, was able to document that the Theraputae rejoiced in hymns and dances.[4] There is certainly no reason to suspect that dancing did not remain an integral part of the worship system throughout the entire, widespread Essene establishment.

Having presented the foregoing as historical background, Davidic dancing has been a key feature of the praise and worship of Messianic Judaism since its reemergence in the 1960s. It is hard to imagine a Messianic congregational celebration without the presence of a formal "dance team" performing before the congregation during praise and worship or a group of devotees gathered in circles in some open space, joyfully communicating with their creator through this ancient means of expression. Even in our own small (twenty or so member) home congregation in Tiberias, several of our members often gather together to sing and dance during our two meetings each week.

Like learning to play a musical instrument, Davidic dancing, although relatively simple, is an art form that must be learned if it is to be used to its fullest potential as a means of worship. By forming a foundation of a dance language, the dancer is better able to express his or her feelings in the dance. Most Messianic congregations offer instruction in the basic dance steps, and once they are learned the new dancer can completely enter into the praise and worship.

There are about eleven words used in the Tenach that are translated as "dance." These describe in detail the various movements, most of which are used in modern day Davidic dancing: For example:

- Hagag—dance in a circle
- Pase'ah—skip
- Daleg—leap or jump
- Karker—rotated with all his might
- Kafoz—jump with both feet[5]

Davidic dancing is not just for the individual. In a congregational setting it draws the participants closer to one another, but more importantly it draws them closer to Him, the Holy One whom they are worshiping together through dance.

Davidic dance is for everyone: men, women, and children alike. Miriam, Moses's sister, who was at least seven years older than Moses,[6] at her very advanced age took a timbrel and led the women in the dance. (See Exodus 15:20.) David, a man among men, danced before the Lord.

I certainly agree with the Concord Messianic congregation in their view that the widespread and rapidly growing restoration of Davidic dancing is a fulfillment of prophecy. The Tenach speaks of the restoration of the people of Israel back to their land and their God.

> Again I will build thee, and thou shalt be built, O virgin of Israel: thou shalt again be adorned with thy tabrets [tambourines], and shalt go forth in the dances of them that make merry.
>
> —Jeremiah 31:4, kjv

> Hear the word of the Lord, O nations, And declare it in the isles afar off, and say, "He who scattered Israel will gather him, And keep him as a shepherd does his flock"....Then shall the virgin rejoice in the dance, And the young men and the old, together; For I will turn their mourning to joy, Will comfort them, And make them rejoice rather than sorrow.
>
> —Jeremiah 31:10, 13

Moreover, I am firmly convinced that this wonderful restoration of anciently rooted Davidic dancing is inexorably bound to the ongoing and rapidly growing Return to the Jewish Roots of Christianity movement. Davidic dancing is an anointed expression of praise and worship that is regularly celebrated by congregations, both large and small, who are seeking to return to the original understandings and worship practices of The Way.

For those who want to learn how to participate in Davidic dancing, I highly recommend Messianic Rabbi Murray Silberling's book *Dancing for Joy* as an excellent comprehensive guide. Rabbi Silberling is probably the world's top expert on this lovely form of worship.

> To everything there is a season, A time for every purpose under heaven.... A time to weep, And a time to laugh; A time to mourn, And a time to dance.
>
> —Ecclesiastes 3:1, 3

Part VI

The Ways of The Way as a Guide for Today's Church

When I first began planning this book and discussing it with my closest friends, I was challenged to imagine myself standing in the entrance of a first-century Israeli home congregation that was about to begin its daily meeting and, having done so, to share in some detail the specific content and conduct of the gathering as I saw and heard them unfold.

I believe that this "peeking through the door" is the most effective way to develop a scripturally and historically valid baseline for modern day home congregations that are seeking to find and embrace the Jewish roots of our faith. I am hopeful that each of these unique groups will then adapt this first-century precedent as the underpinning of their own varying situation- and composition-dictated modern day understandings and practices.

The obvious appeal of this approach is that these emerging bodies can be reasonably assured they are coming forth from the very same stump of Jesse that first gave rise to the Jewish mother synagogue. Indeed, in thus tapping into these same Jewish roots planted deeply in the rich spiritual soil of Mount Zion, they will have become modern day extensions of the congregations that began to emerge throughout all of Israel and beyond only some five years after Yeshua ascended into heaven.

I have done my best to answer this challenge. I am certain that the Lord set me about this work for this very purpose. However, before I begin to weave together all that has preceded these concluding chapters into some hopefully meaningful guidance, let me first make it clear for whom this guidance is intended and, even more importantly, for whom it is not.

Chapter 32
Who Is Returning, and From Where?

The Gentile Christians, for Whom I Have Written

Is it any wonder that there are literally thousands upon thousands of different Christian denominations, more of them seemingly springing up all the time with no end in sight?

How could anyone expect any meaningful unity among these myriad branches of the worldwide church when, for instance, the Council of Jerusalem decided in A.D. 49 that "the brethren who are of the Gentiles in Antioch, Syria, and Cilicia," in order to become members of the emerging body of Yeshua, needed only "abstain from things polluted by idols, from sexual immorality, from things strangled, and from blood" (Acts 15:23, 20)? These are essentially purity rules. It would be impossible in my opinion to found and develop a viable religion based solely upon these few preliminary necessities.

Moreover, the Council dismissed any direct requirement that those who were to become the very foundation of the Gentile Christian Church should have any understanding of the Tenach (Old Testament), much less those of its scriptures which would be continued in the New Testament, which was only just then being written. James, after all, made no bones about the Jewish focus of his ministry. He addressed his epistle to "the twelve tribes which are scattered abroad" (James 1:1).

Let me be clear on this point. I am not saying that James or any other of the early fathers purposefully closed the door or even discouraged newly born-again Gentiles from studying the Old Testament. I am simply saying that the Council of Jerusalem's ground rules for Gentile membership into the body did not establish or even imply such a requirement.

The historical facts are that during the first Diaspora,[1] Judaism attracted a great number of conversions from God-fearing Gentiles who were disenchanted by paganism and seeking higher truth and social justice in this time of progressive enlightenment. Indeed, through these accelerating conversions, Judaism grew numerically to over 10 percent of the population of the Roman Empire.[2]

Moreover, the Jews were not passive participants in what amounted to this quite deliberate missionary outreach. It was common practice in the synagogues of the Diaspora on the Sabbaths and holy days to first read the Torah and Prophet portions in Hebrew from the sacred scrolls and afterward to expound on them in the lingua franca of the common people, most of whom were not Hebrew literate. Afterward, a sermon was delivered in the lingua franca.

Especially in the summer months, the window shutters (there were no glass windows) and doors were left open for the hearing of the women and small children outside. By the fourth century, Gentiles were gathering around outside the Diaspora synagogues in droves to hear wonderful, new, inspiring, and enlightening philosophical teachings. Even many among the senatorial families and upper classes were becoming God-fearers or fully circumcised converts.

This accelerating growth was only arrested when Christianity gained dominance, at first because of competition of the popular new faith and then in the time of Constantine and thereafter by a church-driven and enforced imperial ban on conversion to Judaism. Conversion to Judaism became a capital offense for both the converter and the converted. This marked the historical end of the formally active Jewish missionary mission.[3]

My central point in all of this is that the Council of Jerusalem addressed what was minimally necessary for Gentiles to move, so to speak, inside the emerging messianic synagogues to worship Yeshua alongside their ethnically Jewish brethren.

By no means did James or the Council mean to suggest that Gentiles should not closely study the Tenach. Indeed, the apostle Paul in his several letters to the emerging Gentile Church made specific reference to the Old Testament scriptures no less than thirty-seven times, which certainly implies that this great evangelist whose outreach was focused upon the Gentiles realized that he could more effectively teach them about the gospel of Yeshua by frequently referencing the Torah.

The fact is, Paul was teaching the Gentiles Jewish ethics from the Jewish holy books. Moreover, he taught from these Jewish holy books because behind virtually every New Testament teaching there is a foundation in the Torah, which it has amplified.

My bottom line in the foregoing discussion is simply this: it is equally necessary for both Jewish and Gentile believers in Yeshua to explore, understand, and embrace the biblical Jewish roots of their common faith. It is only though such a common understanding that any meaningful restoration of The Way's thoroughly ecumenical "one new man" belief and worship system as it existed during the late first through fifth centuries can be restored.

Admittedly, what I've said so far in this chapter is an oversimplification of a great historical problem. In any event, however, I believe that the very simple and undemanding requirements for Gentile participation in The Way, as they were handed down by the Council of Jerusalem, were key factors in the development of what we know today as replacement theology, the understanding that the church has replaced Israel, the New Testament has superseded the Old, and the Jewish people are no longer relevant.

While there are no reliable statistics concerning the actual numbers of modern day Christians who embrace this replacement theology, most estimates suggest that at least half of the worldwide body of Christ holds to this understanding. Moreover, the denominations that embrace "replacement" include all top ten liberal groups that I suggested at the outset of this writing are most urgently in need of and are presumably seeking Nazarene-Jewish-based guidance for home congregations.

No, I haven't "lost it," nor am I am speaking at cross-purposes. Certainly, there are many within these most liberal oriented groups who are perfectly content with what they are being taught and are quite satisfied to remain planted in the long-enjoyed comfort of their venerable pews. But, as we have seen earlier, there are still many others within these most liberal branches of the church who are not at all comfortable and are thus leaving their local churches and denominations.

Some but by no means all who are fleeing the mainstream liberal denominations have heard somewhere along the way about the Jewish roots of Christianity. Some have already come to embrace this understanding and are seeking to learn more about the substance of what has become the Return to the Jewish Roots movement. Many of these very same dear ones have also heard about home congregations as an alternative to larger denominational and non-denominational churches from which, for a variety of reasons, they have most recently departed. While not excluding any of the others, it is principally for these very special brothers and sisters that I have written this book.

To Those Who Call Themselves Jews and Are Not

"I love Israel so much *I know that I must be Jewish*!"

Like the old adage goes, if I had a dollar for every time I have heard some version of this passionate heartfelt assertion made by Gentile Christians during their visits to the Land over these sixteen years of my blessed citizenship, I wouldn't be rich but I could probably pay for a business class upgrade to my annual economy class visit with my kids and grandkids in the States.

It just doesn't make much sense to me how otherwise seemingly rational, mostly American Gentile Christians find themselves suddenly overcome, even consumed, by the irrational notion that they have somehow become ethnically Jewish and therefore have been "called home" to take up their inheritance in the land of Israel. Some base their dramatic ethnic metamorphosis upon divine revelation, some upon a misreading of the Scriptures, some upon the recollection of an often distant relative who "looked Jewish." Still others claim that since they have a "Jewish heart," they therefore must have "Jewish blood;" ergo, they must be Jewish.

Since I wrote extensively on this subject in my earlier book, *Full Circle*,[4] I will not dwell on it again at length here. Even so, this isn't a minor issue that can be easily dismissed. The King of the universe Himself saw fit to speak out against this heretical understanding twice in His assessment of the seven churches.

> These things says the First and the Last, who was dead, and came to life: "I know your [the church at Smyrna] works, tribulation, and poverty (but you are rich); and I know the blasphemy of those who say they are Jews and are not, but are a synagogue of Satan."
>
> —REVELATION 2:8–10

> [To the church at Philadelphia] "Indeed I will make those of the synagogue of Satan, who say they are Jews and are not, but lie—indeed I will make them come and worship before your feet, and to know that I have loved you."
>
> —REVELATION 3:9–10

I am speaking here of those dear ones who come to the land of Israel on tourist visas, grow irrationally enamored with it, and decide to stay *forever*. Never mind that they have no legal status for doing so and that it is only after they leave, according to a rule issued in 2008, that they can extend their tourist visa for another three months. However, after this second three-month extension they must wait another full year before they can return for another three-month visit to the Land.

Before this ruling that restricts tourists to remain in the Land for only six months each year, tourists were allowed to renew their three-month visas by leaving the country for a short time and then returning for another three months. For many Gentile Christians who felt called to remain in the Land permanently, this come and go cycle became their way of life for many years, even decades. Many of these individuals, perhaps realizing that they might one day be told to leave the country permanently, didn't bother to renew their tourist visas. I know of a few such families who managed to keep up this tenuous "residency" for several years until finally, without notice, they were denied reentry at the airport passport control while attempting to return to their adopted home.

In any event, since these non-Israeli brothers and sisters remain officially tourists, they are not allowed to be legally employed. Some who are so excluded from legal employment find some sort of low-paying work in the extensive black market world of Israel. Many others who eventually run out of their cash on hand and life's savings look in desperation to the legally enfranchised body in Israel for their support. Since most members of this local body are barely making it themselves, these illegal immigrants to the Land often impose a difficult burden.

Then, there are still a few others who manage to gain legal employment and, with it, temporary work visas that must be renewed each year. As an example of the several I can point to, one such young man—the son of yet another who had taken up the same perilous course—found employment with a local Christian-owned company, married a lovely Christian girl, and proceeded to bring forth a house full of children, all of them without any legal status, all the while hanging on to the hope that they would one day be granted permanent status here in the Land. It didn't happen. Finally, after several more children and several more annual extensions of his work visa, a further annual renewal was denied by the Ministry of Interior, and he and his family were given thirty days to leave the country.

Instead of simply leaving as ordered, they embarked upon a long, expensive, emotionally and financially draining, and futile-from-the-outset legal appeal of this ruling. They lost round after round until there were at last no further rounds to be explored. Nonetheless, they still did not leave, although they were given firm orders by the government to do so. Instead, they continued to sit tight and waited to be physically thrown out of the country, praying for a miracle.

Sadly, the young man's mother died, and he felt compelled to return to the States for her funeral. Not surprisingly, upon his return to Israel, he was denied reentry at the airport.

In extremely rare cases, a token few of these long-suffering, genuine lovers of

Israel are finally granted some form of official residency status. Most, however, are finally forced to permanently leave the Land.

I have not written this book as a means to fuel the misguided fires of such as these among my dear Gentile brothers and sisters who have so terribly lost their way with respect to the identities and callings given to them by their Creator. I earnestly pray that nothing I have written here will encourage others to literally attempt to take up a divine inheritance which is not theirs. My great hope is that all such Gentiles who might struggle in vain to find permanent residence in Israel might instead be content with finding and worshiping with other like-minded brothers and sisters in home congregations founded upon the ways of The Way. However, by His grace, let these dear ones first come to understand that it isn't the land of Israel they are to worship but rather the Lord God of Israel, who gave this land to His Jewish people as their everlasting inheritance.

To Those "Ephraimites," a.k.a. Israelites of the Lost Ten Tribes Who Have Genuinely Lost Their Way

I have also previously written at length about those modern day Gentiles who call themselves Israelites or "Ephraimites" and who subscribe to a "two house" theological invention of their own.[5] These are those who genuinely believe they have descended from the supposed "lost ten tribes of Israel" and are thus yet another misguided offshoot of those Gentiles who would be Jews.

When the Messianic Jewish movement was just beginning to catch on in a big way in the late 1970s and Jewish believers were flocking to join the Messianic Jewish Alliance of America (MJAA), the born-again Jewish leadership of that time was faced with the question of how to deal with those like-minded Gentile brothers and sisters who sought to join the MJAA as fully accepted participants. In the end, the movement's leadership reasoned that Messianic Jewish heritage was based on one having ethnically Jewish parent(s) when one became involved in the movement. (Or one could simply be married to someone who met the requirement.)

Having accepted Yeshua as their Messiah, these physical Jews were also now deemed by the MJAA to be "spiritual Jews." Gentiles who joined the movement, however, were thought of as only spiritual heirs. This conflicting understanding quickly resulted in two classes of membership: full members who were Jewish and "spiritual" members who were non-Jews.

Serious problems soon followed. Many Gentile participants began to complain that they were made to feel like second-class citizens.

Seeking to resolve the problem, a leader of the Gentile faction appealed to the MJAA leadership to establish a "conversion procedure" that would consider everyone equal, both physically and spiritually. The leadership immediately rejected this proposal. It was also rejected out of hand by other frustrated Gentile believers who were, presumably as a result of this situation, inspired to found the Messianic Israel Alliance (MIA) for like-minded Gentiles.[6]

Unfortunately, the movement that resulted from the formation of the MIA quickly gave birth to several divergent spin-off movements that have adopted increasingly more unbiblical understandings, such as:

- Gentiles (either all Gentile Christians or all non-Jews) are "Israelites" who are defined as blood descendants of the supposed "lost tribes;" ergo, they either always have been or have somehow become Jews.
- Gentiles (called "Israelites") have replaced Jews as the recipients of God's covenant promises, though they were made exclusively to the Jewish people through Abraham, Isaac and Jacob. These "Israelites" have thus fallen heir to ten-twelfths of the land of Israel, which they are strongly encouraged to "repopulate."[7]

I have not written this book for these ethnically Gentile "Israelites" in all or any of their several different denominational groupings, lest I should feed even more grist to their highly creative mill, which continues to grind out one successive misreading of Scripture after another. I do, however, earnestly pray that they will return to the biblical Jewish roots of their faith as they were written down and first taught by those Jews on Mount Zion who physically walked with Yeshua and who established their belief systems accordingly.

Chapter 33
Whither Shall They Go?

Yeshua, in a heated exchange with the Pharisees, cried out to them:

> Hypocrites! Well did Isaiah prophesy about you, saying: "These people draw near to Me with their mouth, And honor Me with their lips, But their heart is far from Me. And in vain they worship Me, Teaching as doctrines the commandments of men."
>
> —Matthew 15:7–9 (See Isaiah 29:13.)

Some years ago, not long after we had settled in the Land, we felt led to meet in our home with a number of other like-minded believers. At the outset, it was agreed that I would lead this group, along with a dear born-again brother who had come into the Messianic Jewish movement from a more or less agnostic Rabbinical Jewish background. As we began to establish a small home congregation, we sometimes found ourselves at cross-purposes. I was trying to find ways to gracefully rid myself of the life-long held pagan trappings of my faith while at the same time striving to make my fundamental Christian foundation more reflective of its Jewish roots. My brother, on the other hand, was making every effort to exegete and color his very new fundamental Christian understandings with rabbinical sources, such as the Talmud, Rashi, Akiva, and Rambam.

On one such occasion when I objected to including a rabbinically rooted ceremony in our services, he cried out to me in his frustration, "Rabbinical Judaism may have its problems, but it is the only kind of Judaism we have!" Indeed, the simple truth of his statement took me aback, and it has stayed with me all of these ensuing years as a constant reminder of the true origins of modern day Messianic Judaism.

The mostly Essene-rooted understandings of The Way, as they were promulgated on Mount Zion by James, Peter, and the others, were not to be long lived. As we have already seen, The Way, with few exceptions (such as the group that settled in Tiberias), was forced to endure seemingly unceasing persecution from the Roman government, their fellow Jews, and even from their Gentile Christian progeny. According to what we have so far surmised, by the middle of the second century, most if not all of the spiritual descendants of these original orthodox members of The Way had fled eastward into Coele-Syria and "the Region of Damascus."[1]

It should be clear at this point that what began as the entirely Jewish Way on Mount Zion remained, with its ever-increasing Gentile participation, the dominant expression of the worship of Yeshua in Israel until well into the fourth century. Then, not too long following the Council of Nicea in 325, the Byzantine Church movement in Israel began to emerge in a big way.

History and archaeology tell us that the Nazarenes of The Way essentially lost the battle for the souls of their fellow Israeli Jews. Thus, they were ultimately forced into exile in the "outback" of Syria by the Romans acting in concert with the rabbis of Pharisaic-rooted Rabbinical Judaism, which had caught on and begun to thrive. It was there, thus banished but finally free from their fellow Jews who had long and vigorously opposed them, that the Nazarenes of The Way managed to survive in relative peace for more than another two centuries.

The Romans were the most dangerous and deadly of all those who stood against The Way. They evidently perceived those who called for a new "King" and "kingdom" as a threat, revolutionary to the extreme. (See Acts 17:6–7.) The Pharisees conspired with the Romans to put down these "sectarians," including the Nazarenes of The Way, by damning them; however, they normally did not use violence but rather excommunication and slander. Thus, the curse against them was added to the Pharisees' daily prayers.

Isolated as they were, this was a renaissance of sorts for the Nazarenes of The Way, during which they often settled in spiritually integrated communities where there were synagogues of The Way and pre-Byzantine Gentile Christian churches in close proximity.[2] This setting seems not unlike the varying denominational churches that can be found on opposite street corners of most American residential communities.

However, as it is written, there is "A time to break down, And a time to build up" (Eccles. 3:3). In much the same way that they flourished in Tiberias for more than two centuries before the appearance of the Sanhedrin in their very neighborhood, the now exiled Way similarly flourished during their two centuries in the East. And thus it continued until the rapidly expanding Byzantines spread their influence into Syria. These Nazarene descendants of the original Way were once again beleaguered until they were finally outnumbered, divided, marginalized, and sadly slipped away into what, at least up to now, has seemingly been their final obscurity.

There is an underlying truth in all of this that has long escaped the understanding of many born-again Jews, myself included. We have struggled under the woefully wrong impression that modern day Messianic Judaism as it reemerged in the 1970s and has since flourished is a movement that:

- is generally homogeneous and unified,
- stands in agreement on a body of generally shared theological and doctrinal positions, and
- can be traced directly back to the very first believers in Yeshua, to wit, the Nazarenes of The Way, who first met on Mount Zion.

While it may come as a shock to some as it did to me, not one of these three basic assumptions concerning modern day Messianic Judaism is correct. Let's take a closer look at each of these wrong assumptions in turn.

1. Messianic Judaism is largely a homogeneous movement.

The modern day Messianic movement is anything but like-minded. Rather, it is characterized by a general lack of agreement on even some of the most foundational understandings as they were first held by James, the twelve apostles, and the original core group of their followers. Sadly, the movement is fractionalized, mostly along differing theological and doctrinal understandings, into several large alliances that now stand as alternatives to the Messianic Jewish Alliance of America (MJAA) as it reemerged in the 1970s. To name a few:

- Messianic Bureau International (MBI)
- Union of Messianic Jewish Congregations (UMJC)
- Messianic Jewish Alliance of Canada (MJAC)
- International Messianic Jewish Alliance (IMJA)
- International Alliance of Messianic Congregations and Synagogues (IAMCS)
- International Federation of Messianic Jews (IFMJ)
- Chosen People Ministries (CPM)
- Messianic Israel Alliance (MIA)
- The Association of Messianic Congregations (AMC)

Since I am currently more familiar with the Messianic Jewish movement in Israel, let me point out that we have more than 120 groups, ranging in size from 300-plus members to a growing number of home congregations with twenty or even fewer active participants. Seemingly every theological understanding and doctrinal position that has ever been proposed or even considered, from the most rigidly orthodox to the most blatantly unbiblical, can be found represented somewhere within these widely scattered, entirely independent groups.

While some well-intentioned brothers have attempted on several occasions to implement the semblance of a national structure upon which these largely independent believers in Yeshua might attach themselves for even the simplest purpose of establishing open lines of communication, no such national level structure with any lasting effectiveness has yet emerged. Recently, however, an ad hoc Messianic Action Committee has made some headway in the area of congregational cooperation and communication. This is thanks mostly to the generous pro bono contributions of some genuinely selfless believing lawyers who have been standing by the side of a growing number of Messianic believers who have been under the threat of the government revoking their citizenship on the sole basis of their expressed religious understandings.

2. Basic theological and doctrinal understandings are generally shared throughout Messianic Judaism.

A recent exciting report from credible leaders I know personally reveals that there has been a tremendous growth of the body of Yeshua in Israel in the past ten years. The report notes that although nobody knows for sure how many Messianic Jews live in Israel, it's believed there are now about 120 congregations and 10,000 to 15,000 Jewish believers in Yeshua. Ten years ago, it adds, there were only about 3,500 Jewish believers and 80 congregations.[3]

Given there are some six million Jews in Israel and assuming the highest estimate from the recent report, the believing body of Yeshua in Israel still represents no more than a miniscule one-fourth of one percent of the entire Jewish population. One might reasonably assume that this tiny minority-within-a-minority of professed believers hold in common some of the most basic theological and doctrinal understandings as they were embraced by The Way.

While, admittedly, there is certainly agreement on many such foundational issues, there is also widespread disagreement on the very nature of the Godhead itself. There is, in fact, a nationwide movement of Jewish "believers" in Israel (which has also caught on and is growing in the United States) who flatly deny the divinity of Yeshua, teaching instead that the triune Godhead is an invention of the Christian church. One well-known leader of this movement in Israel with whom I debated this issue told me emphatically that more than half of the Jewish "believers" in Israel subscribe to this Unitarian position, as does his entire congregation, which is one of the largest in the country.

I very much wish I could report that the other half of the Messianic body, those who do embrace Yeshua as God incarnate, were otherwise in general agreement on most other basic theological understandings and doctrine. Sadly, with one notable exception, I cannot.

In truth, the Messianic body of Yeshua is, theologically and doctrinally, a microcosm of the highly fractionalized denominational Christian Church. At one extreme of our reported 120-plus-group Israeli Messianic body, one can find the most conservative hard-shell fundamental expression of evangelical Christianity with only a hint of Jewish trappings. At the other end of this spectrum are those groups that continue to embrace much of the Oral Torah, that is, what Yeshua called the "commandments of men" (Mark 7:7) as they are written in the Talmud and in other rabbinical writings, most notably the Siddur, the Jewish prayer book.

While there are enormous differences in understanding on a wide range of issues at every level between these two extremes, there is one central, formative aspect all groups generally hold in common. I dare to suggest that there is most likely not a single Messianic organization within either Israel or the United States that is not at least in some small way influenced by the theology, doctrine, and the traditions of the Pharisees that have come down to us in their modern day expression in Rabbinical Judaism.

It is this universally shared influence of Pharisaic understanding and practice that brings me to the third and last of what I see as commonly held wrong assumptions concerning the nature of modern day Messianic Judaism.

3. Modern day Messianic Jewish understandings and traditions are rooted in those of The Way on Mount Zion.

We recently left the last vestiges of the Nazarenes of The Way during the closing decades of the fifth century in the far recesses of Syria, where they were finally driven into extinction. Certainly, these first believers in Yeshua left a legacy that reveals much about who they were and what they believed. This, our priceless inheritance, can be found in two sources.

First and foremost, the theology, doctrine, and even some of the traditions of The Way are, by His grace, very much living still in the writings of Matthew, Mark, Luke, John, Paul, Peter, James, and the other New Testament writers, who, as earlier pointed out were all ethnic Jews (with the exception of Luke). It is this very fundamental truth that the Jewish Roots of Christianity movement seeks to promulgate throughout the entire worldwide church.

Second, The Way's legacy includes a wealth of additional theological understandings, doctrine, traditions, and worship practices that have long been buried in the obscurity of nearly two millennia. Again, my central purpose in writing this book is to restore these long-lost treasures as guidance for the modern day church.

Please remember that "the only Judaism we have," modern day Rabbinical Judaism, is inarguably a further development of the Judaism of the Pharisees, the very "commandments of men" with which, as it is recorded in all four canonized gospels, Yeshua repeatedly took strong issue. Thus, it seems fair to say that modern day Messianic Judaism has its roots in the fundamental understandings and practices of two principal sources: from The Way, which have come down to the movement indirectly via the Gentile Christianity to which it gave birth; and also from the unique "commandments of men" that have been passed down to them directly from its authors, the Pharisees, who Yeshua so strongly opposed.

While there are no reliable statistics available to prove the point, I believe it is reasonable to say that most modern day Jews who have come into the kingdom by grace through faith were first observant members of some form of Rabbinical Judaism. Relatively few, such as myself, came into the kingdom without having to carry with them the attendant baggage of the Pharisees. This is not to say that we didn't have baggage of our own to carry though the portal of our own born-again spiritual mansions, that is, the significant body of pagan-compromised teachings and traditions of the church.

Having said all this, let me be clear on an important point: from a Christian perspective, there is much in the teachings of the rabbis that is unbiblical. These are obviously the very understandings and practices that all true born-again believers need to avoid, particularly those highly vulnerable, spiritually wounded brothers and sisters who are fleeing from the liberal church and are sometimes even desperately or blindly seeking to reestablish themselves within some Messianic Jewish expression.

By no means, however, am I suggesting that they or we are to avoid all things rabbinical. There are a number of things that have come down to us from the rabbis that are biblically sound, constructive, and edifying. Certainly, the very rich body of Jewish tradition that has survived through the centuries, those very unique customs and practices that in a real way constitute the very essence of what is distinctively Jewish and what is not, have been passed on to us not only from familial generation to generation but also via the good offices of Rabbinical Judaism.

Thus, inescapably, each of us must very carefully pick and choose from the vast body of rabbinical understandings and traditions what we should and should not embrace. I would suggest that each such evaluation be tested against two simple criteria, to wit:

- Does the understanding or practice under consideration in any way whatsoever conflict with the written or implied precepts of the canonized Bible? If there is even the slightest question on this point, then the understanding or practice under consideration should be rejected.
- Does this understanding or practice, if only in some small way, bring glory to God? If it does not, it should be rejected.

Yeshua Himself lends a strong helping hand in showing us quite clearly what we should include in our understandings and teachings from the rabbis.

> Then Jesus spoke to the multitudes and to His disciples, saying: "The scribes and the Pharisees sit in Moses' seat. Therefore whatever they tell you to observe, that observe and do, but do not do according to their works; for they say, and do not do. For they bind heavy burdens, hard to bear, and lay them on men's shoulders; but they themselves will not move them with one of their fingers. But all their works they do to be seen by men. They make their phylacteries broad and enlarge the borders of their garments. They love the best places at feasts, the best seats in the synagogues, greetings in the marketplaces, and to be called by men, 'Rabbi, Rabbi.' But you, do not be called 'Rabbi'; for One is your Teacher, the Christ, and you are all brethren. Do not call anyone on earth your father; for One is your Father, He who is in heaven. And do not be called teachers; for One is your Teacher, the Christ. But he who is greatest among you shall be your servant. And whoever exalts himself will be humbled, and he who humbles himself will be exalted."
>
> —Matthew 23:1–12

It seems to me Yeshua is telling us here as a main teaching in yet another of His stinging rebukes of the Pharisees that there is only one person worthy of the title "rabbi," and that is Yeshua Himself. His teachings are the Word of God, quite simply because He is God; whereas the teachings of the rabbis are the teachings of men because, despite their Talmudic claim to the contrary,[4] they are simply men.

Again, I believe Yeshua is telling us we are to test rabbinical understandings and traditions against the Word—He is the living Word—and where there is agreement and where God is in some way glorified, these understandings and traditions, and these alone, are worthy for us to embrace. Where there is any question whatsoever regarding these two criteria, then any such rabbinical input should be meticulously avoided.

I would love to be able, in this context, to provide an all-inclusive compendium of what I believe should and should not to be avoided from this vast, multifaceted rabbinical database. Please remember, however, that the most recent versions of the Talmud are set forth in the tediously detailed fifteen thousand pages of its thirty-five thick volumes. Thus, such a compendium, if properly accomplished, would likely mimic the enormity of that which it set out to critique.

Even so, by way of illustration, let me point to just a few of the more obvious understandings of Rabbinical Judaism that should be avoided by anyone seeking to return to the orthodox ways of The Way.

RABBINICAL TEACHING OR PRACTICE TO BE REJECTED OR AVOIDED	SOURCE
the many teachings of the Talmud wherein the commandments of men attempt to correct or supersede the Word of God or wherein these rabbinical inputs conflict in any other way with the Word of God as it is written in the canonized Scriptures	the Talmud[5] and all historical and contemporary rabbinical commentary
the teaching that Jews are superior to Gentiles and the call for the most extreme disunity between them	the Talmud[6]
the teaching that God cannot take on human form	Rambam's third principle
the teaching that God is an absolutely indivisible unity	Rambam's second principle
the requirement for men to cover their heads	Talmud: Tracate Kiddushin
Rabbinical *kashrut*:[7] extra-biblical dietary restrictions that seek to greatly modify and expand the laws of God as they are found in Exodus 22:31 and Leviticus 11, 17:13–15	multiple references throughout almost the entire Talmud and Rashi's Commentary
the edict that the *minim* (believers) are to be cursed three times each day	Talmud: Birkat haMinim
the use of a dash (-) in replacement of the vowel *o* to avoid writing or pronouncing the words *God* and *Lord*[8]	Jerusalem Talmud, Sifra (Chapter 18), Emor, and Rashi's Commentary

It would be almost equally as difficult to provide an all-inclusive compendium of those rabbinical inputs that I believe could and in some cases even should be carried over into the understanding and practice of Jewish and Gentile believers who are seeking to return to the Jewish roots of our faith. Both the Pharisees and the Essenes most likely looked to the same earlier mainline traditional Jewish sources from which they drew much of their understanding and tradition. The multifaceted and often rich traditions of the Pharisees have come down to us in modern day Rabbinical Judaism, "the only Judaism we have." Just what from this huge body of tradition pre-dated the Pharisees and what did not would often at best be difficult to determine. Unfortunately, whatever unique traditions The Way developed in addition to those taken from the traditional sources they shared with the Pharisees were lost with them in the far reaches of the East, where they vanished near the end of the fifth century.

Thus, once again, we must measure those understandings of the Pharisees that we would carry over against the same two criteria we used to determine what should not be included. Moreover, I would add a third consideration. When considering each potential rabbinical input I would ask, Would Yeshua have embraced this understanding or tradition?

Again, since it is well beyond the scope of this writing to offer an all-inclusive compendium of what I believe should be included, I offer, instead, a few examples by way of illustration.

RABBINICAL PRACTICE OR TRADITION TO BE ADOPTED	SOURCE
the weekly Torah portion (in Hebrew, *Parashat ha-Shavua*)	Babylonian captivity, circa the sixth century B.C.
Male circumcision on the eighth day (*brit mila*); required for Jews, entirely optional for Gentiles[9]	Genesis 17:14 and the Talmud[10]
Naming of a baby girl on the first *Shabbat* following her birth (*Simchat Bat*)[11]	Ashkenazi, early 1900s
the Bar/Bat Mitzvah, celebrating a young person's entry into the adult congregational community;[12] the right of "confirmation" in its various forms that has carried over into the church is similar in purpose	Ashkenazi, mid-fourteenth century A.D. for boys, circa 1922 for girls
marriage under a canopy (*chuppa*); liturgy can be flexible and vows personalized[13]	the Talmud: Ketuvot 7b, Hebrew Bible Version (Joel 2:16 and Psalm 19:5)

RABBINICAL PRACTICE OR TRADITION TO BE ADOPTED	SOURCE
celebrating the seven biblically cited Jewish feasts;[14] however, an uncircumcised man should very carefully consider Exodus 12:48: And when a stranger dwells with you and wants to keep the Passover to the LORD, let all his males be circumcised, and then let him come near and keep it; and he shall be as a native of the land. For no uncircumcised person shall eat it.	Leviticus 23
celebrating *Chanukah,*[15] the Festival of Lights	the Talmud (Tracate *Shabbat* 21–23), 1 and 2 Maccabees
sounding the *shofar*, or ram's horn,[16] to quicken the Holy Spirit	There are many references to the *shofar* in the Hebrew Bible, as well as in Talmud, for example Tracate Rosh HaShanah 16
the lighting of candles at the beginning of *Shabbat*[17]	The Talmud: Tracate *Shabbat* 23, 31

In conclusion, let me mention once more that nothing I have suggested in the foregoing chapter is intended to be obligatory, nor by any means are these suggestions intended to be all-inclusive. My prayerful hope is that each home congregation will adopt those things they find best suited to their own unique situations and backgrounds, which of course will vary greatly. Moreover, I am certain that, over time, as these practices are tested, some may be altered or dropped and others added.

My one strong counsel in all of this is that those who undertake to establish such a home congregation be very careful to model the group's celebrations in such a way that they bring glory to God while edifying all who participate.

Chapter 34
The Tiberias Synagogue of The Way

A *Motzei Shabbat* in April, A.D. 140

Now on the first day of the week, when the disciples came together to break bread, Paul, ready to depart the next day, spoke to them and continued his message until midnight.

—Acts 20:7

What I have written to this point has been to provide a basis for what is to follow in this chapter and the next. Again, my central purpose in this writing is to provide guidance to modern day Christian home congregations seeking to return to the original practices and celebrations of the nascent body of Yeshua.

I have given considerable thought to how best to approach the challenge set before me to imagine myself as a witness of a meeting of such a first-century home congregation and to then share its proceedings as they unfolded. After several months of research, when I was well into the first draft, the Lord saw fit to introduce me to the incredible discovery of the remains of a first-century synagogue of The Way located less than five minutes away from where I live. While I have done my best to share with you the great thrill of this discovery, words cannot begin to describe the quickening in my spirit every time I approach this place, even now that its exquisite mosaics have been covered over, awaiting that great day when they will hopefully once again see the light of day.

I marvel at His wonderful grace in leading me next to yet another ancient treasure, a large room located very near to the Messianic synagogue in the area later occupied by the Sanhedrin when they returned to Tiberias circa 220. There, on segments of the badly worn original mosaic floor, revealed through areas of a crude mosaic tile covering that has deteriorated over the ensuing centuries, are still very evident, beautiful *taw* symbols. These beautiful polychrome tiles speak out to me the amazing testimony of the craftsman who placed them there, I surmise, some few years after the failed second revolt against Rome (A.D. 132–135). It was then that Emperor Hadrian openly defied the Lord God of Israel by banishing the last of The Way and all other Jews from Jerusalem "forever." It was also then that he renamed the city Colonia Aelia Capitolina and declared that Israel was from that time forth to be known as Palestine, after the Philistines, an ancient, non-Arab arch-enemy of Israel in the time of David, an abomination that continues even today to stab at the very heart of most Jews.

These two nearly adjacent very special places that are virtually in my front yard beckon to me. I have visited them from time to time for rest, prayer, and contemplation as I have proceeded toward the promised conclusion of this writing. During my now many years in this precious land, I have been blessed to visit numerous archaeological ruins, only one of which—the area of the temple in Jerusalem—even began to excite within me the still alive reality I sense in the ruins of the Tiberias synagogue of The Way. When I am physically alone in these precincts, I can almost feel the presence of those dear ones who once worshiped there, longing to share their exciting testimonies while affirming their own deep love of Yeshua.

It thus occurred to me that I should use the form of a novelette to best share the spiritual excitement these sites have evoked in me, while providing their lovely setting as a backdrop for the guidance I have set out to convey.

Stephanos, like most young teenagers of his time, had never thought much about God, the hereafter, or other such things; that is, until Reuven ben Israel, his best friend and life-long constant companion, had of late begun to share with him about Yeshua, the one he called his Messiah. Very early in these discussions, beyond his understanding, Stephanos had come to think of this historical figure as someone holy who somehow was still living.

Stephanos was the only child of a "pagan" family of tenant farmers. Along with several other such families, they worked the fields of the huge plantation near the southern end of the Sea of Galilee that was owned by his dear friend Reuven's very prosperous, generous, and loving family.

After Reuven's introduction to the one he called his Messiah, Stephanos immediately developed a deep hunger to learn more about this person, Yeshua, and the more he hungered, the more Reuven provided him with the spiritual nourishment he sought. Perhaps even more wonderful to Stephanos than the personal testimony Reuven had so lovingly shared was the very special gift his dear friend had given him on the occasion of his seventeenth birthday—a copy of the Gospel of Matthew, beautifully hand-scribed in Greek letters on fine parchment.

It took only one reading of this Gospel before Stephanos pleaded with Reuven to arrange for him to begin the three-month discipling program that was required for prospective new members of the Tiberias synagogue of The Way. How very wonderfully edifying this time had been, and how quickly it had passed. Stephanos had already learned so much about the Holy Scriptures of the Tenach, and he had virtually consumed the four Gospels and many of the other writings of The Way that were a part of his intensive curriculum. Even so, he still hungered to learn ever more about the great triune God, the Father, Son, and Holy Spirit who had become the very center of his existence.

Stephanos felt very unworthy of this greatest of moments in his still young life to which he had now come, but Pastor Joshua ben Isaac, who was the greatly loved leader of the synagogue, assured him that he was ready.

The Baptism by Immersion

Stephanos looked at the sweet, smiling faces of the congregation who was gathered about him, having come to worship and to share in his great joy. Dressed in a long white robe, he was standing near the top of the seven-step ladder that led down into the living water of the *mikvah*.

Stephanos hugged and exchanged a kiss on each cheek with each of his soon-to-be brothers and sisters of the congregation who had come to greet and pray for him. He was moved to tears of joy as he welcomed and embraced his thrilled and rightfully excited mother and father, who themselves were already nearly halfway finished with their own discipleship training. Their glowing countenances revealed their great love and deep appreciation for their only son, who had in turn led them to their own eternal salvation in Yeshua.

Suddenly, the sharp, loud reports of the congregation's *shofar* were sounded by Pastor Joshua the moment he was able to count the third star to appear in the azure evening sky, thus marking the official beginning of *Shabbat*. The sounding of the *shofar* was also the signal for all members of the congregation to withdraw into the privacy of the sanctuary, where they would wait in silent prayer for Stephanos during his momentous transition from the world of darkness into the kingdom of eternal light.

Stephanos was nearly overcome with brotherly love as, moments after all the others had departed, Reuven, his dearest friend, walking at the side of Pastor Joshua, approached the place where he stood.

Reuven, who recently had been anointed as the congregation's newest *mebaqqer* (deacon), had been appointed by Pastor Joshua to oversee Stephanos's triple self-immersion since it was through Reuven's faithful witness that Stephanos had come to this great moment.

"My dear Stephanos," asked Pastor Joshua, who now stood before him, "are you ready to enter the kingdom of God?"

"I *am*!" Stephanos replied emotionally, as he felt the presence of the Holy Spirit descend upon him and fill the place with such power that he had to struggle to keep his balance and remain standing.

Pastor Joshua continued, "Stephanos, it has been my great pleasure to watch your progression during your discipleship. You have learned the scriptures well, but beyond that you have lived honorably, giving special care to the widows, visiting the sick, and doing many other good works."[1] He paused for a moment to hug the one who stood before him and to give him a holy kiss upon each cheek.

"I, too, am certain that you are now ready to enter the kingdom of God and to be admitted to the full fellowship of this congregation," Pastor Joshua continued.

He then took one of the two small flasks containing anointing oil from his newest *mebaqqer*'s extended hand and explained to Stephanos, "This is the oil of exorcism." Then he poured a generous bit of this oil onto the thick carpet of jet black hair that covered Stephanos's head. Some ran down into Stephanos's already prominent beard. Pastor Joshua then gathered a bit of the oil between his right thumb and forefinger and used it to mark the sign of the *taw* on Stephanos's forehead as he proclaimed, "I renounce you, Satan, all your service, and all your works. Let every evil spirit depart from Stephanos!"

Pastor Joshua then charged his *mebaqqer*, "Reuven, in the presence of the archangel Michael, I charge you to descend with Stephanos, as did our Lord Yeshua, down the seven steps of the cosmic ladder into the sacred living waters and there to baptize him according to the holy ordinance that has been handed down to us from James, Peter, and our brothers on Mount Zion."

With that said, Pastor Joshua took a step back and then concluded, "I will await your return."

"Come, my brother," Reuven beckoned, as he turned and stepped upon the first of the seven steps. "Follow me and be buried with Yeshua in the water that represents His grave; and, having been so buried, rise again as did He unto eternal life given to you through your faith by the grace of His Father."

As Stephanos descended the seven steps with Reuven leading the way, the presence of the Holy Spirit was so intense that he was certain he had been miraculously transported to another plane, a spiritual realm where he, in total awe, now stood in the very physical presence of his Creator.

When Stephanos reached the seventh step, he paused, and as he had been previously instructed, he removed his robe and stood totally naked before his baptizer and his Lord. He neatly folded the robe and handed it to Reuven, who was already standing mid-chest deep in the water. Reuven took the robe and placed it on a nearby ledge, where it would remain dry.

Stephanos then joined his brother, and the two of them, *mebaqqer* and catechumen, now stood face to face in the cool, living water of the *mikvah*.

Without further ceremony, Reuven inquired, "Stephanos, do you believe in Yeshua, the Messiah, Son of God, who was born of the Holy Spirit and the Virgin Miriam, who was crucified under Pontius Pilate; died; was buried; rose on the third day, living from the dead; ascended into heaven; and sat down at the right hand of the Father, the one coming to judge the living and the dead?"

"*I believe*!" Stephanos replied earnestly.

Then, with the forefinger of his right hand, Reuven traced the sign of the *taw* on Stephanos's forehead, after which he gently placed both of his hands on top of Stephanos's head, saying, "Stephanos, I baptize you in the name of the Father."

With that, Stephanos went straight down into the water, while Reuven made certain that he was entirely immersed.

When Stephanos emerged once again, his entire countenance radiating the majestic joy of the moment, Reuven once again traced the sign of the *taw* on his forehead, saying, "Stephanos, I baptize you in the name of the Son," after which Reuven went down into the water.

When he had joyfully emerged for the second time, Reuven traced the sign of the *taw* on his forehead for a third time, saying, "Reuven, I baptize you in the name of the Holy Spirit," after which Reuven once again went down into the water. When he emerged this time, the two of them shouted for joy, singing out their praises to the God they both adored as full-fledged born-again brothers in the body of Yeshua.

After he had drip-dried for a short time, Stephanos once again put on his robe, and, following Reuven, the two of them ascended the seven steps of the cosmic ladder, as Yeshua had done before them when He had risen from the grave and gone to sit at the right hand of His Father.

Pastor Joshua was waiting for them at the top of the stairs. He hugged Stephanos and gave him a holy kiss, then greeted him, saying, "Welcome into the kingdom of God, my brother, and welcome into the fellowship of this congregation!" Then Pastor Joshua took a bit of oil from the second flask that Stephanos had earlier brought to the ceremony, and as Stephanos kneeled before him, he once again traced the sign of the *taw* on his forehead, exclaiming, "This is the oil of thanksgiving. Stephanos, I anoint you in the name of the Father, Son, and Holy Spirit. Thanks be to God for what He has done!"

The Baptism with the Holy Spirit

After a short time, the three of them entered the sanctuary. Stephanos's countenance was still glowing, and he was still enrobed in his white linen garment. Because this would be his first taking of the Lord's Supper he remained so dressed to signify the continuing holy cleansing and purification of his initiation.

When the congregation saw him enter into their midst, they struggled to suppress the outburst of their great joy until the final element of his initiation had been accomplished.

Pastor Joshua, who stood at the table of the Lord's Supper, which stood upon a pedestal in the very center of the large room, beckoned for Stephanos to join him. When Stephanos was kneeling before him at the table, Pastor Joshua took a lovely floral crown from the table and placed it on Stephanos's head. As he did so, the entire congregation, accompanied by the worship team, sang "Putting on the Crown of the Lord":

> The Lord is on my head like a crown, and I shall never be without Him.
> Plaited for me is the crown of truth, and it caused Your branches to
> blossom in me.
> For it is not like a parched crown that blossoms not;
> For You live upon my head, and have blossomed upon me.
> Your fruits are full and complete; they are full of Your salvation....[2]

As the sounds of the ode faded, Pastor Joshua laid his hands upon Stephanos and beseeched the Lord: *Lord God, you have made Stephanos worthy of the removal of sins through the bath of regeneration. Make him now worthy to be filled with Your Holy Spirit. Grant to him Your grace, that he might serve You in Your holy body according to Your will. For to You is the glory, Father, Son, and Holy Spirit, now and throughout the ages of ages. Amen.*

Pastor Joshua then poured some anointing oil into his hand. After first tracing the sign of the *taw* on Stephanos's forehead, he placed both of his hands upon his head, saying, "I anoint you with holy oil in God the Father Almighty, and Yeshua the Messiah, His Son, and the Holy Spirit."

What happened in the next moment remained deeply with Stephanos as the most thrilling moment of all of the many remaining years of his life. In an indescribable instant he felt as if he had been struck by a tongue of fire that emanated directly from the throne of God. He was completely filled with an overwhelming joy that far surpassed the sum of all the previous emotions he had ever known. He wept, totally out of control, as he found himself crying out the strange words of a language he had not known and did not now understand. Even so, he somehow knew that these amazing, to him unintelligible utterances were praises from the depths of his own spirit being offered up directly through his lips to the very Spirit of God.

After a few minutes of this incredible experience, he began to realize that the entire congregation had joined in with him, each of his now brothers and sisters, offering up their own praises each in their own unique spiritual language, which were known only to Him to whom they were directed.

All at once, Stephanos found himself singing his praises rather than simply speaking them. He sang this lyric of praise in the words of his new language, perfectly orchestrated with a hauntingly lovely melody that he had never before heard. The effect was beautiful and edifying beyond description. Then, even more amazing to him still, as he sang out this indescribably beautiful song of praise, the entire congregation joined in with him, each person singing in their own God-given language and each with a seemingly different part of harmony. The overall effect was beyond the human capacity to entirely perceive, yet somehow, by the grace of God, it was made perceptible.

Stephanos was enraptured; he lost track of time, space, and all other realities except for the awesome, holy thing he was experiencing. He had no idea whatsoever how long this had continued, but when it did finally end, it did so suddenly, as if an unexpected breeze had blown out a candle.

The First Sharing of The Lord's Supper

Stephanos once again fell to his knees in front of the eastern side of the table of the Lord's Supper, where he was beginning to recover from the awesome outpouring of the Holy Spirit he had just experienced. He looked up and beheld the sweet, smiling face of his brother, the *mebaqqer,* Reuven, who was standing beside Pastor Joshua.

When Reuven saw that his dear brother had recovered sufficiently, he handed the first of two cups of the oblation that he had been carrying to Pastor Joshua, who in turn made the sign of the *taw* over it and addressed Stephanos as well as the congregation who was gathered closely together around the table.

"Stephanos," he began, "this first cup is water, given to cleanse your inner self as was your outer self made pure during your three immersions."

After Stephanos had partaken of this first cup, Pastor Joshua took the second from Reuven, blessed it with the sign of the *taw,* and gave it to him. "Stephanos," he explained, "this oblation is a mixture of milk and honey. It is given to you in fulfillment of the promise of our Lord made to the fathers, in which He said, 'a land flowing with milk and honey.' Our beloved Yeshua indeed gave his flesh, through which those who believe are nourished like little children by the sweetness of His Word, softening the bitter heart. Take, drink, and be greatly blessed our brother," Pastor Joshua concluded, as he served the cup to Stephanos, who reverently partook of it all.[3]

As Stephanos thus drank and handed the empty cup back to Pastor Joshua, the congregation, accompanied by several stringed and other musical instruments,[4] began to sing:

> As honey drips from the honeycomb of bees, and milk flows from the woman who loves her children, so also is my hope upon You, O my God. As a fountain gushes forth its water, so my heart gushes forth the praise of the Lord, and my lips bring forth praise to Him. And my tongue becomes sweet by His anthems, and my members are anointed by His odes. My face rejoices in His exultation, and my spirit exults in His love, and my nature shines in Him. And he who is afraid shall trust in Him, and redemption shall be assured in Him. And His possessions are immortal life, and those who receive it are incorruptible. Hallelujah.[5]

As they were singing, five additional *mebaqqerim* made their way through the congregation and took their places beside Pastor Joshua and Reuven.

When the lovely ode was finished, Pastor Joshua took one of six wine-filled chalices from the table and held it up in one hand. Then he took a piece of bread and held it up with his other as he addressed his flock, "The apostle Sha'ul cautioned the congregation in Corinth and his words are meant of us as well: 'Whoever eats this bread or drinks this cup of the Lord in an unworthy manner will be guilty of the body and blood of the Lord. But let a man examine himself, and so let him eat of the bread and drink of the cup. For he who eats and drinks in an unworthy manner eats and drinks judgment to himself, not discerning the Lord's body.'[6]

"Therefore," Pastor Joshua continued, "let each of us examine ourselves, praying that the Lord will bring to our minds those things that we have done that have been sinful in His eyes; also the words of our lips that have been an offense to Him. Let us also repent for the sinful thoughts of our minds upon which we have dwelled instead of quickly dismissing, and all unknowing and forgotten sins."

The entire sanctuary fell silent as the congregation quietly repented. It remained so for several minutes until Pastor Joshua, led by the Holy Spirit, spoke out: *Have mercy on us, O Lord, according to Your unfailing love; according to Your great compassion, wipe out our transgressions. Make us whiter than snow; forgive us for our sins, both known and those of which we are not aware. Lead us now to Your table as Your children come with clean hearts. If anyone is holy, let him come to this table; if any one is not so, then let him further repent.*

Pastor Joshua then once again held up a wine-filled chalice, and he blessed it, chanting:

> *Baruch Atah Adoni Elohaenu, Melech haOlam, Boray Puree haGefen, Amen.*
>
> ("Blessed are You, O Lord our God, King of the universe, who creates the fruit of the vine.")

With that, he took a sip of wine, and then he held it to Reuven's lips so he could do likewise.

Then he turned to the still kneeling Stephanos, addressing him, "Stephanos, my brother," he entreated with great warmth, "because of your faith, you have by the Father's grace been born again by the shed blood of His Son, Yeshua. You can be sure that Yeshua is here with us at this very moment. Spiritually, His precious blood is in and around the wine in this chalice, and I invite you, for the first time, to partake of this cup in recognition and thanksgiving of the great things He has done for you and for us all."

Pastor Joshua held the chalice to Stephanos's lips, and he reverently partook of his inaugural Lord's Supper, then he handed the chalice to *Mebaqqer* Reuven.

This was the unspoken sign for all five *mebaqqerim* to each take a chalice from the table and distribute its contents from one participant to the next. The congregation had by that time, out of much practice, divided themselves into six more or less equally populated informal groups, like the six points of a loosely assembled *Magen David* with the table as its center.

When all had thus partaken of the spiritual blood of the Lamb and the six *mebaqqerim* had returned the chalices to the table and retaken their places,

Pastor Joshua raised his hands and prayed: *We thank You, our Father, for the life and knowledge which You have made known unto us through Yeshua, Your Son. To You be the glory for ever. As this broken bread was once scattered on the mountains, and after it had been brought together became one, so may Your Body be gathered together from the ends of the earth unto Your kingdom; for Yours is the glory, and the power, through Yeshua, for ever.*

He then took the bread, held it up, and blessed it, chanting:

> *Baruch Atah Adonia Elohanu Melech haOlam haMotze Lechem Meen haEretz, Amen*
>
> ("Blessed are You, O Lord our God, King of the universe, who brings bread forth from the earth.")

Then he broke off a small piece, which he retained, and handed the rest to Reuven. When he had done so, the other five *mebaqqerim* took their own respective pieces of the bread from the table and joined Reuven in distributing it among the members of the congregation, as they had the wine. However, with the bread, each participant broke off a small piece and retained it so that the entire congregation could partake of this element together.

Thus, when all had received and retained the bread and the *mebaqqerim* had returned to the table, Pastor Joshua held up the small piece he had retained and reverently declared, "This is the healing, restoring body of our Lord. By His stripes we are healed." With that, he and the congregation partook of this element together.

Pastor Joshua then offered a closing prayer:

> *We thank You, holy Father, for Your holy name, which You have caused to dwell in our hearts, and for the knowledge and faith and immortality which You have made known to us through Yeshua Your Son; to You be the glory for ever.*
>
> *Thou, almighty Master, did create all things for the sake of Your name, and have given both meat and drink, for men to enjoy, that we might give thanks to You, but to us You have given spiritual meat and drink, and life everlasting through Your Son.*
>
> *Above all, we thank You that You are able to save; to You be the glory for ever.*
>
> *Remember, Lord, Your body, to redeem it from every evil, and to perfect it in Your love, and gather it together from the four winds, even that which has been sanctified for Your kingdom, which You have*

prepared for it; for Yours is the kingdom and the glory for ever.
Let grace come, and let this world pass away. Hosanna to the Son of David. Maranatha. ("Come, Lord Yeshua.") Amen.[7]

Without any further prompting, the musicians began to play the haunting strains of Ode 26 of the Odes of Solomon,[8] and the congregation sang out their praise and thanksgiving.

I poured out praise to the Lord, because I am His own.
And I will recite His holy ode, because my heart is with Him.
For His harp is in my hand, and the odes of His rest shall not be silent.
I will call unto Him with all my heart, I will praise and exalt Him with all my members.
For from the East and unto the West is His praise;
Also from the South and unto the North is His thanksgiving.
Even from the crest of the summits and unto their extremity is His perfection.
Who can write the odes of the Lord, or who can read them?
Or who can train himself for life, so that he himself may be saved?
Or who can press upon the Most High, so that He would recite from His mouth?
Who can interpret the wonders of the Lord? Though he who
Interprets will be destroyed, yet that which was interpreted will remain.
For it suffices to perceive and be satisfied, for the odists stand in serenity;
Like a river which has an increasingly gushing spring, and flows to the relief of them that seek it.
Hallelujah.

The Lord's Supper Feast

The entire congregation walked the short distance between the sanctuary and Pastor Joshua's nearby large and lovely residence, which had been provided through the generous offerings of their several very prosperous families. These were among the last to flee from Jerusalem, just before all Jews were banished from the city following the ill-fated revolt of the Pharisees against the Romans, which ended in A.D. 135.

Stephanos looked about the huge *meerpesit* (veranda) of the residence, where the great feast in his honor had been set out on several large tables that were nearly overflowing with the most sumptuous and delicious looking offerings he had ever seen. The men of the congregation had prepared several varieties of meat, which included a pit-roasted fatted calf, several roasted lambs, and an entire table of several varieties of freshly caught fish from the nearby Sea of Galilee, grilled over charcoal.

The women had also outdone themselves. The menu for which they were responsible included several types of breads, both wheat and barley, other goods made of flour, roasted green wheat made into gruel, fresh and roasted young brown beans, and fresh and roasted young lentils. There was also an abundance of honey, butter, and several different types of cheeses and yogurt. Even more, to better satisfy those with a more plebian taste, as was the custom of that time, a variety of vegetables, both cooked and raw, and fruits were also available, including dates, pomegranates, and wild plums.[9]

When the congregation had informally drifted out onto the *meerpesit*, they fell silent as Pastor Joshua offered a blessing on the occasion and the food. He went on to thank everyone who had contributed to the exquisite meal, and then he invited Stephanos and his parents to be the first to take up the high-quality clay tableware[10] and make their way among the tables heavily laden with food. They would be the first to have their choice of where to recline among the several beds, soft sofas, exquisitely carved wooden benches and chairs, and numerous other square-shaped wooden chairs that were scattered about the very large area as they ate their meals.[11]

It was just after nine o'clock when Pastor Joshua determined that the feast had run its course, but it was by no means time for him to dismiss his flock and send them home to their waiting beds. This was a baptismal *Motzei Shabbat*, and the evening had only just begun.

The *Motzei Shabbat* Congregational Service

Pastor Joshua thought it was a wonderful thing indeed when he could sound the *shofar* twice on the same *Motzei Shabbat*, as was always the case when the regular, once-weekly congregational service began with the initiation of new members. On these very special occasions the regular proceedings were necessarily interrupted by the Lord's Supper feast, which had been in this case, Pastor Joshua concluded, the most successful of the many he and his wife had been blessed to arrange and oversee since he had been chosen by the Tiberias congregation as their leader in A.D. 140, some twenty years earlier.

Ever since, he reflected, he had worked very closely as brothers with his counsel of twelve elders to administer the affairs of their congregation. He had freely shared the pulpit with any of them who felt called to bring a message from the Lord. Moreover, they had worked together, always praying before every decision of any consequence, always yielding one to the other, and in the end, always seeking and trusting in the guidance of the Holy Spirit, whose presence they routinely invoked.

Pastor Joshua then struggled to hold back a moment of personal pride as he considered that the flock's membership had more than doubled to over three hundred during his tenure. Then he quickly gave proper unspoken credit, declaring in his thoughts, *It was only by the grace of God that this congregation is still thriving and growing.*

With that happy thought, he lifted the ram's horn *shofar* to his lips, pointed it toward the ink blue, star-bejeweled sky, and sounded the call to worship in the sanctuary with all of his heart and all of his soul and all of his strength.

The She'ma and Opening Prayer

The entire congregation jumped to their feet and joined in as Pastor Joshua began to chant the *She'ma*.

> *Sh'ma Yis'ra'eil Adonai Eloheinu Adonai Echad.*[12]
>
> ("Hear, O Israel, the Lord is our God, the Lord is One.")

"Let us pray," Pastor Joshua began, as he looked across the packed sanctuary. His devoted sheep had quickly assembled and once again had taken their seats on finely finished wooden benches that had been arranged in rows facing where he stood, facing east at the opening of the synagogue's singular apse. As always, he was deeply blessed to behold the great anticipation written all over the smiling countenances of his dear ones as they awaited the outpouring of the Holy Spirit, which had never failed to come down and bring God's holy light into even the darkest corners of their earthly realities.

He smiled, acknowledging their obvious deep affection and excitement, and he began the meeting as always: *Our Father who art in heaven, hallowed be Your Name. Your kingdom come. Your will be done on earth, as it is in heaven. Give us today the bread we need, and forgive us our trespasses as we also forgive those who trespass against us. And bring us not into temptation, but deliver us from the evil one; for Yours is the power and the glory for ever.*[13]

The pastor continued with a brief prayer of invocation and thanksgiving, praising God that He had once again called them to this place so that they might be able to worship Him together in spirit and in truth.

What follows is the continuation of my attempt to peak through the door of the Tiberias Messianic Synagogue for a first-person description of the remaining elements of the *Motzei Shabbat* service as they unfold.

Reading of the Word

Torah Reading

An elder reads an entire chapter from the pre-selected "portion"[14] that the pastor will later use as his primary preaching text.

Gospel Reading

Another elder reads a pre-selected passage from one of the four New Testament Gospels that is as closely related as possible to the message the pastor will later deliver.

Epistle Reading

A third elder reads a pre-selected passage from one of the apostolic letters written by Peter, James, John, or Paul that is in some way illustrative of the forthcoming pastoral message.

Optional Reading

A *mebaqqer* may conclude the readings with an appropriate portion of some other writing of The Way, as pre-selected by the pastor for being especially supportive of his forthcoming message.

Praise and Worship

The ordained worship leader works very closely with the pastor to select musical offerings that are connected to and supportive of the pastor's weekly messages. We can reasonably conclude that the worship leader of the Tiberias Messianic Synagogue had a great number of Old Testament and Essene-authored psalms, as well as at least forty-two New Testament odes from which to make his carefully chosen weekly selections.

I would suggest that the worship leader, supported by the ensemble of musical instruments and a number of singers, constituted the worship team that led the congregation through a time of praise and worship. This portion of the service would have lasted for some thirty to sixty minutes or, from time to time as the Spirit may have led, perhaps even longer.[15]

As we have already seen evidenced, The Way was closely led by the Holy Spirit. It is thus reasonable to conclude that they operated very much in the Spirit during their times of congregational praise and worship. I would therefore suggest that they most likely paused between musical offerings to wait upon the Spirit, during which times various words of prophecy or knowledge, sometimes spoken in tongues and sometimes not, would freely come forth from the congregation.

As also previously noted, I would further suggest that Davidic dancing would have been an integral part of The Way's praise and worship. Thus, it is reasonable to conclude that perhaps even many members of the congregation gathered in the open areas of the presumed semi-circular sanctuary, where they joyfully danced their praises while they sang them.[16]

I would further suggest that Davidic dance become a regular feature of each modern day home congregation's praise and worship. Toward this end, I strongly recommend Rabbi Murray Silberling's book, *Dancing for Joy*, as an excellent teaching guide.

The Pastoral Teaching

When the time of praise and worship drew to its own Holy Spirit led conclusion, Pastor Joshua would have returned to his pulpit and called his congregation to assemble for the continuation of this *Motzei Shabbat* service. One can only surmise that this pastor/teacher would have systematically worked his way through the entire Torah each year using some organized arrangement of the Scriptures set to this purpose.

In modern practice, both the content and length of teaching will be guided by the leading of the Spirit. Thus, from time to time, the message may depart entirely from the previously planned Torah-portion-centered content. In the same way, while these messages usually are no less than forty-five minutes and no more than ninety, from time to time they may be shorter or longer.

For modern day home congregations, I would suggest that the weekly *Motzei Shabbat* pastoral teaching be centered upon an exegesis of some selected verse or verses taken from one of the chapters of the applicable published *Parashat haShavua,* or weekly reading. While these listings, referred to collectively as the *Parashot*, provide a well-considered means to cover the entire Torah during any given year, any other such organized schedule with this same purpose would be equally appropriate.

It would be difficult to find any *parasha* whose central message is not clearly foundational to some parallel teaching of Yeshua or the epistles of the New Testament. My sense is that these teachings should always strive to demonstrate that the Old Testament provides a solid foundation for the New and that the fulfillment of Judaism is to be found in Yeshua.

The Lord's Supper

The Lord's Supper would normally, when there was no initiation of new members, be served immediately after the pastoral message. However, in our example, which included the first communion of a newly baptized member, the taking of this sacrament was placed immediately after the water baptism, as the opening feature of the *Motzei Shabbat* service.

The liturgy and proceedings of this sacrament during a regular *Motzei Shabbat* service would have been identical with that set forth in our foregoing example, except that the oblation of milk, honey, and water, which were served only to the newly baptized, would not have been included.

A Time for Physical Healing

Pastor Joshua would then begin a time of prayer for divine healing by first calling on all those present who are in such need to come forward to where he was standing, looking east from the opening of the apse. Once those requiring healing had assembled, the pastor then read for their hearing from the Epistle of James (5:13–16). This finished, those in need would come in turn to the pastor, who had been joined by at least one elder to stand with him in officiating this time of healing.

The pastor and the elders would then lead each person in need of healing in a time of confession and repentance. When each, in turn, had thus privately confessed and repented, the one who had heard them asks them to state the specific nature of their physical need. Having heard the specific need, the officiating pastor or elder makes a sign of the *taw* on the seeker's forehead using anointing oil and, while he laid his hands on the afflicted person, would pray earnestly and specifically for the requested divine healing. This healing service continued in a like manner until all in need had been so served.

A Time for Testimony

Pastor Joshua would then have called upon any of those who had experienced divine healing to share their testimony with the congregation. When all such testimonies concerning healing had been shared, the pastor then called upon any other members of the congregation to freely share any other testimony concerning some divine intervention the Lord had accomplished for them since their last meeting

The Pastoral Prayer

Next, Pastor Joshua would have offered up general petitions to the Lord on behalf of the congregation. This pastoral prayer, which may be of any length, generally addressed more global needs that impacted the entire congregation, community, or nation. For example, we might have heard him praying for the soon second coming of Yeshua to Jerusalem, which will only be possible once the city is restored to its original status and its Jewish residents have been allowed to return to their homes, and the believers to Mount Zion. We might also hear him praying for more local matters, such as the continued conversion of unsaved members of the local community.

This is not to say that the pastor would not have also used this time to lift up the more urgent, specific needs of families or individual members of the congregation who were to his personal knowledge in need of divine intervention.

Congregational Prayer

When he had finished his pastoral prayer, Pastor Joshua would likely have recited Yeshua's prayer of agreement: "Again I say to you that if two of you agree on earth concerning anything that they ask, it will be done for them by My Father in heaven" (Matt. 18:19). He then called upon any members of the congregation to offer up any prayer need, as they may be led by the Holy Spirit, with the expectation that their earnest pleas would be given the great added emphasis afforded to them by the agreement of their assembled brothers and sisters.

Announcements

A *mebaqqer* who served as the secretary of the congregation would then make any administrative, schedule-related, or other general announcements that were of interest to the entire congregation or to some of its members.

Aaronic Blessing

It is now just past midnight, and the first day of the week is already well begun. Pastor Joshua, being greatly blessed, whispers a silent prayer of his own great thanksgiving, raises his hands, and intones, "This is how Aaron and his sons were told to bless the people."

He then dismisses his congregation by chanting with great emotion:

> *Y'varekh'ka Adonai v'yishmerekha.* ("The LORD bless you and keep you.")
>
> *Ya'er Adonai panav eleikha vichunekka.* ("The LORD make his face shine upon you And be gracious to you.")
>
> *Yissa Adonai panav eleikha v'yasem l'kha shalom.* ("The LORD lift up His countenance upon you, And give you peace.")
>
> —NUMBERS 6:24–26

Chapter 35
The Ben Ezra Plantation, Near Tiberias

A Home Group Meeting, April, A.D. 140

So continuing daily with one accord in the temple, and breaking bread from house to house, they ate their food with gladness and simplicity of heart, praising God and having favor with all the people.
—Acts 2:46–47

To best reflect the presumed structure of the Tiberias synagogue of The Way, what follows is a "peeking through the door" recounting of the proceedings of one of its perhaps as many as fifteen or twenty home groups.

Once again, please remember that my principal objective in writing this book is to provide specific guidance to emerging modern day, independent home congregations. Thus, the first-century home groups I show in these pages as meeting each day other than on *Shabbat* then coming together each *Motzei Shabbat* for an assembly in their synagogue are, for the purposes of this writing, to be considered analogous to the contemporary home congregations for which I seek to provide guidance.

Yakov and Rachel ben Ezra had regularly welcomed Stephanos into their home during almost the entire span of his young life. After all, Reuven, their son, and Stephanos had been best friends for as long any of them could remember, and they had long considered Stephanos to be a member of their family.

While traditional orthodox Jews would never have abided such a close, personal relationship between a Jew and a non-Jew, to Yakov and Rachel, who were steadfast believers in Yeshua, Stephanos's pagan ethnicity and the family of lower social class from which he came made absolutely no difference to them.

They had long embraced the teaching of the apostle Paul that "there is neither Jew nor Greek, there is neither slave nor free, there is neither male nor female; for you are all one in Christ Jesus" (Gal. 3:28). Thus, as far as they were concerned, Reuven and Stephanos had always been as close as brothers in the flesh. But now that Stephanos had been born-again in Yeshua, they had become and would always remain "brothers" in the full, deep meaning of that relationship.

That day would herald something very different and very wonderful: they would have the great joy of welcoming the newly baptized Stephanos into the intimacy of their home group. He would, for the first time, join them and the other sixteen dear ones who met to worship together at six thirty each morning in their large and well appointed salon. The meetings usually ended at or near eight. However, there was nothing rigid about their length or content, which could vary considerably, as led by the Holy Spirit.

The ben Ezra family was well known and greatly admired throughout the greater Tiberias area. They were wealthy, but they did not flaunt their affluence; rather, they generously shared it. While it was little known, largely owing to their own great humility, it was Yakov and Rachel who had underwritten a generous part of the great expense involved in building and appointing their congregation's large and lovely residence, which was currently occupied by Pastor Joshua and his family.

As giving as they were with the things of this world, the entire ben Ezra family was all the more generous with their outreach of love and caring. This was true for all whom they encountered, but especially to this home group, which over the years had become their extended family.

It was thus that just before six thirty, all but two of their now nineteen members having taken their places, they were all the more thrilled when Reuven and Stephanos bounced into the room, barely able to contain their own exceeding happiness. The two of them quickly took their places in the remaining unoccupied, comfortable chairs, which were arranged in a loose circle surrounding a large table in the center of the spacious room.

Greeting and Introductory Prayer

After Yakov and Rachel had effusively welcomed Stephanos, he made his way around the group to receive, in turn, warm hugs and holy kisses from each of his new brothers and sisters.

It isn't that they were total strangers who had only just met. All of them had been on hand at the previous evening's *Motzei Shabbat* service. Moreover, they had all become at least casually acquainted with Stephanos during his three-month discipleship. The effect of all this was that Stephanos felt immediately comfortable and accepted, and in turn the other members of the home group immediately accepted him as one of their own.

When they all were once again seated, Yakov, as always, opened the meeting with the Lord's Prayer, which they recited in unison. Then, Yakov, joined by the others, fervently prayed that the Holy Spirit would become manifest among them. They prayed towards this end in Aramaic, their every day language, as well as in the personally unique tongue that each of them had received, freely moving from one language to the other.

As this invocation of the Holy Spirit began to grow in intensity, one of them began to sing out their petition, only to be immediately joined by another, then another, until finally all nineteen of those present were blending their voices in a heavenly chorus of perfectly blended harmony that sounded like a mighty rush of living water.[1] When several minutes later, as their voices had begun to fade and it had once again grown silent, the presence of the Holy Spirit in their midst was awesome, nearly overpowering. This, too, was a consistent aspect of each of their meetings.

Then, in the great majesty of His presence, each of the nineteen reached out to their neighbors and joined hands, forming a completed circle around the table of the Lord's Supper. And so they continued, joined as one in the name of the Lord, praying silently, each to each, until after a time the spiritual intensity of the moment had moderated sufficiently for Yakov to proceed.

Praise and Worship

It was the group's great blessing that, Leah, one of their members, was a talented musician. She moved to the nearby harp that was a central feature of the ben Ezra's beautifully furnished salon, and without any comment, she began to play the first of four Odes of Solomon that had been centrally selected by the congregation's body of elders. They were always in some way connected to the daily teaching that Yakov and the other home group leaders would present following this time of praise and worship.

The Teaching

Yakov, like the other home group leaders of Pastor Joshua's congregation, was very well prepared for the great responsibility of this office he had undertaken in answer to a clear calling from the Lord. He, like the other leaders, had undergone extensive training, administered by the elders of the congregation before he had been ordained and anointed by them to this holy office.[2]

Thus, Yakov was quite ready to teach where he had left off at their last meeting with the next daily lesson, which had been prepared in the form of a detailed outline by the congregation's body of elders to be used by all the home groups that would be meeting this day. These centrally created, daily outlines were intended as a guide to enable the home group leaders to present and oversee a congregation-wide program of more or less uniform, approximately ninety-minute long daily meetings.[3]

Yakov was a particularly anointed teacher, and when his twenty-five minute homily on the fruit of the Holy Spirit, centered on both Old and New Testament Scriptures, drew to an end, everyone present had been edified and was anxious for this teaching to continue the next morning.

The Lord's Supper

Whenever they met in home groups or as a full congregation on *Motzei Shabbat*, the central feature of their coming together was the taking of the Lord's spiritualized body and blood at the table of the Lord's Supper. Yeshua Himself had initiated this sacrament. Thus, they reveled in doing it as often as they were able since it blessed them abundantly, filling them each time they so partook of these elements with a resurgence of their indescribably intense first love of the Lord and an ever-strengthening of their faith.

And so, in the same manner as Pastor Joshua had done the night before, Yakov first took the wine, blessed it, and distributed it among the members of the group. Then he did the same with the bread that Rachel had prepared for this purpose.

Blessing and Healing

Perhaps the greatest blessing of home groups is that in a very real way they are extended *mishpochot* (families) of their twenty or so members. While I am suggesting that it is certainly reasonable for a contemporary home congregation to grow to as many as forty members, from my own experience and observation of such groups, there is an inversely proportional relationship between the size of the group beyond twenty members and the degree of intimacy that exists between its members. That is to say, the bigger the group gets, the less intimate its members become.

Again, looking at the enormously successful contemporary model we have in David Yonggi Cho's Yoido Full Gospel Church, when one of Cho's cell groups grows to ten families (twenty-plus members), it is divided into two units, five families for each. The assistant leader of the original cell group, also a trained and ordained deacon or deaconess, is elevated to the leadership of the newly created group. Then each of the two leaders selects his or her own assistant leader, who will then receive formal training for this position at the church. This procedure is repeated as the size of the cell grows.[4]

The focal point of such a home group system as an adjunct to a mother congregation is its members and their individual needs, be it the Tiberias Messianic Synagogue of the first century or the contemporary Yoido Full Gospel Church. In reality these groups include not only those already registered in the church, but also those who will first be attracted to them and their members before they ultimately become a part of the greater body.

For Yakov, the reality of this focus on the individual needs of the members of his home group came into particular focus during the time at the end of each meeting when he anointed each one with oil and prayed for their individual needs, be it physical healing or any other matter that they saw fit to bring to his attention.

Thus, filled with love for each of these who were most precious to him, he took a small flask of anointing oil from the table and proceeded from one seated member to the next, anointing each of them in turn with oil in the name of the Father, Son, and Holy Spirit. He then sealed it with the sign of a *taw* that he traces on their foreheads, blessing and praying for each of their specific needs until all have been so served.

Chapter 36

Guidance for Home Congregations Seeking to Follow the Model of the First Jewish Believers of The Way

A Summary

In the foregoing pages I have done my best to identify, bring together, and present what I believe are the most germane, edifying, and often surprising things we can learn about The Way, a small group of Nazarene Jews who assembled in the Upper Room on Mount Zion immediately following the ascension of Yeshua and were the very first to embrace Him as their Messiah, the Son of God, and God incarnate. This information has been compiled from canonized Scripture and uncanonized writings, history, archaeology, and other sources concerning this fascinating group of believers.

Most of what I have thus gleaned and presented here is factual and well documented. Those things that cannot be documented and are partly or entirely anecdotal are identified as such.

Some of the more important, well-documented things concerning The Way we can point to are:

- They derived much of their theology, doctrine, and worship practice from the Essenes. As I have demonstrated, virtually all of the points of Pauline understandings were first written in the Dead Sea Scrolls. The same can be said for the teachings of Peter, James, and John. Even more importantly, many of the teachings of Yeshua can be found there as well. Why is the theology and doctrine that became the foundation of Christianity also foundational to the Essenes' understanding? Neither the question nor its answer need be perplexing. Both Christianity and Essenism are deeply rooted in the same rich holy soil of Judaism, which in turn is rooted in the Torah, written by the finger of God.[1]

- The well-developed theology, doctrine, and worship practice they mostly brought forth from this Essenic baseline was later deemed orthodox by the church fathers and ultimately became the very foundation of Christianity.
- The sum of this Essenic influence is that we can say with assurance that Christianity is a fulfillment of Judaism, more specifically a fulfillment, in turn, of the Judaism of the Essenes and the Messianic Judaism of The Way.
- The Way, in the face of unrelenting persecution from the Roman government, the church, and from their fellow Jews, dispersed from Jerusalem in waves centered around A.D. 35, following the martyrdom of Stephan; 62, after James the Just had been assassinated, just before the first Jewish revolt against Rome; and 135, when all Jews were forced by royal edict to leave Jerusalem, by then renamed Aelia Capitolina.
- There were places of Messianic Jewish worship established throughout this new diaspora that resulted from these persecution-driven dispersions from Jerusalem, most notably in Dura Europa, Megiddo, and Capernaum. Based upon its extant remains, other historical evidence, and substantial expert scholarly agreement, we may add to this list the most recently discovered Tiberias synagogue of The Way with an associated facility less than one hundred meters away, which perhaps was the residence of the pastor or some other highly appointed or prosperous believer.
- The first of two sacraments celebrated by The Way was an elaborate initiation of new believers that included water baptism by three immersions; baptism with the Holy Spirit; the serving of an oblation of milk, honey, and water; and a variety of other traditions that have hitherto been essentially long forgotten.
- The Way's second sacrament was the Lord's Supper, which, according to Scripture, they celebrated every time they came together.

There are other beliefs and practices of The Way I have pointed to that are only partly documented and are thus based in part upon an extrapolation of what we do specifically know. Some of the more important among these are the following.

- While we haven't learned with precision exactly how a Messianic synagogue such as the Tiberias synagogue of The Way conducted its services, we can make a very well educated supposition based upon an extrapolation of what we do know to be factual. First, we learn from Scripture that The Way met each day in their homes and that they came together for a congregational assembly each *Motzei Shabbat*. Next, we have a historical reference in the Apostolic Tradition of Hippolytus of Rome, which was composed in approximately A.D. 215 in Rome. (This was during the presumed last days of The Way's tenure in Tiberias.) Apparently the purpose of this writing was to preserve what were originally older Nazarene Jewish practices, which were then in danger of falling to disuse or innovation. Hippolytus shares with us the specific order of worship that was presumably taken directly from the still-contemporary Messianic Jewish model.[2]
- We know that believers of The Way met each day in their homes, where they celebrated the Lord's Supper and did not cease teaching and preaching that Yeshua was the Messiah. (See Acts 5:42.) We can only extrapolate a presumed order of worship and liturgy with which these things were accomplished from what we do specifically know and from our broad general database.
- We have been able to examine a large body of the worship songs that The Way most likely regularly used in their various meetings, some drawn from the vast collection of psalms and hymns that came down to them from the Essenes and also a body of some forty-two New Testament odes, twenty-six of which have now been reworked in form and set to new, highly anointed music. We also know what musical instruments of that day were used in religious services. Moreover, from Scripture and other historical references we know that Davidic dance was a deeply rooted expression of Jewish praise and

worship. From all of this and our general knowledge database, I believe it is reasonable to extrapolate both the presence and process of The Way's praise and worship.

The list of what is and is not well documented, as I have shared above, is by no means all-inclusive and is presented to underscore a central concluding point. The guidance for home congregations I have presented in this book is not in any way meant to be a cast-in-iron, absolute blueprint to be applied in every detail by those who are seeking to establish such groups and are looking for how they should proceed. My intention and prayerful expectation is that many Holy Spirit-inspired variations and adaptations will be forthcoming based on some mix of the collective backgrounds, understandings, and goals of those who have come together to establish such new home congregations.

There are, in my thinking, however, several cardinal understandings that I strongly recommend be embraced by all such emerging, as well as already established, home congregations. These include:

- The apostle Paul makes it clear that in Yeshua there are no distinctions between born-again Jewish and Gentile believers who have become "one new man" in the body, as all branches of that body are equally fed by the spiritually Jewish roots they hold in common. (See Ephesians 2:14–18 and Romans 11:13–24.)
- Jew and Gentile should cherish and give thanks to God for having created them as who and what they are. It is therefore heretical for a Gentile to say he is a Jew or—while it is not specifically stated—for a Jew to say he is a Gentile. (See Revelation 2:9 and 3:9.) Also, therefore, the cultist understanding known variously as "two house," "Ephraimite," or "Israelite," which proposes all Gentiles are in fact descended from the so-called "lost ten tribes of Israel" and are thus "Israelites," is a false teaching that should be flatly rejected.
- Yeshua declared unequivocally that He and He alone is the exclusive means of salvation. (See John 14:6.) Therefore the widespread and growing understanding known as "two covenant," holding that Jews do not need salvation in Yeshua since they already know the Father, must be rejected.

Finally, as I bring this writing to a conclusion, there is an underlying, two-part scriptural imperative that I would offer as a closing bit of guidance for all my dear Gentile brothers and sisters who have recently come to understand that the roots of their faith are spiritually in Judaism and that they are thus, in a way, physically planted in the deep and rich soil of Israel.

The first part of this imperative concerns the word *idols*, which appears some 128 times in my New King James Version of the Bible. The abundantly clear message of the Scriptures on this topic being that we are to avoid making any obeisance whatsoever to anyone or anything other than our creator, the Lord God of Israel.

> Let all be put to shame who serve carved images, Who boast of idols. Worship Him, all you gods.
>
> —Psalm 97:7

R. A. Torrey (1856–1928), a pillar of the church, wrote and preached:

> If we are to run with patience the race that is set before us, we must always keep looking to Jesus (Hebrews 12:1–3). One of the simplest and yet one of the mightiest secrets of abiding joy and victory is to never lose sight of Jesus.[3]

During the past sixteen glorious years I have been enormously blessed to be a citizen of Israel, the land of my inheritance—the very thought of which stirs my spirit and gladdens my heart. I am especially blessed to observe those who are visiting Israel, especially for the first time, as almost invariably they catch on to this same spirit of excitement and joy that still captivates me when I walk about in the very places where Yeshua walked so long ago.

Sadly, in all of this joy there is a deep-set and serious potential problem of the greatest consequences. Simply, with so much concentration focused upon Israel the land, it is a very common occurrence for otherwise deeply spiritual Christians to turn Israel into an idol and in the process take their eyes off Yeshua.

Over the years I have seen this tragedy repeat itself again and again. First, there was the director of a major Christian outreach who fell so much in love with the Land that she renounced her faith in Yeshua, converted to Judaism, and now resides here with her new Orthodox Jewish husband.

Next, there was the pastor of one of the most successful pro-Israel, pro-Messianic Jewish protestant congregations in the United States, who caught this same "Israel fever," abandoned her congregation (which now is defunct), divorced her husband, and is now dwelling somewhere unknown to me here in the Land.

Then, there was the ministry couple in their sixties who had a special outreach to Israel. She, however, often stayed at home caring for their very large extended family while he traveled to Israel to "minister." In the process, he fell in love with the Land and out of love with his wife. Still married and seeking a divorce from his wife, he now travels about the Land "ministering" as he may in the very close company of a much younger woman, who has fallen from grace.

I could go on with other examples, but suffice it to say that we, all of us, must diligently keep our eyes focused where they belong—on the face of our Lord.

I urge each of you who are seeking to learn more about Israel and the Jewish roots of our shared faith, especially those who are set on joining or establishing new home congregations that are founded upon the understandings of The Way, to visit the Land on a professionally guided tour. I know that you will find such a typical two-week adventure to be one of the richest and most rewarding experiences of your entire Christian walk.

I particularly pray that one day soon all of you who visit the Land will be able to stand in awe as you behold the fully excavated and restored Tiberias synagogue of The Way. It would be my very great blessing to break bread and pray with you there.

Appendix I
The Gospel According to the Nazarenes

The following fragments of the Gospel According to the Nazarenes are excerpted from Ron Cameron's *The Other Gospels: Non-Canonical Gospel Texts* (Philadelphia: The Westminster Press, 1982), 99–102. Philipp Vielhauer and George Ogg of *New Testament Apocrypha* originally made the translation.

> To these [citations, in which Matthew follows not the Septuagint but the Hebrew original text] belong the two: "Out of Egypt have I called my son" and "For he shall be called a Nazaraean."
>
> —Jerome, De viris inlustribus 3

> Behold, the mother of the Lord and his brethren said to him: John the Baptist baptizes unto the remission of sins, let us go and be baptized by him. But he said to them: Wherein have I sinned that I should go and be baptized by him? Unless what I have said is ignorance [a sin of ignorance].
>
> —Jerome, Adversus Pelagianos 3.2

> The Jewish Gospel has not "into the holy city" but "to Jerusalem."
>
> —Variant to Matthew 4:5 in the Zion Gospel Edition

> The phrase "without a cause" is lacking in some witnesses and in the Jewish Gospel.
>
> —Variant to Matthew 5:22, ibid.

> In the so-called Gospel According to the Hebrews instead of "essential to existence" I found "mahar," which means "of tomorrow," so that the sense is: "Our bread of tomorrow"—that is, of the future—"give us this day."
>
> —Jerome, Commentary on Matthew 1 (on Matthew 6:11)

The Jewish Gospel reads here as follows: "If ye be in my bosom and do not the will of my Father in heaven, I will cast you out of my bosom."

—Variant to Matthew 7:5,
or better, to Matthew 7:21–23,
in the Zion Gospel Edition

The Jewish Gospel: (wise) more than serpents.

—Variant to Matthew 10:16, ibid.

The Jewish Gospel has: (the kingdom of heaven) is plundered.

—Variant to Matthew 11:12, ibid.

The Jewish Gospel has: I thank thee.

—Variant to Matthew 11:25, ibid.

In the Gospel which the Nazarenes and the Ebionites use, which we have recently translated out of Hebrew into Greek, and which is called by most people the authentic [Gospel] of Matthew, the man who had the withered hand is described as a mason who pleaded for help in the following words: "I was a mason and earned [my] livelihood with [my] hands; I beseech thee, Jesus, to restore me to my health that I may not with ignominy have to beg for my bread."

—Jerome, Commentary on Matthew 2
[on Matthew 12:13]

The Jewish Gospel does not have: three d(ays and nights).

—Variant to Matthew 12:40
in the Zion Gospel Edition

The Jewish Gospel: corban is what you should obtain from us.

—Variant to Matthew 15:5, ibid.

What is marked with an asterisk [i.e., Matthew 16:2–3] is not found in other manuscripts, also it is not found in the Jewish Gospel.

—Variant to Matthew 16:2–3, ibid.

The Jewish Gospel: son of John.

—Variant to Matthew 16:17, ibid.

He [Jesus] said: If thy brother has sinned with a word and has made three reparations, receive him seven times in a day. Simon his disciple said to him: Seven times in a day? The Lord answered and said to him: Yea, I say unto thee, until seventy times seven times. For in the prophets also after they were anointed with the Holy Spirit, the word of sin [sinful discourse?] was found.

—Jerome, Adversus Pelagianos 3.2

The Jewish Gospel has after "seventy times seven times": For in the prophets also, after they were anointed with the Holy Spirit, the word of sin [sinful discourse?] was found.

—Variant to Matthew 18:22
in the Zion Gospel Edition

The other of the two rich men said to him: Master, what good thing must I do that I may live? He said to him: Man, fulfil the law and the prophets. He answered him: That have I done. He said to him: Go and sell all that thou possessest and distribute it among the poor, and then come and follow me. But the rich man then began to scratch his head and it [the saying] pleased him not. And the Lord said to him: How canst though say, I have fulfilled the law and the prophets? For it stands written in the law: Love thy neighbor as thyself; and behold, many of the brethren, sons of Abraham, are begrimed with dirt and die of hunger—and thy house is full of many good things and nothing at all comes forth from it to them! And he turned and said to Simon, his disciple, who was sitting by him: Simon, son of Jona, it is easier for a camel to go through the eye of a needle than for a rich man to enter into the kingdom of heaven.

—Origen, Commentary on Matthew 15:14
[on Matthew 19:16–30]

In the Gospel which the Nazarenes use, instead of "son of Barachias" we have found written "son of Joiada."

—Jerome, Commentary on Matthew 4
[on Matthew 23:35]

But since the Gospel (written) in Hebrew characters which has come into our hands enters the threat not against the man who had hid (the talent), but against him who had lived dissolutely—for he (the master) had three servants: one who squandered his master's substance with harlots and flute-girls, one who multiplied the gain, and one who hid the talent; and accordingly one was accepted (with joy), another merely rebuked, and another cast into prison—I wonder whether in Matthew the threat which is uttered after the word against the man who did nothing may not refer to him, but by epanalepsis to the first who had feasted and drunk with the drunken.

—Eusebius, Theophania 22
[on Matthew 25:14–15]

The Jewish Gospel: And he denied and swore and damned himself.

—Variant to Matthew 26:74
in the Zion Gospel Edition

Barabbas...is interpreted in the so-called Gospel according to the Hebrews as "son of their teacher."

—Jerome, Commentary on Matthew 4
[on Matthew 27:16]

But in the Gospel which is written in Hebrew characters we read not that the veil of the temple was rent, but that the lintel of the temple of wondrous size collapsed.

—Jerome, Epistula ad Hedybiam 120.8

The Jewish Gospel: And he delivered to them armed men that they might sit over against the cave and guard it day and night.

—Variant to Matthew 27:65
in the Zion Gospel Edition

He (Christ) himself taught the reason for the separations of souls that take place in houses, as we have found somewhere in the Gospel that is spread abroad among the Jews in the Hebrew tongue, in which it is said: "I choose for myself the most worthy: the most worthy are those whom my Father in heaven has given me."

—Eusebius, Theophania 4.12
[on Matthew 10:34–36]

Appendix II

Principal Points of Contact Between the Didache and the New Testament

The following table shows the specific points of contact between the Didache and the canonized Gospels, as well as the three noted epistles.[1]

DIDACHE	MATTHEW	MARK	LUKE	JOHN	JAMES	1 PETER	1 JOHN
1:1	7:13–14	–	13:24	–	–	–	–
1:2	22:39	12:31	10:27	–	2:8	–	–
1:2e	7:12	–	6:31	–	–	–	–
1:3b	5:44	–	6:28	–	–	2:23; 3:9	–
1:3c	5:46–47	–	6:32	–	–	2:20	–
1:4b	5:39	–	6:29	–	–	3:9	–
1:4b	5:48; 19:21	–	6:36, 40	–	1:4	1:15	–
1:4b	5:40	–	6:29	–	–	–	–
1:5a	5:42	–	6:30	–	2:15–16	–	–
1:5a	5:44–45	–	6:35	–	–	2:23; 3:9	–
1:5c	5:26	–	12:59	–	–	–	–
2:2	19:18	10:19	18:20	–	2:10–11	–	–
2:3	5:33	–	–	–	5:12	–	–
3:2	5:21–22	–	–	–	–	–	3:15
3:3	5:27–28	–	–	–	1:14–15	–	2:16
3:7	5:5	–	–	–	–	–	–
5:1b	15:19	7:21–23	–	–	–	–	–
7:1 c, d	28:19	–	–	–	–	–	–
8:1	6:16	–	–	–	–	–	–

DIDACHE	MATTHEW	MARK	LUKE	JOHN	JAMES	1 PETER	1 JOHN
8:2a	6:2, 5, 16	12:38–39	11:42–43; 20:46	–	–	–	–
8:2c	6:9–13	–	11:2–4	–	–	–	–
9:5b	7:6	–	–	–	–	–	–
11:1	5:17, 19	–	16:17	–	–	–	–
11:7	12:31	3:28–30	12:10	–	–	–	5:16
13:1	10:9–10	–	10:7	–	–	–	–
14:2	5:24	–	–	–	–	–	–
16:1	24:42, 25:13	13:33–37	12:35–40	–	–	–	–
16:3	24:11–12	13:22	21:8	–	–	–	2:18–19, 26, 4:1
16:4a, 5	24:10	13:12	21:16	–	–	–	–
16:6, 8	24:30	13:26	21:27	–	–	–	–
16:8a	16:27; 25:31	8:38; 14:62	9:26; 22:69	1:51	–	–	–
16:9	25:34, 46	9:44	16:26	3:16, 36	–	–	2:25

Appendix III
The Didache

The Lord's Teaching Through the Twelve Apostles to the Nations (Roberts-Donaldson Translation)

Chapter 1. The Two Ways and the First Commandment

There are two ways, one of life and one of death, but a great difference between the two ways. The way of life, then, is this: First, you shall love God who made you; second, love your neighbor as yourself, and do not do to another what you would not want done to you. And of these sayings the teaching is this: Bless those who curse you, and pray for your enemies, and fast for those who persecute you. For what reward is there for loving those who love you? Do not the Gentiles do the same? But love those who hate you, and you shall not have an enemy. Abstain from fleshly and worldly lusts. If someone strikes your right cheek, turn to him the other also, and you shall be perfect. If someone impresses you for one mile, go with him two. If someone takes your cloak, give him also your coat. If someone takes from you what is yours, ask it not back, for indeed you are not able. Give to every one who asks you, and ask it not back; for the Father wills that to all should be given of our own blessings (free gifts). Happy is he who gives according to the commandment, for he is guiltless. Woe to him who receives; for if one receives who has need, he is guiltless; but he who receives not having need shall pay the penalty, why he received and for what. And coming into confinement, he shall be examined concerning the things which he has done, and he shall not escape from there until he pays back the last penny. And also concerning this, it has been said, Let your alms sweat in your hands, until you know to whom you should give.

Chapter 2. The Second Commandment: Grave Sin Forbidden

And the second commandment of the Teaching; You shall not commit murder, you shall not commit adultery, you shall not commit pederasty, you shall not commit fornication, you shall not steal, you shall not practice magic, you shall not practice witchcraft, you shall not murder a child by abortion nor kill that which is born. You shall not covet the things of your neighbor, you shall not swear, you shall not bear false witness, you shall not speak evil, you shall bear no grudge. You shall not be double-minded nor double-tongued, for to be double-tongued is a snare of death. Your speech shall not be false, nor empty, but fulfilled by deed. You shall not be covetous, nor rapacious, nor a hypocrite, nor evil disposed, nor haughty. You shall not take evil counsel against your neighbor. You shall not hate any man; but some you shall reprove, and concerning some you shall pray, and some you shall love more than your own life.

Chapter 3. Other Sins Forbidden

My child, flee from every evil thing, and from every likeness of it. Be not prone to anger, for anger leads to murder. Be neither jealous, nor quarrelsome, nor of hot temper, for out of all these murders are engendered. My child, be not a lustful one, for lust leads to fornication. Be neither a filthy talker, nor of lofty eye, for out of all these adulteries are engendered. My child, be not an observer of omens, since it leads to idolatry. Be neither an enchanter, nor an astrologer, nor a purifier, nor be willing to look at these things, for out of all these idolatry is engendered. My child, be not a liar, since a lie leads to theft. Be neither money-loving, nor vainglorious, for out of all these thefts are engendered. My child, be not a murmurer, since it leads the way to blasphemy. Be neither self-willed nor evil-minded, for out of all these blasphemies are engendered.

Rather, be meek, since the meek shall inherit the earth. Be long-suffering and pitiful and guileless and gentle and good and always trembling at the words which you have heard. You shall not exalt yourself, nor give over-confidence to your soul. Your soul shall not be joined with lofty ones, but with just and lowly ones shall it have its intercourse. Accept whatever happens to you as good, knowing that apart from God nothing comes to pass.

Chapter 4. Various Precepts

My child, remember night and day him who speaks the word of God to you, and honor him as you do the Lord. For wherever the lordly rule is uttered, there is the Lord. And seek out day by day the faces of the saints, in order that you may rest upon their words. Do not long for division, but rather bring those who contend to peace. Judge righteously, and do not respect persons in reproving for transgressions. You shall not be undecided whether or not it shall be. Be not a stretcher forth of the hands to receive and a drawer of them back to give. If you have anything, through your hands you shall give ransom for your sins. Do not hesitate to give, nor complain when you give; for you shall know who is the good repayer of the hire. Do not turn away from him who is in want; rather, share all things with your brother, and do not say that they are your own. For if you are partakers in that which is immortal, how much more in things which are mortal? Do not remove your hand from your son or daughter; rather, teach them the fear of God from their youth. Do not enjoin anything in your bitterness upon your bondman or maidservant, who hope in the same God, lest ever they shall fear not God who is over both; for he comes not to call according to the outward appearance, but to them whom the Spirit has prepared. And you bondmen shall be subject to your masters as to a type of God, in modesty and fear. You shall hate all hypocrisy and everything which is not pleasing to the Lord. Do not in any way forsake the commandments of the Lord; but keep what you have received, neither adding thereto nor taking away therefrom. In the church you shall acknowledge your transgressions, and you shall not come near for your prayer with an evil conscience. This is the way of life.

Chapter 5. The Way of Death

And the way of death is this: First of all it is evil and accursed: murders, adultery, lust, fornication, thefts, idolatries, magic arts, witchcrafts, rape, false witness, hypocrisy, double-heartedness, deceit, haughtiness, depravity, self-will, greediness, filthy talking, jealousy, over-confidence, loftiness, boastfulness; persecutors of the good, hating truth, loving a lie, not knowing a reward for righteousness, not cleaving to good nor to righteous judgment, watching not for that which is good, but for that which is evil; from whom meekness and endurance are far, loving vanities, pursuing revenge, not pitying a poor man, not laboring for the afflicted, not knowing Him Who made them, murderers of children, destroyers of the handiwork of God, turning away from him who is in want, afflicting him who is distressed, advocates of the rich, lawless judges of the poor, utter sinners. Be delivered, children, from all these.

Chapter 6. Against False Teachers, and Food Offered to Idols

See that no one causes you to err from this way of the Teaching, since apart from God it teaches you. For if you are able to bear the entire yoke of the Lord, you will be perfect; but if you are not able to do this, do what you are able. And concerning food, bear what you are able; but against that which is sacrificed to idols be exceedingly careful; for it is the service of dead gods.

Chapter 7. Concerning Baptism

And concerning baptism, baptize this way: Having first said all these things, baptize into the name of the Father, and of the Son, and of the Holy Spirit, in living water. But if you have no living water, baptize into other water; and if you cannot do so in cold water, do so in warm. But if you have neither, pour out water three times upon the head into the name of Father and Son and Holy Spirit. But before the baptism let the baptizer fast, and the baptized, and whoever else can; but you shall order the baptized to fast one or two days before.

Chapter 8. Fasting and Prayer (the Lord's Prayer)

But let not your fasts be with the hypocrites, for they fast on the second and fifth day of the week. Rather, fast on the fourth day and the Preparation (Friday). Do not pray like the hypocrites, but rather as the Lord commanded in His Gospel, like this:

> Our Father who art in heaven, hallowed be Thy name. Thy kingdom come. Thy will be done on earth, as it is in heaven. Give us today our daily (needful) bread, and forgive us our debt as we also forgive our debtors. And bring us not into temptation, but deliver us from the evil one (or, evil); for Thine is the power and the glory for ever.

Pray this three times each day.

Chapter 9. The Lord's Supper

Now concerning the Lord's Supper, give thanks this way. First, concerning the cup:

> *We thank thee, our Father, for the holy vine of David Thy servant, which You madest known to us through Jesus Thy Servant; to Thee be the glory for ever.*

And concerning the broken bread:

> *We thank Thee, our Father, for the life and knowledge which You madest known to us through Jesus Thy Servant; to Thee be the glory for ever. Even as this broken bread was scattered over the hills, and was gathered together and became one, so let Thy Church be gathered*

together from the ends of the earth into Thy kingdom; for Thine is the glory and the power through Jesus Christ for ever.

But let no one eat or drink of your Lord's Supper, unless they have been baptized into the name of the Lord; for concerning this also the Lord has said, "Give not that which is holy to the dogs."

Chapter 10. Prayer After Communion

But after you are filled, give thanks this way:

We thank Thee, holy Father, for Thy holy name which You didst cause to tabernacle in our hearts, and for the knowledge and faith and immortality, which You modest known to us through Jesus Thy Servant; to Thee be the glory for ever. Thou, Master almighty, didst create all things for Thy name's sake; You gavest food and drink to men for enjoyment, that they might give thanks to Thee; but to us You didst freely give spiritual food and drink and life eternal through Thy Servant. Before all things we thank Thee that You are mighty; to Thee be the glory for ever. Remember, Lord, Thy Church, to deliver it from all evil and to make it perfect in Thy love, and gather it from the four winds, sanctified for Thy kingdom which Thou have prepared for it; for Thine is the power and the glory for ever. Let grace come, and let this world pass away. Hosanna to the God (Son) of David! If any one is holy, let him come; if any one is not so, let him repent. Maranatha. Amen.

But permit the prophets to make thanksgiving as much as they desire.

Chapter 11. Concerning Teachers, Apostles, and Prophets

Whosoever, therefore, comes and teaches you all these things that have been said before, receive him. But if the teacher himself turns and teaches another doctrine to the destruction of this, hear him not. But if he teaches so as to increase righteousness and the knowledge of the Lord, receive him as the Lord. But concerning the apostles and prophets, act according to the decree of the Gospel. Let every apostle who comes to you be received as the Lord. But he shall not remain more than one day; or two days, if there's a need. But if he remains three days, he is a false prophet. And when the apostle goes away, let him take nothing but bread until he lodges. If he asks for money, he is a false prophet. And every prophet who speaks in the Spirit you shall neither try nor judge; for every sin shall be forgiven, but this sin shall not be forgiven. But not every one who speaks in the Spirit is a prophet; but only if he holds the ways of the Lord. Therefore from their ways shall the false prophet and the prophet be known. And every prophet who orders a meal in the Spirit does not eat it, unless he is indeed a false prophet. And every prophet who teaches the truth, but does not do what he teaches, is a false prophet. And every prophet, proved true, working unto the mystery of the Church in the world, yet not teaching others to do what he himself does, shall not be judged among you, for with God he has his judgment; for so did also the ancient prophets. But whoever says in the Spirit, Give me money, or something else, you shall not listen to him. But if he tells you to give for others' sake who are in need, let no one judge him.

Chapter 12. Reception of Christians

But receive everyone who comes in the name of the Lord, and prove and know him afterward; for you shall have understanding right and left. If he who comes is a wayfarer, assist him as far as you are able; but he shall not remain with you more than two or three days, if need be. But if he wants to stay with you, and is an artisan, let him work and eat. But if he has no trade, according to your understanding, see to it that, as a Christian, he shall not live with you idle. But if he wills not to do, he is a Christ-monger. Watch that you keep away from such.

Chapter 13. Support of Prophets

But every true prophet who wants to live among you is worthy of his support. So also a true teacher is himself worthy, as the workman, of his support. Every first-fruit, therefore, of the products of wine-press and threshing-floor, of oxen and of sheep, you shall take and give to the prophets, for they are your high priests. But if you have no prophet, give it to the poor. If you make a batch of dough, take the first-fruit and give according to the commandment. So also when you open a jar of wine or of oil, take the first-fruit and give it to the prophets; and of money (silver) and clothing and every possession, take the first-fruit, as it may seem good to you, and give according to the commandment.

Chapter 14. Christian Assembly on the Lord's Day

But every Lord's day gather yourselves together, and break bread, and give thanksgiving after having confessed your transgressions, that your sacrifice may be pure. But let no one who is at odds with his fellow come together with you, until they be reconciled, that your sacrifice may not be profaned. For this is that which was spoken by the Lord: "In every place and time offer to me a pure sacrifice; for I am a great King, says the Lord, and my name is wonderful among the nations."

Chapter 15. Bishops and Deacons; Christian Reproof

Appoint, therefore, for yourselves, bishops and deacons worthy of the Lord, men meek, and not lovers of money, and truthful and proved; for they also render to you the service of prophets and teachers. Therefore do not despise them, for they are your honored ones, together with the prophets and teachers. And reprove one another, not in anger, but in peace, as you have it in the Gospel. But to anyone that acts amiss against another, let no one speak, nor let him hear anything from you until he repents. But your prayers and alms and all your deeds so do, as you have it in the Gospel of our Lord.

Chapter 16. Watchfulness; the Coming of the Lord

Watch for your life's sake. Let not your lamps be quenched, nor your loins unloosed; but be ready, for you know not the hour in which our Lord will come. But come together often, seeking the things which are befitting to your souls: for the whole time of your faith will not profit you, if you are not made perfect in the last time. For in the last days false prophets and corrupters shall be multiplied, and the sheep shall be turned into wolves, and love shall be turned into hate; for when lawlessness increases, they shall hate and persecute and betray one another, and then shall appear the world-deceiver as Son of God, and shall do signs and wonders, and the earth shall be delivered into his hands, and he shall do iniquitous things which have never yet come to pass since the beginning. Then shall the creation of men come into the fire of trial, and many shall be made to stumble and shall perish; but those who endure in their faith shall be saved from under the curse itself. And then shall appear the signs of the truth: first, the sign of an outspreading in heaven, then the sign of the sound of the trumpet. And third, the resurrection of the dead—yet not of all, but as it is said: "The Lord shall come and all His saints with Him." Then shall the world see the Lord coming upon the clouds of heaven.

Notes

Introduction

1. Pew Forum, *U.S. Religious Landscape Survey*, June 2008, http://religions.pewforum.org/portraits.

2. *Charisma*, "The Decline of the Mainline Church," March 2000, 61; also, National Council of Churches, "Membership Statistics for the National Council of Churches Member Communions," www.electronicchurch.org/2002/NCC_members.htm.

3. Steven Katz, "The Jewish Roots Movement: Flowers and Thorns," http://jewsforjesus.org/publications/havurah/4_1/jewishroots.

4. Raymond Robert Fischer, *The Children of God*, 52–53. While the de-Judaizing of the church came into full swing at the Council of Nicea in 325 and later, there is evidence that this process began even earlier. For example, the Messianic Seal seemingly faded into obscurity on Mount Zion when the fish was pulled away from the Star of David and the *menorah* to become the stand-alone symbol of the church.

5. *Time*, "Why Home Churches Are Filling Up," February 27, 2006.

6. Tricia Tillan, "Transforming the Church, *Cross+Word*, http://intotruth.org/apostasy/cell-church4.htm#cho.

7. *The Economist*, "O Come All Ye Faithful, Special Report on Religion and Public Life," November, 2007.

8. David Yonggi Cho, *Successful Home Cell Groups*, v–vii.

9. The Apocryphal Gospel of Thomas, verse 12: "The disciples said to Jesus, 'We know that you are going to leave us. Who will be our leader?'" Jesus said to them, "No matter where you are you are to go to James the Just, for whose sake heaven and earth came into being."

10. Craig A. Evans, "The Synoptic Gospels and the Dead Sea Scrolls," James H. Charlesworth, ed., *The Bible and the Dead Sea Scrolls*, Vol. 3, 92.

11. Bellarmino Bagatti, *The Church From the Circumcision*, 43–49.

12. Emmanuel Testa, *The Faith of the Mother Church*, 146–157.

13. Eusebius, *The History of the Church*, 37.

14. Raymond Robert Fischer, *The Door Where It Began* (Olim Publications, 2005).

15. Ernest Renan, *The History of the Origins of Christianity*, Vol. 2, 117–124.

16. Ibid. 15, 73. (While little known and seldom discussed in scholarly references to the very early church, there is compelling evidence that the migrations of The Way most likely included various end locations in what is modern day Jordan. For example, Pella, the site generally agreed to be the first stop of The Way circa 62 on their way to forming the second Great Diaspora, is in fact just east of the Jordan River in the Kingdom of Jordan. Even more interesting is the St. Georges Church, in Northern Jordan, dated to A.D. 230 by Jordanian Archaeologist Abdul Qader

Hussan, head of the Rihab Centre for Archaeological Studies. Source: *The Jordan Times*, June 10, 2008.)

17. While no precise date can be fixed for the transfer of the Mother Church to Damascus, the beginning of this process can be seen following Paul's conversion on the road where he was going to persecute an already well-established, believing Jewish community in that city. Another benchmark can be found in Dr. Lee W. Woodard's *Codex W: Old and Holy*, which sets forth his analysis of forensic evidence that the original Gospel of Matthew was completed in Aramaic in Damascus in 37, only seven years following Yeshua's ascension. According to Woodard, the final version of this Gospel was completed in Damascus in 67. This date remarkably corresponds with considerable scholarly support that all but a small remnant of Jewish believers, having been divinely forewarned of the impending first revolt against Rome, fled from Jerusalem circa 65 to safety in Pella, a city in the Decapolis, followed by the destruction of the Temple in 70. It seems reasonable to suggest that there was a close communication and coordination between these two main centers of The Way. (See Eusebius, 68–75.)

18. Jósef T. Milik, *Ten Years of Discovery in the Wilderness of Judea*, 88–91, 142.

19. Flavius Josephus, *Jewish Antiquities*, xx.9.

20. Eusebius, 107.

21. Eusebius, 68.

22. Ray A. Pritz, *Nazarene Jewish Christianity*, 35, 42.

23. The Mishna is the written version of the Oral Torah that was redacted by the Pharisees beginning soon after 70, in Yavne where the Sanhedrin moved following the destruction of the temple. The process was finally completed soon after their final relocation to Tiberias circa 220. The Gemara is a very lengthy rabbinical commentary on the Mishna. Together, the Mishna and the Gemara become the Talmud.

24. Mary T. Boatwright, *Hadrian and the Cities of the Roman Empire*, 197.

25. Dom Touttee, *Dom Touttee's St. Cyril (1790)*. From the church historians and his works collected by Dom Touttee in his edition of them at Paris, in 1790.

26. Ilan Tal, "Dance in the Ancient World," *Near Eastern Archaeology*, Vol. 66, No. 3 (Sep. 2003): 135–136.

27. Bible teacher and scholar John McTernan provides an excellent teaching on the reconstruction of the temple at his Web site http://branchofdavid.org/temple.htm#king%20messiah%20temple.

28. Mancini, *Archaeological Discoveries Relative to the Judeo-Christians*, 176–177.

29. Ibid.

Chapter 1
The Founding of the Jewish Mother Congregation on Mount Zion

1. While the Roman Catholics base much of their teaching upon Mary's supposed continuing virginity until her death, the early understanding of The Way and that of most Protestant groups is quite different, holding that Mary gave birth to several children following the virgin conception and birth of Yeshua. While there

is scriptural evidence that speaks to this understanding (Luke 1:26–38), there is also much in the NT apocrypha, attributed to Jewish Christian authorship, that adds another dimension to this understanding. For example, in the Second Apocalypse of James, dated to the late first or early second century, we read what is said to be the teaching (in part) of James as presented from the steps leading up to the temple:

> Once when I was sitting deliberating, he [Yeshua] opened the door. That one whom you hated and persecuted came in to me. He said to me, "Hail, my brother; my brother, hail." As I raised my face to stare at him, [my] mother said to me, "Do not be frightened, my son, because he said 'My brother' to you. For you were nourished with this same milk. Because of this he calls me 'My mother'. For he is not a stranger to us. He is your step-brother...

2. John Painter, *Just James, The Brother of Jesus in History and Tradition*, 269–279.

3. Jerome, *De viris illustribus, The Catholic Encyclopedia*, accessed at New Advent Online, http://www.newadvent.org/fathers/2708.htm.

4. The Gospel of Thomas, 12, English translation by Stephen Patterson and Marvin Meyer, http://www.misericordia.edu/users/davies/thomas/Trans.htm.

5. See Acts 1:12–14.

6. There are five Vatican documents that cite the Pope as the "Sweet Christ on Earth," for example: Pope John Paul II, Apostolic Exhortation *Vita Consecrata* (*On the Consecrated Life and Its Mission in the Church and in the World*), March 25, 1996, http://www.wayoflife.org/fbns/popeidentifies.htm:

> In founders and foundresses [of the consecrated orders of nuns and priests, etc.] we see a constant and lively sense of the Church, which they manifest by their full participation in all aspects of the Church's life, and in their ready obedience to the bishops and especially to the Roman pontiff. Against this background of love towards Holy Church, "the pillar and bulwark of the truth" (1 Tim. 3:15), we readily understand the devotion of Saint Francis of Assisi for "The Lord Pope", the daughterly outspokenness of Saint Catherine of Siena towards the one whom she called "Sweet Christ on Earth."

7. Renan, 58.

8. Painter, 83–84.

9. Renan, 77.

10. Charles H. Spurgeon, *Spurgeon's Sermon Notes*, 244.

11. Eusebius, 37.

12. Fischer, *The Door Where It Began*. This earlier writing speaks in part to the hypothesis that the Gentile Christian Church began in nearby Hippos of the Decapolis, shortly after Yeshua fed the multitude of four thousand at Tel Hadar.

13. See Chapter 26, 200.

14. Bagatti, 7.

15. It is unclear just when Symeon died. According to Hegesippus he lived until the ripe old age of 120 and he died during the reign of Trajan (98–117). Source: Hegesippus, *Fragments From His Five Books of Commentaries on the Acts of the Church*, www.EarlyChristianWritings.com.

16. Eusebius, 4.5, 43–44, 58–61.

17. Oskar Skarsaune and Reidar Hvalik, eds., *Jewish Believers in Jesus*, 757–758.

18. Mancini, 176–177.

Chapter 2
The Organization and Structure of the Nazarenes and Their Mother Congregation of The Way on Mount Zion

1. Raymond Robert Fischer, *Full Circle*, Part One 21–134.

2. Israel Law of Return (Amendment No. 2) 5730–1970 (4B), which states, "For the purposes of this Law, 'Jew' means a person who was born of a Jewish mother or has become converted to Judaism and who is not a member of another religion."

3. For example, see Dead Sea Scrolls 4Q246 I 7–9, II 1–7, 1Qp Mic 1–5 all, 4Q522 8II 3–4, 4Q20 4 2–10, 4Q434 1–4, CD–B, XIX, 5–13, 15.

4. Abraham Cohen, *Everyman's Talmud: The Major Teachings of the Rabbinic Sages*, 405.

5. Dead Sea Scrolls, 4Q541 9, 1, 1–6.

6. James H. Charlesworth, ed., *The Bible and the Dead Sea Scrolls*, preface to Vol. 1, xxvii.

7. Dead Sea Scrolls, "Community Rule" (1QS) 8.1–4.

8. Fischer, *Full Circle*, 90. The Essenes celebrated a type of the Lord's Supper at every communal meal when they understood that the Messiah of Israel was present.

9. Dead Sea Scrolls, "Damascus Document," CD 13:7–13.

10. *The NIV Study Bible*, "Introduction to the Epistle of James," 1879.

11. George Brook, "Biblical Interpretation at Qumran," James H. Charlesworth, ed., *The Bible and the Dead Sea Scrolls*, Vol. 1, 309.

12. Didache, Roberts-Donaldson Translation, 8:1.

Chapter 3
The Way's Understanding and Celebration of Water Baptism

1. "The *mikvah*, the Jewish ritual bath, has an important place in the history of traditional Judaism, Christianity, and Messianic Judaism. God told Moses that Jews are to take a *mikvah* on quite an array of occasions: after contact with seminal fluid (Lev. 15:16, 18 and Deut. 23:11) or menstrual blood (Lev. 15:21–22, 27), upon being cured from certain skin diseases (Lev. 14:8–9), after exposure to certain diseases (Lev. 15:5–6, 8, 10–11, 13), after contact with a dead animal (Lev. 17:15–16) or human (Num. 19:7–8, 19), upon becoming a *cohen* (priest) (Exod. 29:4; 40:12), and during the Yom Kippur ritual (Lev. 16:4, 24, 26, 28)." From Glen Penton, *Mikvah*, http://beth-abraham.org/Mikvah.html.

2. War 2:129.

3. War 2:150.
4. Dead Sea Scrolls, 1QS III 4–9.
5. Bellarmino Bagatti, *The Church From the Gentiles in Pal*estine, 303.
6. The Essenes called themselves "Lebanon," which means "white," because they habitually wore sparklingly white robes of fine linen. From *History and the Essenes Classical Authors on the Essenes and Galileans or Zealots (On the writings of Josephus)* http://www.thenazareneway.com/classical_authors_on_the_essenes.htm#pliny.
7. Dead Sea Scrolls, 1QS 6:13–23; also, *The Apostolic Tradition of Hippolytus of Rome*, 27.
8. Jean Danielou, *The Theology of Jewish Christianity*, 323. The baptismal formula of the triple effusion (pouring) is an entirely Jewish Christian initiated practice not rooted in Judaism that speaks exclusively to immersion.
9. The Didache, Alan J. P. Garrow, trans., "The Gospel of Matthew's Dependence on the Didache," xxiii.
10. Theodotus, *Excerpta Ex Theodoto*, 7, 24, http://www.gnosis.org/library/excr.htm.
11. "The Odes of Solomon Lyrics," *The Odes Project*, from text found in Odes 4, 8, 23, and 24, http://www.theodesproject.com/listen.
12. Lee Woodard, *First Century Gospels Found*! 294. The word *mark* in Ezekiel 9:4 is translated as *taw* in the Hebrew Bible.
13. Bagatti, *The Church From the Circumcision*, 239.

Chapter 4
The Way's Understanding and Celebration of the Lord's Supper

1. Y. Tepper and L. Di Segni, *A Christian Prayer Hall of the Third Century*, 26.
2. (Pronouns have been updated to modern American English usage.) *The Didache, or Teaching of the Twelve Apostles*, Charles H. Hoole, trans., www.EarlyChristianWritngs.com.
3. Dead Sea Scrolls 1QSA II 11– 21. It seems clear that the Essenes genuinely believed that the Messiah (Yeshua) was present with them by the power of His Holy Spirit during their regular daily meals (communal celebrations) when they participated, according to in the elements of the new wine and bread, and that they looked forward to His expected physical incarnation, near the end of which He would be physically present to officiate at the historical Lord's Supper in the Upper Room on Mt. Zion.
4. *Shabbat* ends at nightfall, when three stars are visible, approximately forty minutes after sunset. From "Shabbat," *Judaism 101*, http://www.jewfaq.org/Shabbat.htm.
5. Didache, Charles H. Hoole, trans., 10.1, 10.3.
6. Rabbi Tzvi Rosen, "The Art of Kosher Wine Making," Star-K Kashrus, admin.; Kashrus Kurrents, Ed., http://www.star-k.org/kashrus/kk-thirst-wine.htm.
7. The fascinating account of Dr. Thomas B. Welch and how he came to develop Welch's Grape Juice as a nonalcoholic substitute for communion wine is available online at "The Chalice Reconsidered," www.standrewslaramie.org/files/chalice.pdf.

8. The four cups used in the traditional Passover *Seder* represent the four "I wills" uttered by God as promises to Moses, recorded in Exodus 6:6–8.

The elements of the Passover *Haggadah* were put together in Talmudic times (circa 10 B.C.E. to about 200 C.E.) and were based on the Passover Seder conducted by five rabbis in Bnai Brak in Palestine during Roman times. This is told in the tractate (essay) called "Pesachim" in the Mishnah, which is part of the Talmud (also known as the Mishnah Talmud). The rituals contained in the Passover Haggadah are discussed in Pesachim 10 of the Mishnah Talmud. Although the Passover Haggadah was formed in Talmudic times, its contents changed over time. The contents of the Passover Haggadah only became stable in the 9th and 10th centuries when the great rabbis (also known in Hebrew as the "Geonim") in the Jewish academies of learning in Babylonia, established a stable Passover Haggadah text, starting with the Passover Haggadah text of Sa'adiah Gaon in Sura, Babylonia. The first printed Haggadah came from Guadalajara, Spain circa 1482 and Italy in 1505, respectively. From "Passover," http://4passover.tripod.com/.

9. See Matthew 26:27, Mark 14:23, and Luke 22:17.

10. Pentecost comes from the harvest festival called the Feast of Weeks, which occurs fifty days (seven weeks) following Pesach. It is a feast prepared from the first fruits of the grain in the form of leavened bread. The leavened as opposed to unleavened bread is symbolic of the power of the Holy Spirit, for the leavening that fills the dough with air and makes it rise has been long regarded as a symbol of the Holy Spirit.

11. "In the Roman Catholic Church, the issue has doctrinal implications and was the subject of an edict from Joseph Ratzinger, the German cardinal who became Pope Benedict XVI in 2005. He ruled that bread used at Holy Communion must contain at least a tiny amount of gluten in order for it to be 'valid matter for the celebration of the Lord's Supper.' It seems that canon law requires that the wafers be made from wheat which naturally contains gluten, a protein. Hence, wafers made from rice would not suffice. As a result, wafer manufacturers supplying Catholic churches have developed a product with a gluten content so small that Catholics can eat it without any ill effects." From "Special Communion Wafers Issued to Clergy so Worshippers with Food Allergies Don't Fall Ill," *The Daily Mail*, January 13, 2008.

Chapter 5
The Initiation of New Members of The Way in First Century Jerusalem

1. While The Way regularly celebrated both baptism and the Lord's Supper, the "sacraments" were first institutionalized by the early Roman Church and are not, as such, specifically to be found in traditional or believing Jewish practice. In Gentile Christian belief and practice, a sacrament is a rite instituted by Christ that mediates grace, constituting a sacred mystery. Views concerning both what rites are

sacramental and what it means for an act to be sacramental vary among Christian denominations and traditions.

2. The doctrine of the "two ways" is central to Essene understanding and is the central theme of the entire sixteen chapters of the Didache, which begins, "There are two ways, one of life, the other of death, and there is a great difference between the two ways" (Didache 1.1). This understanding is the very essence of Essene thought and a central theme of the Dead Sea Scrolls. For example, Frag. 1 2 says, "He is setting [before you a blessing and a curse. These are] t[wo] ways, one goo[d and one evil. If you walk in the good way,] He will bless you. But if you walk in the [evil] way, [He will curse you in your going out] Sand in your [ten]ts. He will exterminate you, [smiting you and the product of your toil with blight and mildew, snow, ice, and hai[l…] along with all…" (Dead Sea Scrolls 4Q473).

3. Bagatti, *The Church From the Gentiles in Palestine*, 303.

4. Dead Sea Scrolls, "The Manual of Discipline," IV, 13–23.

5. Testa, 143.

6. Didache, 7.1b.

7. Dead Sea Scrolls, "Rule of the Community," 1QS VI, 13–23.

8. The Epistle of Barnabas, Roberts-Donaldson translation, 18:1.

9. Dead Sea Scrolls, "Rule of the Community," 1 QS V, 8.

10. Didache, 7.4.

11. Bagatti, *The Church From the Circumcision*, 239–240; also, Testa, *The Faith of the Mother Church*, 146–149.

12. The striking carryovers of The Way's initiation process into the Christian Church circa 215 can be seen in The Apostolic Tradition of Hippolytus of Rome, which is available online at www.bombaxo.com/hippolytus.html.

13. Before *The Messianic Seal of the Jerusalem Church* (1999), by Reuven Efraim Schmalz and Raymond Robert Fischer, was published, the authors counted seven separate entrances to the elaborate catacombs that according to reliable witnesses run crisscross under the entire area of Mount Zion. Soon thereafter, all but one of these entrances were sealed by either the Roman Catholic and/or Greek Orthodox Church in order to keep the curious away. Both Ludwig Schnieder, who holds the nine remaining artifacts bearing the "Messianic Seal" and Bethie Schmalz, now the wife of coauthor Reuven Schmalz, who used to play with her friends in these catacombs when she was a young teenager circa 1967, testify as to this elaborate and intricate network of interlaced caves. For Ludwig's testimony, see *The Messianic Seal of the Jerusalem Church*, iv–vii.

14. Bagatti, 246. Those being baptized by fire held a lamp in their hands, not only to illuminate their anointed bodies but to further symbolize the light to darkness motif frequently mentioned by the Essenes in the Dead Sea Scrolls.

15. J. P. Migne, ed., *Patrologia Graeca*, 9, 710–711.

16. St. Cyril of Jerusalem, "Lectures on the Christian Sacraments: The Procatechesis and the Five Mystagogical Catecheses," Frank L. Cross, ed., *Catechetical Lecture #20.*

17. Bagatti, 239–240.

18. Testa, 147.

19. Ode 25 is one of twenty-six of the forty-two Odes of Solomon that have so far been recreated by The Odes Project, offering an exquisite and anointed body of modern day praise songs based upon this first-century model. See http://www.theodesproject.com.

20. *New American Bible*, Ezekiel 9, footnote 1: "Ezekiel is preeminently the prophet of personal retribution; the innocent inhabitants of Jerusalem are to be spared when the idolatrous are punished. An X: literally, the Hebrew letter *taw*, which had the form of a cross."

21. Dead Sea Scrolls, "Damascus Document," XIX, 12.

22. The Essenes frequently adopted orphans. There is much scholarly conjecture that John was orphaned at an early age. John spent his adolescence in the Judean wilderness; the Essenes were locally based at Qumran in the Judean desert. John the Baptist and the Essenes had a shared interest in priestly matters and a priestly Messiah, and a shared focus on Isaiah 40:3. Both parties adhered to Spartan diets and ascetical behavior. Similar interests in water immersion also link John to the Essenes (in that John's water rite was comparable to Qumran ablution rights). Of the three main Jewish sects, John the Baptist's eschatological orientation is closest to the Essene position. From James Eglington, "John the Baptist," http://www.applesofgold.co.uk/john_the_baptist.htm.

23. It is a common sight to see new immigrants from Ethiopia wandering about the cities of Israel displaying very prominent equilateral crosses (*taws*) tattooed upon their foreheads. These new immigrants have come to Israel as "former believers" in Yeshua known as *Falashas* who are required by our orthodox-dominated government to undergo conversion to Orthodox Judaism. The tattoos, however, remain as indelible testimony to a former identity and sealing.

24. Bagatti, *Church From the Circumcision*, 239.

25. St. Cyril of Jerusalem, "Catechism, III, II, 33, 427."

26. Schmalz and Fischer, *The Messianic Seal of the Jerusalem Church*, v.

27. See Chapter 17, 187–190.

28. Testa, 151.

29. Ibid.

30. See Isaiah 11:2–3 and Romans 12:6–8.

31. Testa, 151.

32. The Shepherd of Hermas, Simlitude IX, 16, 5–7.

33. The Ascension of Isaiah, 10, 8–10; cf., The Epistle of Barnabas, XI, 4; also, The Gospel of Nichodemus, V, 1–3.

34. Justin Martyr, Dial. LXXXVIII, 3, 6, 686.

35. Sibylline Oracles, VI, 3–7, Milton S. Terry, trans. (1899).

36. Testa, 154.

37. Ibid., 156.

38. Bagatti, 241.

39. Testa, 156.

40. Flavius Josephus, *Jewish War* 2.137–142.

41. Bagatti, 241.
42. Ibid., 270.
43. Ibid., 256–257.
44. Schmalz and Fischer, 131–135.
45. Bellarimino Bagatti, *The Church from the Circumcision*, 256, cf Figure 129.
46. Bagatti, 270–272.
47. Schmalz and Fischer, 131–135. (Also see Testa, Plates, 7, Figure 13.)
48. Hippolytus of Rome, *The Apostolic Tradition of Hippolytus of Rome*, 21:27–32, http://www.bombaxo.com/hippolytus.html.
49. Rick Aharon Chaimberlin, "Anti-Judaism and the Council of Nicea," http://messianicfellowship.50webs.com/nicea.html.
50. Hippolytus of Rome, *The Apostolic Tradition of Hippolytus of Rome*, selected verses from Chapter 28.
51. Dom R. Hugh Connolly, *The So-Called Egyptian Church Order and Derived Documents*, 92–93.

Chapter 6
Discovery and Initial Identification

1. Testimony given to the author by Carrie Holland and approved by her (August 18, 2008).
2. Israel Antiquities Authority, press release (August 8, 2007), http://www.antiquities.org.il/article_Item_eng.asp?sec_id=25&subj_id=240&id=1273&module_id=#as.
3. Ibid.
4. Excerpt from an e-mail from Professor Jay Thompson to the author (August 6, 2008).
5. Ibid. (April 17, 2008).

Chapter 7
The Tiberias Messianic Synagogue's Mosaics

1. David W. Chapman, *Ancient Jewish and Christian Perception of Crucifixion*, 179–182; citing Erwin Goodenough, *Jewish Symbols*, 1:132 (cf. plates 225–29 in Vol. 3).
2. Excerpts from the text of two e-mails from Dr. Woodard to the author (respectively, May 15 and May 20, 2008).

Dr. Lee Woodard concurs with the foregoing assessment:

> The ancient Aramaic-Hebraic form for *Taw* has always been associated with the cross and cross shape. Additionally, the Teth form of "T" or "Th" had a circle around the + like cross shape.... And the A.D. 67–74-dated crosses upon pages of Codex W feature crosses with horizontal and perpendicular segments that are nearly equal in length. That is why I consider that small cross in the Tiberias Mosaic as reflecting First Century artistic style, and the Greek alphabetic script within that Mosaic

is also consistent with some samples from First Century. From what I can judge, the style of Greek Uncial script within the Tiberias Mosaic tiles is consistent with samples known or thought to be from the Late First Century. For instance, I compared Tiberias samples with some that the late great Sir Frederick Kenyon dated in the First Century.

3. Alan Johnson, *The Expositor's Bible Commentary* Vol. 12, Frank E. Gaebelein, ed., 478–479.

4. Excerpt from the text of an e-mail from Dr. Lee Woodard to the author (March 31, 2008).

5. "Plant Symbols in Christian Art," *Suite 101*, http://arthistory.suite101.com/article.cfm/plant_symbols_in_christian_art.

6. From the text of an e-mail from Professor Thompson to the author (August 6, 2008).

7. Excerpts from two e-mails from Dr. Woodard to the author (respectively, March 29 and May 15, 2008).

8. From the text of an e-mail from Professor Thompson to the author (August 6, 2008).

9. "Symbols and Their Meanings," Cross Road Ministries, http://www.crossroad.to/Books/symbols1.html.

10. Robert Graves, *The White Goddess*, 150.

11. Steven Alexander and Karen Alexander, *Crop Circles: Signs, Wonders and Mysteries*. This book provides a succinct history with beautiful illustrations of this ongoing phenomenon, which may or may not be entirely a hoax.

12. Schmalz and Fischer, 68–69.

13. Ibid., iv–vii.

Chapter 8
The Mikvah of the Tiberias Synagogue of The Way

1. Rabbi Aryeh Kaplan, *Waters of Eden: The Mystery of the Mikveh*.

2. Ron Moseley, PhD, *Mystical Mikveh Immersion*, http://www.essene.com/B'nai-Amen/MysticalImmersion.htm.

3. There is a large *mikvah* associated with the synagogue in the Essene quarter of the old city of Jerusalem. More to the point, a *mikvah* was used in the three-part initiation of The Way on Mount Zion. (See Bagatti, *The Church From the Circumcision*, 237–246.)

Chapter 9
The Way's Presumed Late-First-Century Movement from Mount Zion to Tiberias

1. Bagatti, for instance, briefly introduces some 576 early sites in his three-volume *Ancient Christian Village* study. Of these, by my own preliminary review, some 222 may first have been sites of The Way scattered along the several pathways

of their dispersion. (See *Ancient Christian Villages of the Galilee, Ancient Christian Villages of Judea and Negev*, and *Ancient Christian Villages of Samaria.)*

2. Skarsaune and Hvalvik, 757.

3. Ibid., 419–462.

4. Jonathan Reed, "Excavating Jesus," http://www.bibleinterp.com/articles/excavating_Jesus.htm.

5. "The Ancient History of Tiberias," Chabag.org, http://www.chabad.org/.

6. For example, according to the Talmud, all plants of the cemetery are not pruned, grass is not mowed, and only the paths are paved and maintained. However, it has been traditional for Jewish communities to carry out routine cleaning and clearing of vegetation at cemeteries and to undertake remedial work when cemeteries have suffered from destruction and subsequent neglect. Even so, removal of vegetation often requires approval from both secular and religious authorities. Further, the Talmud is specific in stating that animals should not be pastured nor grass collected in a cemetery. Yet, if any one collected grass, it had to be burnt immediately out of respect due to the dead (Sanhedrin 46a). It is thus totally unthinkable and a gross violation of Jewish religious law that anyone should consciously erect a dwelling, much less and entire city, upon the remains of an ancient cemetery.

7. Josephus, *Antiquities*, XVIII, 36–38.

8. J. J. Rousseau and R. Arav, *Jesus and His World*, 318.

9. Seth Schwartz, *Imperialism and Jewish Society 200 B.C.E. to 640 C.E.*, 143.

10. Flavius Josephus, *The Life of Flavius Josephus*, 277.

11. "Israel," Chabad.org, http://www.chabad.org/special/israel/points_of_interest_cdo/aid/606244/jewish/Tiberias.htm.

12. Y. Kilayim, 9–4, 32b.

Chapter 10
Tiberias in the Late First Century: The Setting for a New Congregation of The Way

1. Skarsaune and Hvalvik, 757.

2. "Newly discovered ruins of the Sanhedrin at Tiberias," TheSanhedrin.org (July 27, 2005), www.thesanhedrin.org/en/tiberias/.

3. An e-mail from Dr. Woodard to the author (May 25, 2008).

4. Bagatti, *Church From the Circumcision*, 227.

Chapter 11
The End of an Era: The Way Takes Leave of Tiberias

1. "What Is Messianic Judaism?" http://www.yashanet.com/library/nazarene_judaism.html.

2. Epiphanius, *Panarion* 29.

3. "What Is Messianic Judaism?"

Chapter 12
The Amazing Saga of Count Joseph

1. Excerpt from an e-mail from Professor Thompson to the author (August 6, 2008).
2. "Epiphanius of Salmas," *The Catholic Encyclopedia,* accessed at New Advent Online.
3. Skarsaune and Hvalvik, 530.
4. T. C. G. Thornton, "The Stories of Joseph of Tiberias," *Vigiliae Christianae* 44 (1990): 54–63.
5. Ibid., 58.
6. Ibid., 54–55.
7. Skarsaune and Hvalvik, 533.
8. Ibid., 534.
9. Ibid., 535.
10. Yizhar Hirschfeld and Eran Meir, Israel Antiquities Authority, Journal 118, Tiberias (2004).
11. "Bet She'an (Scythopolis)," *Archaeological World,* http://www.archaeology-classic.com/Israel_E/Beth_She'an.html.
12. Fischer, R.R., *The Door Where it Began,* 176–177
13. Thomas Kocik, "Return to the East?" *Adoremus Bulletin* (November 1999), http://www.adoremus.org/1199-Kocik.html.
14. "History of the Church Altar," *The Catholic Encyclopedia,* accessed at New Advent Online, http://www.newadvent.org/cathen/01362a.htm.
15. "Capernaum, table insert, 'Chronological Summary' 3," *Biblical Archaeology,* www.bibarch.com/Archaeological Sites/Capernaum.htm.
16. Skarsaune and Hvalvik, 528.

Chapter 13
The "Byzantine Church" on Mount Berenice: Another Tiberias Nazarene Site of The Way?

1. "Excavations at Tiberias Reveal Remains of Church and Possibly Theater," *The Biblical Archaeologist* Vol. 54, No. 3 (September 1991): 170–171.
2. "Antipas (Herod Antipas)," *The Jewish Encyclopedia,* http://www.jewishencyclopedia.com/view.jsp?letter=A&artid=1597.
3. Josephus, *Antiquities,* 18.116–119.
4. *The Jewish Encyclopedia.*

Chapter 14
Two Other Early Sites of The Way

1. Frank Senn, "Sacraments and Social History: Postmodern Practice," *Theology Today* (October 2001).
2. Tepper and Di Sengi, "A Christian Prayer Hall of the Third Century C.E. at Kefar Othnay (Legio)," 5–9.

3. Ibid., 24.
4. Ibid., 17–18.
5. Ibid., 31–34.
6. Ibid., 25.

Chapter 15
The Transition From Nazarene to Pre-Byzantine and Early Byzantine Christianity (Circa Late First to Early Fourth Centuries a.d.), as Evidenced by the Original Floor Mosaics at Tabgpha and Kursi

1. Excerpt from an e-mail from Professor Thompson to the author (August 6, 2008).
2. "Church of the Multiplication of the Loaves and the Fishes," *Jewish Virtual Library*, http://www.jewishvirtuallibrary.org/jsource/Archaeology/Tabgha.html.
3. Israel Ministry of Foreign Affairs, "Kursi-Christian Monastery on the Shore of the Sea of Galilee" (December 19, 1999), http://www.mfa.gov.il/MFA/History/Early%20History%20-%20Archaeology/Kursi-%20Christian%20Monastery%20on%20the%20Shore%20of%20the%20Sea.
4. Ibid.
5. "Kursi (Gergesa)," *BibleWalks*, http://www.biblewalks.com/Sites/Kursi.html.
6. Charles R. Page, II, "Kursi Excavation Project 2001," Jerusalem Institute for Biblical Exploration, http://www.bibleinterp.com/excavations/kursi_2001.htm.
7. Charles R. Page, II, "Kursi-Gergesa Excavation 2002 Report," Jerusalem Institute for Biblical Exploration, December 2003, http://www.bibleinterp.com/excavations/kursi_2002.htm.
8. Ibid.

Part III
The Theology and Doctrine of The Way

1. Irenaeus, *Against Heresies,* XXIX, PG 41, 387–406.
2. Testa, 18.
3. "Ebionites," *Britannica Online Encyclopedia*, http://www.britannica.com/EBchecked/topic/177608/Ebionites#tab=active~checked%2Citems~checked&title=Ebionite%20--%20Britannica%20Online%20Encyclopedia.
4. Ibid, XXX, 11, 405–473.
5. Charlesworth, *The Bible and the Dead Sea Scrolls*, Vol. 1, xxiii, xxvii.

Chapter 16
Christology: The Way's Understanding of the Nature of Yeshua

1. David Flusser, *Judaism and the Origins of Christianity*, 31–37.
2. Dead Sea Scrolls, 4Q246 I 7–9, II 1–7.
3. Ibid., 4Q541 9, 1, 1–6.
4. Ibid., 4Q Messianic Apocalypse [4Q521].
5. Ibid., 1QIs 44:5–22.

6. "Ancient Tablet Ignites Debate on Messiah and Resurrection," *The New York Times* Middle East Edition, July 6, 2008, http://www.nytimes.com/2008/07/06/world/middleeast/06stone.html (accessed February 17, 2009).
7. Ibid.
8. "Dead Sea tablet suggests Jewish resurrection imagery predates Jesus," Haaretz.com, July 16, 2008, http://www.haaretz.com/hasen/spages/999719.html (accessed February 17, 2009).
9. "Ancient Tablet Ignites Debate on Messiah and Resurrection."
10. Ibid.
11. Ibid.
12. Aryeh Kaplan, "The Book of Creation," *Sefer Yetzirah.*
13. Adolphe Franck, with I. Sossnitz, trans., *The Kabbalah*, 77.
14. Kaplan, xii.
15. Aryeh Kaplan, *Sefer Yetzirah*, The Book of Creation, xii.
16. Grant Jeffrey, "The Handwriting of God," *The Sacred Mystery of the Trinity*, www.grantjeffry.com.
17. *Zohar*, Vol. ii. Amsterdam edition, 43.
18. Ibid., vol. iii, 65.
19. Ibid., 288.
20. Fischer, *Full Circle*, 108–110. For a more detailed discussion on the emergence of the doctrine of the Trinity from mainline Judaism, please refer to Chapter 6 of this earlier writing.

Chapter 17
The Way's Understanding of the Name

1. *Talmud*, Kiddushin, 71a.
2. Ibid., Sanhedrin, 101a.
3. Danielou, 148.
4. Ibid., 157.
5. Hermas, *Simlitude* IX, 14:5.
6. J. L. Teicher, "The Christian Interpretation of the Sign × in the Isaiah Scroll," *Vetus Testamentum* Vol. 5 (April 1955): 189–198.
7. The word translated as "mark" ("to be placed on the foreheads") in the English language versions of the Bible is translated as *taw* in the Hebrew Bible.
8. Danielou, 155.
9. Didache, X, 2–3.

Chapter 18
The Way's Understanding of Redemption

1. Ascension of Isaiah, X:12.
2. Ibid., X, 7–12.
3. Ibid., XI, 17.
4. Danielou, 213.

5. James E. Keifer, "Creeds, Confessions and Catechisms," *The Hall of Church History*, www.spurgeon.org/~phil/creeds.htm; cf., Danielou, 233, 235.
6. Irenaeus, *Against Heresies*, 4.27.1–2.
7. Universal Declaration of Human Rights, "Christianity and its Persecutions of Jews," www.christianityandhumanrights.com.
8. Ibid.
9. Martin Luther, "Part 12," *On the Jews and Their Lies* (1543), University of Pennsylvania reprint of a 1948 abridged translation, http://onlinebooks.library.upenn.edu/webbin/book/lookupid?key=olbp38498.
10. Irenaeus, *Against Heresies*, V, 17:4.
11. Danielou, 279–283.
12. Chapter 28, 275–278, with captioned photographs of two *taw* symbols.
13. Irenaeus, *Demonstatio*, 34.
14. The Gospel of Peter, Sam Gibson, trans., fragments 9–10.
15. *The Apocalypse of Peter, The Ethiopic Text*, M. R. James, trans. (Oxford: Clarendon Press, 1924).
16. *The Epistula Apostolorum*, M. R. James, trans., 16.
17. This Vatican fresco, "Constantine's Vision with Cross and Serpent" by Raphaello, is posted online at the Vatican Museum site, http://mv.vatican.va/3_EN/pages/x-Schede/SDRs/SDRs_01_01_003.html.
18. C. Burk, "Cyril of Jerusalem," *A Religious Encyclopedia*, 3rd ed., Vol. 1 (London: Funk and Wagnalls, 1894), 595; cf. Danielou, 270.
19. Danielou, 292.
20. The Testament of Benjamin, IX, 5.
21. The Gospel of Peter, 13.
22. See John 20:17.
23. Ascension of Isaiah 9:16.
24. Acts 1:1 makes this interval to be 40 days rather than the apocryphal 545.
25. Danielou, 255.

Chapter 19
The Way's Understanding of Predestination

1. Charlesworth, "John the Baptizer and the Dead Sea Scrolls," *The Bible and the Dead Sea Scrolls*, Vol. 3, 18.
2. Magen Broshi, "Predestination in the Bible and the Dead Sea Scrolls," James Charlesworth, ed., *The Bible and the Dead Sea Scrolls* Vol. 2, 235–236.
3. Dead Sea Scrolls 1QS 3.15–16, F. Garcia Martinez, trans.
4. Dead Sea Scrolls 1Q "Hymns" 1, 20–21, F. Garcia Martinez, trans.
5. *Clementine Homilies*, IX, 22, *Christian Classics Ethereal Library*, http://www.ccel.org/ccel/schaff/anf08.toc.html.
6. The Apocalypse of Peter, M. R. James, trans.
7. Hermas, Vision I, 3:5.
8. Odes of Solomon, IX, 12–13.

9. "Catechism 1037" (618–620), United States Conference of Catholic Bishops, http://www.usccb.org/catechism/text/pt1sect2chpt3art12.htm.

10. "World Christian Database," Gordon-Conwell Theological Seminary, http://www.worldchristiandatabase.org/wcd/about/denominationlist.asp.

Chapter 20
The Way's Understanding of the Body of Yeshua, the Church

1. Walter Lowrie, *Art in the Early Church*, 105.

2. A modern day traditional synagogue is a *Bet Kenesset*, and the seat of the Israeli government is the *Kenesset.*

3. Danielou, 306–307.

4. Dead Sea Scrolls, "Rule of the Community," 1QS VIII, 5 and XI, 8, F. Garcia Martinez, trans.

5. Ascension of Isaiah, IV, 3.

6. Hermas, Vision II, 4.

7. Second Clement, XIV.

Chapter 21
Angelology: The Way's Understanding of the Angels

1. Danielou, 119–120.

2. Hermas, IX, 12:7–8.

3. Second Enoch, XXIX, 3.

4. Danielou, 181.

5. Second Enoch I, 4.

6. The Gospel of Peter, 41.

7. Irenaeus, *Against Heresies*, Book I, Chapter 5, 2.

8. Second Enoch, XX, 3–4, and XXI, 1.

9. James H. Charlesworth, ed., *The Old Testament Pseudepigrapha* Vol. 1 (Garden City, New York: Doubleday & Co., 1985); also II Enoch, XVIII, 131.

10. Ibid., 111.

11. Ibid., 133.

12. Pseudo-Clement, *Recognitions,* II, 42; cf. Testa, 107.

13. Testa, *The Faith of the Mother Church*, 107.

14. Dead Sea Scrolls, 1 QS III, 15b–26.

15. The Apocalypse of Peter, M. R. James, trans., Frag. 2, 48.1.

16. Testa, 154.

17. Bagatti, *The Church of the Circumcision*, 240–241.

18. Testa, 149–152.

19. *Testaments of the Twelve Patriachs, Testament of Asher* 6, Roberts-Donaldson translation.

Chapter 22
Demonology: The Way's Understanding of the Fallen Angels

1. Bagatti, *The Church From the Circumcision*, 261.
2. Ibid., 47.
3. First Enoch, 7:11.
4. Fragments of Papias from the Exposition of the Oracles of the Lord, 7:1, Roberts-Donaldson translation.
5. Second Enoch, 33:11–12.
6. Dead Sea Scrolls, "Rule of the Community," 1 QS IV 23–25.
7. Ascension of Isaiah, X, 30.
8. *Testaments of the Twelve Patriarchs, Testament of Reuben*, Roberts-Donaldson translation, Chapter I, 12–30.
9. Danielou, 191.
10. Abaddon, in demonology, was chief of the demons of the seventh hierarchy. He was called the Destroyer and, in the Book of Revelation, John called him the King of the locusts (Rev. 9:7–11). From "Abaddon," *The Catholic Encyclopedia*, New Advent Online, http://www.newadvent.org/cathen/01005a.htm.
11. Dead Sea Scrolls, 11QapocrPs 2.2 abridged.
12. Danielou, 192.

Chapter 23
Millenarianism: The Way's Understanding of Eschatology, the End of Days

1. "Christian History Institute is a non-profit Pennsylvania corporation. We are tied to no particular denomination. Instead, we seek to serve the entire Christian community (and the secular world, too) by showing the part that Christians and Christianity have played in the development of world civilization—how the church has given our planet values, freedoms, and morals that have made life better for millions. Our aim is to make Christian history a delight to the widest possible public through modern media such as video and the Internet. We strive to make our output look good and communicate well while sticking to the facts. Consequently, we are involved in film and video production and book publishing." From "Who Are We?" Christian History Institute, http://chi.gospelcom.net/about/index.shtml.
2. "Cyrus Ingerson Scofield Passed to His Judgment," Christian History Institute, July 24, 1921.
3. The Ascension of Isaiah, IV, 14–17.
4. Danielou, 380.
5. Irenaeus, *Against Heresies*, V, 33:3.
6. Ibid.
7. Methodius, Conv. IX, 5, as quoted by Danielou, 382.
8. Irenaeus, V, 33:1.
9. "Chapter 4," R. H. Charles, trans., *Book of Jubilees* (Oxford: Clarendon Press, 1913).

10. Septuagint, Isaiah 65:20–22.
11. Irenaeus, *Against Heresies*, V, 23:2.
12. Justin Martyr, *Dialogue* LXXXI, 3–4.
13. Danielou, 393.
14. First Enoch X, 17.
15. Danielou, 394.
16. *Sibylline Oracles* VII, 200.
17. The Epistle of Barnabas, XV, 3–8.
18. Emperor Constantine, *Edict of March 7, A.D. 321,* Corpus Juris Civilis Cod., lib. 3, tit. 12, 3.
19. Council of Laodicea, Canon XXIX.

Part IV
The Sacred Writings of The Way

1. Renan, Vol. 2, 70.
2. "The Fathers of the Church," Wesley Center of Applied Theology, http://wesley.nnu.edu/biblical_studies/noncanon/fathers.htm.

Chapter 24
The Canonical Gospels of The Way and the Rediscovered Codex Washington

1. Woodard, *First Century Gospels Found!* 12–13.
2. "Biblical Manuscripts," *Freer Galleries*, http://www.asia.si.edu/collections/biblicalHome.htm.
3. Dr. Woodard's scholarly explanation of the contents of Codex W means simply that the codex is comprised of copies of the four Gospels with their original titles, signed and sealed by their authors.
4. Excerpts from two e-mails from Lee Woodard to the author (December 13, 2007).
5. Excerpts from two e-mails from Lee Woodard to the author (February 27, 2008).
6. Woodard, *First Century Gospels Found*, 91.
7. Ibid., 55.
8. Eusebius, 3:5:3.
9. These extant references are from the church fathers: Eusebius in his *History of the Church* (A.D. 325) and Epiphanius in his *Panarion* (374–376) and in *On Measures and Weights* and *Pseudo-Clementines* (fourth century).

Chapter 25
Old Testament Pseudepigraphic Writings Pertinent to The Way

1. There are more than sixty Old Testament pseudepigraphic writings that can be read online at www.EarlyChristianWritings.com. For those with a deeper interest, see James H. Charlesworth, ed., *The Old Testament Pseudepigrapha*.

2. Danielou, 12–13.
3. The Ascension of Isaiah, R. H. Charles, trans., 3:10–14.
4. Ibid., 9:7–10.
5. Ibid., 10:7–14.
6. Evans, Craig, *Noncanonical Writings and New Testament Interpretation*, 23.
7. "Second Enoch," found at: http://yourgoingtohell.com.
8. Danielou, 14.
9. M. de Jong, *The Testaments of the Twelve Patriarchs*, 183.
10. Ursula Treu, *New Testament Apocrypha*, 653–654.
11. Fischer, *The Door Where It Began*, 191.
12. Second Peter was finally permanently canonized in the fifth century by inclusion in the Codex Alexandrinus. Up to that time, principally because its authorship by Peter was disputed, it had been excluded from canon listings on several occasions: Marcion (138), Tertullian (200), Clement (208), Cyprian (206), Origen (250), and Eusebius (330). From F. F. Bruce, *The Canon of Scripture.*
13. Dead Sea Scrolls, 1Q "Hymns," IV, 13–15.

Chapter 26
The New Testament Apocryphal Writings of The Way

1. Docetism was an early Christian doctrine that the sufferings of Yeshua were apparent and not real and that after the crucifixion He appeared in a spiritual body.
2. F. F. Bruce, *Jesus and Christian Origins Outside the New Testament*, 93.
3. Ron Cameron, ed., *The Other Gospels: Non-Canonical Gospel Texts*, 76–82.
4. Serapion, Bishop of Antioch, from a publicly circulated letter circa 190–203, which suggested with respect to the Gospel of Peter that "most of it belonged to the right teaching of the Saviour," but that some parts might encourage its hearers to fall into the Docetist heresy. Serapion's rebuttal of the Gospel of Peter is lost, but it is discussed by Eusebius, 3:2.
5. H. B. Swete, *The Akhmim Fragment of the Apocryphal Gospel of St. Peter*, 44.
6. Danielou, 21–22.
7. Woodard, 78.
8. Cameron, 85–86.
9. Cyril of Jerusalem, Discourse on Mary Theotokos 12a.
10. Jerome, *Commentary on Isaiah 4* [on Isaiah 11:2].
11. Origen, *Commentary on John 2.12.87* [on John 1:3].
12. Clement, Stromateis 2.9.45.5.
13. Ibid., 5.14.96.3.
14. Jerome, *Commentary on Ephesians 3* [on Ephesians 5:4].
15. Jerome, *Commentary on Ezekiel 6* [on Ezekiel 18:7].
16. Jerome, *De viris inlustribus* 2.
17. Danielou, 22–23.
18. Ibid.
19. Woodard, 55.
20. Danielou, 23–24.

21. Ibid.

22. "Introduction to the Gospel of Thomas Collection," *Gnostic Society Library*, http://www.webcom.com/gnosis/naghamm/nhl_thomas.htm.

23. Bruce, 161, 191.

24. The Apocalypse of Peter, Roberts-Donaldson Translation, www.EarlyChristianWritings.com.

25. *The Epistle of the Apostles,* M. R. James, trans., Leaf 2 (Ethiopic) www.EarlyChristianWritings.com.

26. Danielou, 27.

27. *The Epistle of the Apostles*, Leaf 5.

28. Ibid, Leaf 11–12.

29. Ibid., Leaf 16.

30. Ibid., Leaf 19.

Chapter 27
The Didache: The Lord's Teaching Through the Twelve Apostles to the Nations

1. Renan, Vol. 2, 89.

2. The presumed establishment of the first Gentile Christian church at Hippos/Sussita was the central theme of my historical novel, *The Door Where It Began* (Olim Publications, 2005). Following her review of this work, Dr. Jolanta Mlynarczyk from the Polish Academy of Sciences, who was one of the principal leaders of the archaeological dig at Hippos/Sussita, wrote to me personally, saying, "In terms of history/archaeology, your novel opened my eyes to an obvious fact (did anyone discover it before?) that actually, the Gentile Church began at the Decapolis, spreading from the place where the formerly possessed man (your Athanasios) lived (Kursi?) south to Hippos and Gadara, and beyond." (Excerpt from an e-mail from Professor Mlynarczyk to the author [April 12, 2006].)

3. Renan, Vol. 2, 82–85.

4. Eusebius, 97.

5. Parthia was a huge Iranian civilization situated in the northeastern part of modern Iran, but at the height of its power, the Parthian dynasty covered all of Iran proper, as well as regions of the modern countries of Armenia, Iraq, Georgia, eastern Turkey, eastern Syria, Turkmenistan, Afghanistan, Tajikistan, Pakistan, Kuwait, the Persian Gulf, the coast of Saudi Arabia, Bahrain, Qatar, Lebanon, Israel, Palestine, and the UAE. From Parthia.com.

6. Scythia, ancient region of Eurasia, extending from the Danube on the west to the borders of China on the east.

7. The three regions cited encompass a huge area spreading from northwestern Asia Minor through most of what is modern day Turkey.

8. Eusebius, 65.

9. Bruce, *The Canon of Scripture.*

10. Schonfield, 40.

11. James H. Charlesworth, "A Study in Shared Symbolism and Language," *The Bible and the Dead Sea Scrolls*, Vol. 3, 115.
12. Woodard, 91–95.
13. Danielou, 30.

Part V
The Praise and Worship of The Way

1. The Essenes looked for the coming of the Messiah who would be the divine son of God as evidenced in: "...and he will be great over the earth....great will he be called and he will be designated by his name. He will be called the Son of God, and they will call him the Son of the Most High...His kingdom will be an eternal kingdom, and all his paths in truth and uprightness. The earth will be in truth and all will make peace....The sword will cease in the earth and all the cities will pay him homage. He is a great God among the gods." (See 4Q246 I 7–9, II 1–7.) The Holy Spirit, the third member of the Godhead, is addressed elsewhere in the scrolls, for example: "And you [YHWH] chose the land of Judah, and established your covenant with David so that he [Yeshua] would be like a shepherd, a prince over your people, and would sit in front of you on the throne of Israel forever. And all the countries would see your glory, for you have made yourself holy in the midst of your people, Israel....For you have poured out your Holy Spirit upon us....You have removed from us all our failings and have purified us from our sin, for yourself." (See 4Q504 IV, 6–8, V 15, VI 2.)
2. Neil Hawes, "The History of Notation," *Basic Music Theory on the World Wide Web*, http://neilhawes.com/sstheory/theory22.htm.
3. Charlesworth, *The Bible and the Dead Sea Scrolls*, 417.

Chapter 28
The Essene Psalter of Old Testament and Apocryphal Psalms

1. From ancient Jewish hymns circa the early 1900s, http://www.oldandsold.com/articles05/jewish_hymns.shtml.
2. Peter W. Flint, "Psalms and Psalters in the Dead Sea Scrolls," James H. Charlesworth, ed., *The Bible and the Dead Sea Scrolls*, Vol. 1, 233–234.
3. Ibid., 11QPs 24, lines 3–17. Trans. by J. Sanders, The Dead Sea Psalms Scroll.
4. Ibid.
5. Dead Sea Scrolls, 11Q11 I, 4–6.3, F. Garcia Martinez, trans.
6. Dead Sea Scrolls, 11Q5 16, 1–6, J. Sanders, trans., *The Dead Sea Psalms Scroll.*
7. Ibid., 11Q5 27, 2–11. While it is unlikely because of its form and content that this psalm was sung, I include it here to point out the huge number of psalms that it attributes to David. If these numbers are correct, then literally thousands of such psalms have been lost, most likely forever.
8. Ibid., 11Q5 26, 9–15.

Chapter 29
The Hodayoth (Hymns of Thanksgiving)

1. Jacob Chernan, "The Moses at Qumran," James H. Charlesworth, ed., *The Bible and the Dead Sea Scrolls* Vol. 2, 353–354.
2. Dead Sea Scrolls, 1QH 10:31–35, F. Garcia Martinez, trans.
3. Ibid., CD 1:9–11.
4. Ibid., CD 3:12–15.
5. Ibid., 1QpHab 7:5.
6. George J.Brooke, "Biblical Interpretation at Qumran," James H. Charlesworth, ed., *The Bible and the Dead Sea Scrolls* Vol. 1, 311.
7. Dead Sea Scrolls, 1QH 12.22–23, F. Garcia Martinez, trans.
8. Double predestination is the understanding that God preelects both those who are and who are not to be saved. Moreover, in this understanding there is no opportunity to move from one of these groups to the other.
9. Dead Sea Scrolls, 1QH 20.11–12.
10. Ibid., 1QH 7 16–17, 7.25.
11. Émile Puech, "Resurrection: The Bible and Qumran," James H. Charlesworth, ed., The Bible and the Dead Sea Scrolls Vol. 2, 272–273.
12. Ibid., Dead Sea Scrolls, 1QH 9 20–27, Émile Puech, trans.
13. Fischer, *Full Circle*, 55–84.
14. Dead Sea Scrolls, 1QH 12, 35–37, F. Garcia Martinez, trans.
15. Ibid., 1QH 7, 28–29.
16. Ibid., 1QH 4, 11–12.
17. F. Garcia Martinez, *The People of the Dead Sea Scrolls*, 201, note 330.

Chapter 30
The Odes of Solomon

1. "The Origin of the Odes," *The Odes Project*, http://www.theodesproject.com/history.
2. Ibid.
3. "Pliny, *Letters,* 10.96–97," University of Pennsylvania, http://ccat.sas.upenn.edu/jod/texts/pliny.html.
4. Ibid.
5. "Introducing Your Congregation to the Odes Project," The Odes Project, http://www.theodesproject.com/for-leaders-intro.
6. Stanley Burgess, Gary B. Mckee, and Patrick H. Alexander, *Dictionary of Pentecostal and Charismatic Movements*, 2–3.
7. "The number of Protestants—particularly Pentecostals—continues to increase in the United States, with a fourth Pentecostal denomination joining the list of 25 largest U.S. religious bodies." From "Pentecostals lead modest growth in U.S. church membership," Associated Baptist Press, March 16, 2004.
8. Burgess, McGee, and Alexander, 53.
9. For more information, visit http://www.TheOdesProject.com.

10. For more information, visit http://cdbaby.com.
11. Translation by James H. Charlesworth.
12. Ibid.
13. Ibid.
14. Ibid.

Chapter 31
The Rich Jewish Heritage of Davidic Dance

1. Murray Silberling, *Dancing for Joy*, 2–6.
2. "Voice of the Temple Mount Newsletter," Winter 2007, http://www.templemountfaithful.org/index.htm.
3. Ilan Tal, "Dance in the Ancient World," *Near Eastern Archaeology* Vol. 66, No. 3 (September 2003): 135–136.
4. Jean Gould Bryant, et al., "Women in Hellenistic Judaism," *Creating Women: An Anthology of Readings on Women in Western Culture* Vol. I.
5. "Davidic Praise and Worship," Concord Messianic Fellowship, http://messianicfellowship.50webs.com/worship.html.
6. "Moses, Aaron and Miriam," *Judaism 101*, http://www.jewfaq.org/moshe.htm.

Chapter 32
Who Is Returning, and From Where?

1. The first Jewish Diaspora (the pre-Christian dispersal of Jews outside of the land of Israel) is commonly understood to have begun with the eighth-to-sixth-century-B.C. conquests of the ancient Jewish kingdoms, the destruction of the first temple, and expulsion of the enslaved Jewish population. It is also associated with the destruction of the second temple and aftermath of the Bar Kokhba revolt during the Roman occupation of Judea in the first and second century A.D.
2. James Carroll, *Constantine's Sword*, 26.
3. L. V. Rutgers, *The Hidden Heritage of Diaspora Judaism*, 199–224.
4. Fischer, *Full Circle*, 239–297.
5. Ibid.
6. Ibid.
7. Ibid.

Chapter 33
Whither Shall They Go?

1. Adolph von Harnack, *The Mission and Expansion of Christianity in the First Three Centuries*, 5–6.
2. Mancini, *Archaeological Discoveries*, 176–177.
3. "Messianic Movement in Israel Growing and on Brink of a Great Revival," *Breaking Christian News*, July 16, 2008, http://www.breakingchristiannews.com/articles/display_art_pf.html?ID=5571. (From data provided by credible leaders within the Israeli movement who are known to the author.)

4. For example, see Talmud, Baba Mezia 59b; a rabbi debates God and defeats Him. God admits the rabbi won the debate. Also, Talmud, Auburn 21; the commands of the rabbis are more important than the commands of the Bible: "Whosoever disobeys the rabbis deserves death and will be punished by being boiled in hot excrement in hell."

5. Talmud, Soncino edition, Erubin 21b: "My son, be more careful in the observance of the words of the Scribes than in the words of the Torah (Old Testament)."

6. The following are two of many examples from the Talmud: (1) A Jewish man is obligated to say the following prayer every day: "Thank you, God, for not making me a Gentile, a woman or a slave" (Menahoth 43b–44a). (2) This is the saying of Rabbi Simon ben Yohai: "Even the best of the gentiles should all be killed" (Minor Tractates. Soferim 15, Rule 10).

7. Rabbinical Kashrut, or dietary laws as they are presented in the Talmud, cover the general areas of:

- Food preparation—causing pain to creatures; sending away a mother bird; kosher slaughter; covering blood after slaughter; food taken from live animals; animals which were not slaughtered in a kosher fashion; animals which are mortally wounded; kashering meat, preparation of meat for eating; kashering utensils, preparation of utensils for use with kosher food; rabbinic dietary prohibitions; how the method of eating affects the Law
- Specific creatures/foods—*Issurei Hanaah*, items of forbidden benefit; grafted species; *Ben Pekuah*, animals found inside slaughtered animals; *Oto v'et B'no*, an animal and its young, slaughtered on the same day; laws specific to "chayah" class animals; blood; *Gid haNasheh*, the sciatic neurovascular bundle; cooking vessels that were owned by a Nochri; certain forbidden fats; *Basar b'Chalav*, meat and milk mixtures; foods used as idolatry; wine used for idolatry
- Food of debatable Kashrut status: *Taarovet*, mixtures of forbidden and permitted foods; determining the legal status of food; testimony regarding potential prohibitions; trustworthy people; special personal stringencies.

There are almost countless references within each of these sub-categories scattered throughout almost the entire Talmud. From "Kashrut/Dietary Laws," *WebShas*, http://www.webshas.org/kashrus/index.htm.

8. The name of God, in any event "God" or "Lord." God, according to His own words—there are more than 580 uses of "I AM" in the Tenach—does have a personal name comprising the Hebrew letters "Yud-Hei-Vav-Hei." But according to centuries of Jewish understanding, the vowels were lost, thus we do not know how to pronounce the letters. In any event, traditionally, the holy name was only to be pronounced by the *cohein gadol* (high priest) and was considered very powerful (if the *cohein* did it incorrectly, he could be struck dead). By the time of the Talmudic rabbis, the convention developed to pronounce the name "Adonai" (our Lord), each time we came across the four letters in the Siddur (prayer book).

9. Circumcision is a "type" of Yeshua's blood sacrifice. Yeshua Himself was circumcised on the eighth day. (See Luke 2:21.) In Galatians 5:2–6 Paul teaches that it is not necessary for Gentiles to be circumcised. James on the other hand admonishes Paul for teaching Jews who dwell among Gentiles that there is no need for them to be circumcised (Acts 21:21). Bottom line: a Gentile is not in any way made to be "more Jewish" through circumcision.

10. Talmud, Shabbath 133a.

11. "Traditionally, the Simchat Bat ceremony for baby girls takes place in the congregation on the first *Shabbat* following her birth. During the ceremony, either the father or both parents are called to the Torah for a reading and blessing. Today, many families choose to have the ceremony in their own homes." From "Jewish Traditions," Jewish Federation of Greater Kansas City, http://www.jewishkansascity.org/page.html?ArticleID=33677.

12. Ibid., "The Bar/Bat Mitzvah celebrates a young person's entry into the adult Jewish community." Although these observances are not prescribed by the Torah, the Bar Mitzvah has its roots in the Middle Ages and has been celebrated since at least 1492. The Bat Mitzvah has become an important religious tradition over the last half century. "Typically, during the celebration the young person recites a blessing over the Torah, reads the Haftorah or Torah portion for that week and then offers a speech or scholarly comment."

13. Ibid., "The marriage ceremony is a simcha [joy], celebrating the union between two Jewish individuals. The ceremony takes place under a chuppah, or canopy, and the actual marriage involves exchanging wedding rings while the couple (or just the groom in some congregations) recites the following: 'Behold thou art sanctified unto me by this ring according to the law of Moses and Israel.'" The ceremony is concluded with the groom stomping upon a cloth wrapped wine glass. Traditionally, this custom was also incorporated into the ceremony to remind everyone that even at the height of one's personal joy, we must, nevertheless, remember the destruction of the Temple in Jerusalem. The breaking of the glass symbolizes the breaking of our hearts in remembrance.

14. The seven biblical feasts are:

- Passover (Pesach): Exod. 12: 8; liberation from slavery in Egypt
- Feast of Unleavened Bread: Exod.12:15; unleavened bread is eaten for seven days since yeast is a symbol for sin
- Feast of First fruits: Lev. 23:9–14; celebrating the beginning of the grain harvest
- Shavuot (Pentecost): Exod. 32:18–28, Acts 2:40–41. In the Old Testament, three thousand died because of disobedience. In the New Testament the Holy Spirit was poured out in the temple courts and three thousand new members came into the kingdom.
- Feast of Trumpets: Num. 29:1; *Rosh Hashanah,* the Jewish New Year, symbolic of the second coming of Yeshua
- Yom Kippur (Day of Atonement): Lev. 23:27, Matt. 27:50–51a; annual day for fasting and prayer, when Jews pray for remission of

their sin. Believers are now able to pass through the torn curtain leading into the holy of holies, where they have infinite access to their God.

- Feast of Tabernacles (Succoth): Deut. 16:13; celebration of the brining-in of the harvest. The celebrants dwell in tabernacles (huts, tents) for seven days and nights, commemorating the time when the Jews lived in tents for forty years in the desert.

15. *Chanukah*, also known as the Festival of Lights, is an eight-day Jewish holiday commemorating the rededication of the second temple in Jerusalem at the time of the Maccabean Revolt of the second century B.C. Hanukkah is observed for eight nights and may occur from late November to late December on the Gregorian calendar.

16. We read in John 10:22 that Yeshua was on hand to celebrate the Festival of Lights. Chanukah has come to be a sort of surrogate Christmas for Messianic Jews who do not have a traditional connection to this universally celebrated, albeit pagan-rooted, church holiday. Most scholars would agree that there is little likelihood that Yeshua was actually born on Christmas. One frequently mentioned date for the actual advent is on the last day of Succoth. If nothing else, this is a lovely thought since when counting backwards nine months from this day we find that if Yeshua was actually born as it is suggested, He would have been conceived by the Holy Spirit on the last day of Chanukah.

17. The *shofar* is mentioned over eighty times in the Old Testament. The ram's horn was the authentic *shofar*, and it is still in wide use by traditional Jewish groups in Israel. Another form, the Yemenite *shofar*, is taken from an African antelope called the kudu. While the horn of the kudu is much more "showy" than the ram's horn and is often sold to tourists visiting Israel, it was not at all likely that this Yeminite Jewish adaptation was used by The Way or by any traditional group within Israel. The first time the *shofar* is mentioned is in Exodus 19:16–19. when the Israelites had gathered at Mt. Sinai. The "voice of the trumpet [*shofar*] sounded exceeding loud" and "waxed louder and louder." According to the Torah in Exodus 20:18, the sound was so penetrating that the people could actually "see the sounds."

Chapter 34
The Tiberias Synagogue of The Way

1. The baptismal liturgy used here is an adaptation of *The Apostolic Tradition of Hippolytus of Rome*, which was composed in approximately A.D. 215 in Rome. It apparently was written to preserve older second-century Jewish-Christian practices, which were in danger of falling to disuse or innovation.

2. "Ode 1," The Odes of Solomon, James H. Charlesworth, trans.

3. Hippolytus of Rome, *The Apostolic Tradition*, 21:27–32, an adaptation by the author.

4. In Psalm 150, every section of the orchestra is invited to join in the crescendo of praise for the marvelous works of God. (See J. King and E. Stager, *Life in Biblical Israel*, 290–297.)

5. "Ode 40," The Odes of Solomon, translation by the Odes Project.

6. See 1 Corinthians 11:27–29.

7. The liturgy for the foregoing celebration of the Lord's Supper is my adaptation of the Lord's Supper liturgy set forth in the Didache, or Teaching of the Twelve Apostles, English translation by Charles H. Hoole, www.EarlyChristianWritings.com.

8. "Ode 26," The Odes of Solomon, James H. Charlesworth, trans. This Ode has not yet been included in the collection recreated by the Odes Project, but because of its depth and appropriateness I am hopeful that they will soon be inspired to do so.

9. The setting and content of the Lord's Supper feast are the author's adaptation of the one suggested by King and Stager, *Life in Biblical Israel*, 61–68.

10. In ancient Israel, food was served in dishes and bowls, but there were no eating utensils known in this period. The people ate with their fingers and wiped the plate or bowl clean with a piece of bread. From Oded Borowski, *Every Living Thing: The Use of Animals in Ancient Israel*, 19.

11. Ibid.

12. See Deuteronomy 6:4.

13. The Lord's Prayer as adapted by the author from the Roberts-Donaldson translation of the Didache, which states in Chapter 8 that this prayer is to be recited by all believers three times each day.

14. There may or may not have yet been formal, scheduled *Parsha* (Torah) readings, although it would have been very natural for these to have been implemented very early by The Way. In any event, I believe that it is important that such readings be included as a part of every modern day *Motzei Shabbat* gathering.

15. Please bear in mind that these *Motzei Shabbat* services lasted well into the night. (See Acts 20:7.) The praise and worship of modern day home congregations will vary greatly, but hopefully be generally based upon this suggested model of The Way. There might not even be a worship team or a worship leader, or if such exists, it may consist of one instrument or many, with or without one or more singers. As for the selections to be sung, I would urge every home congregation to acquire both volumes of the Odes Project CDs, which may be purchased on the Internet from Amazon.com, CD Baby, or iTunes. The associated lyrics are posted on the Ode Project's Web site. I would suggest that these odes be gradually worked in to the group's praise and worship until they are learned, loved, and permanently adapted. Moreover, I would also suggest that such modern day praise and worship be free to include a mix of contemporary praise songs and early Messianic Jewish offerings from the rebirth of the movement, such as *Israel Hope*. My point here is that it would be good if eventually there were a large if not total representation of the odes in every such group.

16. I would also urge all groups to include Davidic dance as an integral part of their times of praise and worship. For those who are unfamiliar with this form of expression or who want to learn more, I highly recommend Rabbi Murray Silberling's landmark book, *Dancing for Joy*, which is available from Amazon.com and several other sources.

Chapter 35
The Ben Ezra Plantation, Near Tiberias

1. See John 7:38.

2. While we know from Scripture that The Way had formally appointed deacons and deaconesses and from Bagatti that these deacons and deaconesses were active participants in the administration of the body, including baptism, nothing is extant concerning the nature or length of their formal training before ordination. (See Acts 6:1–6; 1 Timothy 3:8–13; Bagatti, *The Church From the Gentiles in Palestine*, 303.)

3. While this standardized, congregation-wide home group meeting guide is my own creation, it is based in part on the extremely successful program established by Paul Yonggi Cho in the 1980s and memorialized in his book, *The Home Cell Group Study Guide Vol. 1* (Milton Keynes, England: Word Books, 1990), which sets up a one-year program consisting of fifty-two one-hour meeting guides intended to be presented at weekly—as opposed to daily—meetings. While this book is no longer in print, it can be found for sale on the Internet, and it is highly recommended as a general guide for contemporary home congregations.

4. Young-hoon Lee, "The Life and Ministry of David Yonggi Cho and the Yoido Full Gospel Church," Asian Journal of Pentecostal Studies 7:1 (2004): 13–14.

Chapter 36
Guidance for Home Congregations Seeking to Follow the Model of the First Jewish Believers of The Way

1. I have written about many of these specific Dead Sea Scroll appearances of Christian theology and doctrine in my earlier work, *Full Circle.* (See Fischer, *Full Circle*, 85–99.)

2. *The Apostolic Tradition of Hippolytus* is available in English at Amazon.com and elsewhere and is also posted online at http://www.bombaxo.com/hippolytus.html.

3. R. A. Torrey, "Looking to Jesus," http://www.gotothebible.com/HTML/Sermons/TorreyLooking2Jesus.html.

Appendix II
Principal Points of Contact Between the Didache and the New Testament

1. Points of contact with Matthew are from J. P. Garrow, *The Gospel of Matthew's Dependence on the Didache*, xiv to xxxiii. Other points of contact were derived by the author.

Glossary

Akiva: Rabbi Akiva ben Joseph (A.D. 50–135) was one of the most central and essential contributors to the Mishna. He is referred to in the Talmud as *Rosh la-Chachomim*, or "Head of All the Sages." He is considered by many to be the father of Rabbinical Judaism.

Ascetism: (Greek: *askēsis*) A lifestyle characterized by abstinence from various sorts of worldly pleasures, often with the aim of pursuing religious and spiritual goals. The Essenes of Qumran were an ascetic group, while the many Essene communities in the Diaspora were not.

Acrostic: A writing in an alphabetic script in which the first letter, syllable, or word of each line, paragraph, or other recurring feature in the text spells out another message. A well-known example is associated with the Christian fish symbol. The Greek word for fish is *ichthus*, spelled with the Greek letters "iota-chi-theta-upsilon-sigma," which form the acrostic "Jesus Christ of God, the Son, the Savior." (*Iesous* [Jesus], *CHristos* [Christ], *THeou* [of God], *Uiou* [the Son], *Soter* [the Saviour].)

***Aelia Capitolina*:** (Latin) Colonia Aelia Capitolina was a city built by Emperor Hadrian in the year 131 on site of Jerusalem, which was in ruins. *Aelia* came from Hadrian's given name, Aelius, while *Capitolina* showed that the new city was dedicated to the pagan god, Jupiter Capitolinus, to whom a temple was built on the site of the former Jewish temple.

Apocalypse: A group of Jewish and Jewish Christian writings that appeared from about 200 B.C. to A.D. 350 and were assumed to make revelations of the ultimate divine purpose, wherein the forces of righteousness triumph over the forces of evil; the Revelation of John is an example of these writings

Apocrypha: A group of fourteen books, not considered canonical, included in the Septuagint and the Vulgate as part of the Old Testament but usually omitted from Protestant editions of the Bible. There are also a vast number of early Christian writings that are not included in the Bible that are considered to be New Testament Apocrypha. Many of these were written by members of The Way.

Apostate: "One who forsakes his religion or faith," from the Greek *apostasia, meaning* "defection, desertion, rebellion." In Christianity, one who denies the person of Yeshua and/or the triune Godhead is considered to be an apostate. Contrast with *heretic*: a professed believer who maintains religious opinions contrary to those accepted by his or her church or rejects doctrines prescribed by that church.

***Bamot*:** The platform from which services are conducted in a synagogue

Byzantine: The eastern part of the later Roman Empire, dating from when Constantine rebuilt Byzantium (modern day Istanbul) and made it his capital; its extent varied greatly over the centuries, but its core remained the Balkan Peninsula and Asia Minor. The empire collapsed when Constantinople fell to the Ottoman Turks in 1453.The Byzantine Church was the first organized denominational Gentile Christian presence in Israel, with the first churches dated to the mid fourth century.

Canon: That body of sacred writings that have been accepted by the Christian Church as genuinely holy Scriptures. There have been 23 main lists of canon with evolving content, beginning with the Marcion List circa 138 and ending with the Westminster List in 1646, when the Canon was "closed."

***Cardo*:** In ancient Roman city planning, a *cardo* or *cardus* was a north-south oriented street in cities, military camps, and colonies. Sometimes called the *cardus maximus*, the cardo served as the center of economic life. The street was lined with shops, merchants, and vendors.

Catechumen: In the early church, this was a person under instruction in the rudiments of Christianity in preparation for baptism and initiation into full fellowship with the body.

Cenacle: A small dining room, usually on an upper floor; the building that houses the Upper Room on Mount Zion is traditionally known as the Cenacle. Approximately 25 percent of the extant building, a part of the foundation, is original.

Cosmic ladder: In Jewish mysticism embraced by the Essenes, there was a cosmic ladder with seven steps, each step of which corresponded with one of the seven heavens. Yeshua was thought to have descended this ladder into Mary's womb, then ascended it following His resurrection.

Decapolis: The Decapolis was a ten-city Greco-Roman federation, or league, occupying all of Bashan and Gilead in northeastern Palestine. The territory was contiguous except for Damascus, which some believe to have been an honorary member. Eusebius records it as the region around Hippos, Pella, and Gadara.

Diaspora: Any dispersion of people from their native land. This writing refers to two diasporas of the Jews. The first was their scattering to countries outside of Palestine after the Babylonian captivity. The second refers to the dispersion of The Way during three distinct waves: centered on A.D. 32–35, with the martyrdom of Stephen; A.D. 62–65, before and following the first revolt against Rome; and A.D. 132–135, following the second revolt against Rome. During this last wave, all Jews were banished from the city by the Roman emperor.

Docetism: The belief that Yeshua's physical body was an illusion, as was His crucifixion. This doctrine assumes that He only seemed to have a physical body and to physically die, but in reality He was incorporeal, a pure spirit, and hence could not physically die.

Domus ecclesia: (Latin) house church

Dominus Flevit: The Franciscan chapel of *Dominus Flevit* (Latin, "the Lord wept") was built in 1955, near the site which medieval pilgrims identified as the place where Jesus wept over the city. The site, acquired by the Franciscans in 1881, was on a procession route from the Mount of Olives to the Church of the Holy Sepulcher. Archaeological excavations carried out prior to construction uncovered the foundations of a fifth-century monastery and chapel. A large first-century Jewish-Christian burial place has been discovered on this site.

Epiphanius: An early second-century church father who was a strong defender of orthodoxy; he was known for tracking down and coming against religious movements he deemed "heretical" during the era following the Council of Nicea (A.D. 325)

Erev Pesach: (Hebrew) The Hebrew day begins and ends just after sundown. *Erev* translates as "evening." Thus, the first day of *Pesach* (Passover) begins the evening before the first full day of the eight-day holiday. In the same way, *Shabbat* (Saturday), the Sabbath, actually begins on *Erev Shabbat*—that is, at shortly after sundown on Friday evening—and ends on Saturday evening.

Flagellation: The act of whipping the human body, as practiced by the Romans. Yeshua was mercilessly so abused. Paul endured this punishment three times. (See 2 Corinthians 11:25.) Peter, John, and others of The Way were also punished by this means. Specialized implements for this torture included rods, switches, and the cat-o-nine-tails.

Gemara: A rabbinical commentary on the Mishna. After the Mishnah was published circa A.D. 220, the work was studied exhaustively by generation after generation of rabbis in Babylonia and Israel. Their discussions were written down in a series of books that became the Gemara, which when combined with the Mishnah to make up the body of the Talmud.

Haggadah: (Hebrew) A Jewish religious text that sets out the order of the Passover Seder

Hegesippus: (circa A.D. 110–180) A Gentile chronicler of the early church who wrote against the heresies of the Gnostics; Hegesippus's works are now entirely lost, save eight passages concerning church history quoted by Eusebius

Hellenism: The assimilation, especially by the Jews, of Greek speech, manners, and culture from the fourth century B.C. through the first centuries A.D.

Heterodox: Any opinion or doctrine at variance with an official or orthodox position. As an adjective, *heterodox* is used to describe that which is characterized by departure from accepted beliefs or standards. The Way's theology and doctrine was considered to be orthodox by the early Gentile church fathers, while that of the Ebionites was deemed heterodox, principally because the Ebionites denied the divinity of Yeshua.

***Hodayoth*:** The scroll of the *Hodayoth,* or Thanksgiving Hymns, was found in Cave One in the spring of 1947, along with several other scrolls. Late in the summer of 1952, numerous fragments of other manuscripts were found in Cave Four. The poems contained in the scroll are similar to the biblical psalms. Primarily they are hymns of thanksgiving that provide both rich theological and doctrinal detail as well as insight into Qumran worship. The two fundamental themes running through the collection are those of salvation and knowledge.

Hypocaust: An ancient Roman system of central heating; the word literally means "heat from below"

***Katyusha*:** Originally a World War II-era Soviet rocket; the Katyusha, or "Little Kate," was a rocket launcher mounted on a heavy truck that fired volleys of up to forty-eight rockets nearly four miles. Current, greatly improved versions of this rocket have ranges exceeding 112 miles. During the 2006 war, Hezbollah fired some six thousand various-range rockets against Israel. Reportedly, both Syria and Hezbollah currently each have as many as forty thousand such rockets poised and ready to launch in the event of resumed hostilities.

***Midrash*:** The term *midrash* can refer to a particular way of reading and interpreting a biblical verse and to a book—a compilation of *midrashic* teachings. *Midrash* can also refer to a particular verse and its interpretation. Thus, one can say, "The *midrash* on Genesis 1:1 says. . . ."

***Mikvah*:** A gathering of "living" (running) water in a pool used by Jewish men and women for a variety of ritual purifications; used by Essenes and The Way for baptism by self-immersion

Mishna: The heavy losses among Jewish sages during the two revolts against Rome were likely the deciding factor that led Rabbi Judah the Prince around the year A.D. 200 to record what had previously been the Oral Law. The process began in Yavne and was completed in Tiberias circa 220–230.

Nazarenes: The first Jewish believers in Yeshua, most of whom were first Essenes, with some converts from the Pharisees and Sadducees. The first Nazarenes met on Mount Zion from Pentecost until the last of them were dispersed into a second great diaspora circa A.D. 135. They were referred to as "The Way" in the New Testament. The name *Nazarene* is attributed variously to two sources: Yeshua's place of birth, Nazareth; and Isaiah 11:1, where the word *netzer* ("shoot") refers to Yeshua as the "Shoot" that will come forth from the stump of Jesse.

Oblation: A solemn offering; for example, newly baptized members of The Way partook of an oblation of water, milk, and honey as an offering to God in celebration of their entry into the kingdom

Ophanim ("Wheels")**:** A higher order of celestial beings that are living symbols of God's justice and authority. They are said to be the carriers of the throne of God and to have the form of great wheels covered in eyes

Orthodox: For the purposes of the writing, *orthodox* means "regarded by the Gentile Christian church fathers as in keeping with their theological and doctrinal understandings."

Parousia: The second coming of Yeshua, during which He will return to Earth to set up His kingdom, where He will reign for one thousand years.

Pontus/Bithynia: An ancient country in northeastern Asia Minor (now Turkey) on the Black Sea coast; on its inland side were Cappadocia and western Armenia. It was not significantly penetrated by Persian or Hellenic civilization.

Predestination: There were two views of predestination operative in the early centuries: single predestination and double predestination. Single predestination is the understanding that God predetermines who and who will not be saved. However, through repentance and righteous living, it is nevertheless possible for those who were not originally chosen for salvation to be saved. Double predestination is the understanding that God pre-elects both those who are and who are not to be saved. Moreover, in this understanding there is no opportunity to move from one of these groups to the other.

Pseudepigrapha: Fifty-two apocryphal texts written between 200 B.C. and A.D. 200 falsely ascribed to the authorship of various prophets and kings; many of these were written by members of The Way and are mostly apocalyptic in nature

Qumran: Site of the Essene monastic community on the northwestern shore of the Dead Sea; most of the Dead Sea Scrolls were discovered in caves at this location

Rambam: *Rambam* is an acrostic of the one named Rabbeinu Moshe ben Maimon (1135–1204). Greatly beloved by Rabbinical Jews, he is buried in an elaborate tomb in Tiberias, where throngs of Jewish tourists come to pray at his grave for various favors. Rambam was strongly opposed to the Jewish Christians of his time. He wrote two of his *Thirteen Principles Faith* (Talmud, tractate Sanhedrin, Chapter 10) denying the possibility that the Godhead could be divided and that God could take on flesh.

Rashi (Rabbi Shlomo Yitzchaki)**:** (1040–1105) He is considered by many to be the outstanding rabbinical biblical commentator of the Middle Ages. His commentary on the Tenach became so popular that there are now more than two hundred commentaries on his commentary. Rashi's commentary on the Talmud is considered even more important than his Bible commentary. The Talmud was written in legalese—terse, unexplained language with no punctuation. Rashi provided a simple explanation of all Gemeara discussions. It became an instant best-seller, and, to this day, it is unthinkable to study the Talmud without studying Rashi's commentary at the same time.

Redact: (verb) To make ready for publication; edit or revise

Rosetta Stone Alpha: The black basalt Rosetta Stone was found in 1799 in a fortress located on the outskirts of Rashid, a year after the French expedition to Egypt began. It measured 113 centimeters tall, 75.5 cm. Long, and 27 cm. thick, and contained three distinct bands of writing. The most incomplete was the top band, containing hieroglyphics; the middle band was written in the Demotic script, and the bottom was in Greek. Studies carried out on the stone by scholars revealed that the stone was a royal decree that stated that it was to be written in the languages used in Egypt at the time. Scholars began to focus on the Demotic script since it was more complete and resembled alphabetical letters rather than the pictorial hieroglyphs. This was essentially a shorthand form of hieroglyphics and had evolved from an earlier shorthand version of Egyptian called "hieratic."

Seder: (Hebrew) An order of prayers that constitutes a liturgy; most often associated with the traditional meal partaken by Jews on the first evening of Pesach (Passover). The Seder is the most important event in the Passover celebration. Usually gathering the whole family and friends together, the Seder is steeped in long-held traditions and customs.

Shofar: The *shofar* is mentioned over eighty times in the Old Testament. The ram's horn was the authentic *shofar*, and it is still in wide use by traditional Jewish groups in Israel. Another form the Yemenite *shofar* is taken from an African antelope called the kudu. While the horn of the kudu is much more "showy" than the ram's horn and is often sold to tourists visiting Israel, it was not at all likely that this Yemenite Jewish adaptation was used by The Way or by any traditional group within Israel proper.

Solomonic Knot: The Solomonic knot is composed of two rings that interlace each other four times with alternating crossing points that go over, under, over, and under as one traces around each of the rings. King Solomon, according to Italian legend, was on a hill and was charged by God with protecting a village from large boulders that were going to roll down and destroy the village. They claim he was holding three large boulders, and took a rope and devised this knot to support the boulders and protect the town.

The design is frequently used in the mosaics of ancient synagogues, which probably gave rise to the symbol's association with King Solomon. In traditional Judaism it is imbued with mystical meaning as a symbol of eternal motion and the intertwining of space and time. When used by Jewish Christians it most often represented the destroyed temple. In the mosaics of traditional Jews, the temple was represented by an artistic depiction or symbol of its sacred implements.

I have found this symbol used in a wide variety of sites in the Galilee, including: the original (presumed circa first-century) mosaics at Tabgpha, the original (presumed second- to third-century) mosaics of the Basilica at Kursi, the first-century mosaics of the chapel at Kursi, the third-century prayer hall at Megiddo Prison, and the first- to second-century Tiberias Synagogue of The Way.

Stadia: Plural of *stadium* (Latin); an ancient Greek and Roman unit of length, the Athenian unit being equal to about 607 feet (185 m.)

Systematic Theology: Systematic theology answers the question, What does the whole Bible teach us about any given topic? This definition indicates that systematic theology involves collecting and understanding all the relevant passages in the Bible on various topics and then summarizing their teachings clearly.

Tenach: The Hebrew Bible; the Old Testament of the Christian Holy Bible

The Way: The scriptural and historical name of the first Jewish believers in Yeshua who met in the Upper Room on Mount Zion immediately after the ascension of Yeshua

Torah: (Hebrew) also called the Pentateuch; the first five books of the Old Testament. Traditional Jewish understanding is that God spoke the Torah to Moses on Mount Sinai, and Moses wrote it down on tablets.

Yeshua: *Yeshua* is the original Hebrew proper name (birth name) for Jesus of Nazareth, who is also known by more than six thousand other language-specific names.

Yeshua haMasiach: (Hebrew) "Jesus the Messiah"

Bibliography

Alexander, Steven, and Karen Alexander. *Crop Circles: Signs, Wonders and Mysteries.* Port St. Lucie, Florida: Arcturus Books, 2006.

Bagatti, Bellarmino. *The Church From the Circumcision.* Jerusalem, Israel: Franciscan Printing Press, 1984.

______. *The Church From the Gentiles in Palestine.* Jerusalem, Israel: Franciscan Printing Press, 1984.

______. *Ancient Christian Villages of the Galilee.* Jerusalem, Israel: Franciscan Printing Press, 2001.

______. *Ancient Christian Villages of Judea and Negev.* Jerusalem, Israel: Franciscan Printing Press, 2002.

______. *Ancient Christian Villages of Samaria.* Jerusalem, Israel: Franciscan Printing Press, 2002.

Beckwith, John. *Early Christian and Byzantine Art.* New Haven, Connecticut: Yale University Press, 1970.

Bennett, Rod. *Four Witnesses: The Early Church in Her Own Words.* San Francisco, CA: Ignatius Press, 2002.

Bingham, Joseph. *The Antiquities of the Christian Church.* London: Henry G. Bohn, 1856.

Boatwright, Mary T. *Hadrian and the Cities of the Roman Empire.* Princeton, New Jersey: Princeton University Press, 2002.

Borowski, Oded. *Every Living Thing: The Use of Animals in Ancient Israel.* Lanham, MA: AltaMira Press, 1999.

Bruce, F. F. *The Canon of Scripture.* Downers Grove, Illinois: InterVarsity Press, 1988.

______. *Jesus and Christian Origins Outside the New Testament.* Grand Rapids, Michigan: William B. Eerdmans Publishing Company, 1974.

Bryant, Jean Gould. *Creating Women: An Anthology of Readings on Women in Western Culture.* Upper Saddle River, NJ: Prentice Hall, 2004.

Burgess, Stanley M., Gary B. McGee, and Patrick H. Alexander, ed. *Dictionary of Pentecostal and Charismatic Movements.* Grand Rapids, MI: Regency, Zondervan.

Burk, C. *A Religious Encyclopedia.* London: Funk& Wagnalls, 1894.

Cameron, Rod, ed. *The Other Gospels: Non-Canonical Gospel Texts*. Philadelphia, PA: The Westminster Press, 1982.

Carroll, James. *Constantine's Sword*. Boston: Houghton Mifflin, 2001.

Charlesworth, James H., ed., *The Bible and the Dead Sea Scrolls* (three vols.). The Princeton Symposium on the Dead Sea Scrolls. Waco, Texas: Baylor University Press, 2006.

______. *The Old Testament Pseudepigrapha* (two vols.). New York: Doubleday.

Cho, David Yonggi. *Successful Home Cell Groups*. Orlando, Florida: Bridge-Logos, 1981.

Cohen, Abraham. *Everyman's Talmud: The Major Teachings of the Rabbinic Sages*. New York: Schocken Books, 1995.

Cureton, W. *Ancient Syriac Documents Relative to the Earliest Establishment of Christianity in Edessa and the Neighboring Countries*. London: Williams and Norgate, 1864.

Cyril of Jerusalem. *Lectures on the Christian Sacraments*. Edited by Frank L. Cross. Yonkers, New York: St. Vladimir's Seminary Press, 1986.

Danielou, Jean. *The Theology of Jewish Christianity*. Translated by John A. Baker. Chicago: The Henry Regnery Company, 1964.

de Jonge, M. *The Testaments of the Twelve Patriarchs: A Study of their Text, Composition, and Origin*. Assen, Netherlands: Van Gorcum, 1953.

Donfried, Karl P. and Richardson, ed. *Judaism and Christianity in First-Century Rome*. Grand Rapids, Michigan: William B. Eerdman, 1998.

Dix, Gregory. *The Treatise on the Apostolic Tradition of St. Hippolytus of Rome, Bishop and Martyr*. London: The Alban Press, 1992.

Eusebius. *The History of the Church*. Translated by G. A. Williamson. London: Penguin, 1965.

Franck, A. and I. Sossintz. *The Kabbalah*. Whitefish, Montana: Kessinger Publishing, 2003.

______. *The Onomasticon, Palestine in the Fourth Century* A.D. Translated by G. S. P. Freeman-Grenville. Jerusalem, Israel: Carta, 2003.

Evans, Craig A. *Noncanonical Writings and New Testament Interpretation*. Peabody, MA: Hendrickson, 1992.

Fischer, Raymond Robert. *The Door Where It Began*. Tiberias, Israel: Olim Publications, 2005.

______. *The Children of God*. Tiberias, Israel: Olim Publications, 2000.

______. *Full Circle.* Tiberias, Israel: Olim Publications, 2002.

Fitzmyer, Joseph A. *The Dead Sea Scrolls and Christian Origins.* Grand Rapids, MI: William B. Eerdmans, 2000.

Flusser, David. *Judaism and the Origins of Christianity.* Jerusalem, Israel: The Magnes Press, The Hebrew University, 1988.

Garrow, Alan J. P. *The Gospel of Matthew's Dependence on the Didache.* London: T&T Clark International, 2004.

Gavin, F. *Jewish Antecedents of the Christian Sacraments.* London: Society for Promoting Christian Knowledge, 1928.

Graves, Robert. *The White Goddess.* Manchester, United Kingdom: Carcanet Press, 1999.

Harnack, Adolph von, *The Mission and Expansion of Christianity in the First Three Centuries.* New York: Harper Torchbooks, 1962.

Hengel, Martin and Anna Maria Schwemer. *Paul, Between Damascus and Antioch, the Unknown Years.* Louisville, KY: Westminster John Knox Press, 1997.

Horne, Thomas Hartwell. *A Compedious Introduction to the Study of the Bible.* New York: Carlton & Porter, 1862 (University of Michigan Library Reprint Series).

House, H. Wayne. *Charts of Christian Theology & Doctrine.* Grand Rapids, MI: Zondervan.

Howson, J. S. *Life and Epistles of St. Paul.* Grand Rapids, Michigan: Wm. B. Eerdmans, Publishers, 1966.

Jeffery, Grant. *The Sacred Mystery of the Trinity.* Carol Stream, Illinois: Tyndale House, 1998.

Johnson, Alan, and Frank E. Gaebelein, ed. *The Expositor's Bible Commentary,* Vol. 12. Charlottsville, VA: Regency Reference Library, 1984.

Jones, A. H. M. *Constantine and the Conversion of Europe.* Toronto, Canada: University of Toronto Press, 1978.

Josephus. *The Works of Josephus.* Translated by William Whiston. Peabody, MA: Hendrickson Publishers, 1987.

Kaplan, Aryeh. *Sefer Yetzirah: The Book of Creation.* York Beach, ME: Weiser Books, 1997.

______. *Waters of Eden: The Mystery of the Mikveh.* New York: Union of Orthodox Jewish Congregations of America, 1993.

Kelley, J. N. D. *Jerome: His Life, Writings, and Controversies.* Peabody, MA: Hendrickson Publishers, 1998.

King, Philip J., and Lawrence E. Stager. *Life in Biblical Israel*. Louisville, Kentucky: Westminster John Knox Press, 2001.

Lowrie, Walter. *Art in the Early Church*. Lowrie Press, 2007.

Luther, Martin. *The Jews and Their Lies*. Florissant, Missouri: Liberty Bell Publications, 2004.

Mancini, Ignazio. *Archaeological Discoveries Relative to the Judeo-Christians*. Jerusalem, Israel: Franciscan Printing Press, 1984.

Martinez, Florentino Garcia. *The Dead Sea Scrolls Translated*. Grand Rapids: William B. Eerdmans, 1996.

Martinez, Florentino Garcia and Julio Trebolle Barrera. *The People of the Dead Sea Scrolls*. New York: E.J. Brill, 1993.

The Zohar: Pritzker Edition, Volume I. Translated by Daniel C. Matt. Palo Alto, CA: Standord University Press, 2003.

McTernan, John, and Ruggiero. *King Messiah in His Holy Temple: Part 2*. Oklahoma City, OK: Hearthstone Publishing, 2003.

Metzger, John B. *The Tri-unity of God Is Jewish*. St. Louis, Missouri: Cenveo-Plus Communicatons, 2005.

Migne, J. P., ed. *Patrologia Graeca #9: St. Clement of Alexandria*. Paris: Granier, 1890.

Milik, J. T. *Ten Years of Discovery in the Wilderness of Judea*. Norwich, United Kingdom: SCM Press, 1963.

Nehunya. *The Bahir*. Translated by Aryeh Kaplan. Amsterdam, the Netherlands: Jason Aronson, 1994.

(The) NIV Study Bible, New International Version. Grand Rapids, MI: Zondervan, 1985.

Painter, John. *Just James, The Brother of Jesus in History and Tradition*. Columbia, SC: University of South Carolina Press, 1997.

Philo. *The Works of Philo*. Translated by C. D. Yonge. Peabody, MA: Hendrickson Publishers, 1993.

Pritz, Ray A. *Nazarene Jewish Christianity*. Jerusalem, Israel: The Hebrew University, E. J. Brill, 1988.

Renan, Ernest. *The History of the Origins of Christianity* (Vols.2, 3, 4 and 5). Ithaca, NY: The Cornell University Library Digital Collections, 1991.

Rousseau, J. J., and R.Arav. *Jesus and His World*. Minneapolis, MN:Fortress, 1995.

Rutgers, L. V. *The Hidden Heritage of Diaspora Judaism.* Leuven, Belgium: Peeters Publishers, 1998.

Schmalz, Reuven Efriam, and Raymond Robert Fischer. *The Messianic Seal of the Jerusalem Church.* Tiberias, Israel: Olim Publications, 1999.

Schneemelcher, Wilhelm, ed. *New Testament Apocrypha: Writings Relating to the Apostles Apocalypses and Related Subjects.* Translated by R. McL. Wilson. Cambridge, England: James Clarke and Company, 1992.

______. *New Testament Apocrypha.* Translated by R. McL. Wilson. Cambribge, England: James Clarke and Company, 1991.

Schonfield, Hugh J. *The History of Jewish Christianity.* London: Duckworth, 1936.

Schurer, Emil. *A History of the Jewish People in the Time of Jesus Christ.* Peabody, MA: Hendrickson Publishers, 1998. (Originally published by T&T Clark, Edinburgh, 1890.)

Schwartz, Seth. *Imperialism and Jewish Society, 200 B.C.E. to 640 C.E.* Princeton, NJ: Princeton University Press, 2004.

Silberling, Murray. *Dancing for Joy.* Baltimore, MD: Lederer Books, 1995.

Skarsaune, Oskar. *In the Shadow of the Temple, Jewish Influences on Early Christianity.* Downers Grove, IL: InterVarsityPress, 2002.

Skarsaune, Oskar, and Reidar Hvalvik, ed. *Jewish Believers in Jesus.* Peabody, MA: Hendrickson Publishers, 2007.

Spurgeon, Charles H. *Spurgeon's Sermon Notes.* Grand Rapids, MI: Kregel Publicatons, 1990.

Tepper, Y., and L.Di Sengi. *A Christian Prayer Hall of the Third Century C.E. at Kefar 'Othnay (Legio).* Jerusalem, Israel: Israel Antiquities Authority, 2005.

Testa, Emmanuel. *The Faith of the Mother Church.* Jerusalem, Israel: Franciscan Printing Press, 1992.

Van de Sandt, Huub, and David Flusser. *The Didache: Its Jewish Sources and Its Place in Early Judaism and Christianity.* Minneapolis, MN: Fortress Press, 2002.

Woodard, Lee W. *First Century Gospels Found!* (Pre-publication edition) Tahlequah, OK: LaSalle Monument, 2008.

Zinman Institute of Archaeology. *Hippos-Sussita, Sixth Season of Excavations.* Haifa, Israel: University of Haifa, 2005.

To Contact the Author

olim@012.net.il

www.olimpublications.com

P.O. Box 2111
Tiberias, Israel 14116

About the Cover

Two well-known first century A.D. archaeological relics of *The Way* are depicted. The "Loaves and the Fishes" mosaic is believed to have been placed by early Jewish believers to mark the site where Yeshua (Jesus) performed His first miraculous feeding of the multitude (Mark 6:30–44). Three *taws*, the last letter of the ancient Hebrew alphabet rendered as an equilateral cross ("+" symbol), are depicted in the breadbasket, pointing to its very early Jewish believer origination.

The "Messianic Seal of the Jerusalem Church" symbol pointing down to the mosaic is believed to be an early logo of *The Way*. This rendition of the three-part symbol was taken as a "strike" directly from the face of one of eight surviving artifacts found on Mount Zion in the 1960s by an old Greek Orthodox monk. These surviving artifacts are privately held by a prominent Christian family in Jerusalem and are, reportedly, all that remain from a cache of 30–40 such "Seal"-marked artifacts, the rest of which have disappeared and are thought by some to have been suppressed. The three parts of this ancient symbol are a menorah at the top and a fish at the bottom. Between them, the stand of the menorah and the tail of the fish interlace to make up the *Magen David* (Star of David).